EXTRA
Large

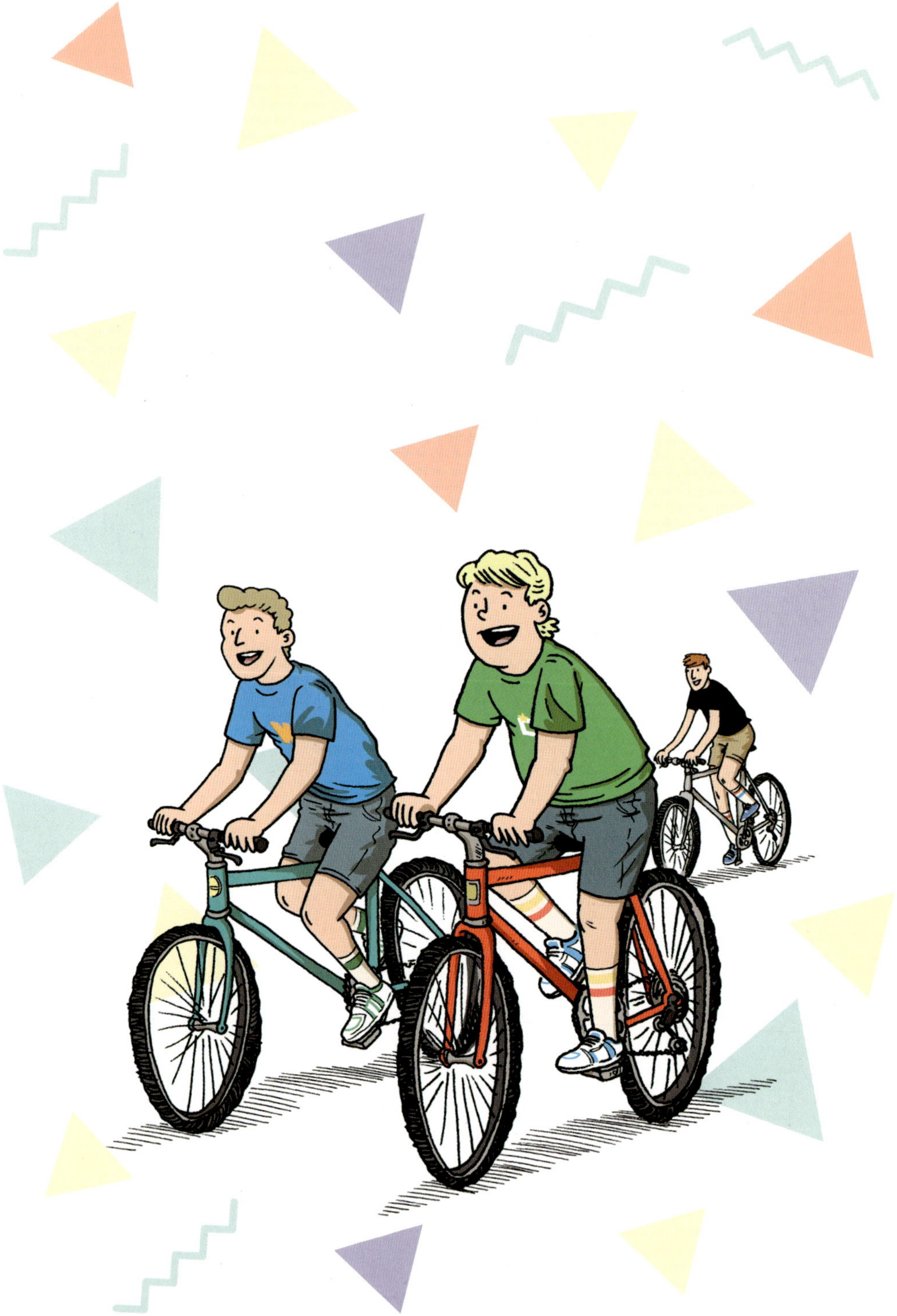

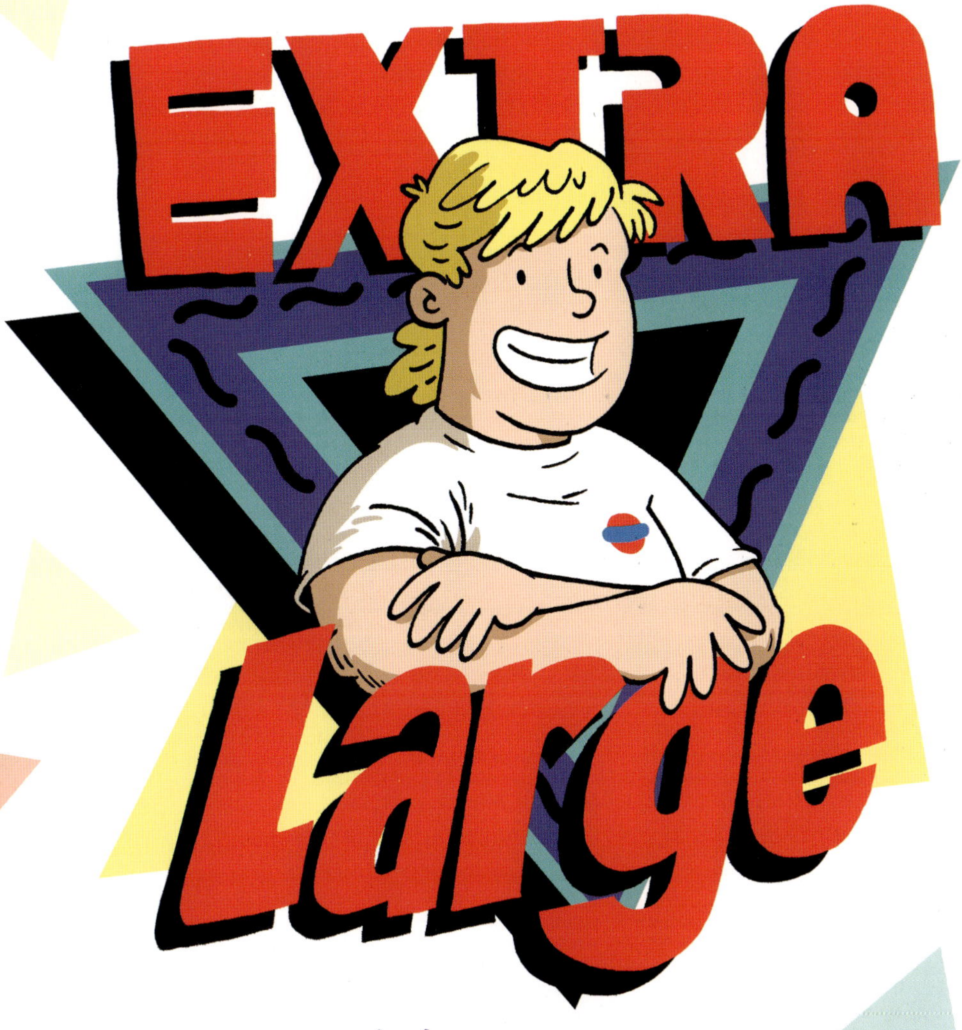
EXTRA
Large

tyler page

:01
First Second
New York

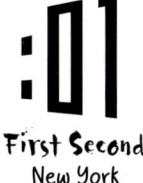

First Second

Published by First Second
First Second is an imprint of Roaring Brook Press, a division of Holtzbrinck Publishing Holdings Limited Partnership
120 Broadway, New York, NY 10271
firstsecondbooks.com
mackids.com

© 2025 by Tyler Page
All rights reserved

Library of Congress Control Number: 2024935323

Our books may be purchased in bulk for promotional, educational, or business use.
Please contact your local bookseller or the Macmillan Corporate and Premium Sales Department
at (800) 221-7945 ext. 5442 or by email at MacmillanSpecialMarkets@macmillan.com.

First edition, 2025
Edited by Calista Brill and Alex Lu
Cover design by Sunny Lee
Interior book design by Casper Manning
Production editing by Avia Perez

Special thanks to Samantha Puc

Penciled with a mechanical pencil on copy paper. Scanned into Photoshop, converted to non-photo blue and printed on 9x12 Bristol paper. Inked with various-size Micron pens. Colored digitally in Photoshop.

Printed in China by 1010 Printing International Limited, Kwun Tong, Hong Kong

ISBN 978-1-250-85156-7 (paperback)
10 9 8 7 6 5 4 3 2 1

ISBN 978-1-250-85157-4 (hardcover)
10 9 8 7 6 5 4 3 2 1

Don't miss your next favorite book from First Second! For the latest updates go to
firstsecondnewsletter.com and sign up for our enewsletter.

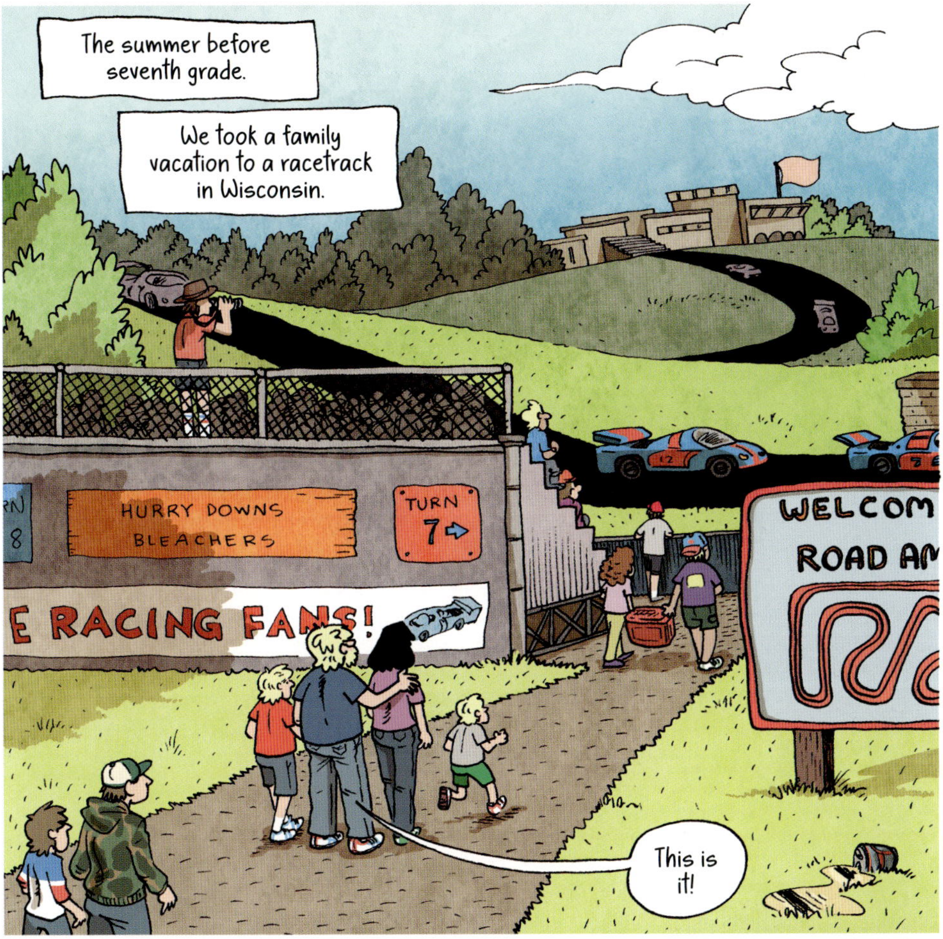
The summer before seventh grade.
We took a family vacation to a racetrack in Wisconsin.
HURRY DOWNS BLEACHERS
TURN 7
E RACING FANS!
WELCOM
ROAD AM
This is it!

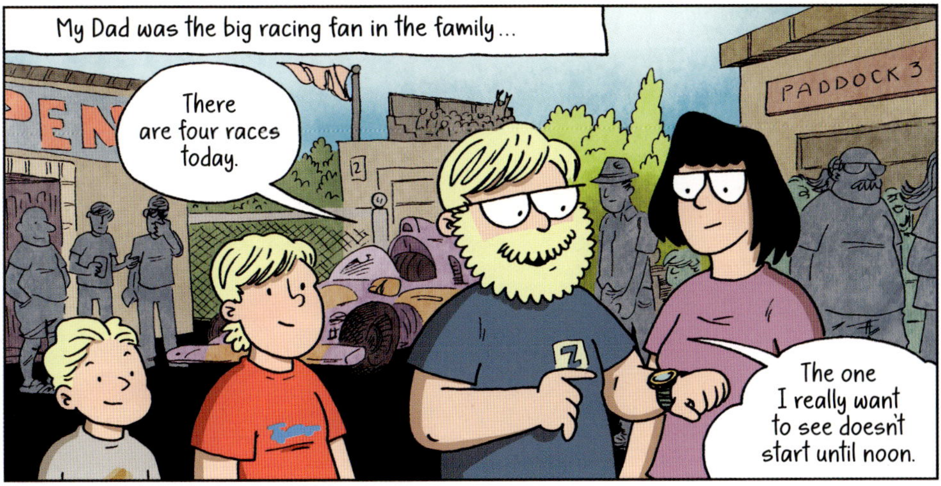
My Dad was the big racing fan in the family...
PADDOCK 3
There are four races today.
The one I really want to see doesn't start until noon.

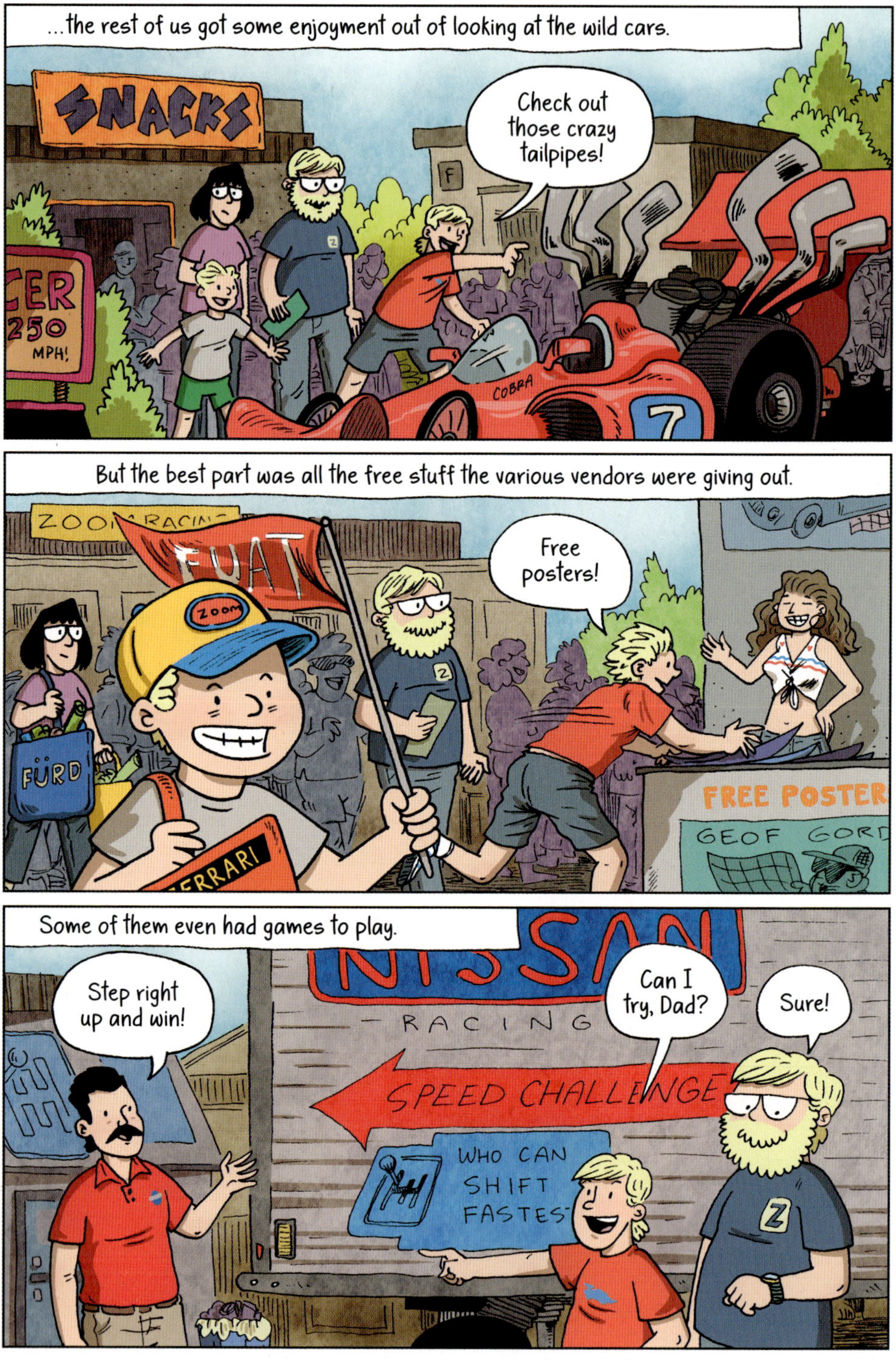
...the rest of us got some enjoyment out of looking at the wild cars.
SNACKS
Check out those crazy tailpipes!
COBRA
But the best part was all the free stuff the various vendors were giving out.
FUAT
ZOOM
FÜRD
Free posters!
FREE POSTER
Some of them even had games to play.
Step right up and win!
RACING
Can I try, Dad?
Sure!
SPEED CHALLENGE
WHO CAN SHIFT

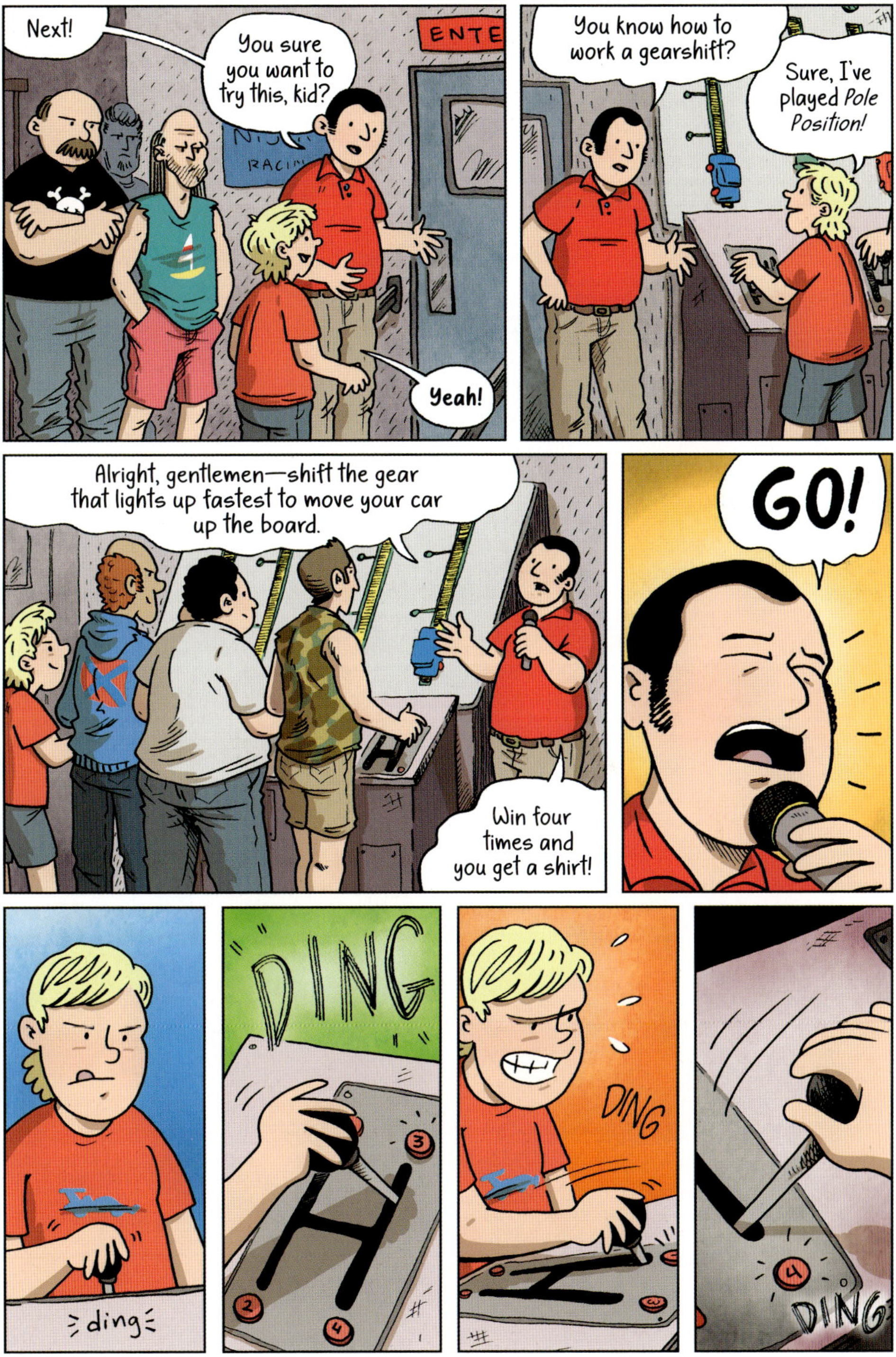

Next!
You sure you want to try this, kid?
Yeah!
ENTE
RACIN
You know how to work a gearshift?
Sure, I've played *Pole Position!*
Alright, gentlemen—shift the gear that lights up fastest to move your car up the board.
Win four times and you get a shirt!
GO!
ding
DING
DING
DING

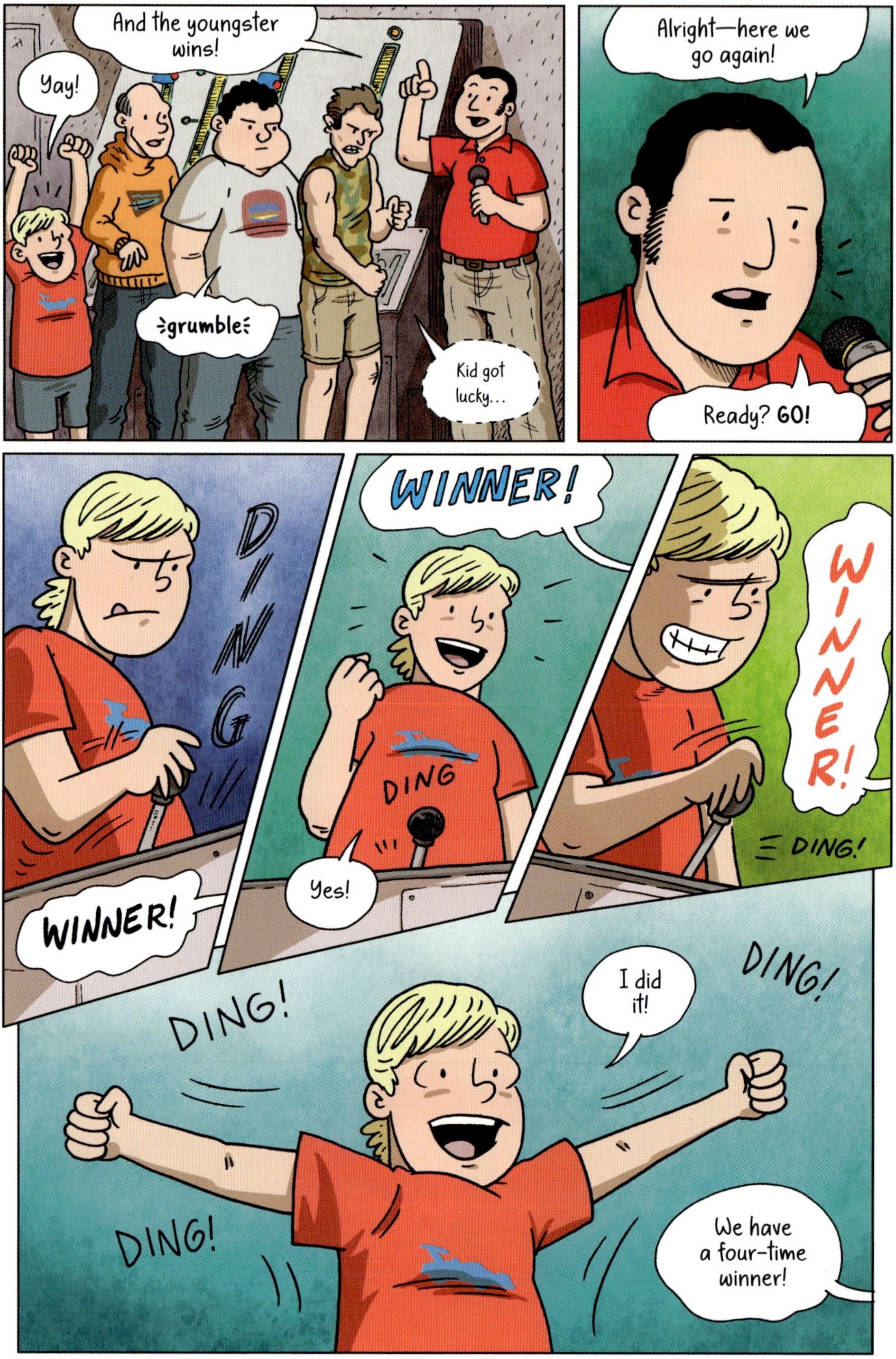
And the youngster wins!
Yay!
grumble
Kid got lucky...
Alright—here we go again!
Ready? GO!
DING
WINNER!
WINNER!
DING
Yes!
WINNER!
DING!
I did it!
DING!
DING!
DING!
We have a four-time winner!

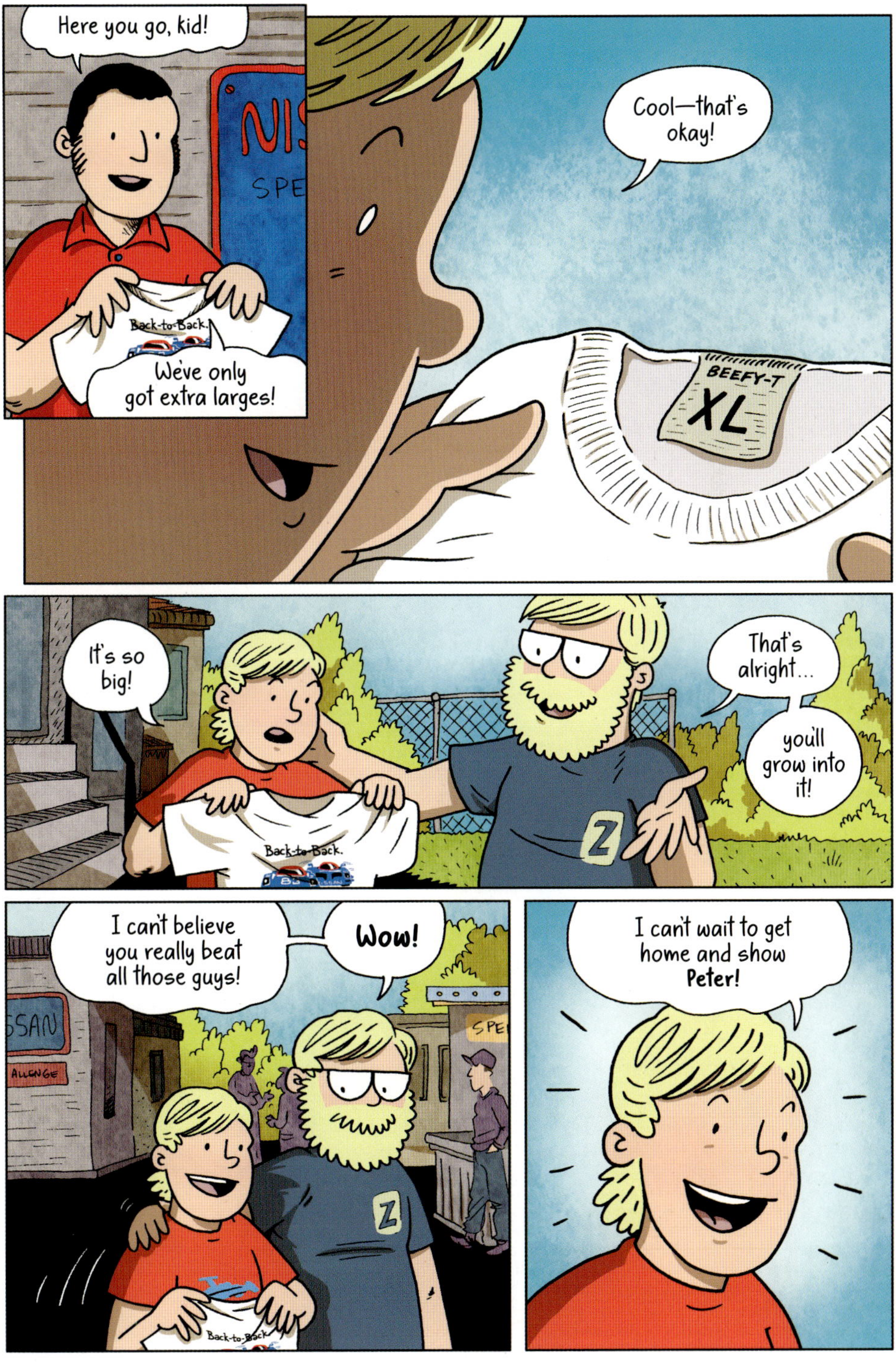
Here you go, kid!
NIS
SPE
Back-to-Back.
We've only got extra larges!
Cool—that's okay!
BEEFY-T
XL
It's so big!
That's alright...
you'll grow into it!
Back-to-Back.
I can't believe you really beat all those guys!
Wow!
SSAN
ALLENGE
SPE
Back-to-Back.
I can't wait to get home and show **Peter!**

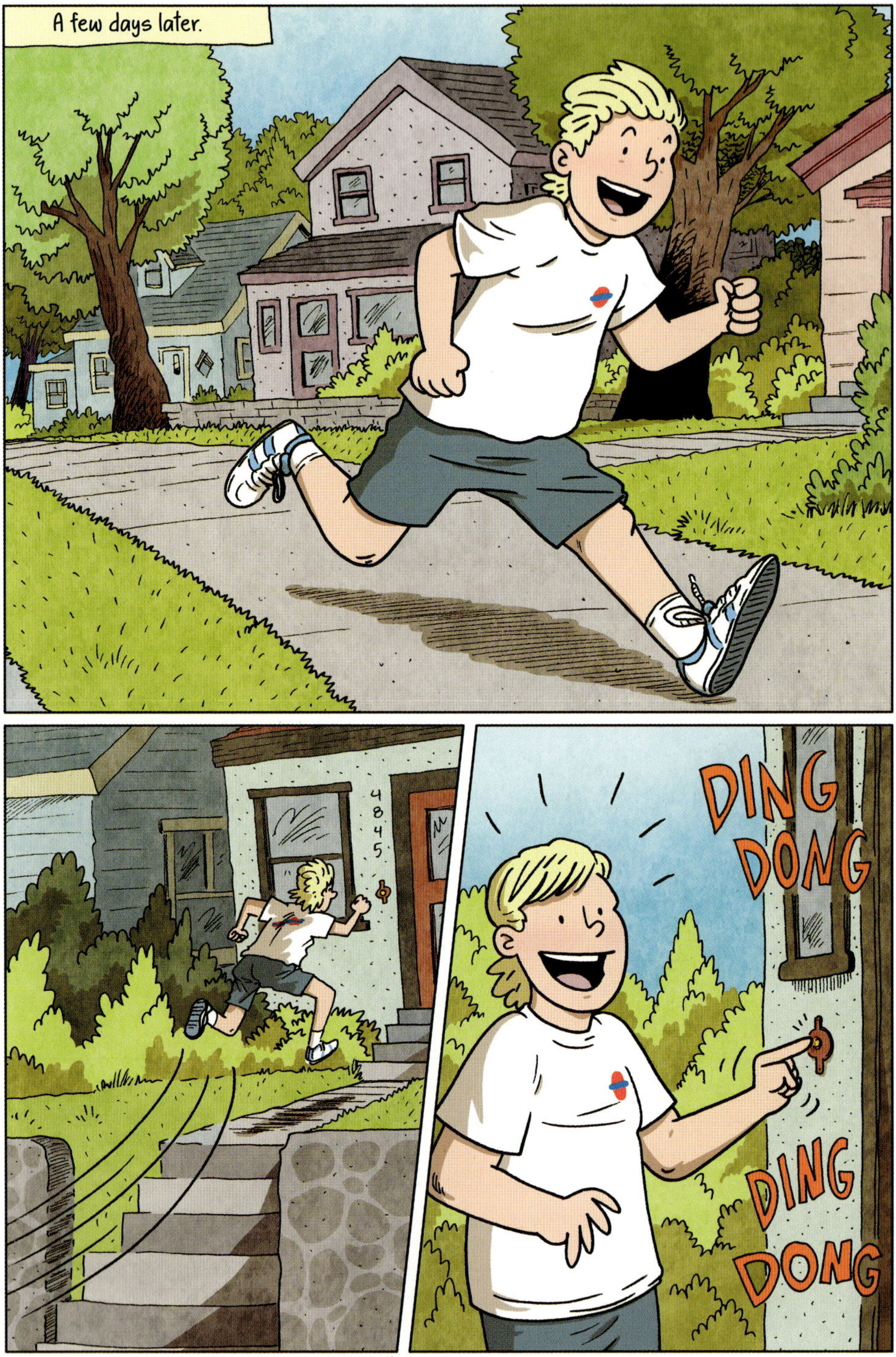
A few days later.
4845
DING DONG
DING DONG

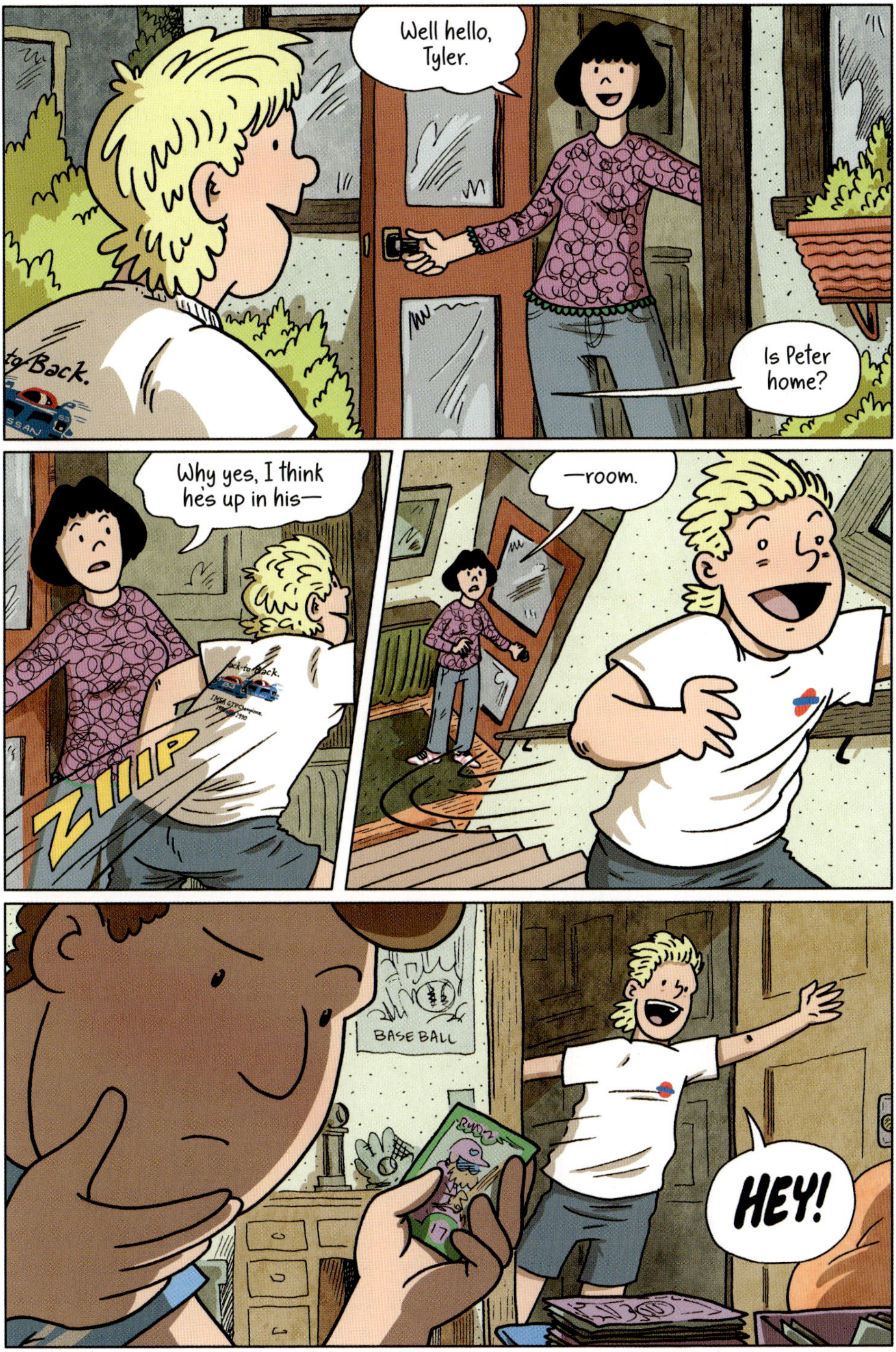
Well hello, Tyler.
Is Peter home?
Why yes, I think he's up in his—
ZIIIP
—room.
BASEBALL
HEY!

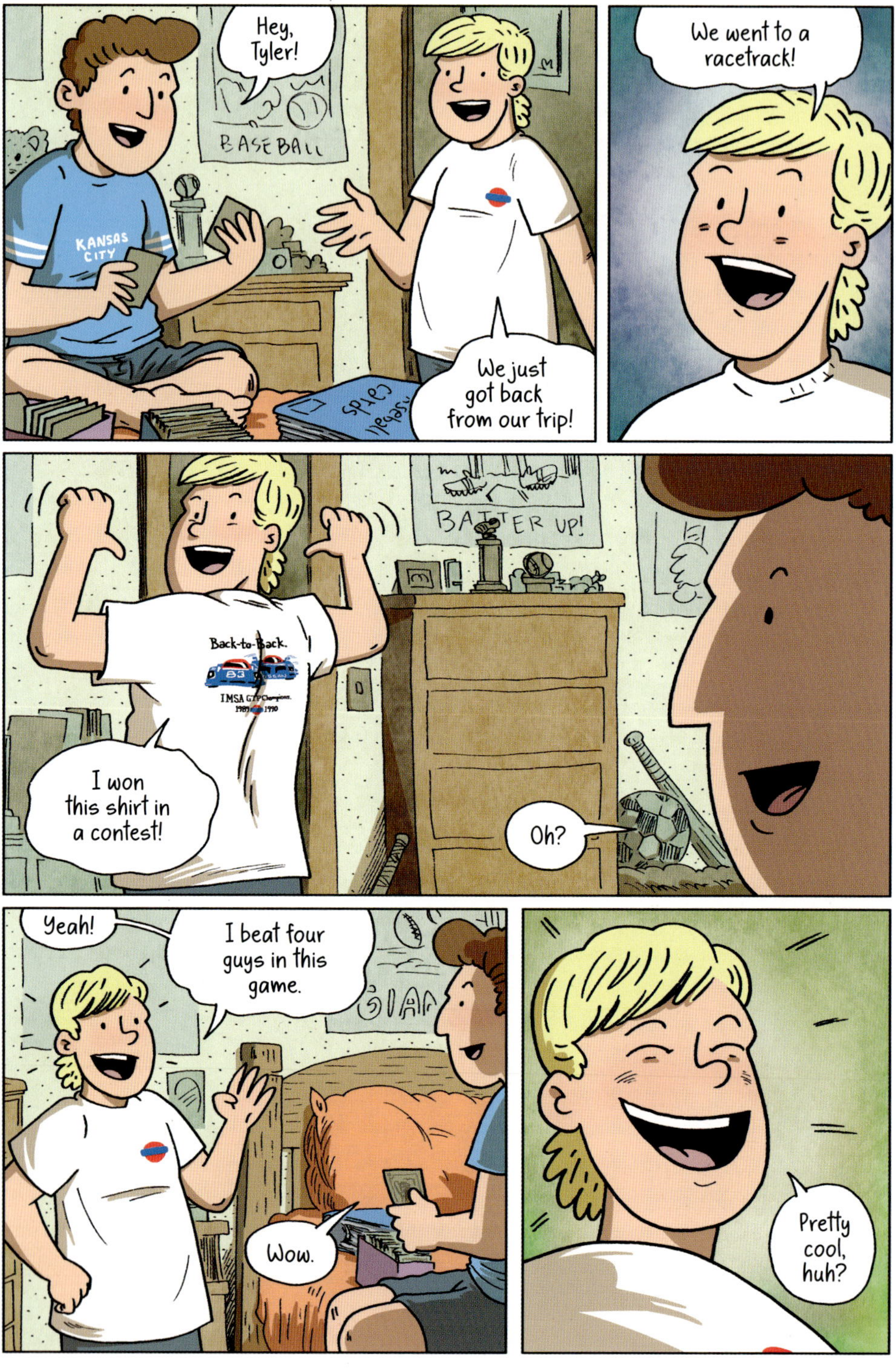
Hey, Tyler!
BASEBALL
KANSAS CITY
We just got back from our trip!
We went to a racetrack!
BATTER UP!
Back-to-Back.
I won this shirt in a contest!
Oh?
Yeah!
I beat four guys in this game.
Wow.
Pretty cool, huh?

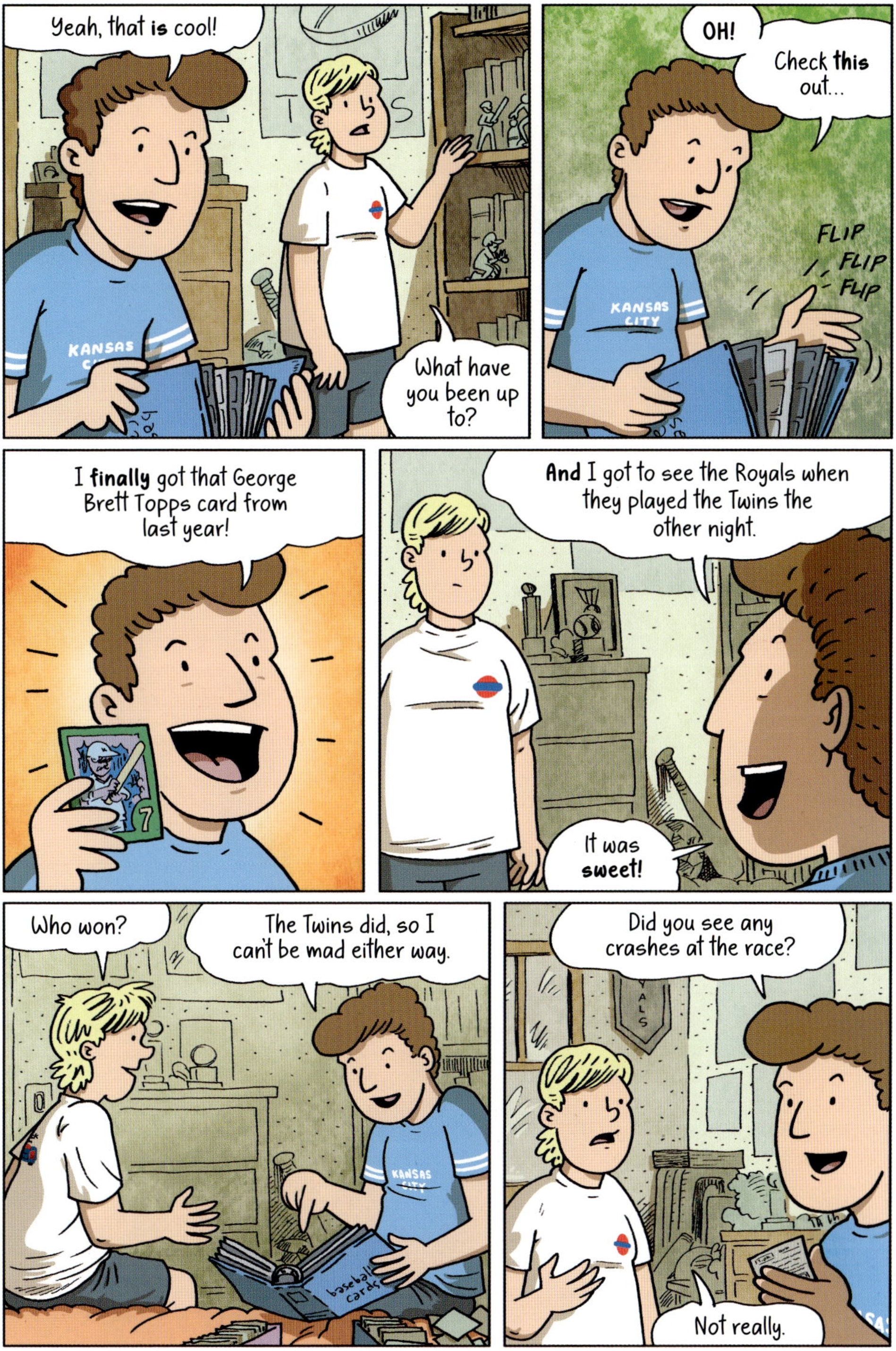
Yeah, that **is** cool!
What have you been up to?
OH!
Check **this** out...
FLIP FLIP FLIP
KANSAS CITY
I **finally** got that George Brett Topps card from last year!
And I got to see the Royals when they played the Twins the other night.
It was **sweet!**
Who won?
The Twins did, so I can't be mad either way.
baseball cards
Did you see any crashes at the race?
Not really.

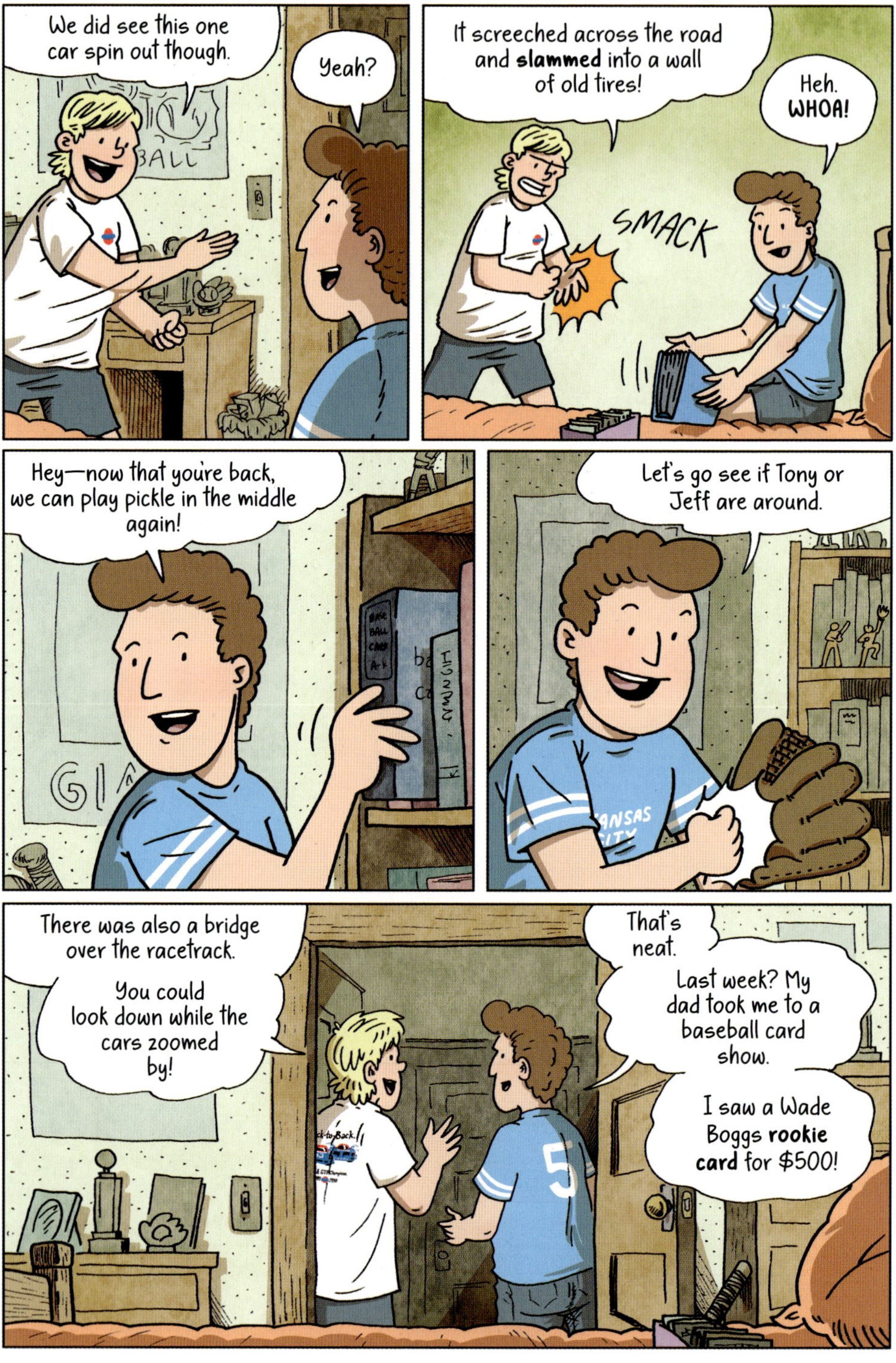
We did see this one car spin out though.
Yeah?
It screeched across the road and **slammed** into a wall of old tires!
Heh. **WHOA!**
SMACK
Hey—now that you're back, we can play pickle in the middle again!
Let's go see if Tony or Jeff are around.
There was also a bridge over the racetrack.
You could look down while the cars zoomed by!
That's neat.
Last week? My dad took me to a baseball card show.
I saw a Wade Boggs **rookie card** for $500!

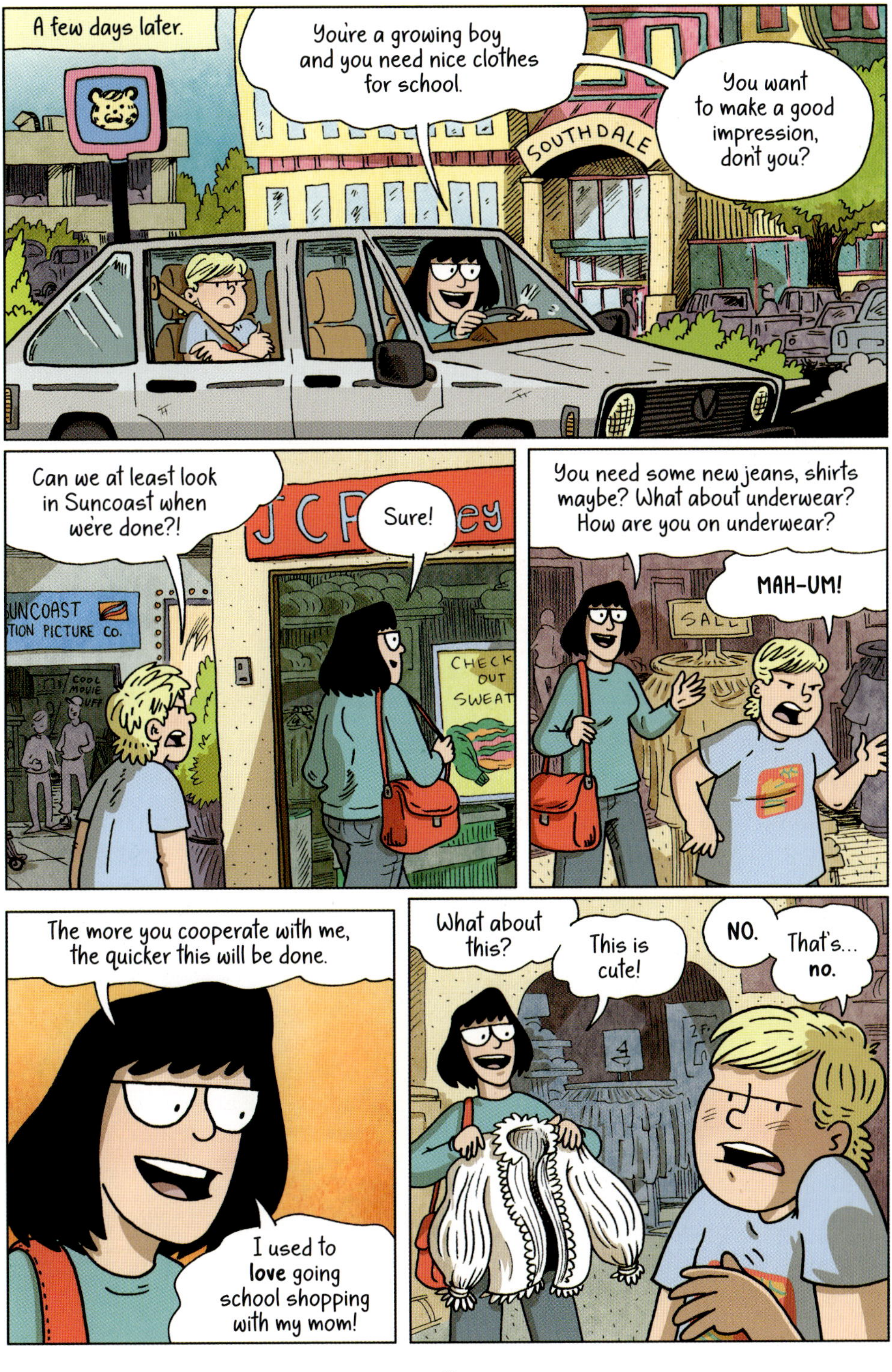

A few days later.
You're a growing boy and you need nice clothes for school.
You want to make a good impression, don't you?
SOUTHDALE
Can we at least look in Suncoast when we're done?!
Sure!
SUNCOAST MOTION PICTURE CO.
COOL MOVIE STUFF
CHECK OUT SWEAT
You need some new jeans, shirts maybe? What about underwear? How are you on underwear?
MAH-UM!
SALE
The more you cooperate with me, the quicker this will be done.
I used to **love** going school shopping with my mom!
What about this?
This is cute!
NO.
That's... **no.**

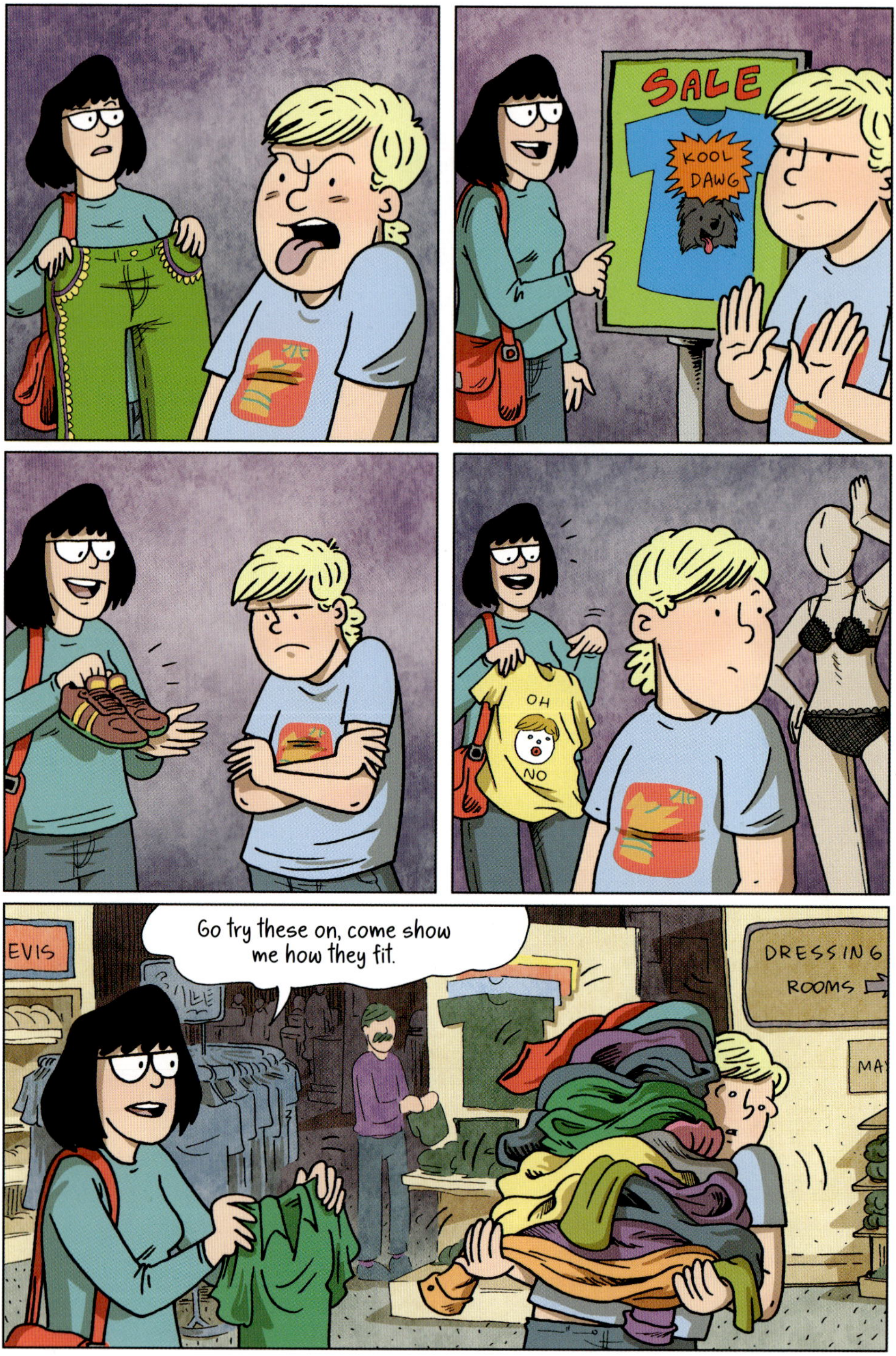
SALE
KOOL DAWG
OH
NO
EVIS
Go try these on, come show me how they fit.
DRESSING ROOMS

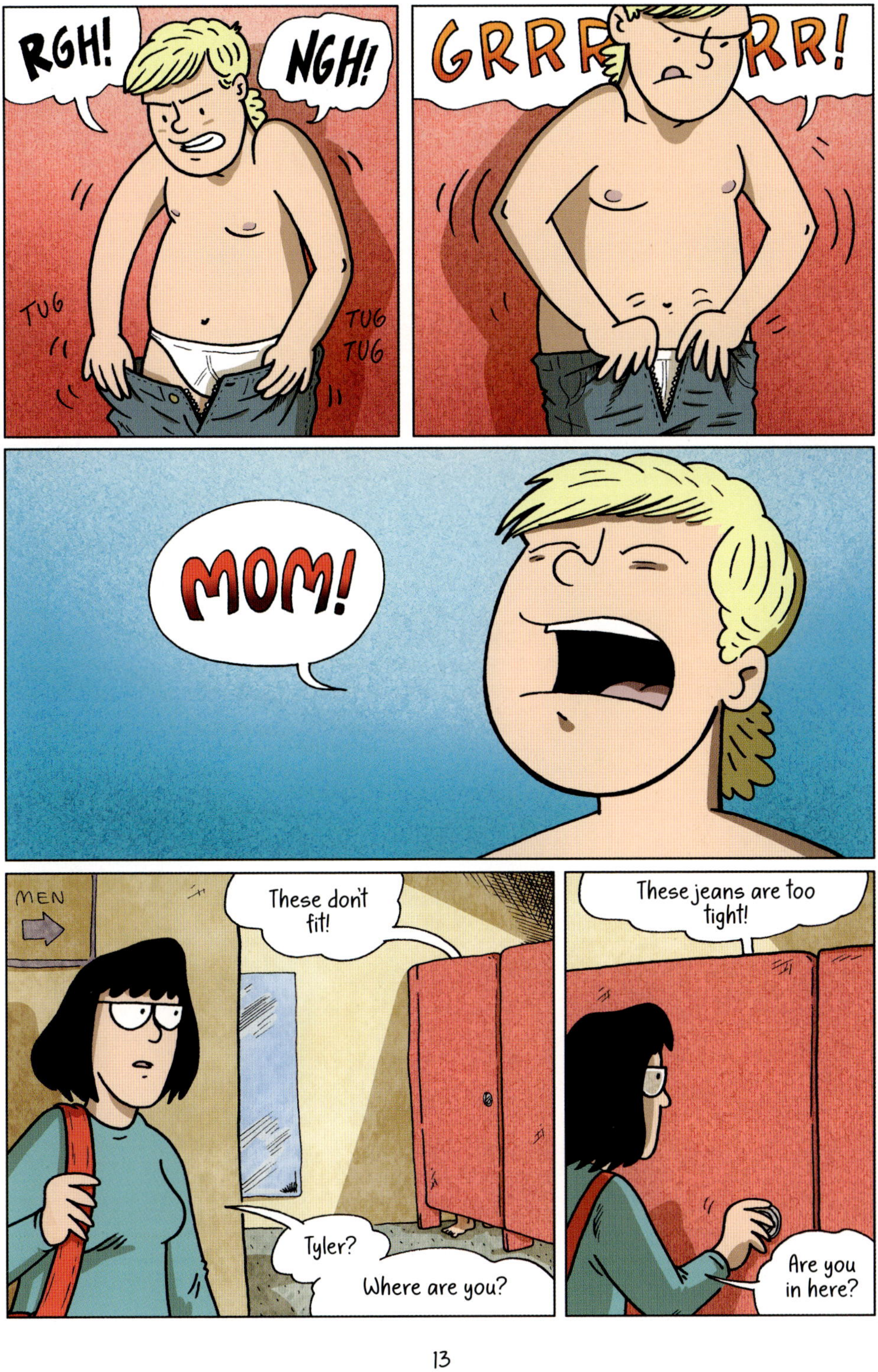
RGH!
NGH!
TUG
TUG
TUG
GRRRRR!
MOM!
MEN
These don't fit!
Tyler?
Where are you?
These jeans are too tight!
Are you in here?

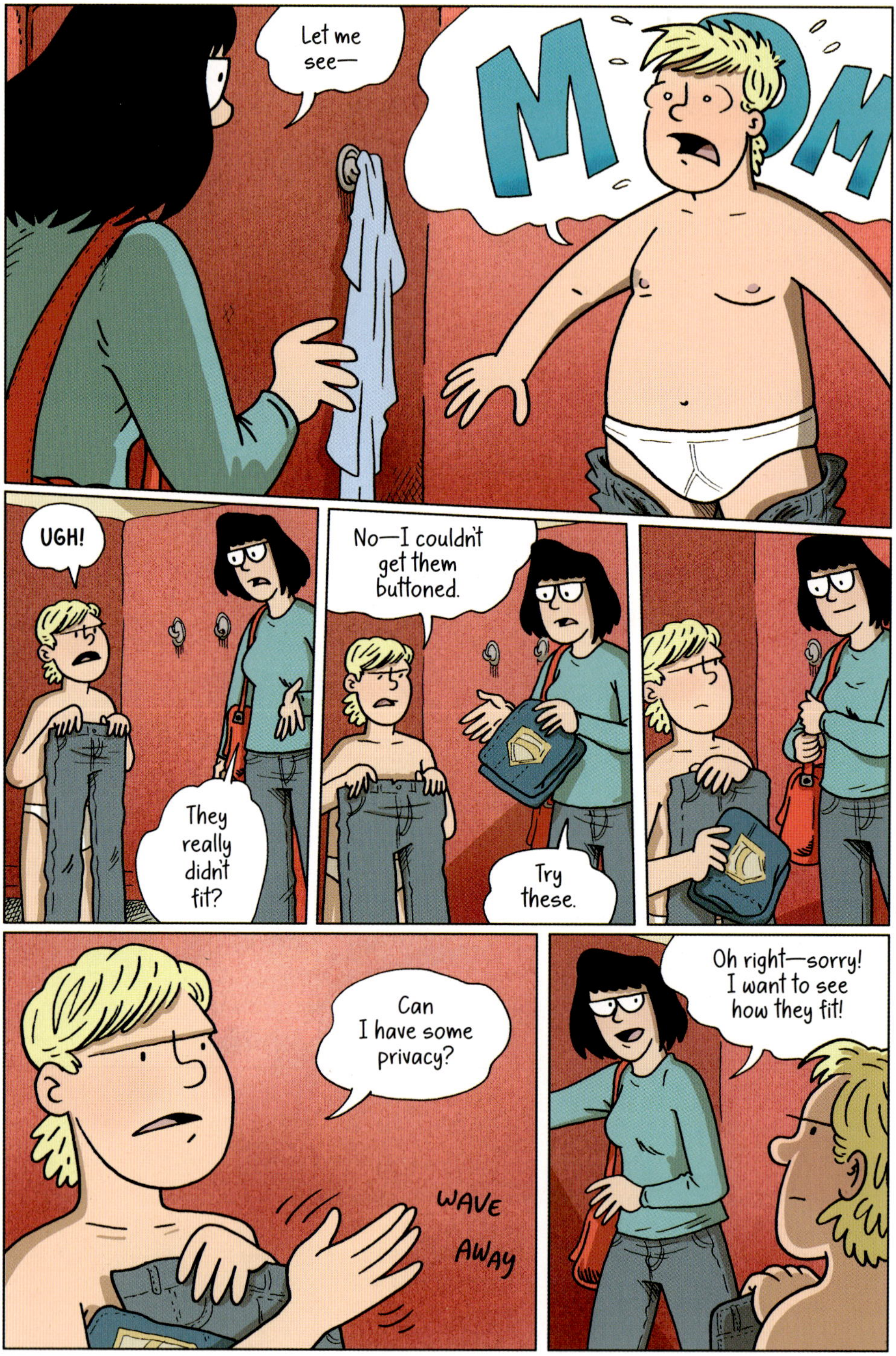
Let me see—
MOM
UGH!
They really didn't fit?
No—I couldn't get them buttoned.
Try these.
Can I have some privacy?
WAVE
AWAY
Oh right—sorry! I want to see how they fit!

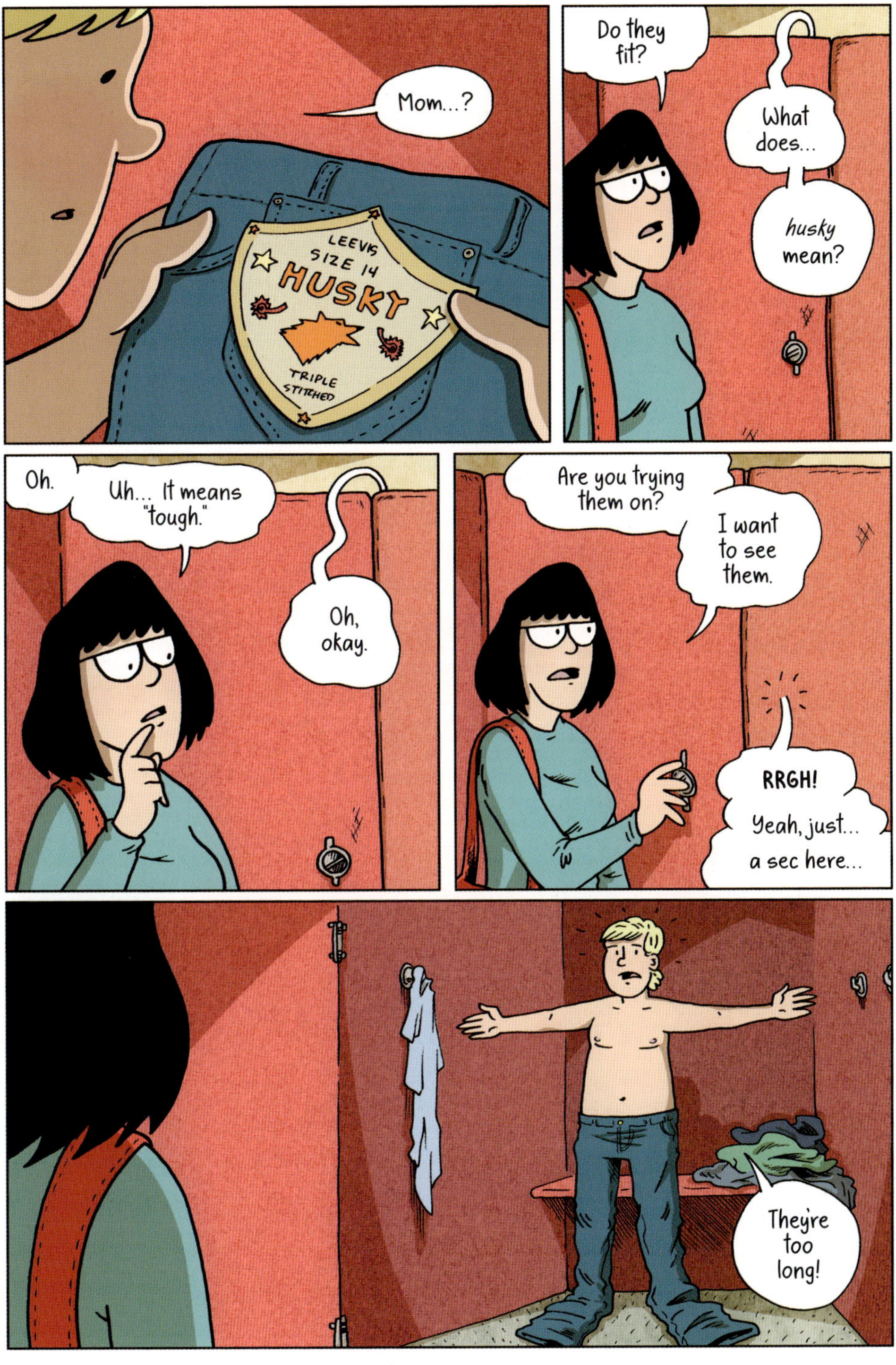
Mom...?
LEEVIS
SIZE 14
HUSKY
TRIPLE STITCHED
Do they fit?
What does...
husky mean?
Oh.
Uh... It means "tough."
Oh, okay.
Are you trying them on?
I want to see them.
RRGH!
Yeah, just... a sec here...
They're too long!

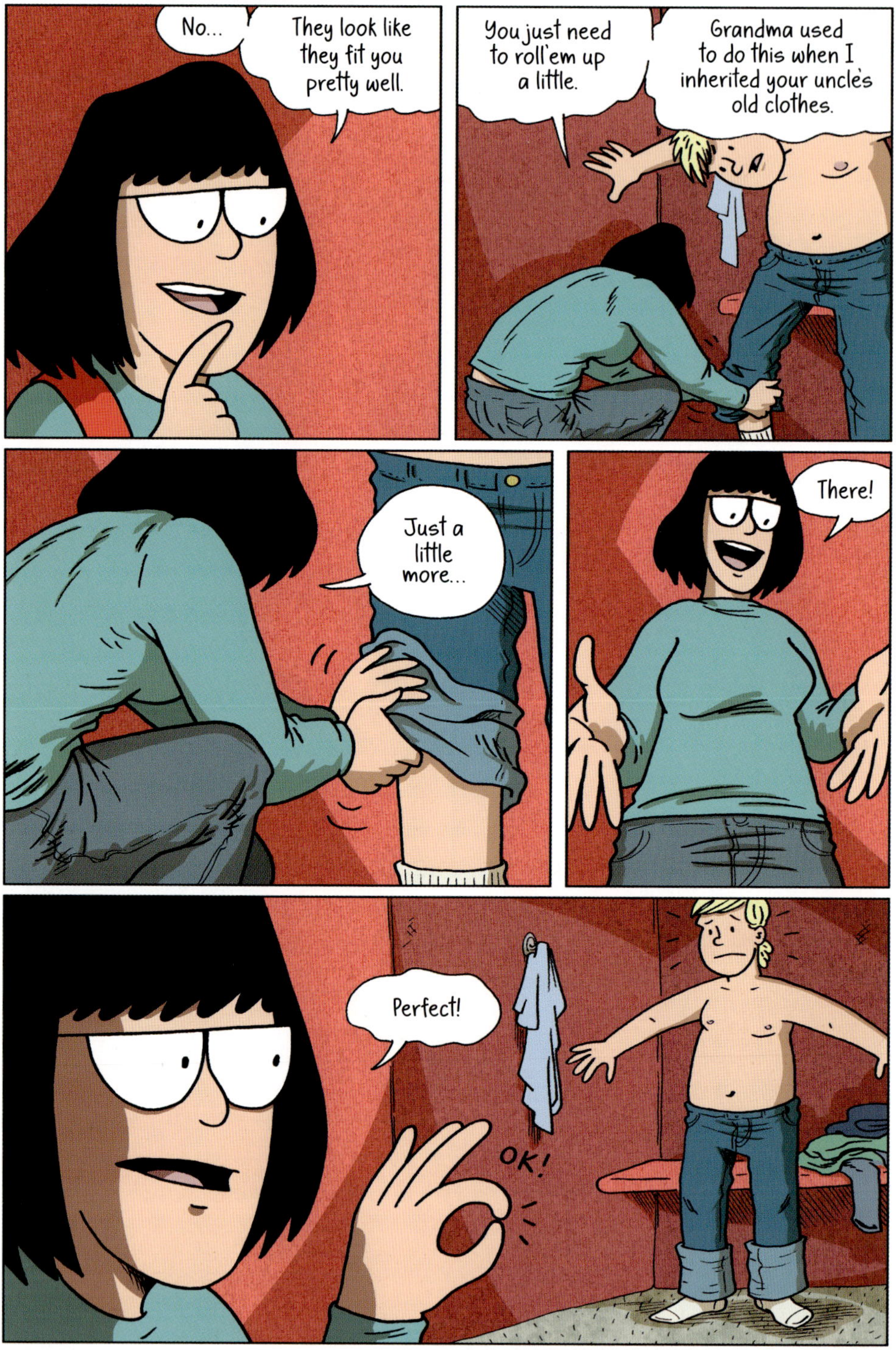
No...
They look like they fit you pretty well.
You just need to roll'em up a little.
Grandma used to do this when I inherited your uncle's old clothes.
Just a little more...
There!
Perfect!
OK!

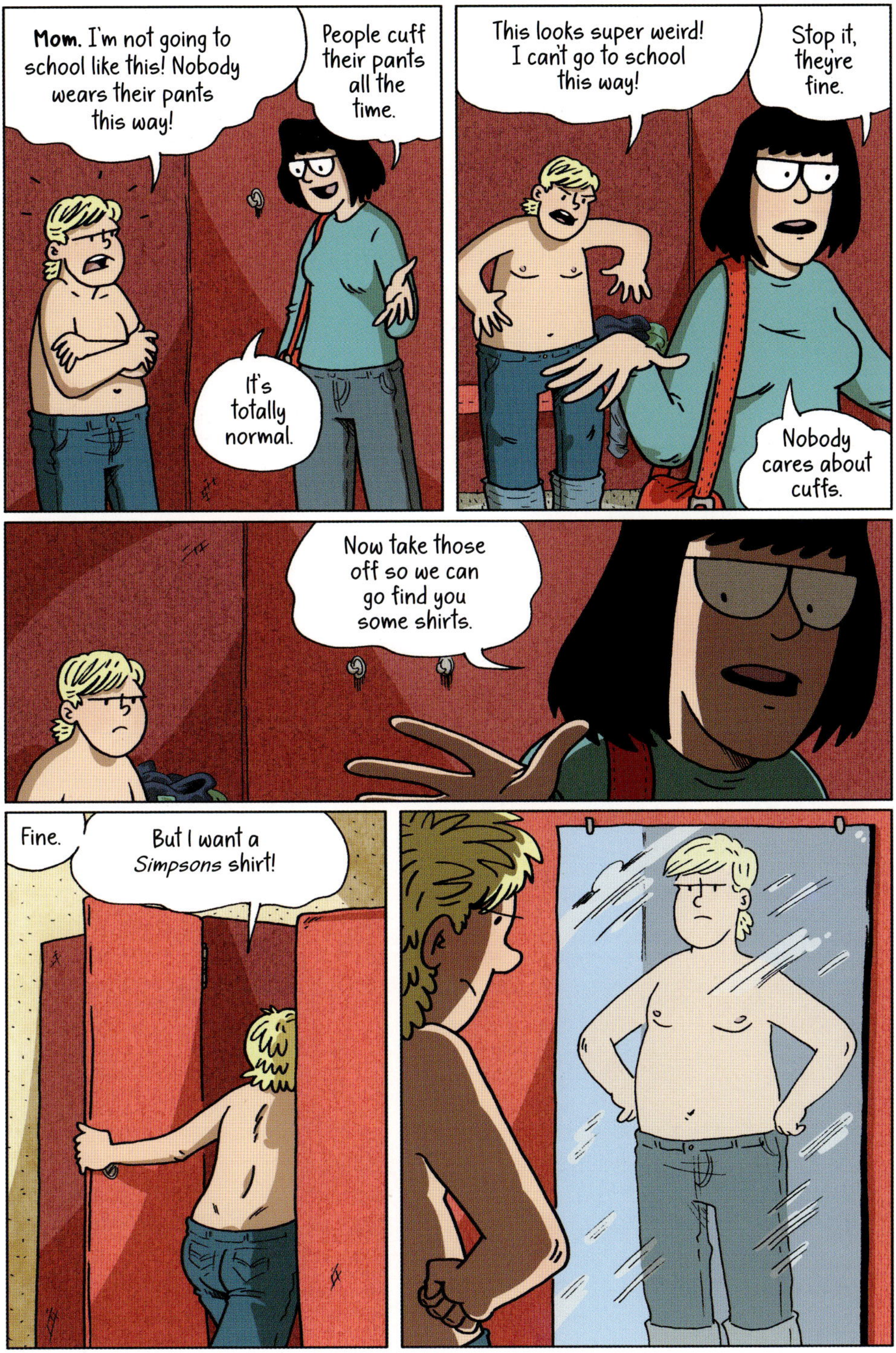
Mom. I'm not going to school like this! Nobody wears their pants this way!
People cuff their pants all the time.
It's totally normal.
This looks super weird! I can't go to school this way!
Stop it, they're fine.
Nobody cares about cuffs.
Now take those off so we can go find you some shirts.
Fine.
But I want a *Simpsons* shirt!

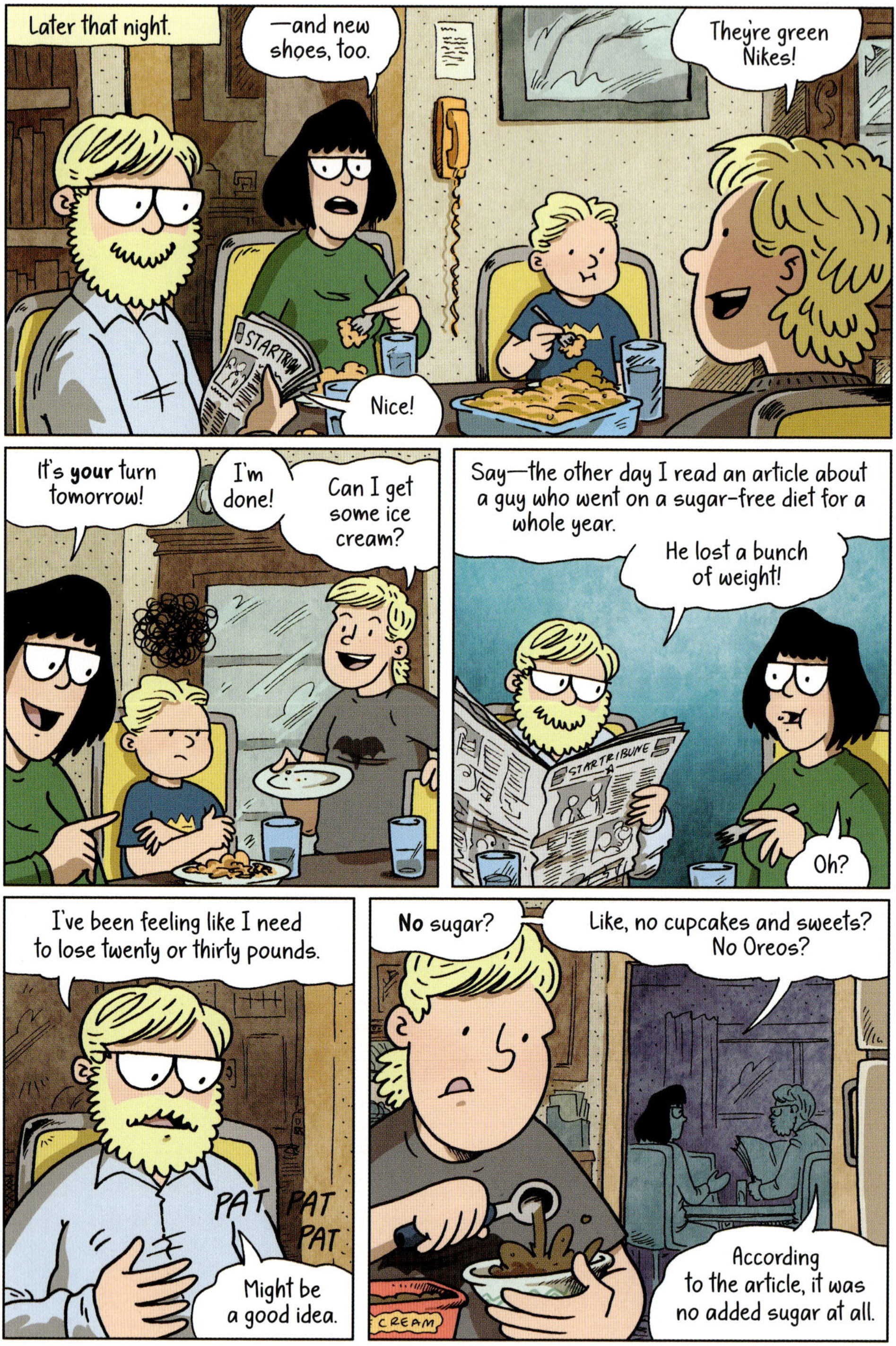
Later that night.
—and new shoes, too.
They're green Nikes!
STARTRIB
Nice!
It's **your** turn tomorrow!
I'm done!
Can I get some ice cream?
Say—the other day I read an article about a guy who went on a sugar-free diet for a whole year.
He lost a bunch of weight!
STARTRIBUNE
Oh?
I've been feeling like I need to lose twenty or thirty pounds.
PAT PAT PAT
Might be a good idea.
No sugar?
Like, no cupcakes and sweets? No Oreos?
CREAM
According to the article, it was no added sugar at all.

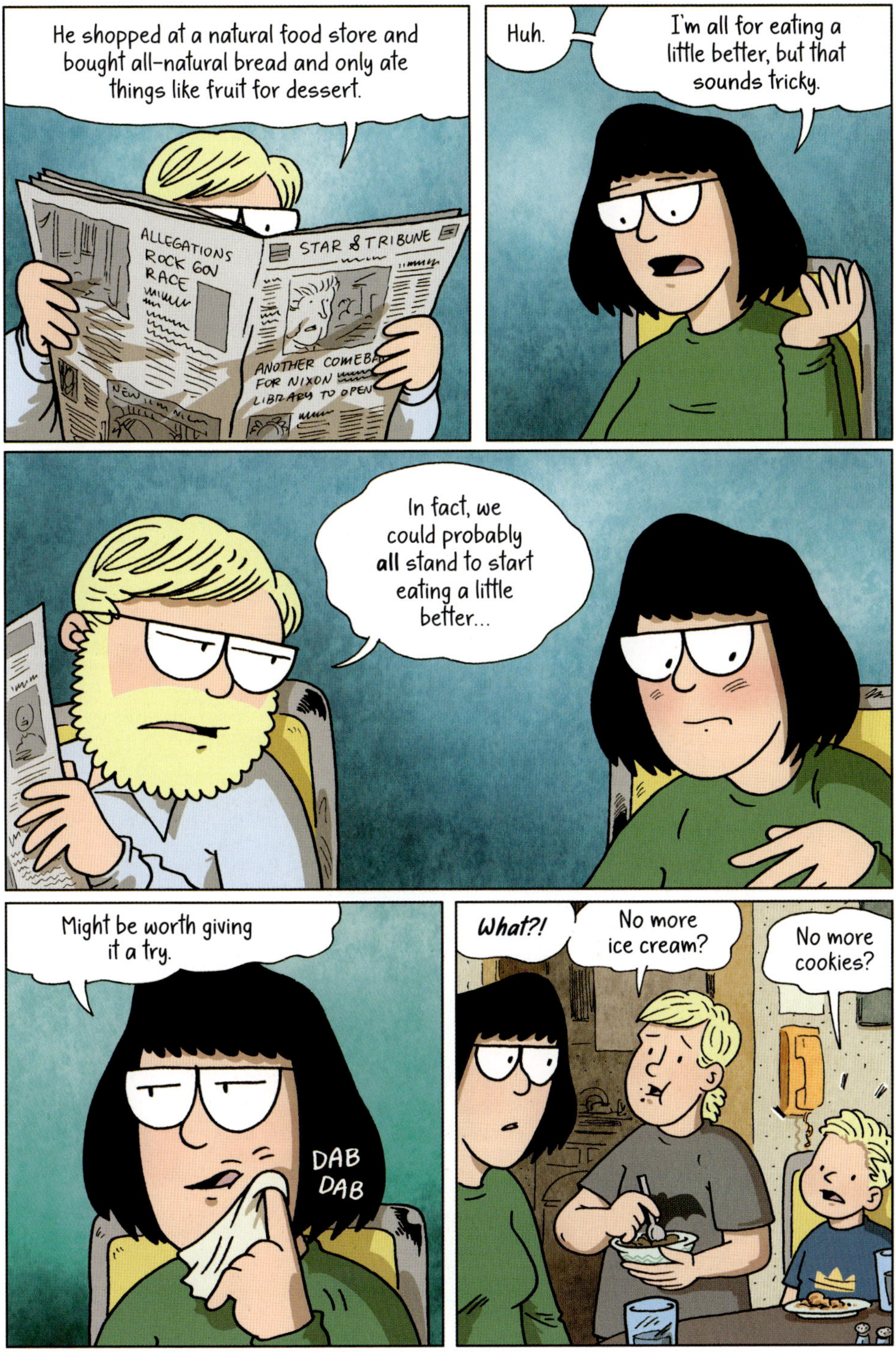
He shopped at a natural food store and bought all-natural bread and only ate things like fruit for dessert.
ALLEGATIONS ROCK GOV RACE
STAR & TRIBUNE
FOR NIXON
LIBRARY TO OPEN
Huh.
I'm all for eating a little better, but that sounds tricky.
In fact, we could probably **all** stand to start eating a little better...
Might be worth giving it a try.
DAB DAB
What?!
No more ice cream?
No more cookies?

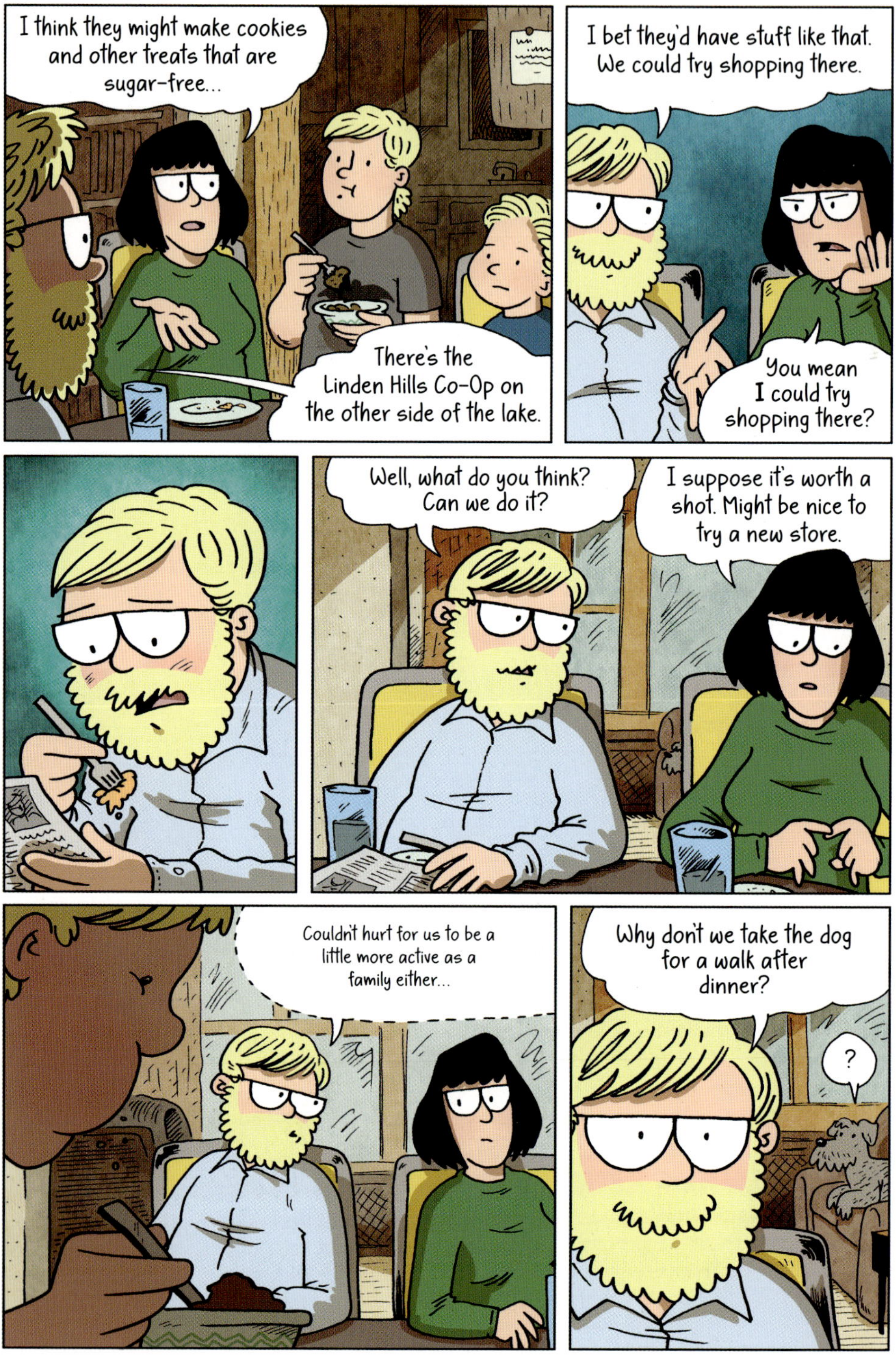
I think they might make cookies and other treats that are sugar-free...
There's the Linden Hills Co-Op on the other side of the lake.
I bet they'd have stuff like that. We could try shopping there.
You mean I could try shopping there?
Well, what do you think? Can we do it?
I suppose it's worth a shot. Might be nice to try a new store.
Couldn't hurt for us to be a little more active as a family either...
Why don't we take the dog for a walk after dinner?
?

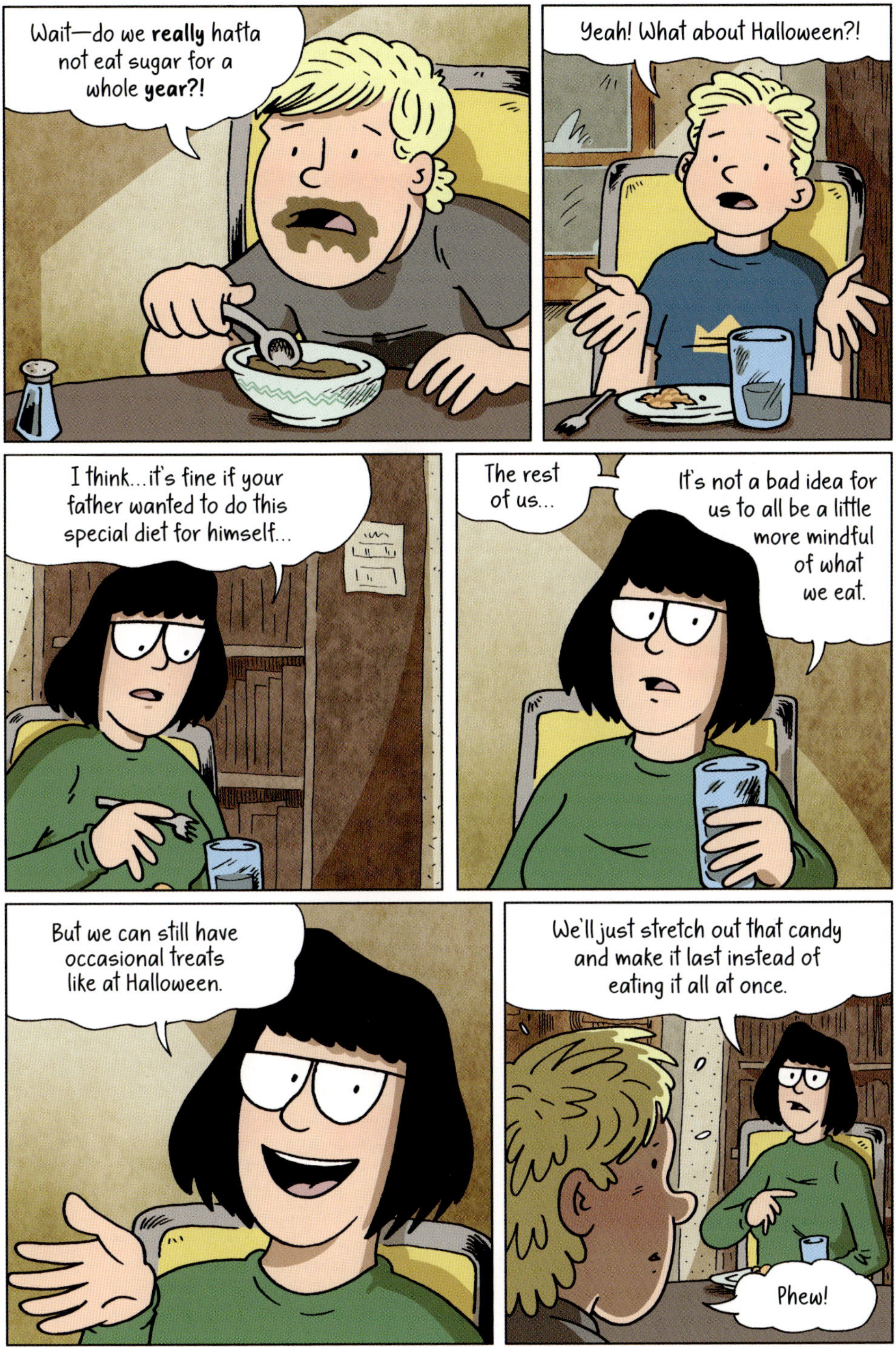
Wait—do we **really** hafta not eat sugar for a whole **year**?!
Yeah! What about Halloween?!
I think...it's fine if your father wanted to do this special diet for himself...
The rest of us...
It's not a bad idea for us to all be a little more mindful of what we eat.
But we can still have occasional treats like at Halloween.
We'll just stretch out that candy and make it last instead of eating it all at once.
Phew!

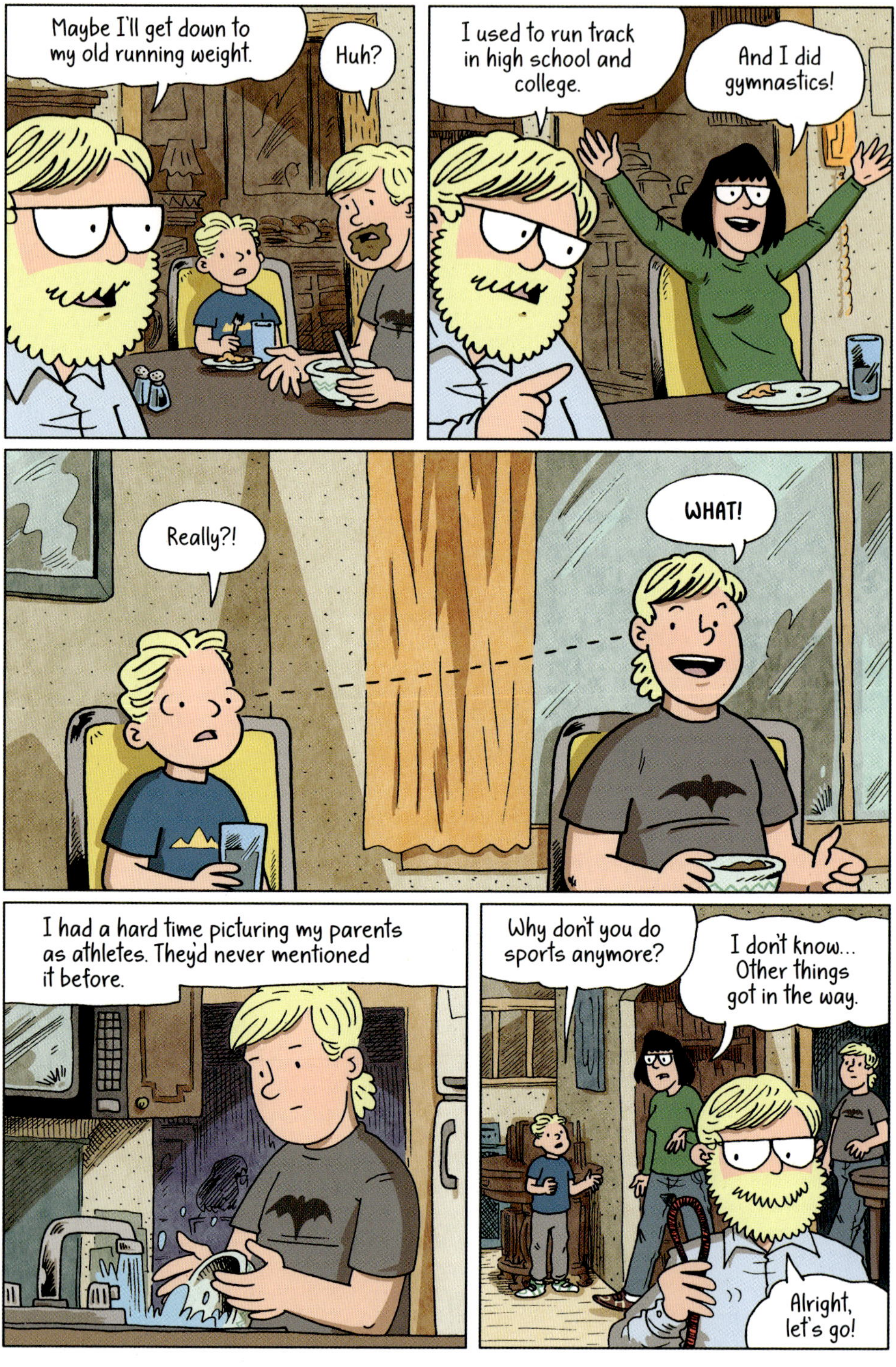

Maybe I'll get down to my old running weight.
Huh?
I used to run track in high school and college.
And I did gymnastics!
Really?!
WHAT!
I had a hard time picturing my parents as athletes. They'd never mentioned it before.
Why don't you do sports anymore?
I don't know... Other things got in the way.
Alright, let's go!

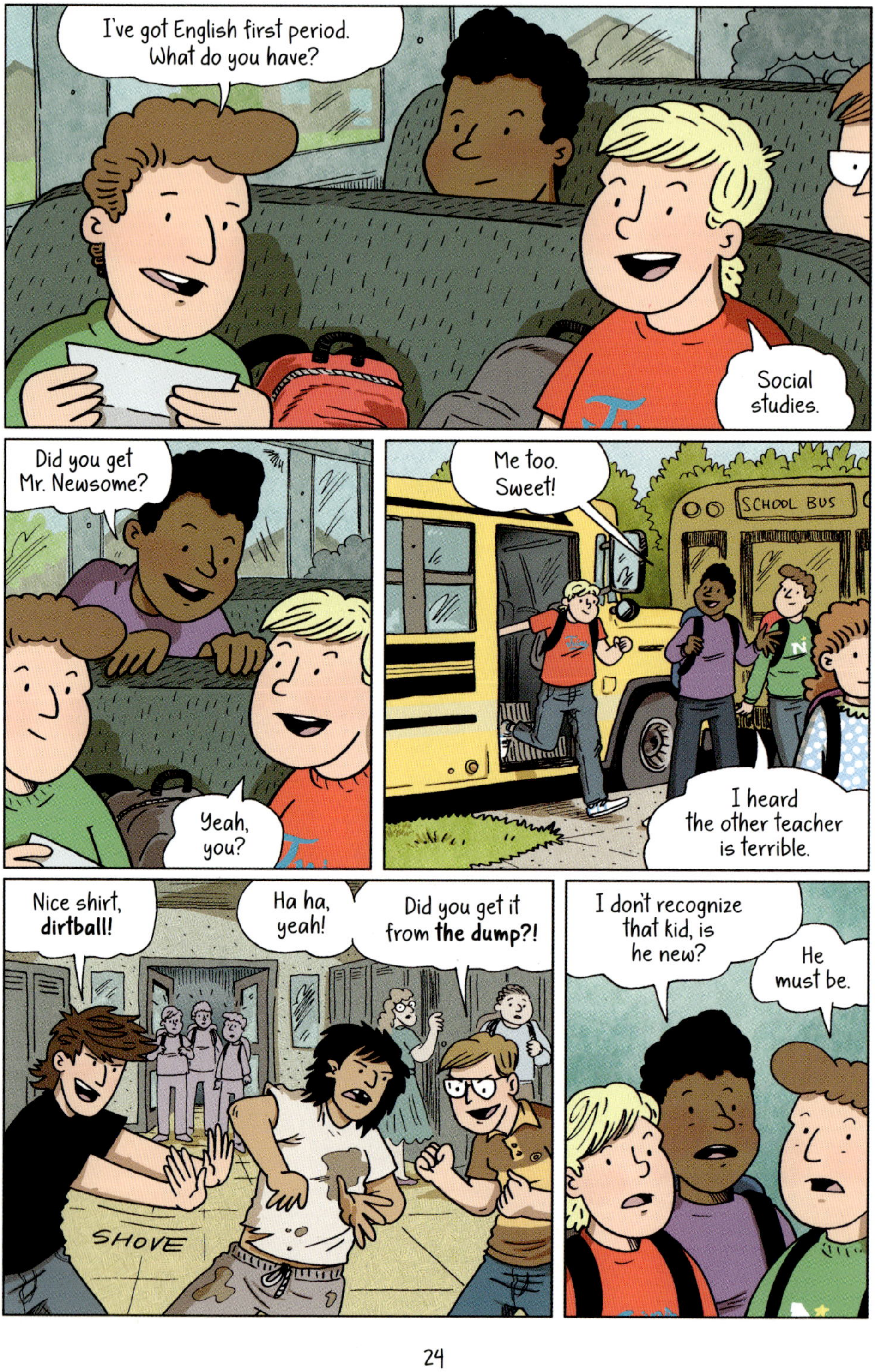

I've got English first period. What do you have?
Social studies.
Did you get Mr. Newsome?
Yeah, you?
Me too. Sweet!
I heard the other teacher is terrible.
Nice shirt, **dirtball!**
Ha ha, yeah!
Did you get it from **the dump?!**
SHOVE
I don't recognize that kid, is he new?
He must be.

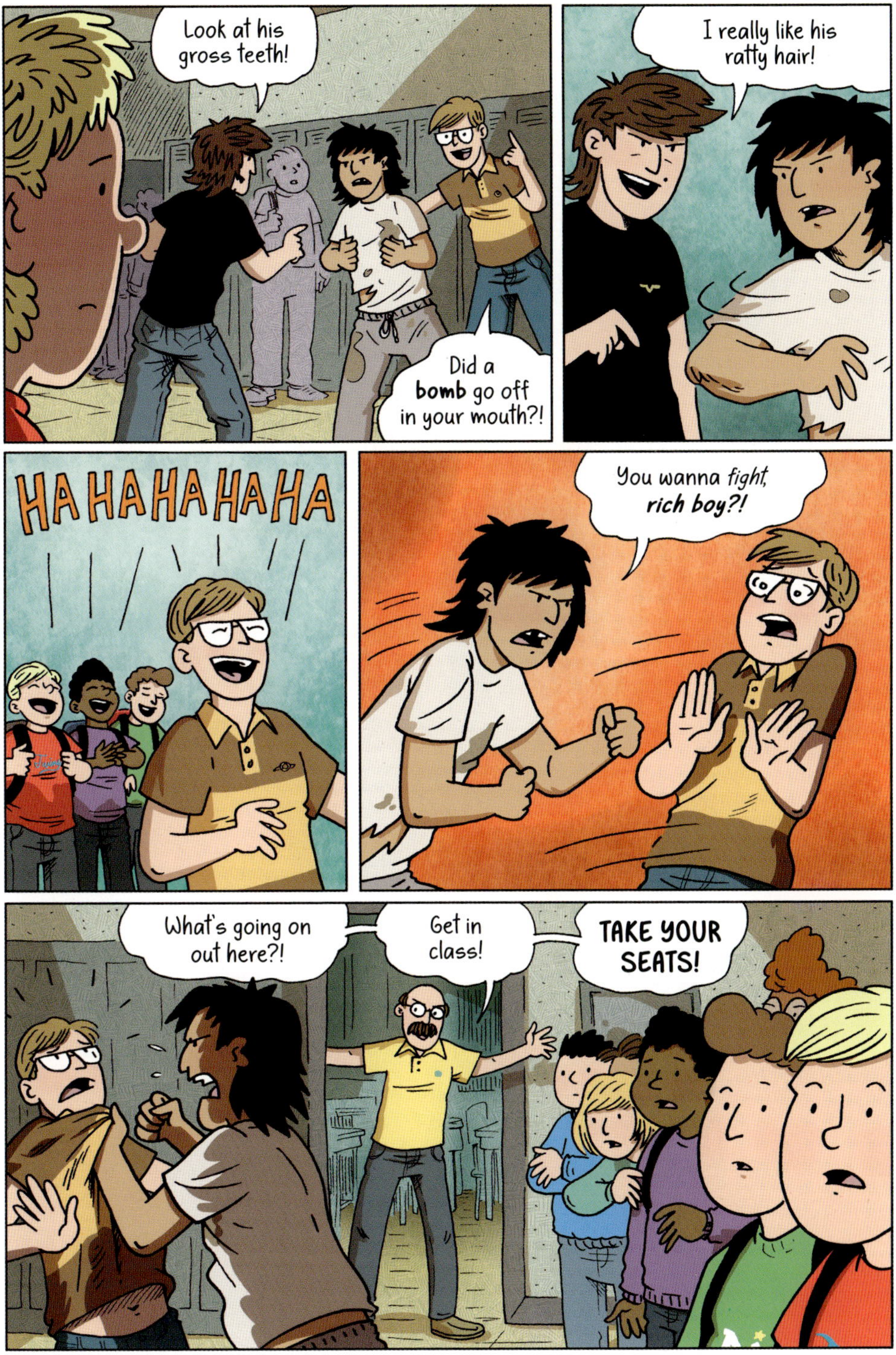
Look at his gross teeth!
Did a **bomb** go off in your mouth?!
I really like his ratty hair!
HAHAHAHAHA
You wanna *fight*, ***rich boy?!***
What's going on out here?!
Get in class!
TAKE YOUR SEATS!

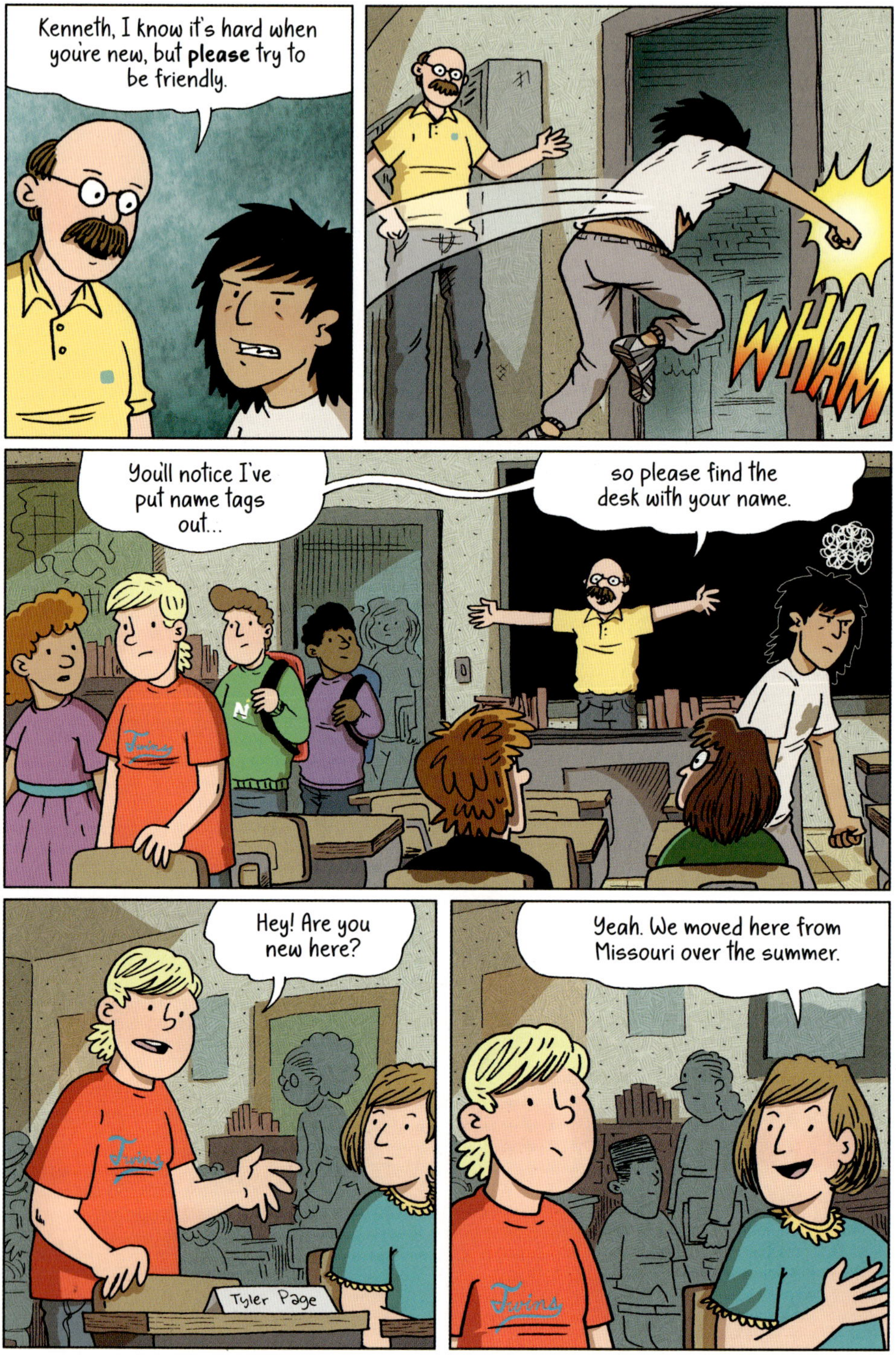

Kenneth, I know it's hard when you're new, but **please** try to be friendly.
WHAM
You'll notice I've put name tags out...
so please find the desk with your name.
Hey! Are you new here?
Tyler Page
Yeah. We moved here from Missouri over the summer.

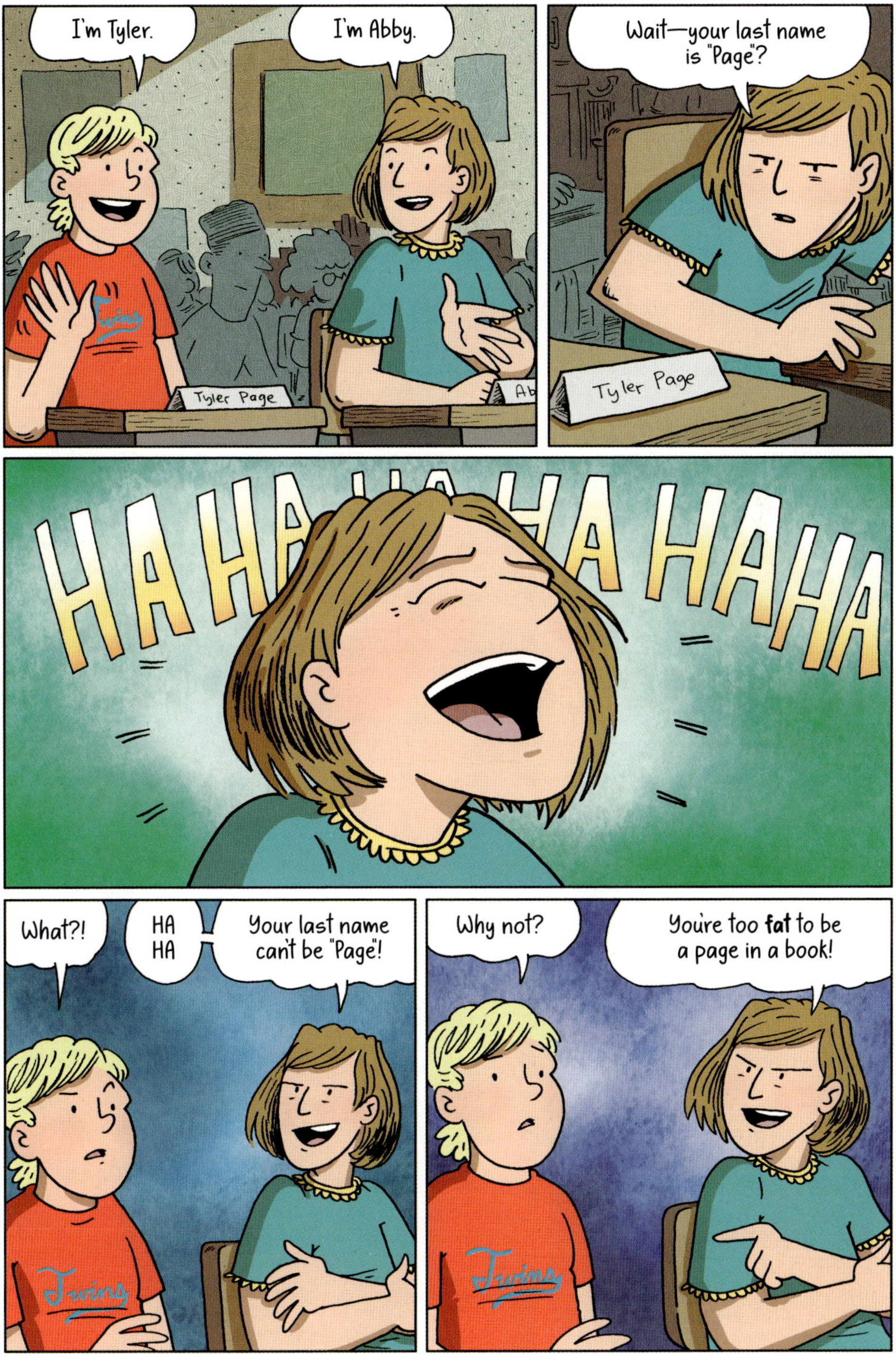
I'm Tyler.
I'm Abby.
Tyler Page
Wait—your last name is "Page"?
Tyler Page
HAHAHAHAHAHAHAHA
What?!
HA HA
Your last name can't be "Page"!
Why not?
You're too **fat** to be a page in a book!

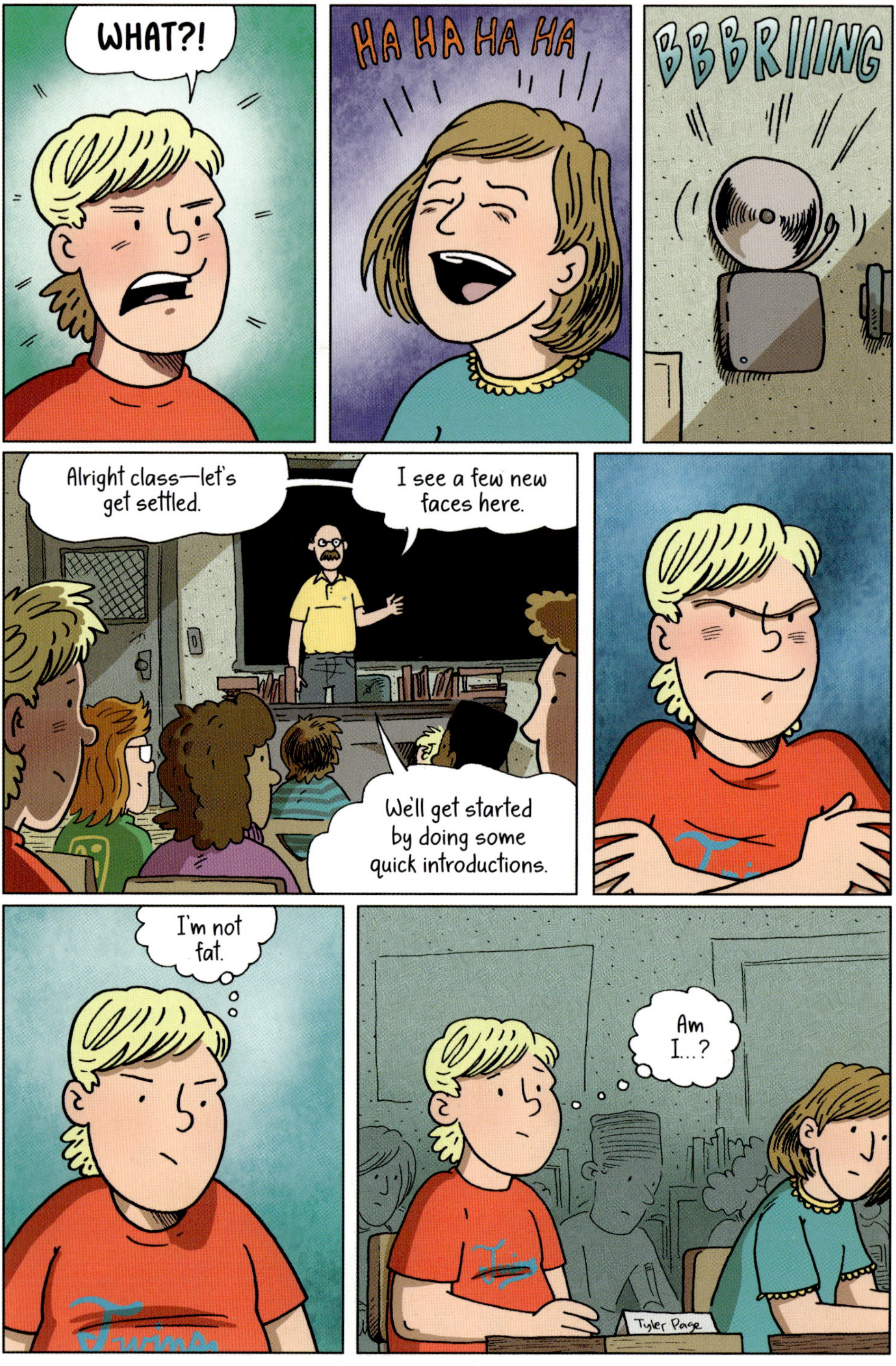
WHAT?!
HA HA HA HA
BBBRIIING
Alright class—let's get settled.
I see a few new faces here.
We'll get started by doing some quick introductions.
I'm not fat.
Am I...?
Tyler Page

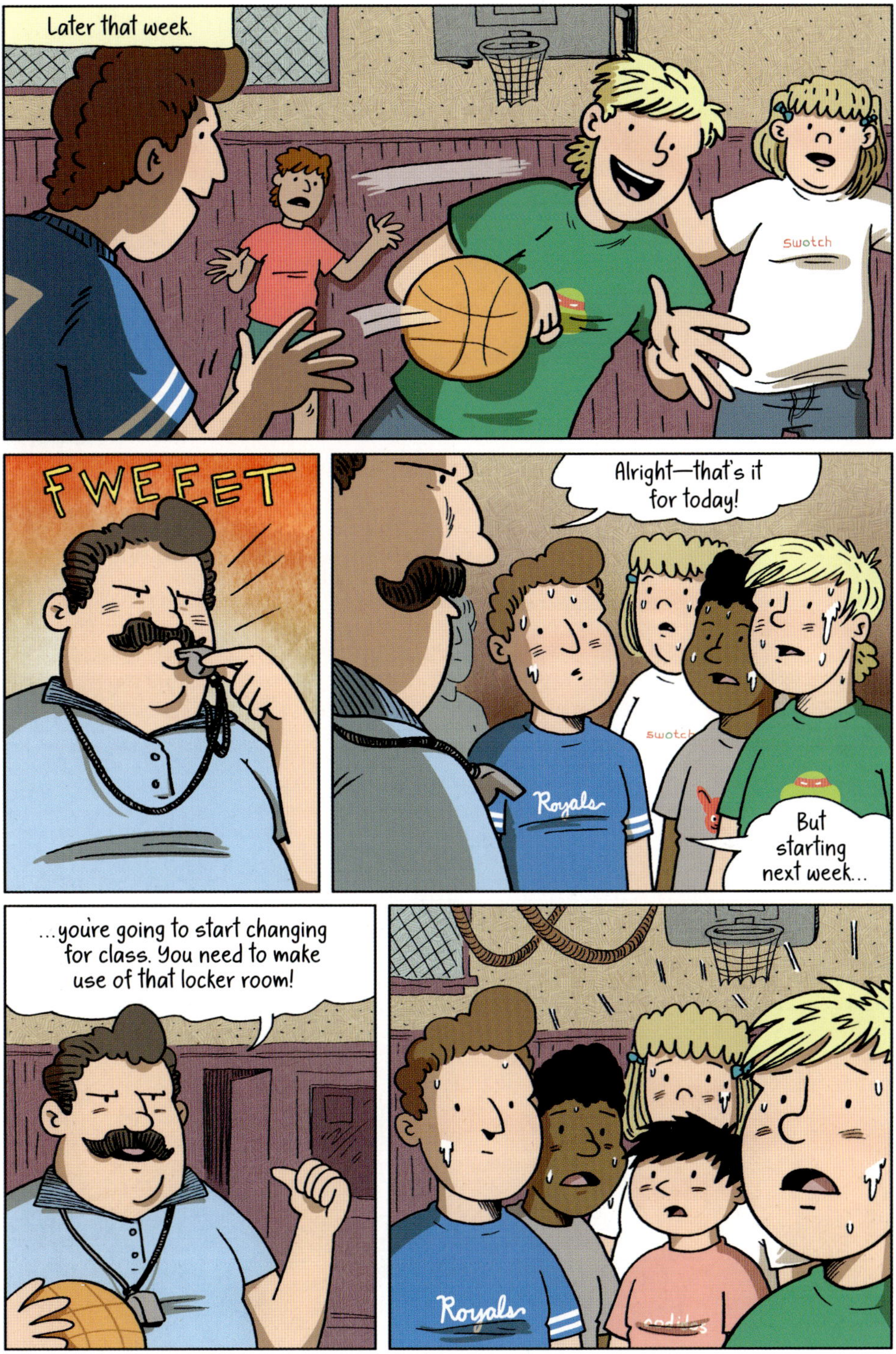
Later that week.
FWEEET
Alright—that's it for today!
But starting next week...
...you're going to start changing for class. You need to make use of that locker room!

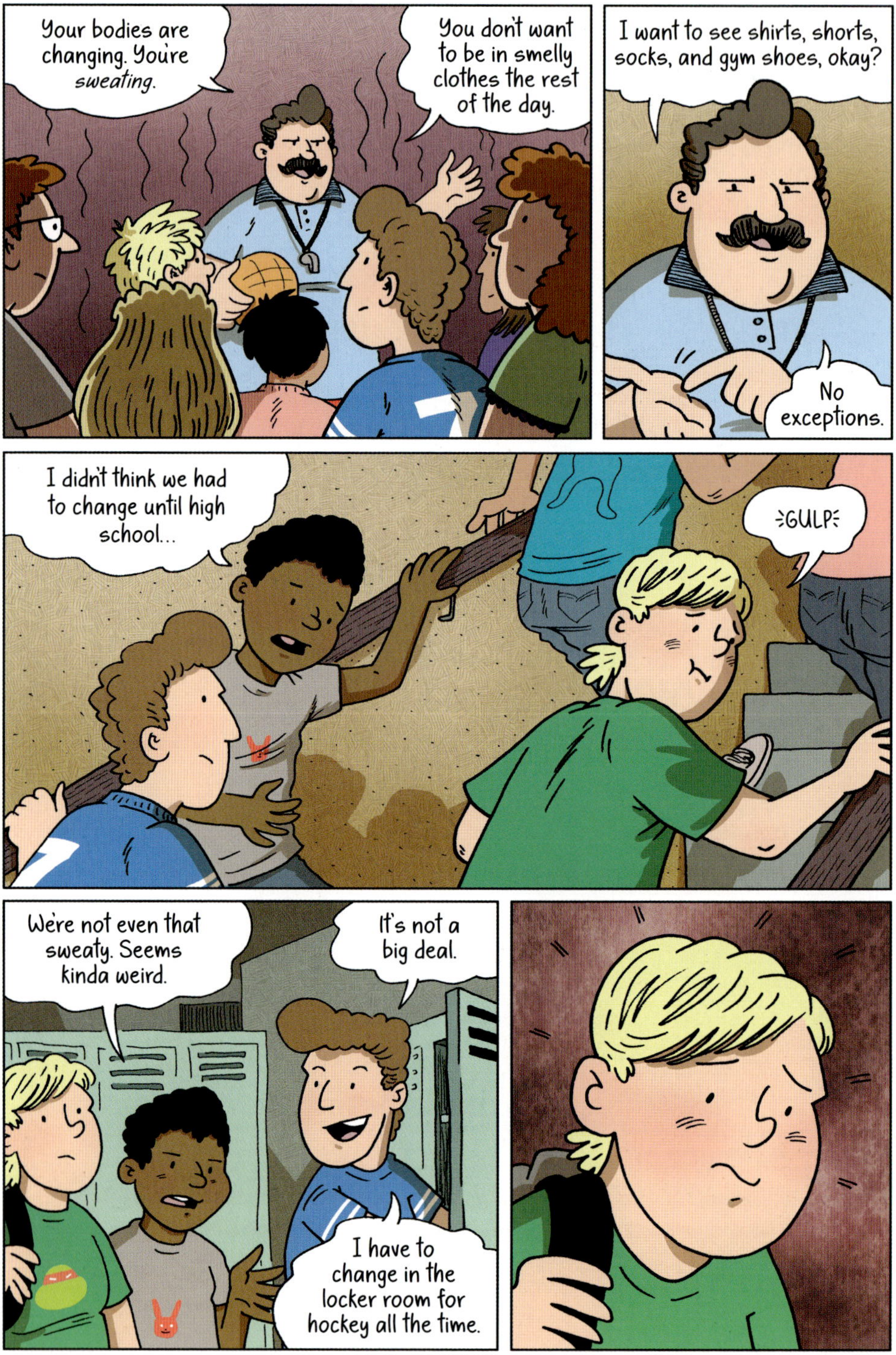
Your bodies are changing. You're *sweating*.
You don't want to be in smelly clothes the rest of the day.
I want to see shirts, shorts, socks, and gym shoes, okay?
No exceptions.
I didn't think we had to change until high school...
GULP
We're not even that sweaty. Seems kinda weird.
It's not a big deal.
I have to change in the locker room for hockey all the time.

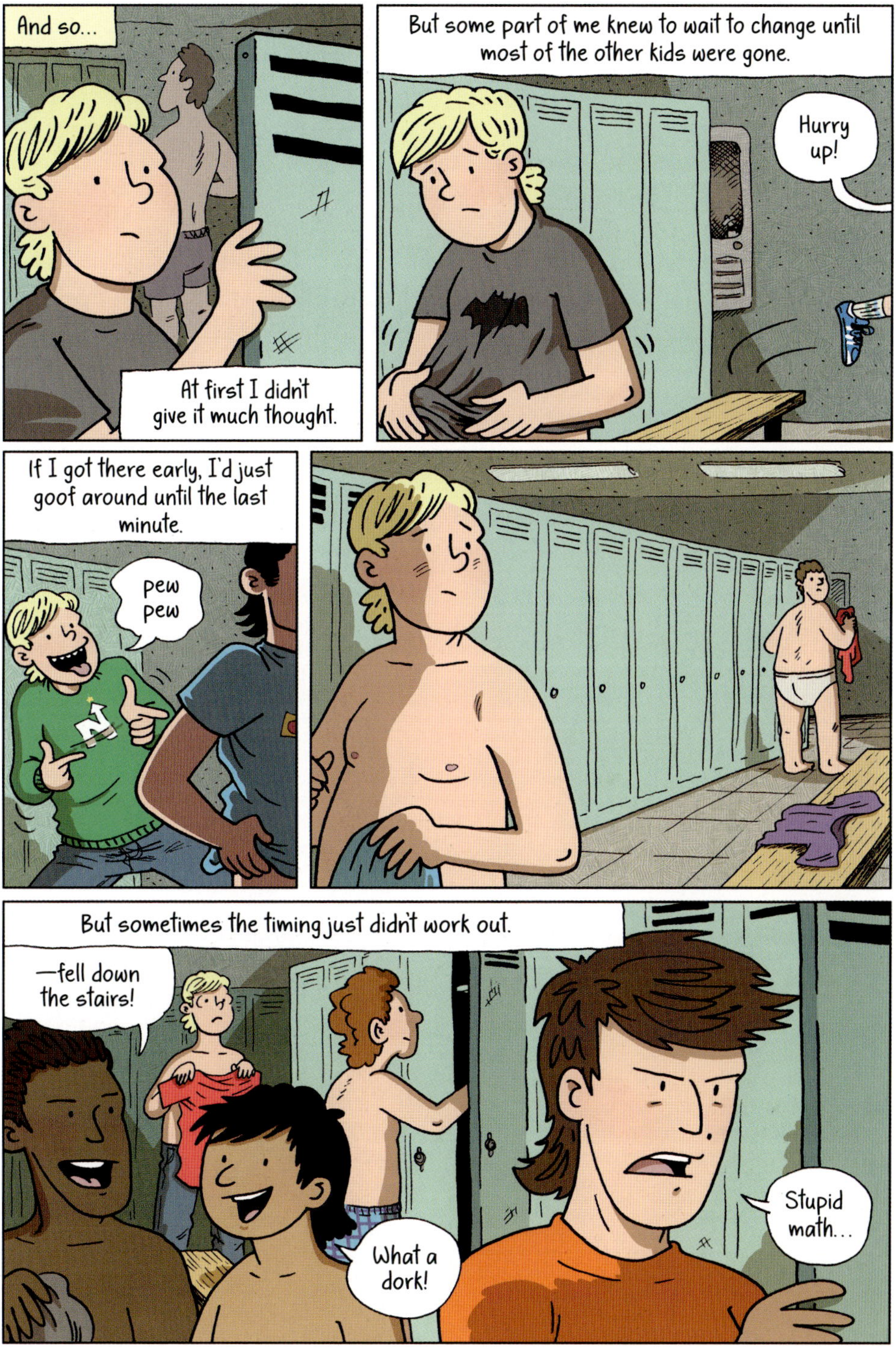
And so...
At first I didn't give it much thought.
But some part of me knew to wait to change until most of the other kids were gone.
Hurry up!
If I got there early, I'd just goof around until the last minute.
pew pew
But sometimes the timing just didn't work out.
—fell down the stairs!
What a dork!
Stupid math...

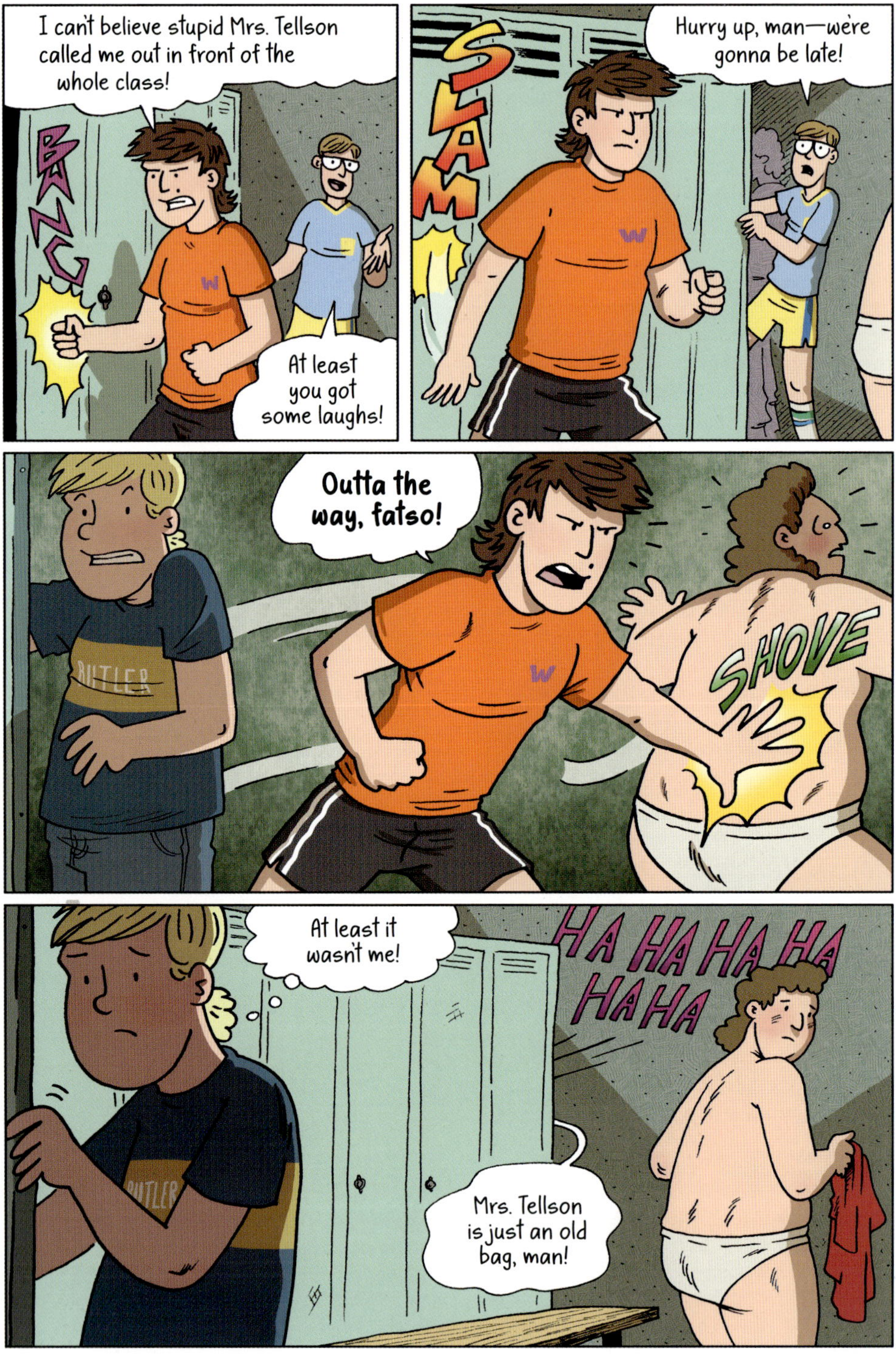
I can't believe stupid Mrs. Tellson called me out in front of the whole class!
BANG
At least you got some laughs!
SLAM
Hurry up, man—we're gonna be late!
Outta the way, fatso!
SHOVE
BUTLER
At least it wasn't me!
HA HA HA HA HA HA HA
BUTLER
Mrs. Tellson is just an old bag, man!

It was hard not to notice things were changing.
It seemed like a lot of my classmates had been working out.
Sculpted muscles...
...and bulging veins had suddenly appeared.
They were paying more attention to their appearances, too...

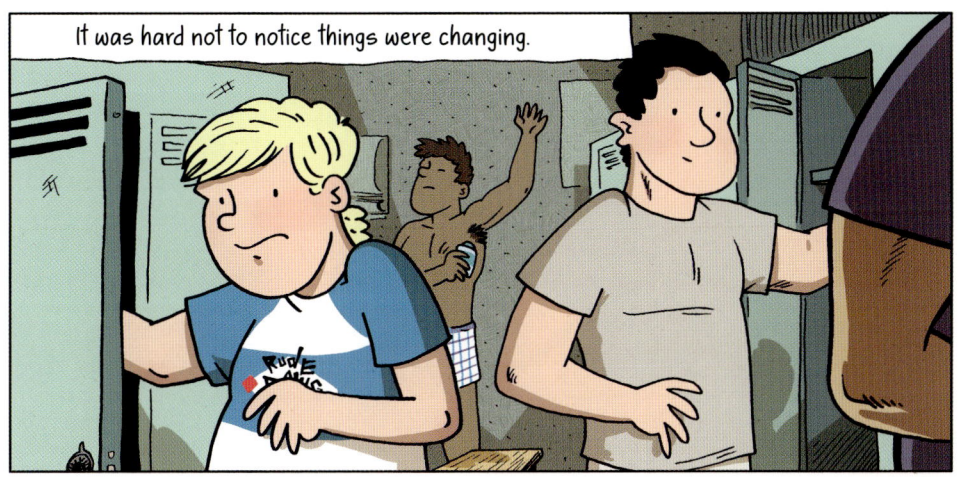

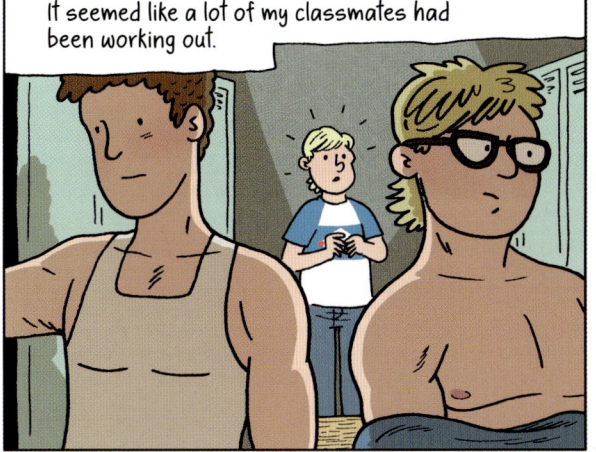

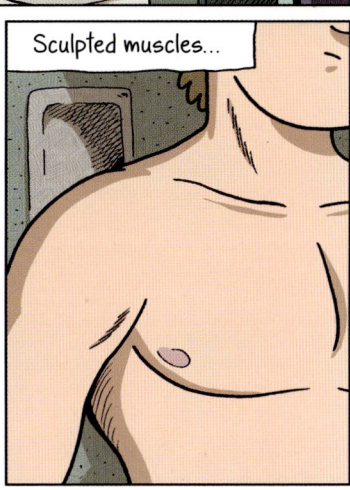

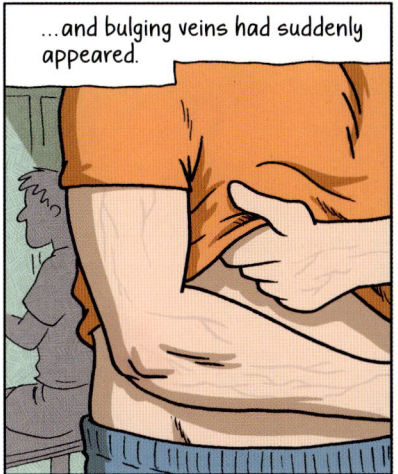

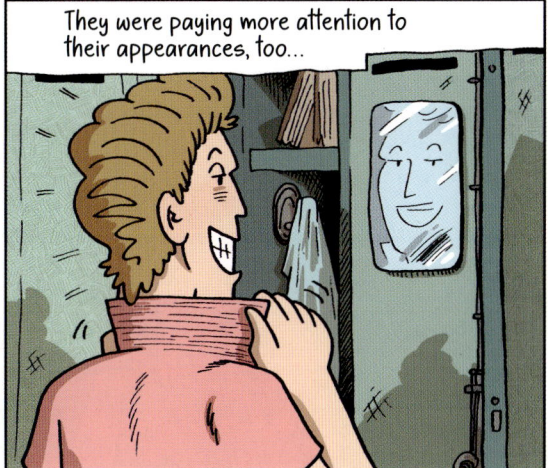

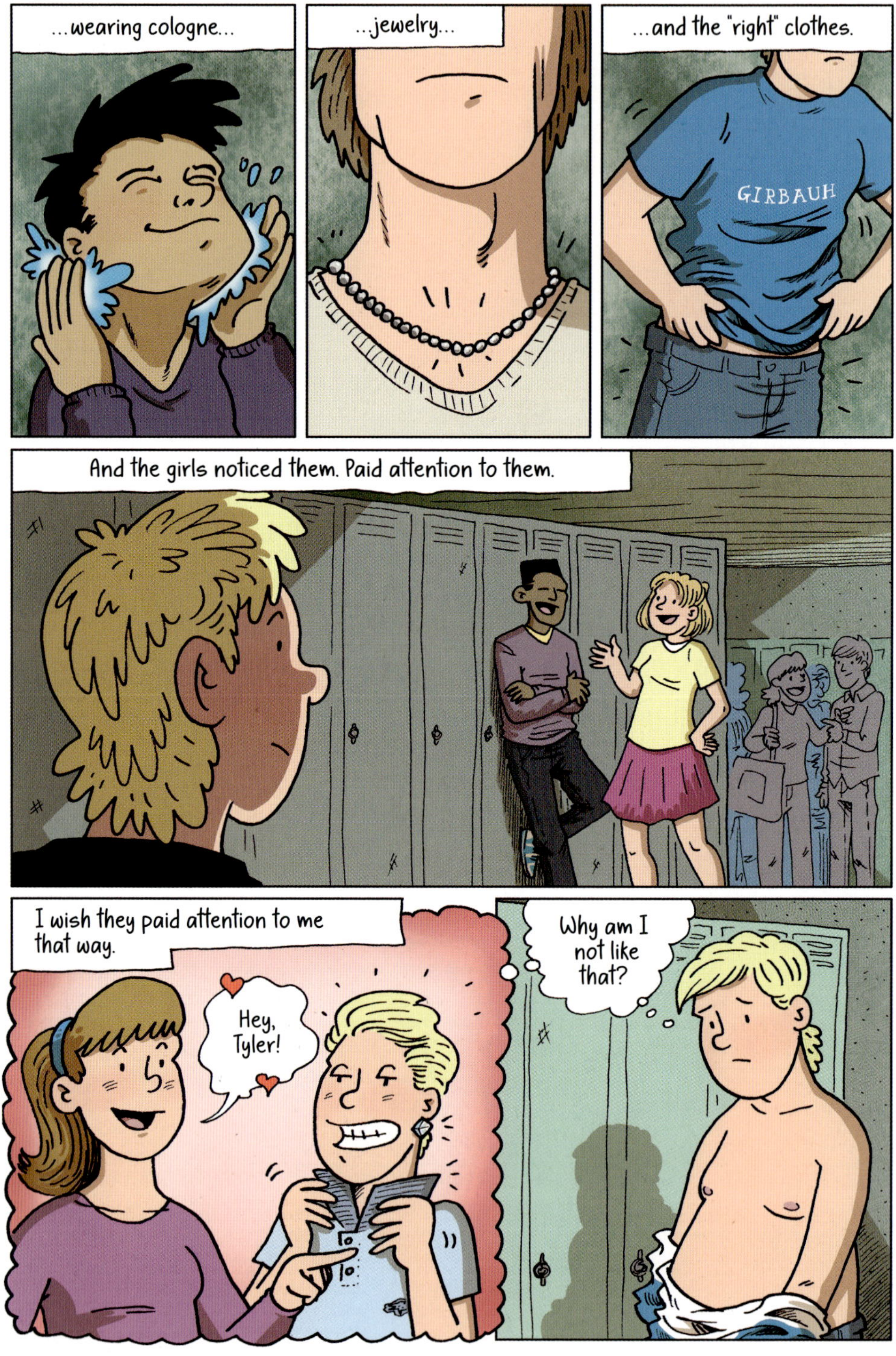
...wearing cologne...
...jewelry...
...and the "right" clothes.
GIRBAUH
And the girls noticed them. Paid attention to them.
I wish they paid attention to me that way.
Hey, Tyler!
Why am I not like that?

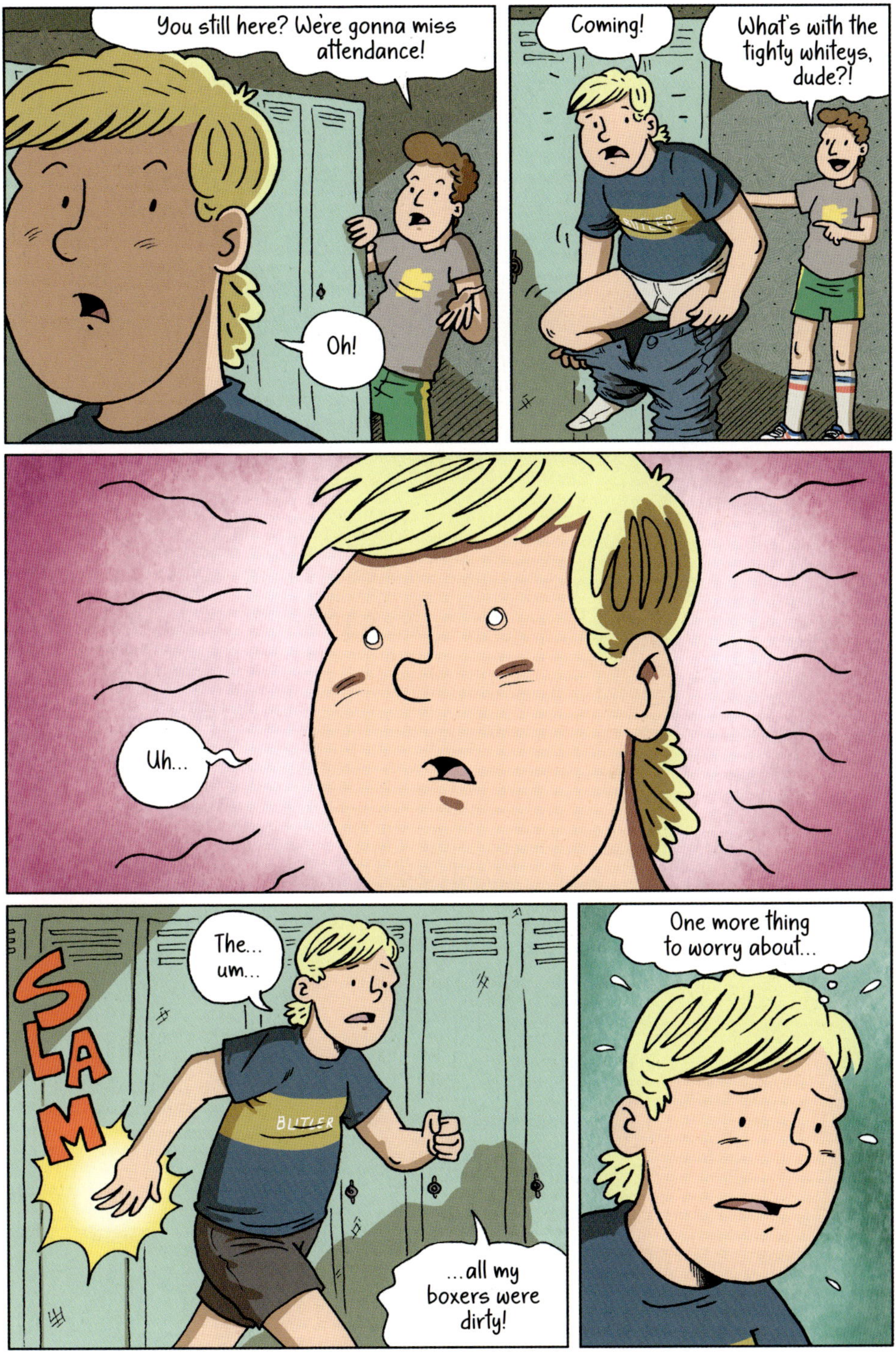
You still here? We're gonna miss attendance!
Oh!
Coming!
What's with the tighty whiteys, dude?!
BUTLER
Uh...
SLAM
The... um...
BUTLER
...all my boxers were dirty!
One more thing to worry about...

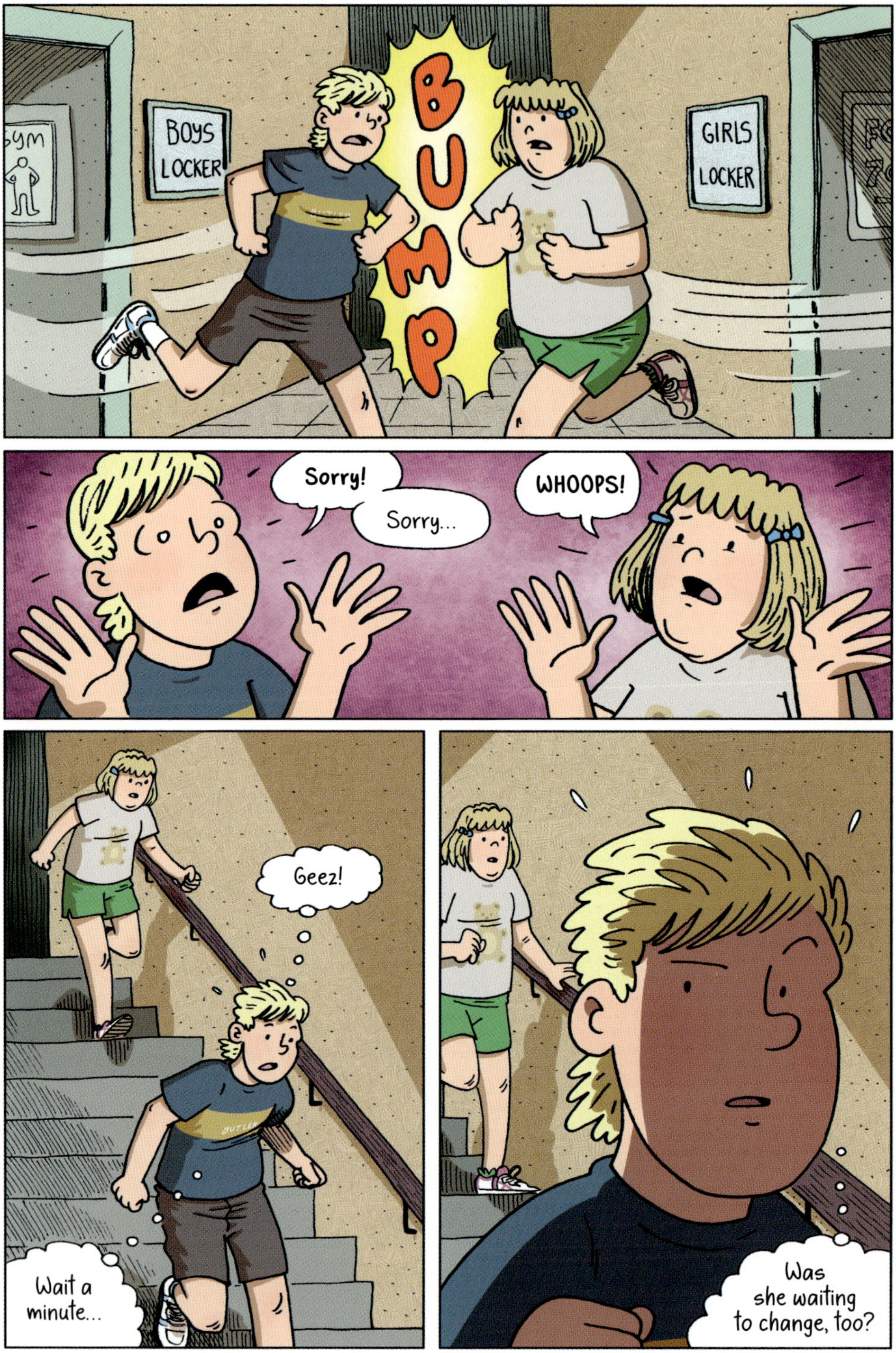
BOYS LOCKER
GYM
BUMP
GIRLS LOCKER
Sorry!
Sorry...
WHOOPS!
Geez!
Wait a minute...
Was she waiting to change, too?

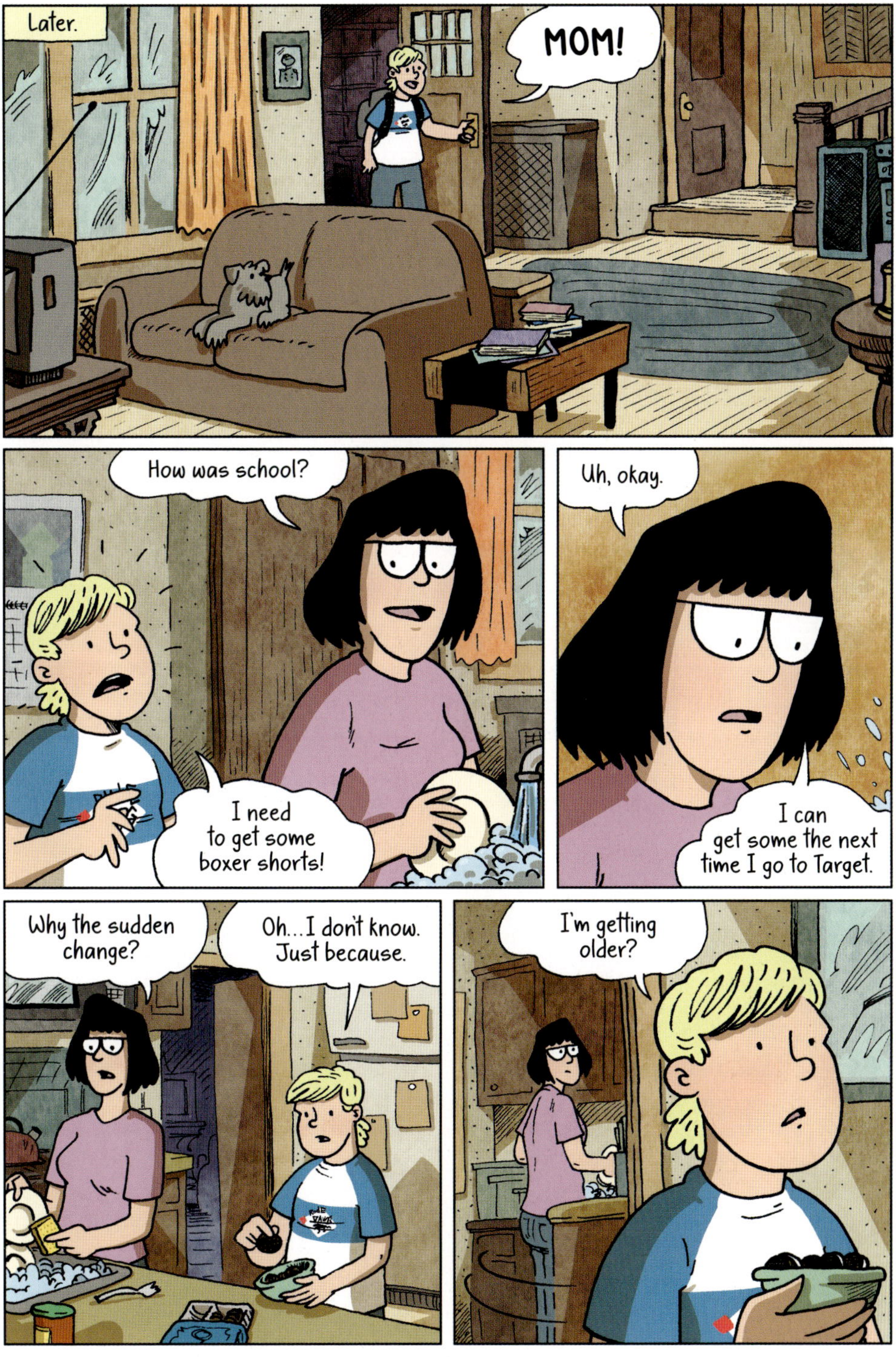
Later.
MOM!
How was school?
Uh, okay.
I need to get some boxer shorts!
I can get some the next time I go to Target.
Why the sudden change?
Oh... I don't know. Just because.
I'm getting older?

Ah, this is better...
RudE DAWG
CLICK
HE-MAN AND THE MASTERS OF THE UNIVERSE
Alright! Just in time!
RudE DAWG
Is that what a man is *supposed* to look like?

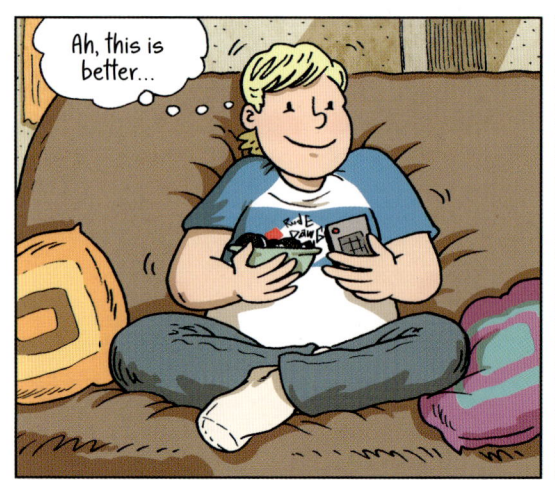

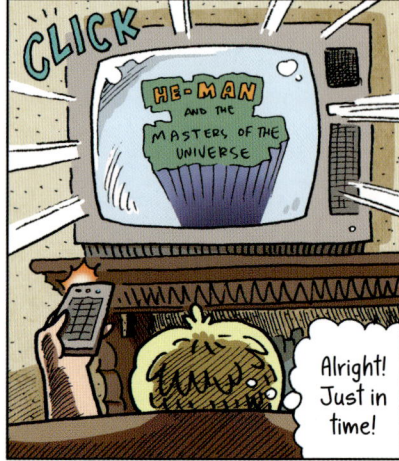

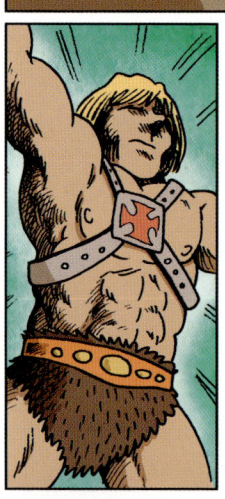

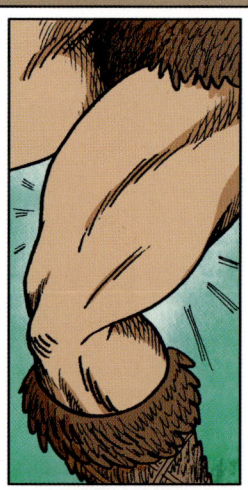

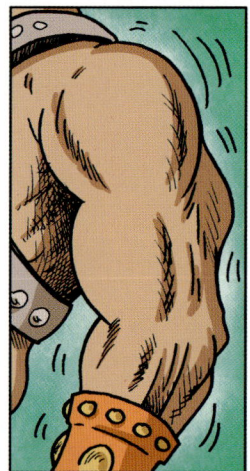

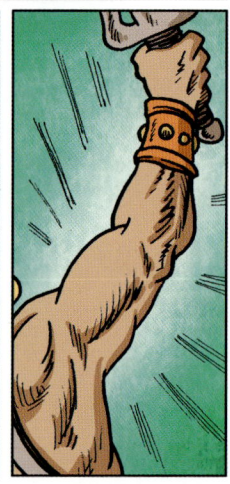

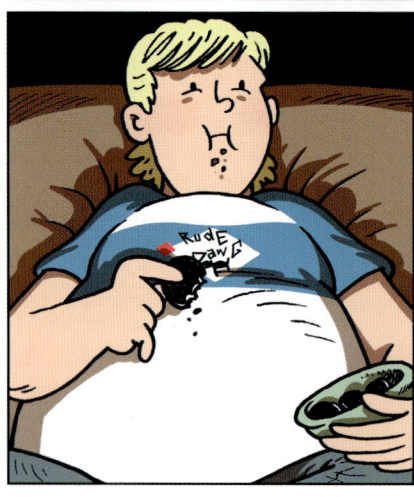

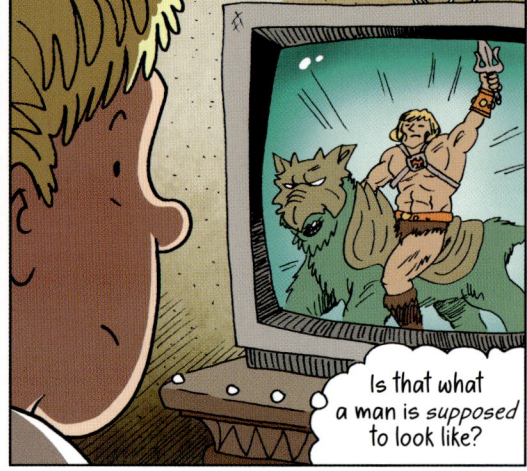

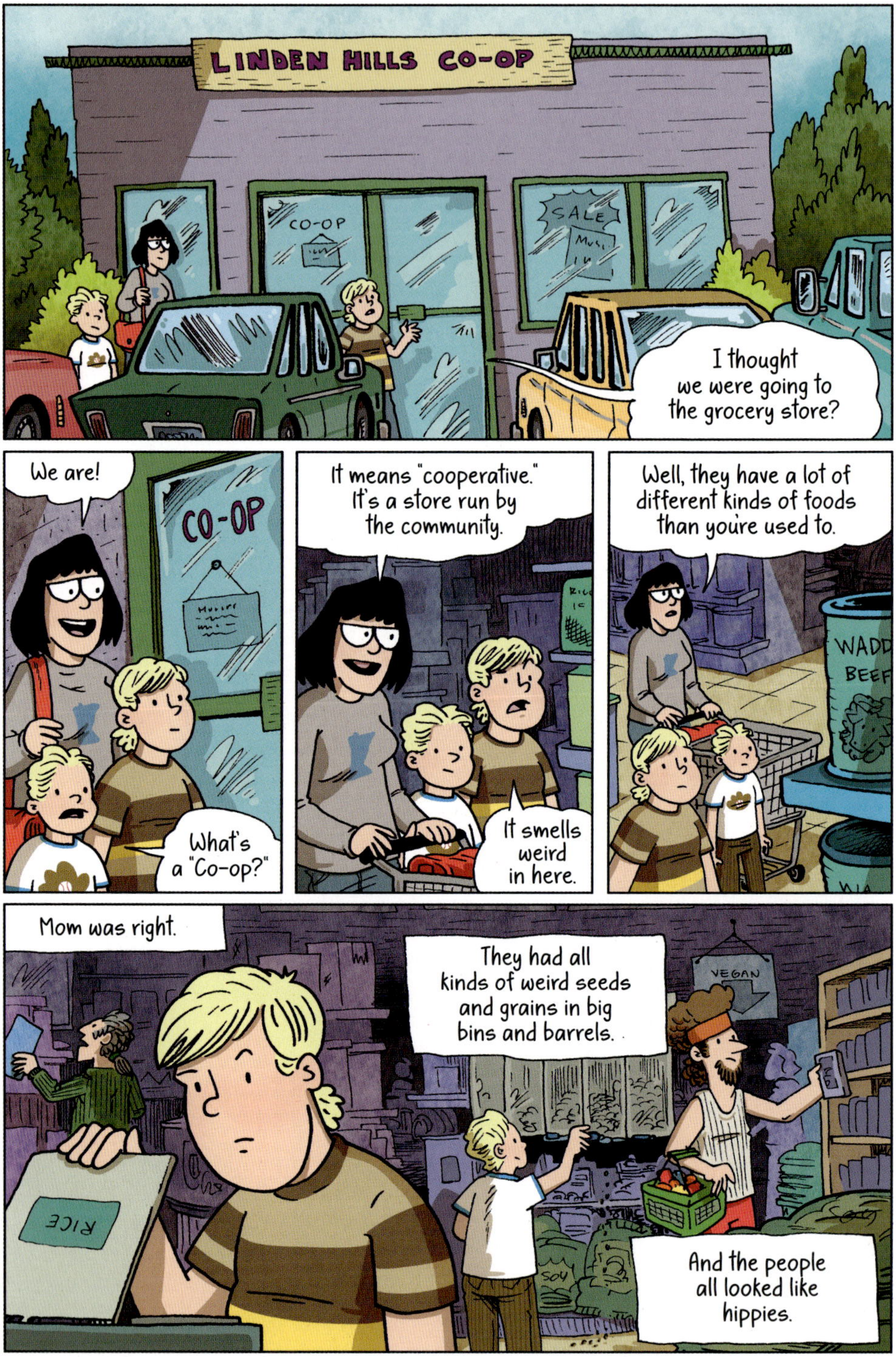
LINDEN HILLS CO-OP
CO-OP
SALE
I thought we were going to the grocery store?
We are!
CO-OP
What's a "Co-op?"
It means "cooperative." It's a store run by the community.
It smells weird in here.
Well, they have a lot of different kinds of foods than you're used to.
Mom was right.
They had all kinds of weird seeds and grains in big bins and barrels.
VEGAN
RICE
SOY
And the people all looked like hippies.

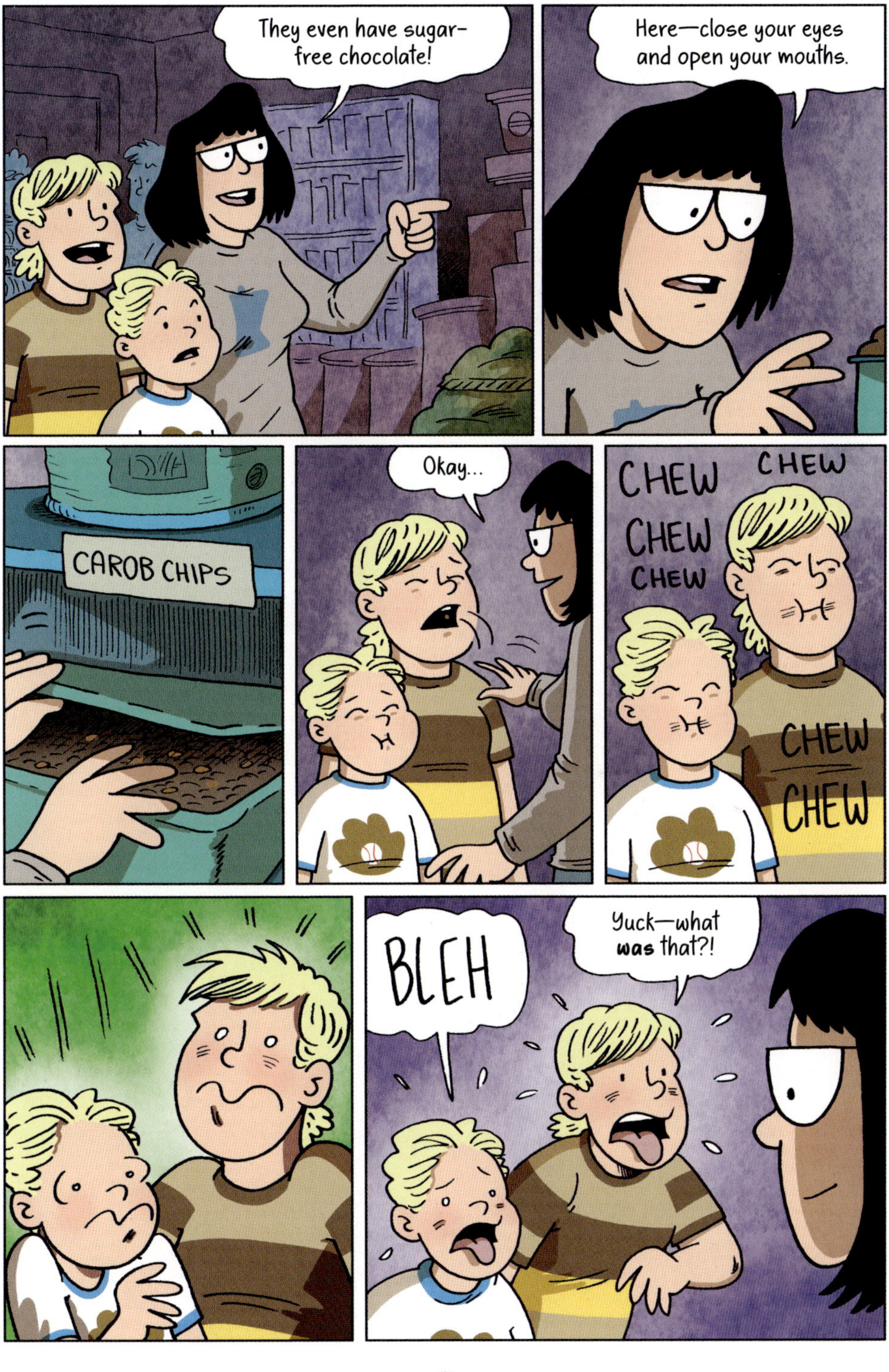
They even have sugar-free chocolate!
Here—close your eyes and open your mouths.
CAROB CHIPS
Okay...
CHEW CHEW CHEW CHEW
CHEW CHEW
BLEH
Yuck—what **was** that?!

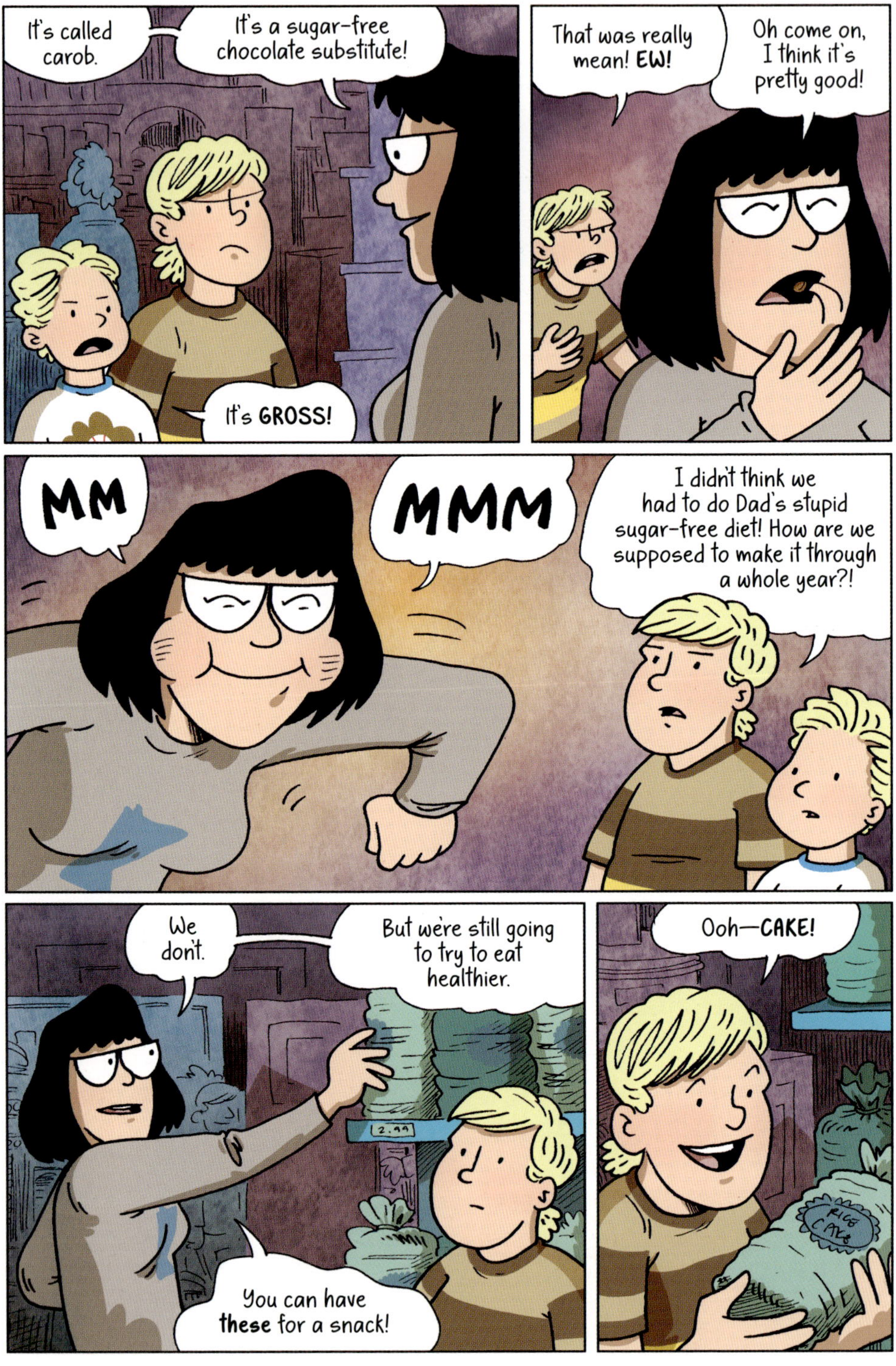
It's called carob.
It's a sugar-free chocolate substitute!
It's **GROSS!**
That was really mean! **EW!**
Oh come on, I think it's pretty good!
MM
MMM
I didn't think we had to do Dad's stupid sugar-free diet! How are we supposed to make it through a whole year?!
We don't.
But we're still going to try to eat healthier.
You can have **these** for a snack!
Ooh—**CAKE!**
RICE CAKE

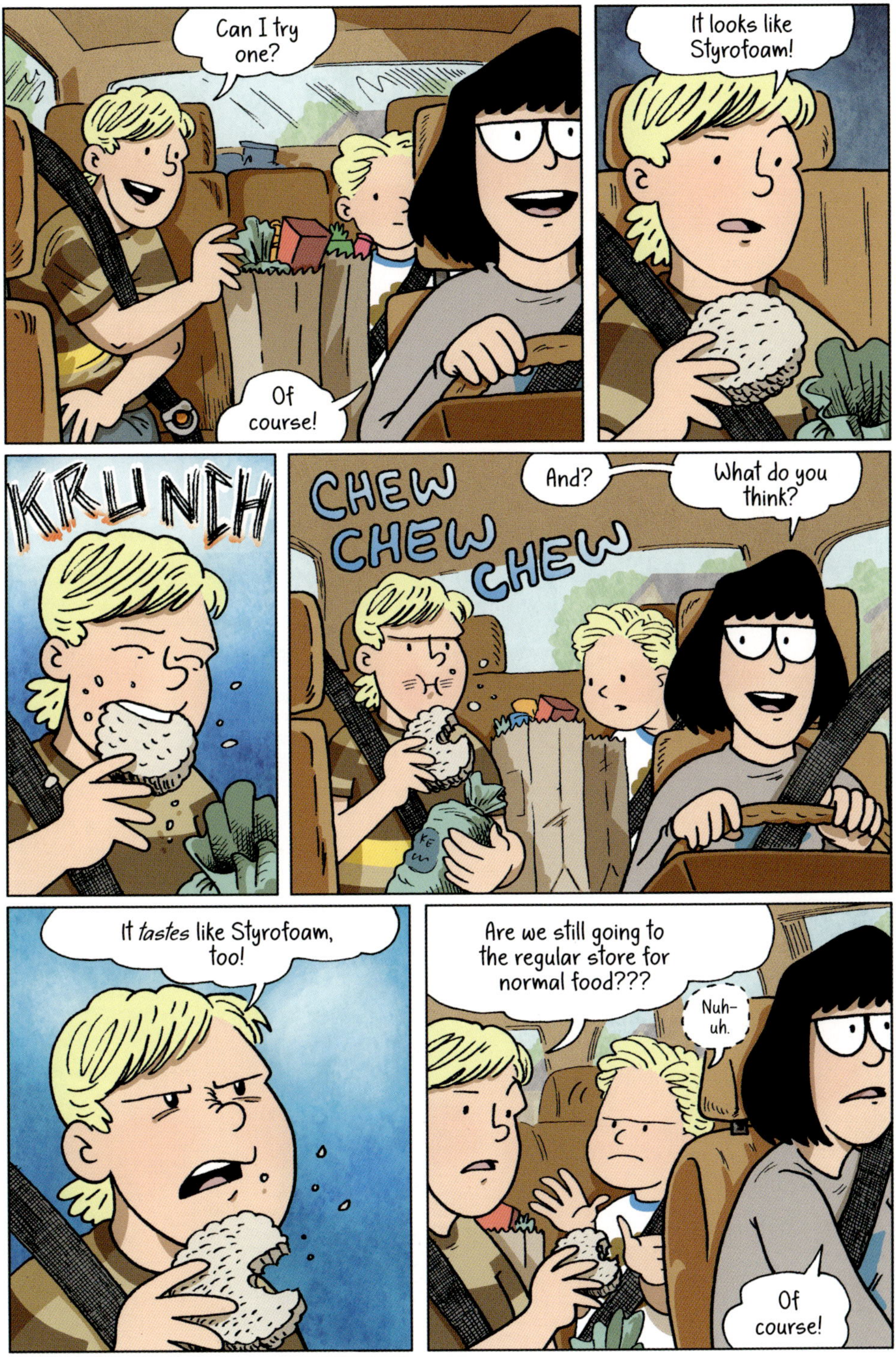
Can I try one?
Of course!
It looks like Styrofoam!
KRUNCH
CHEW CHEW CHEW
And?
What do you think?
It *tastes* like Styrofoam, too!
Are we still going to the regular store for normal food???
Nuh-uh.
Of course!

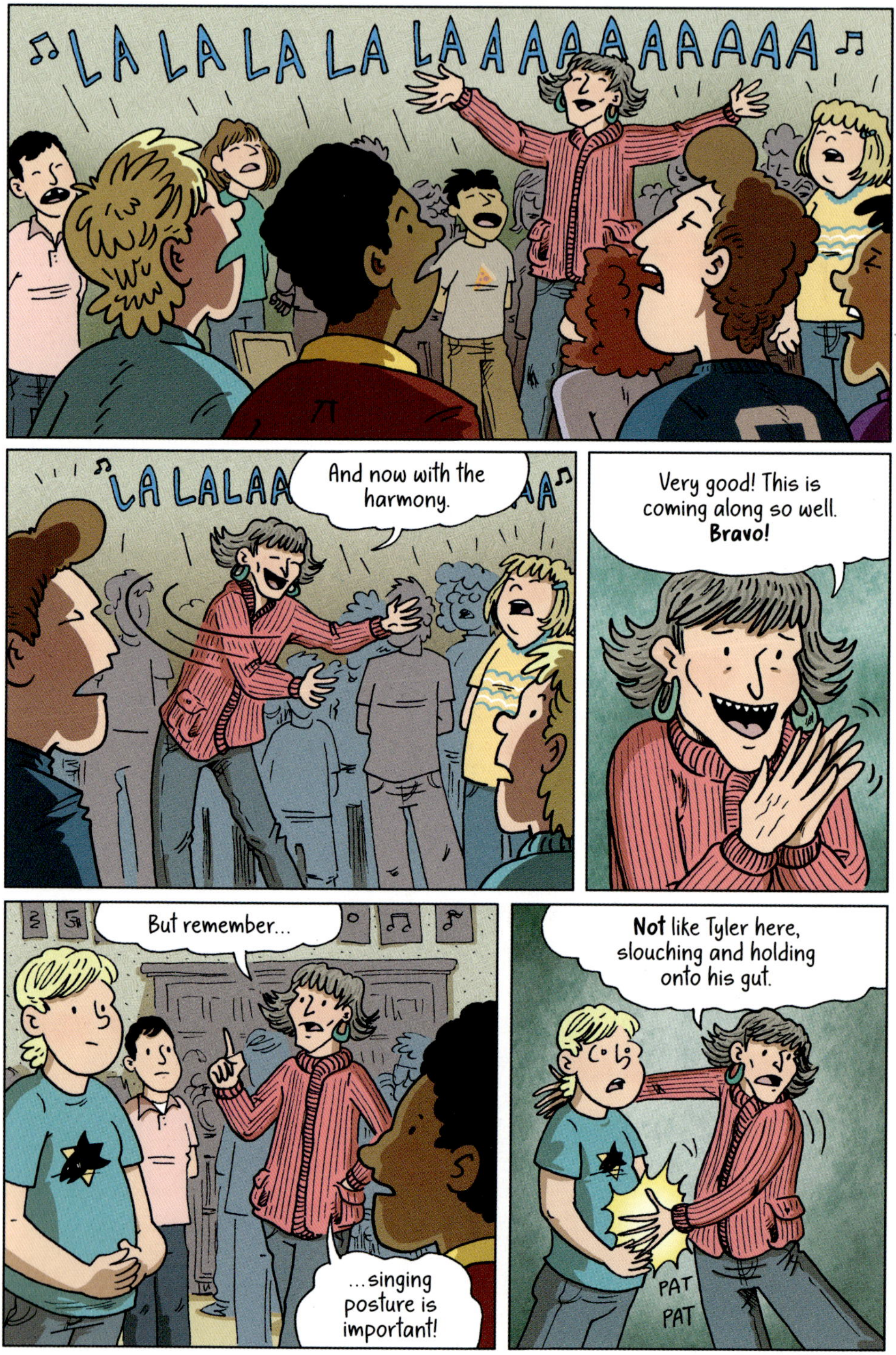

LA LA LA LA LAAAAAAAAAA
LA LALAA AA
And now with the harmony.
Very good! This is coming along so well. **Bravo!**
But remember...
...singing posture is important!
Not like Tyler here, slouching and holding onto his gut.
PAT PAT

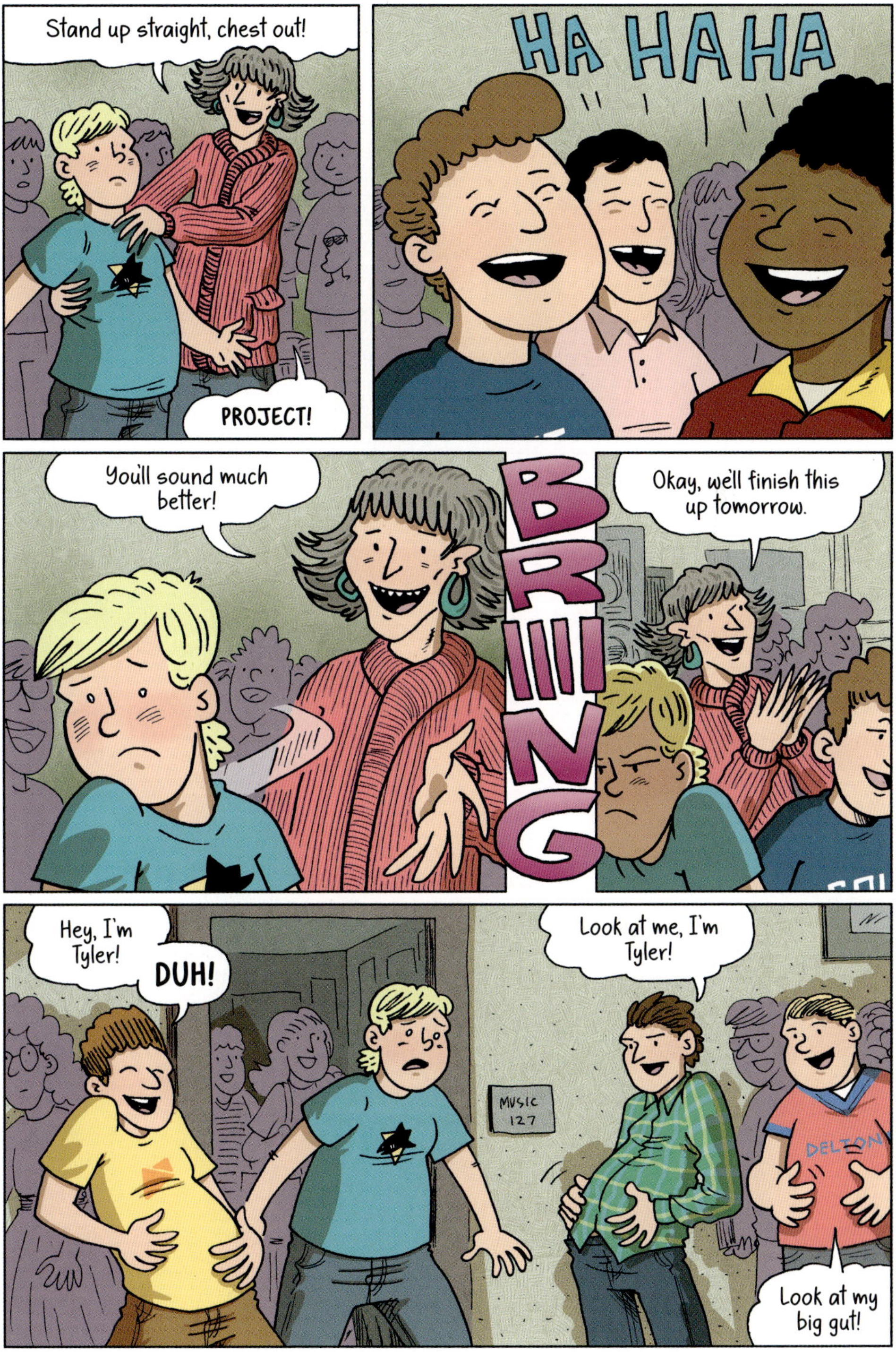
Stand up straight, chest out!
PROJECT!
HA HAHAHA
You'll sound much better!
BRIIIING
Okay, we'll finish this up tomorrow.
Hey, I'm Tyler!
DUH!
MUSIC 127
Look at me, I'm Tyler!
DELTON
Look at my big gut!

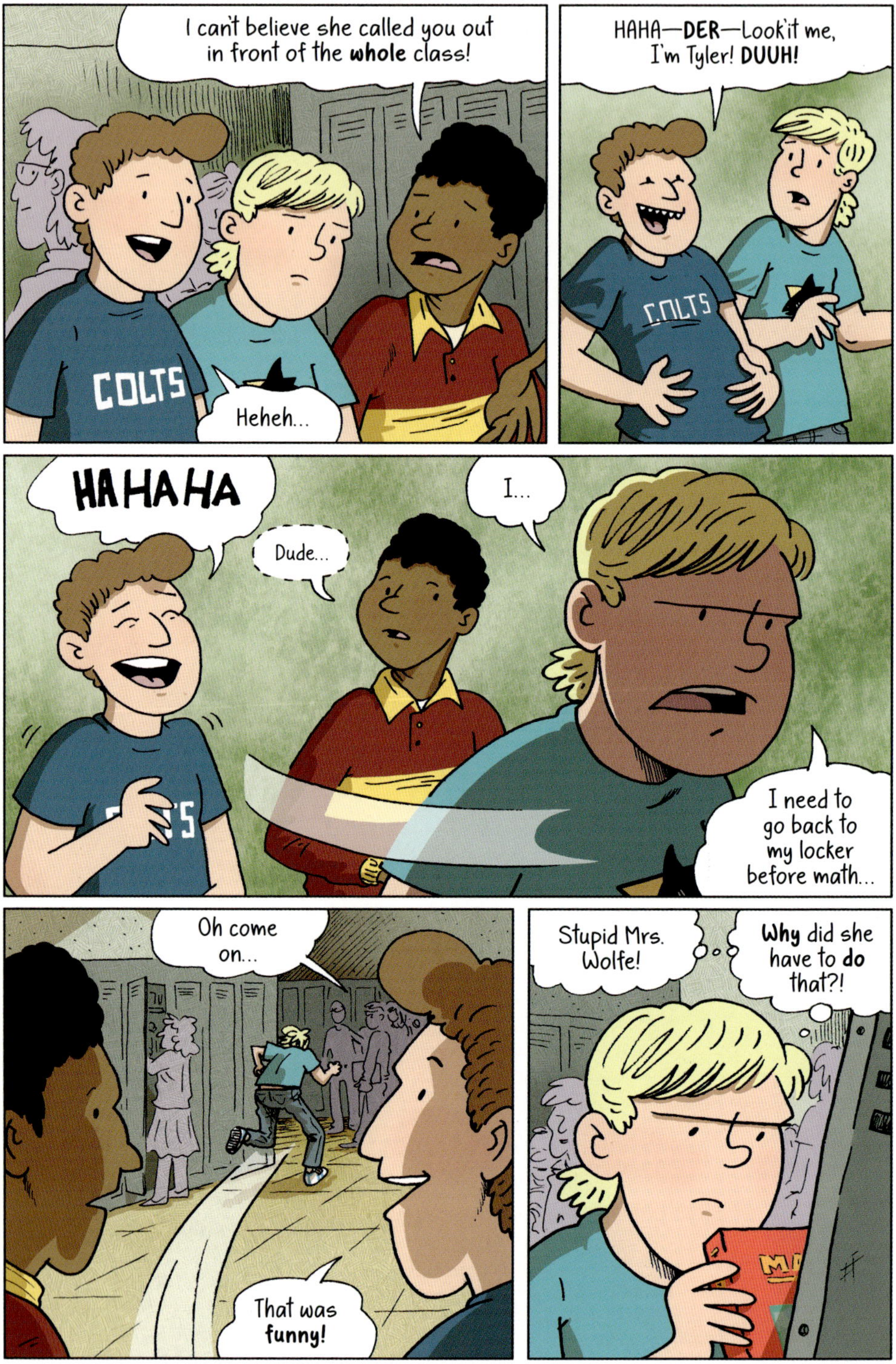

I can't believe she called you out in front of the **whole** class!
Heheh...
HAHA—**DER**—Look'it me, I'm Tyler! **DUUH!**
COLTS
HAHAHA
Dude...
I...
I need to go back to my locker before math...
Oh come on...
That was **funny!**
Stupid Mrs. Wolfe!
Why did she have to **do** that?!

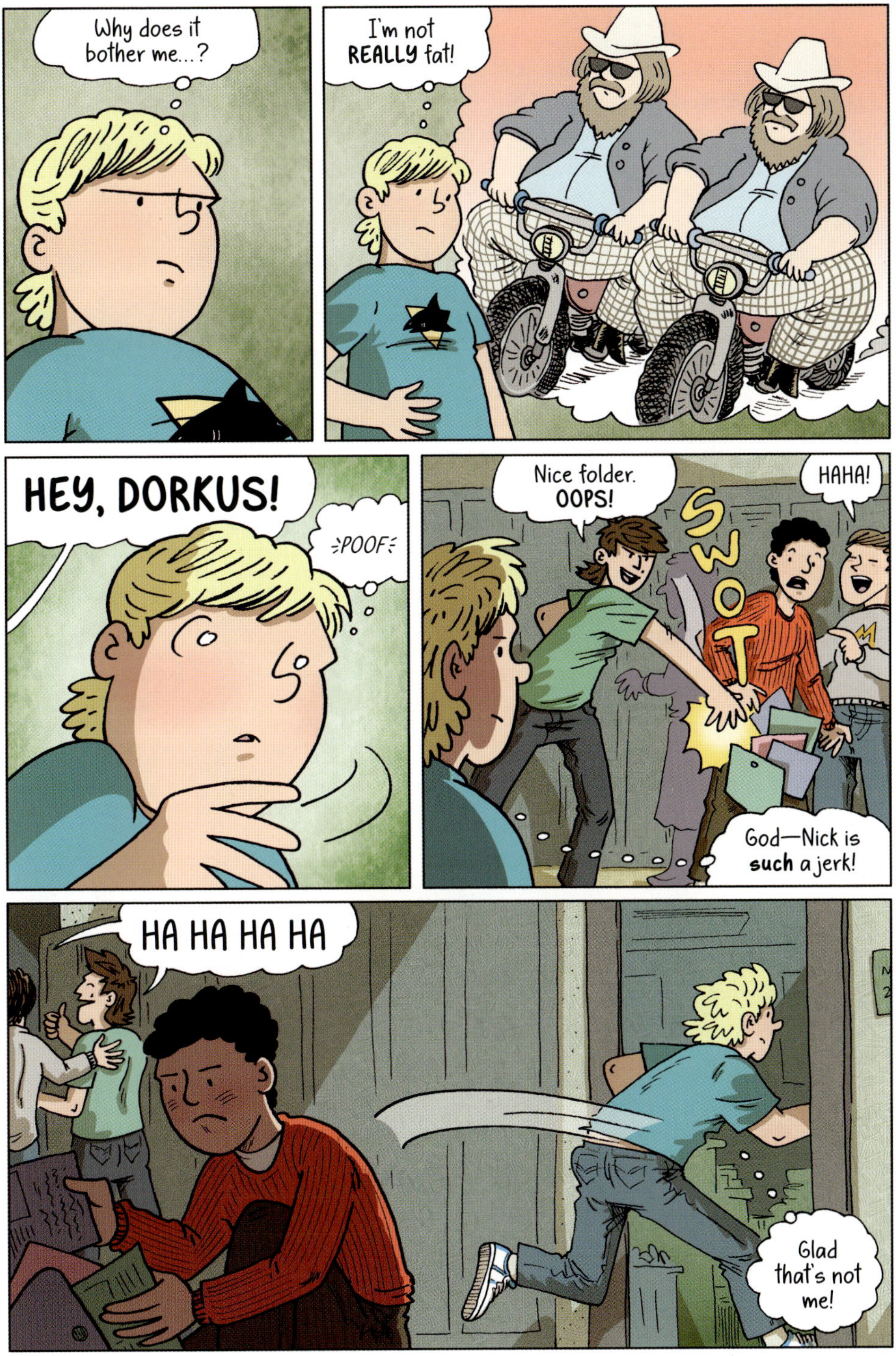
Why does it bother me...?
I'm not REALLY fat!
HEY, DORKUS!
POOF
Nice folder. OOPS!
SWOT
HAHA!
God—Nick is such a jerk!
HA HA HA HA
Glad that's not me!

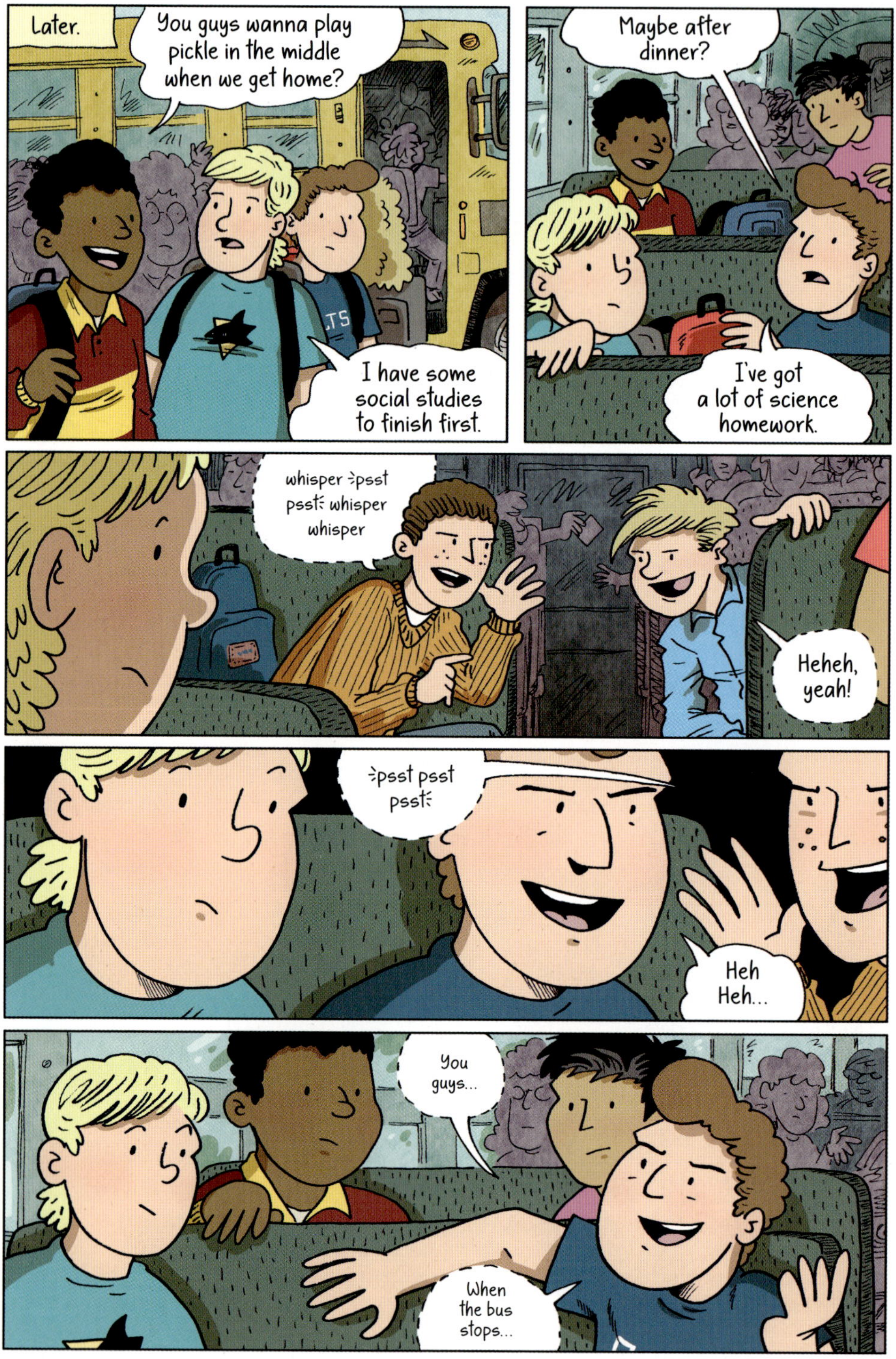
Later.
You guys wanna play pickle in the middle when we get home?
I have some social studies to finish first.
Maybe after dinner?
I've got a lot of science homework.
whisper psst psst whisper whisper
Heheh, yeah!
psst psst psst
Heh Heh...
You guys...
When the bus stops...

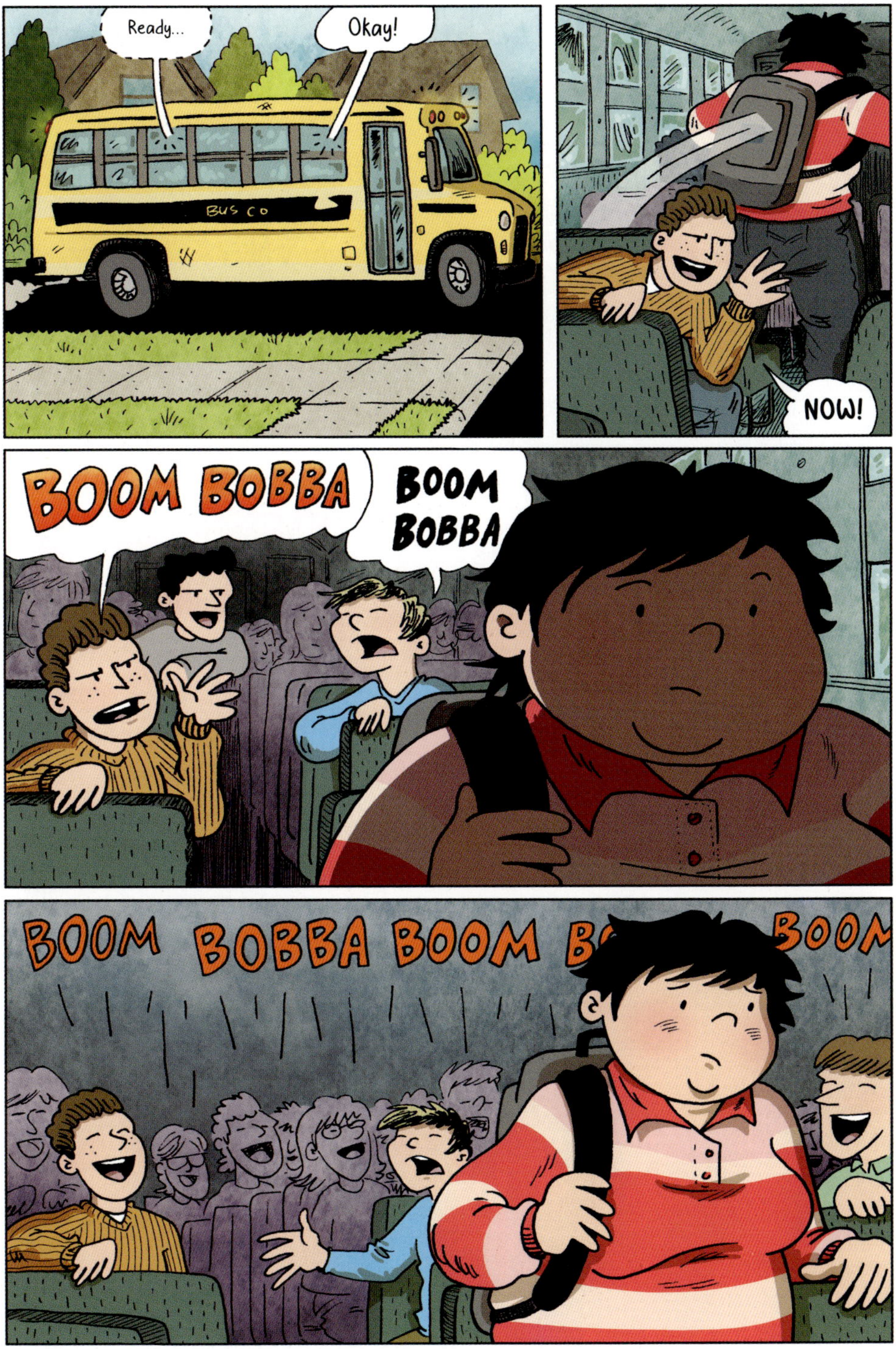
Ready...
Okay!
BUS CO
NOW!
BOOM BOBBA
BOOM BOBBA
BOOM BOBBA BOOM
BOOM

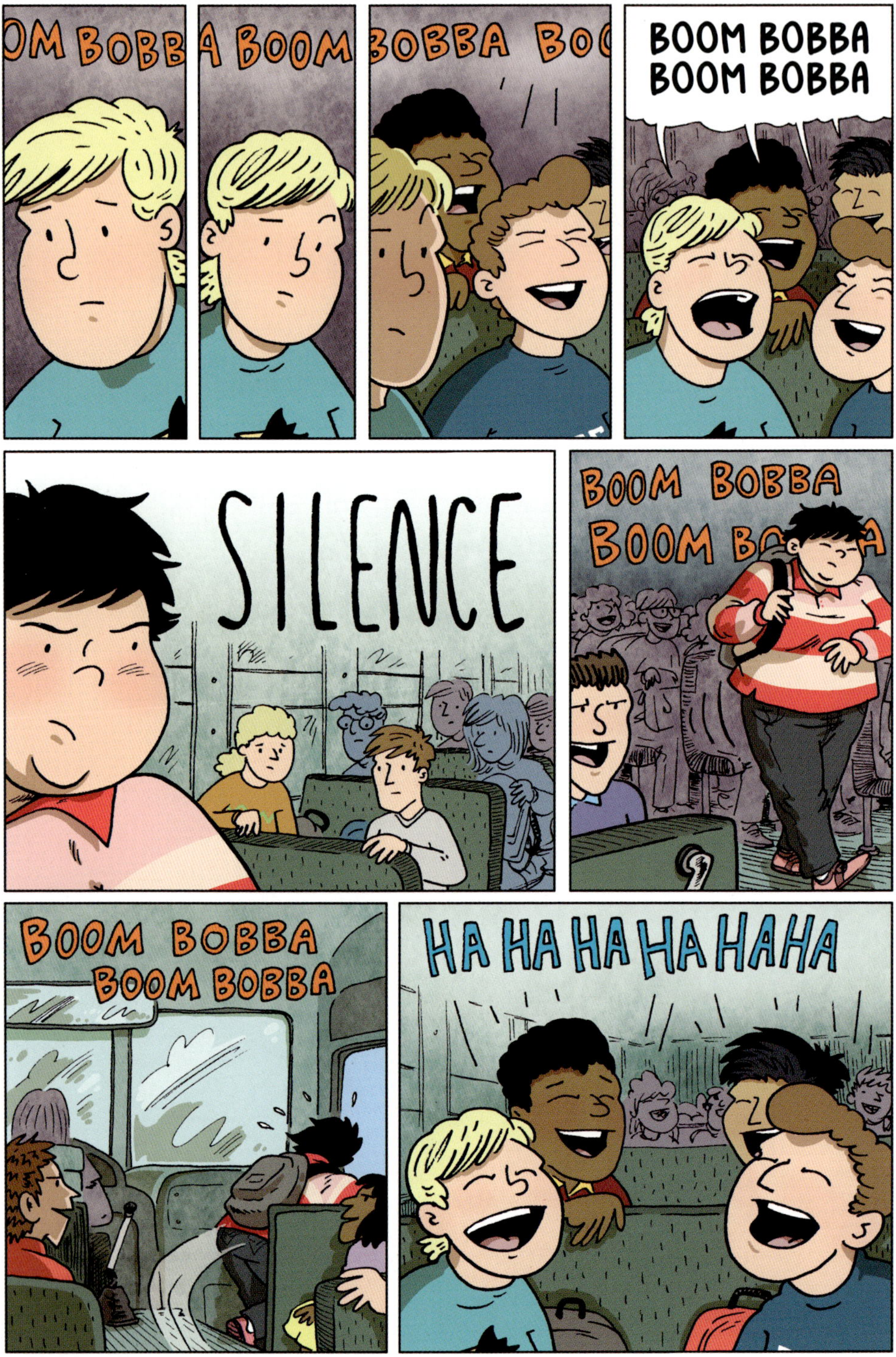
OM BOBB
A BOOM
OBBA BO
BOOM BOBBA
BOOM BOBBA
SILENCE
BOOM BOBBA
BOOM
BOOM BOBBA
BOOM BOBBA
HA HA HA HA HAHA

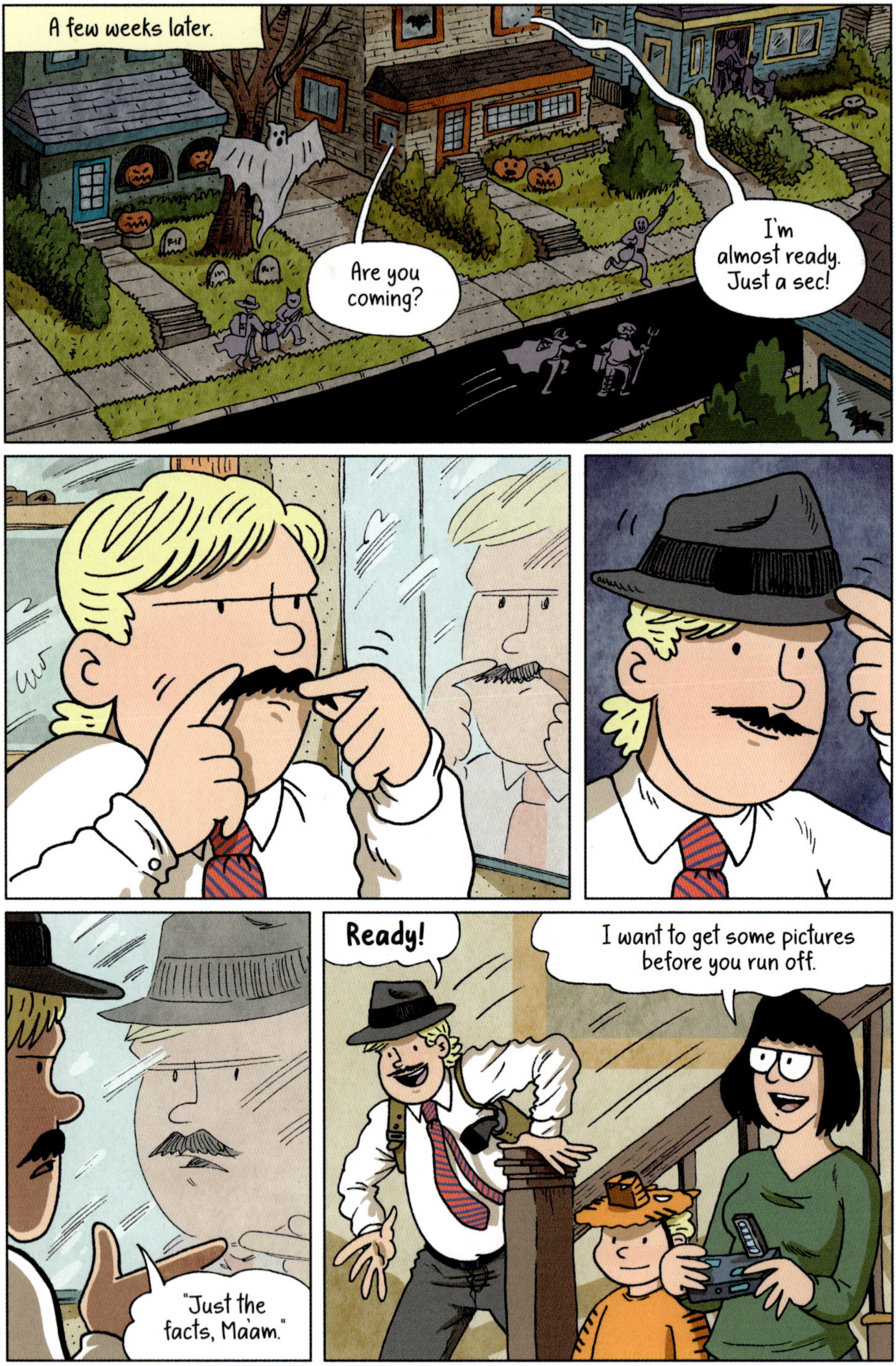
A few weeks later.
Are you coming?
I'm almost ready. Just a sec!
Ready!
I want to get some pictures before you run off.
"Just the facts, Ma'am."

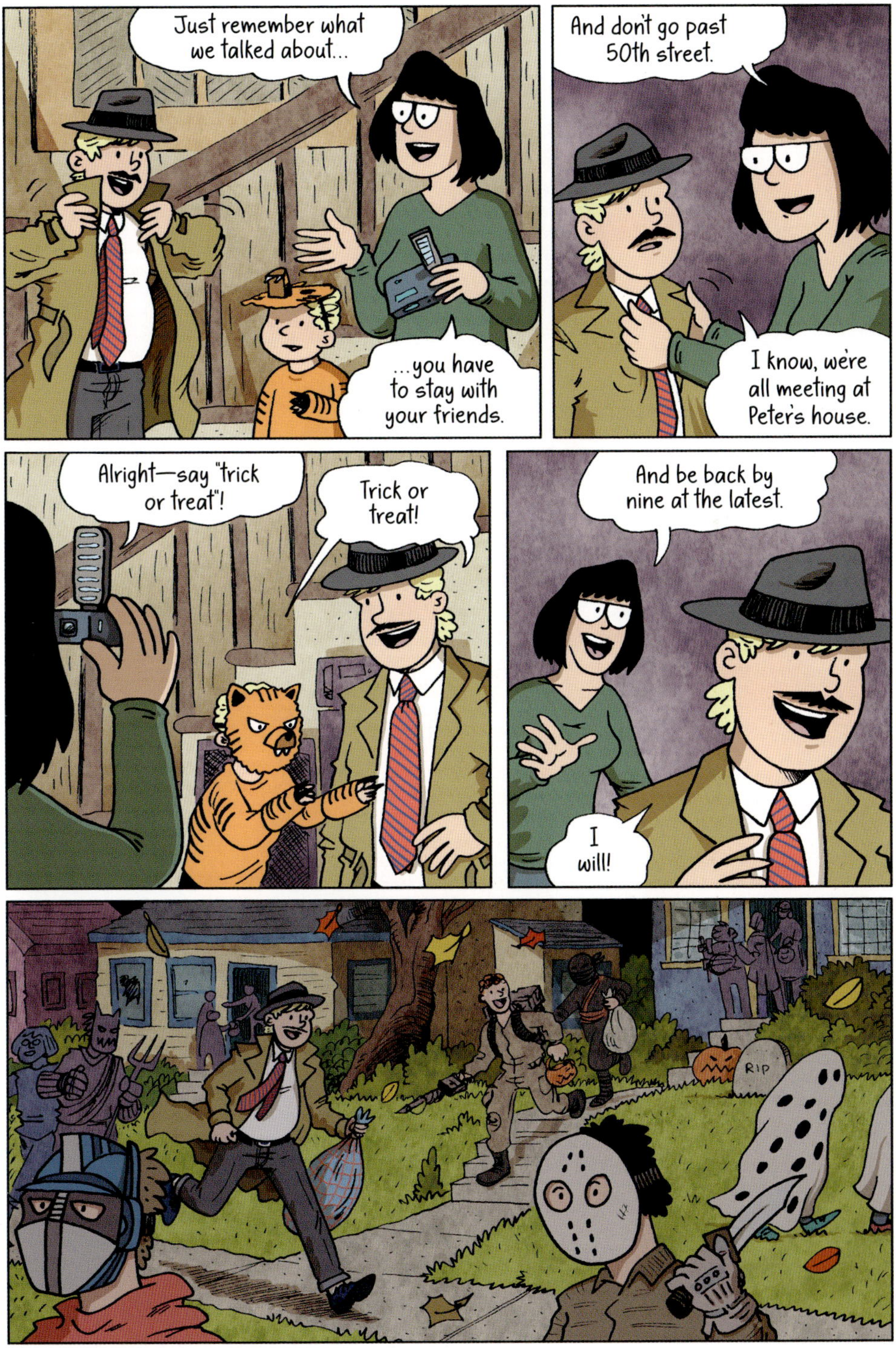
Just remember what we talked about...
...you have to stay with your friends.
And don't go past 50th street.
I know, we're all meeting at Peter's house.
Alright—say "trick or treat"!
Trick or treat!
And be back by nine at the latest.
I will!
RIP

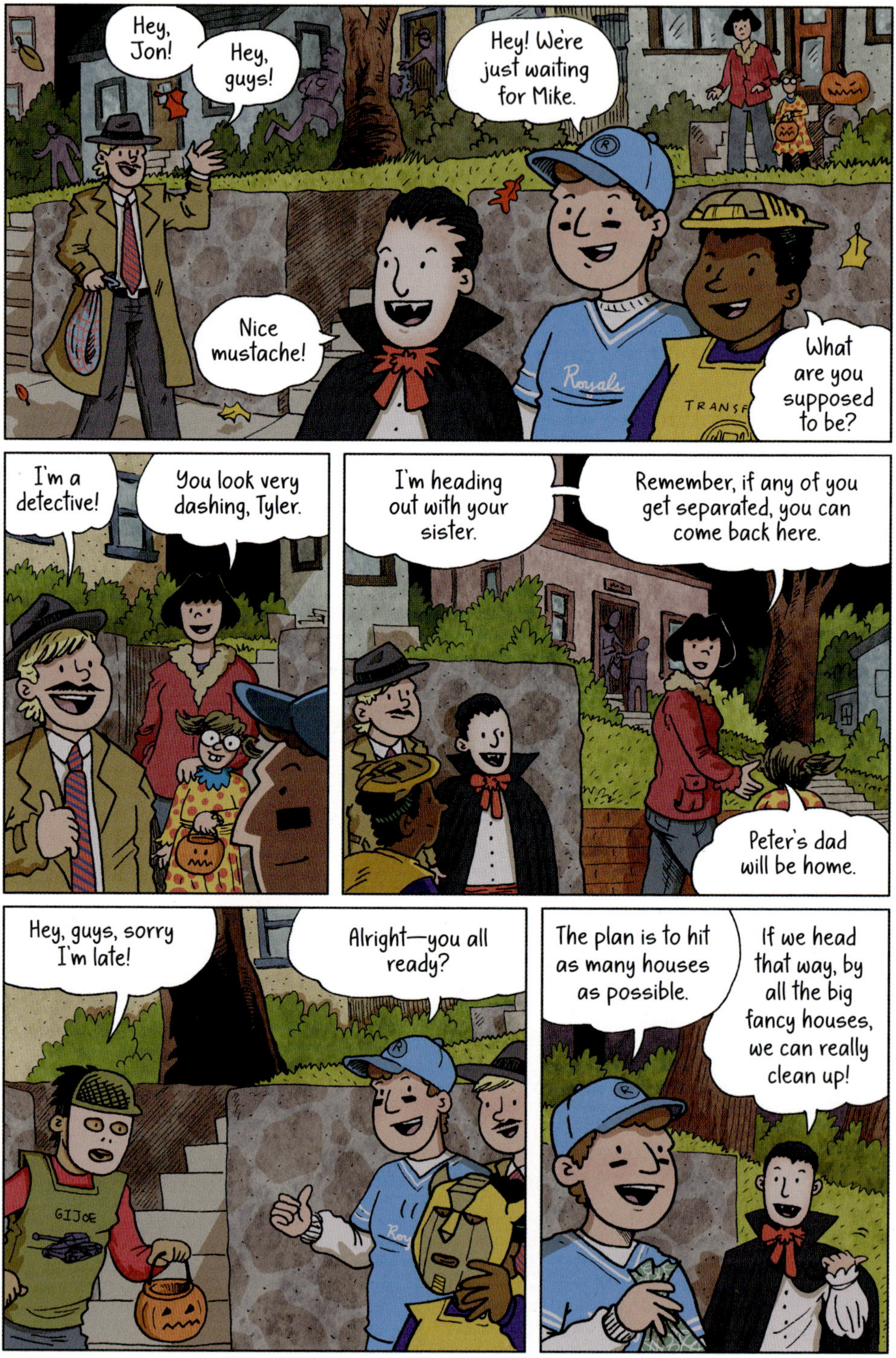
Hey, Jon!
Hey, guys!
Hey! We're just waiting for Mike.
Nice mustache!
What are you supposed to be?
I'm a detective!
You look very dashing, Tyler.
I'm heading out with your sister.
Remember, if any of you get separated, you can come back here.
Peter's dad will be home.
Hey, guys, sorry I'm late!
Alright—you all ready?
The plan is to hit as many houses as possible.
If we head that way, by all the big fancy houses, we can really clean up!
Royals
TRANSF
GIJOE

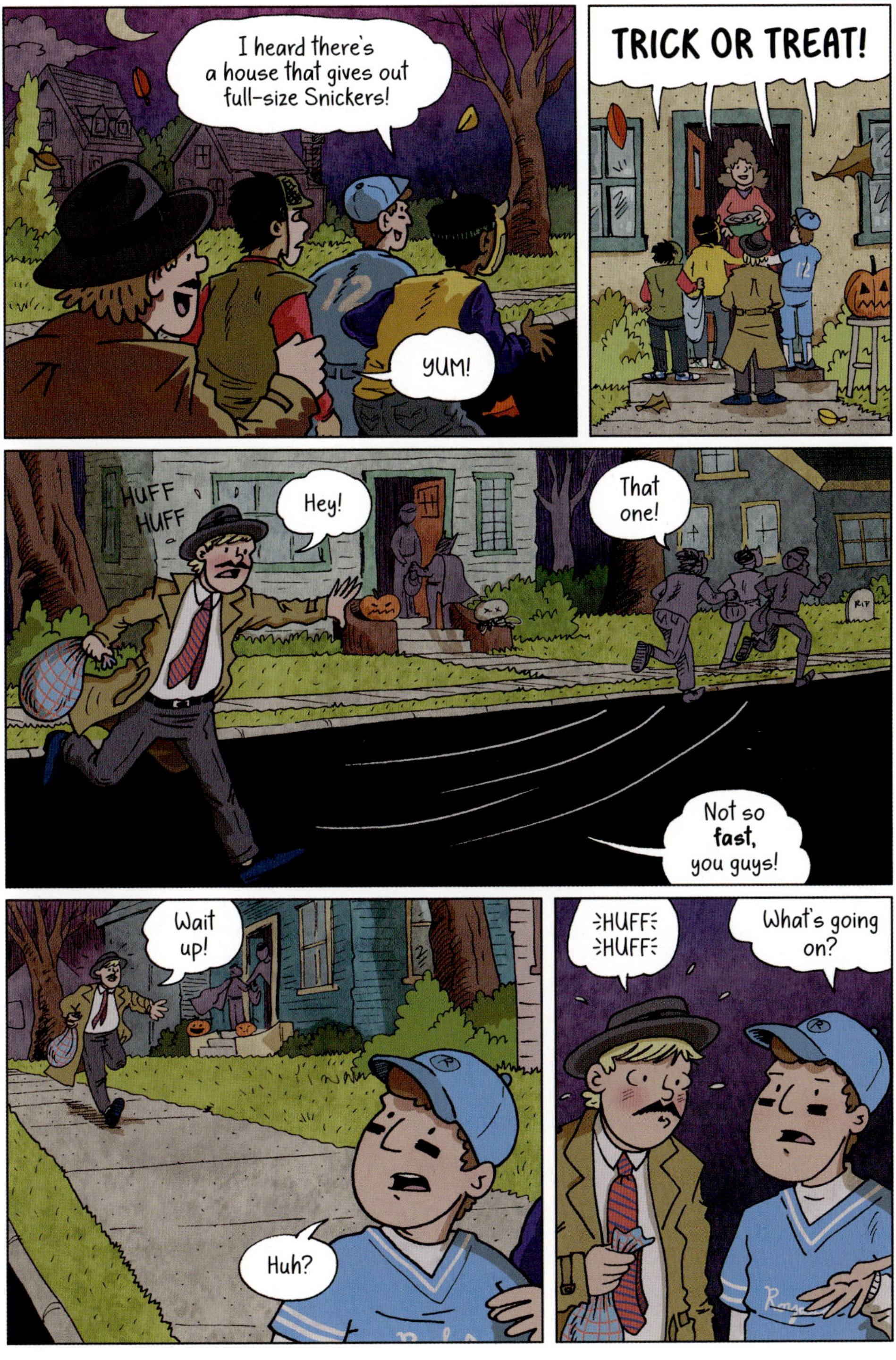
I heard there's a house that gives out full-size Snickers!
YUM!
TRICK OR TREAT!
HUFF HUFF
Hey!
That one!
Not so **fast**, you guys!
Wait up!
Huh?
HUFF HUFF
What's going on?

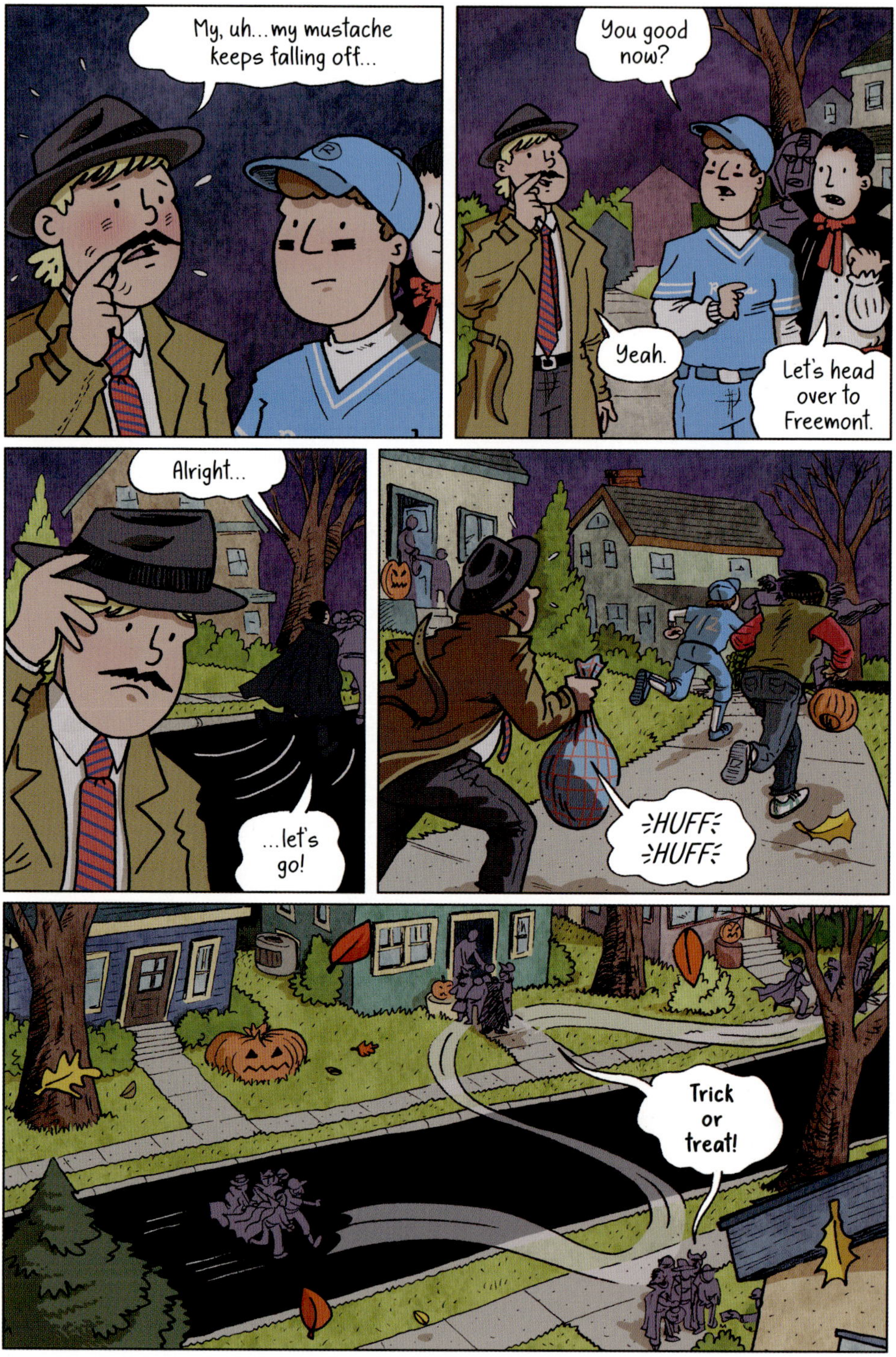
My, uh... my mustache keeps falling off...
You good now?
Yeah.
Let's head over to Freemont.
Alright...
...let's go!
HUFF
HUFF
Trick or treat!

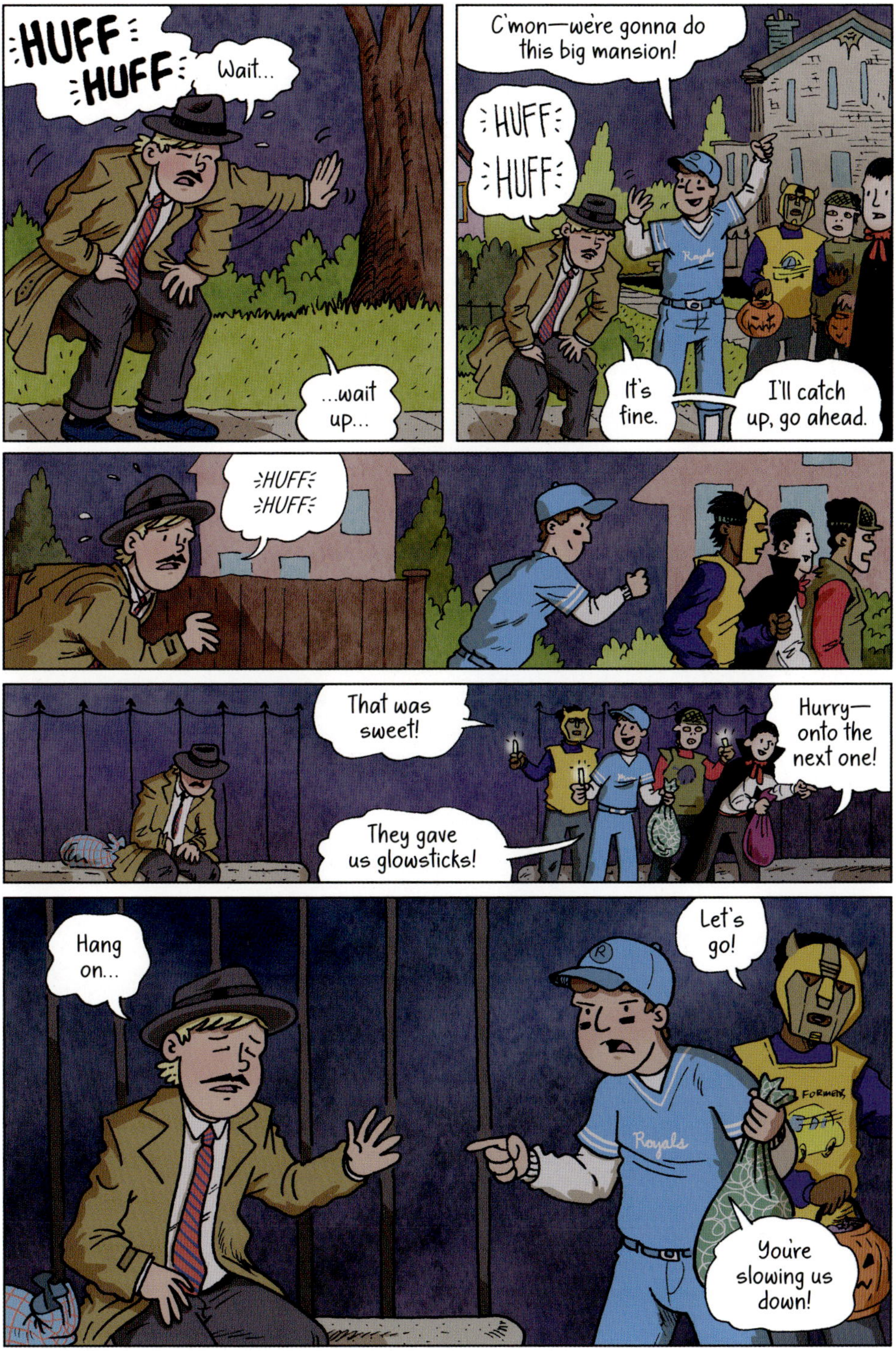
HUFF HUFF
Wait...
...wait up...
C'mon—we're gonna do this big mansion!
HUFF HUFF
It's fine.
I'll catch up, go ahead.
HUFF HUFF
That was sweet!
Hurry—onto the next one!
They gave us glowsticks!
Hang on...
Let's go!
You're slowing us down!

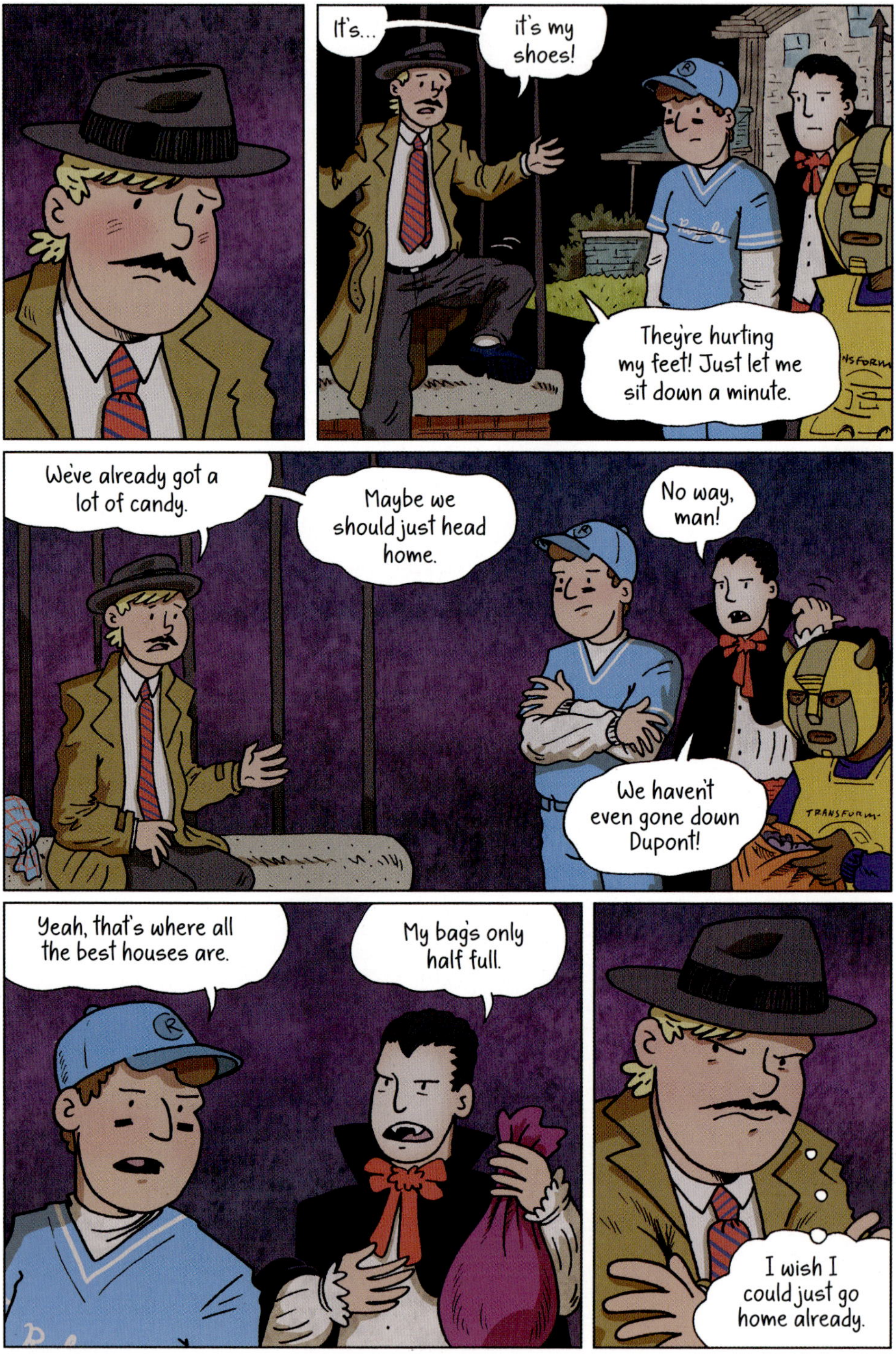

It's...
it's my shoes!
They're hurting my feet! Just let me sit down a minute.
We've already got a lot of candy.
Maybe we should just head home.
No way, man!
We haven't even gone down Dupont!
Yeah, that's where all the best houses are.
My bag's only half full.
I wish I could just go home already.

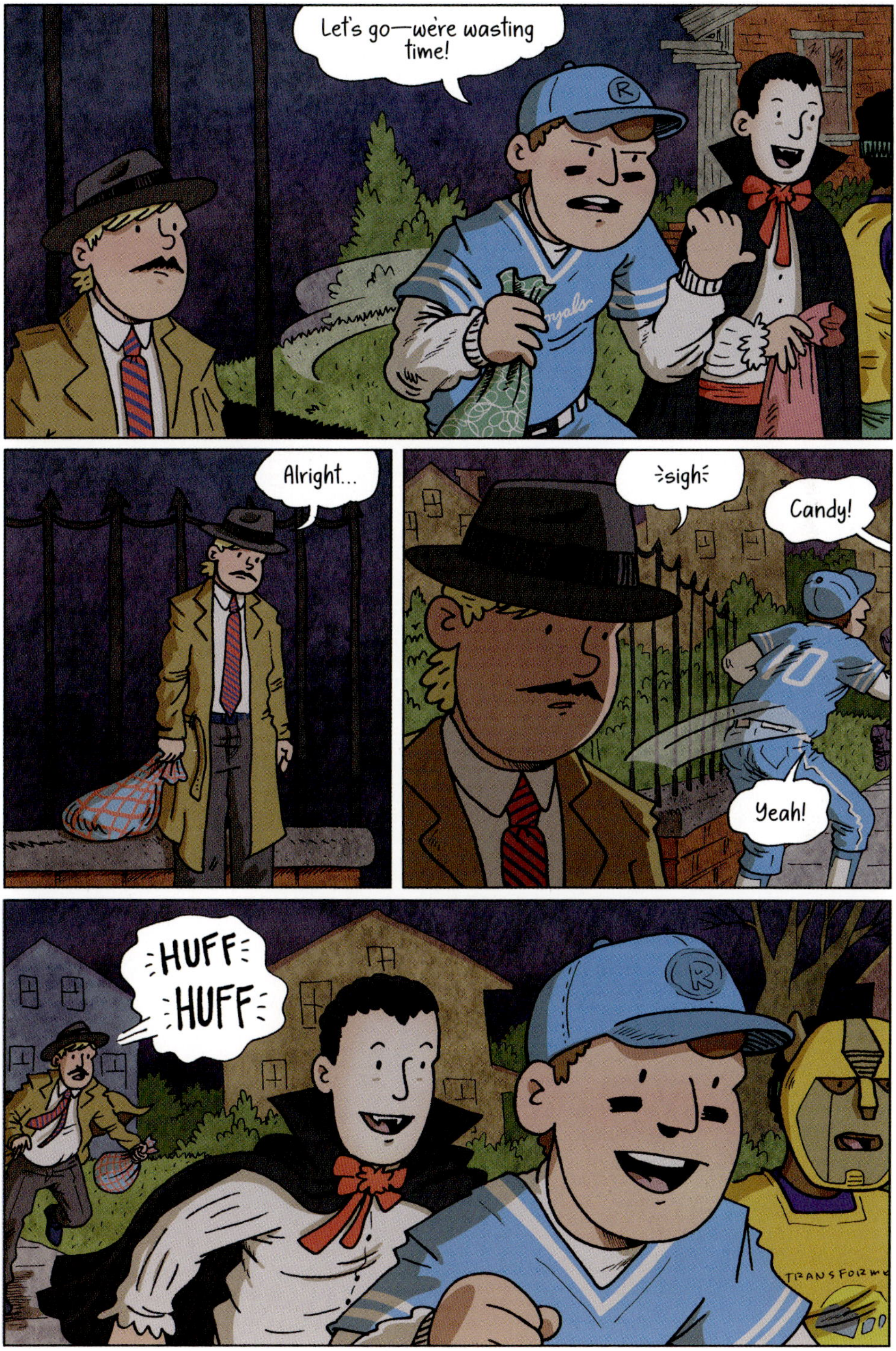
Let's go—we're wasting time!
Alright...
sigh
Candy!
Yeah!
HUFF
HUFF
TRANSFORM

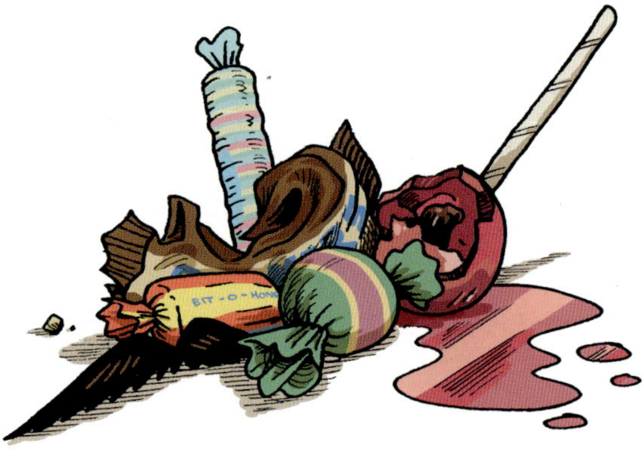
BIT - O - HON

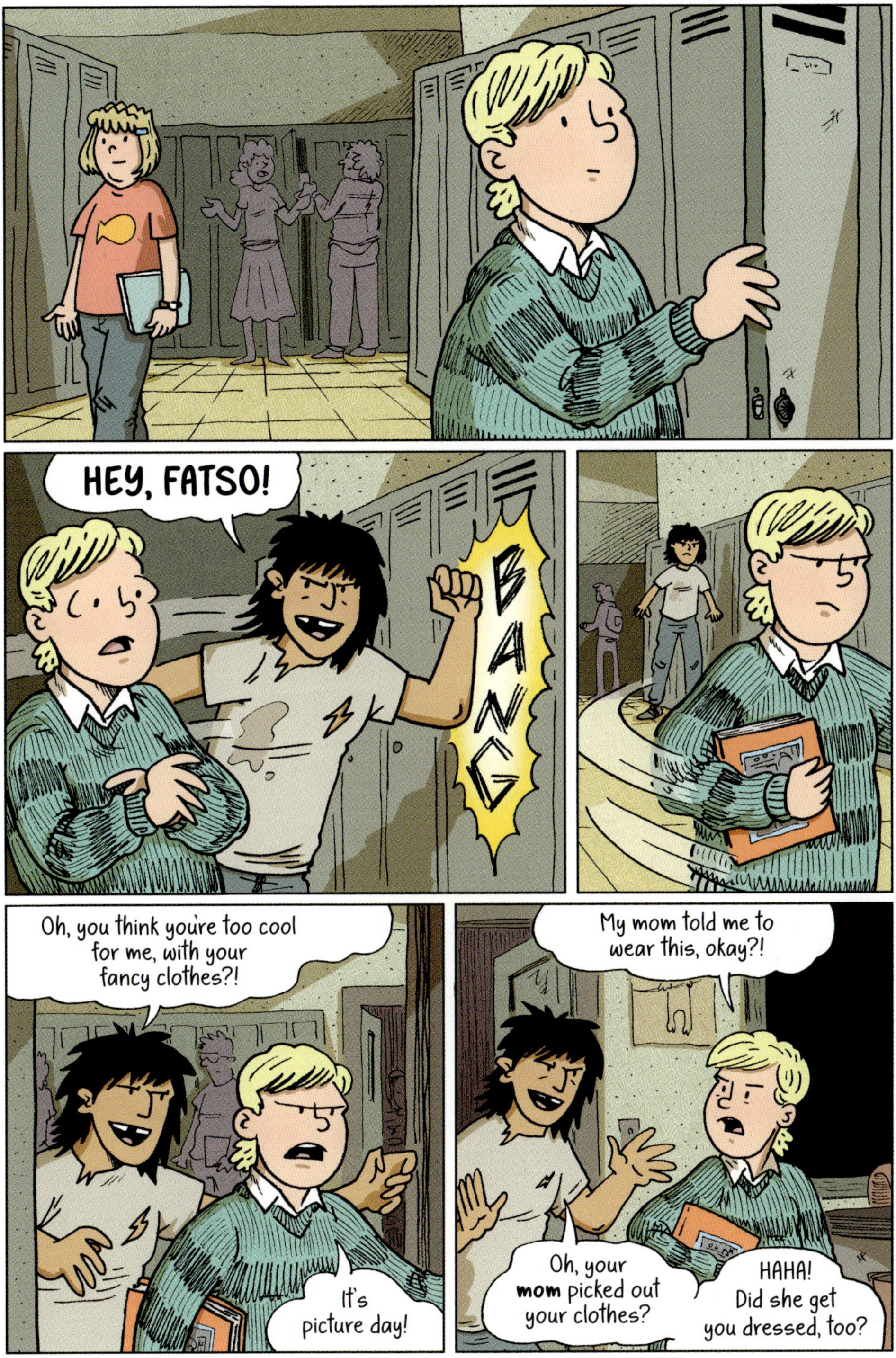
HEY, FATSO!
BANG
Oh, you think you're too cool for me, with your fancy clothes?!
It's picture day!
My mom told me to wear this, okay?!
Oh, your **mom** picked out your clothes?
HAHA! Did she get you dressed, too?

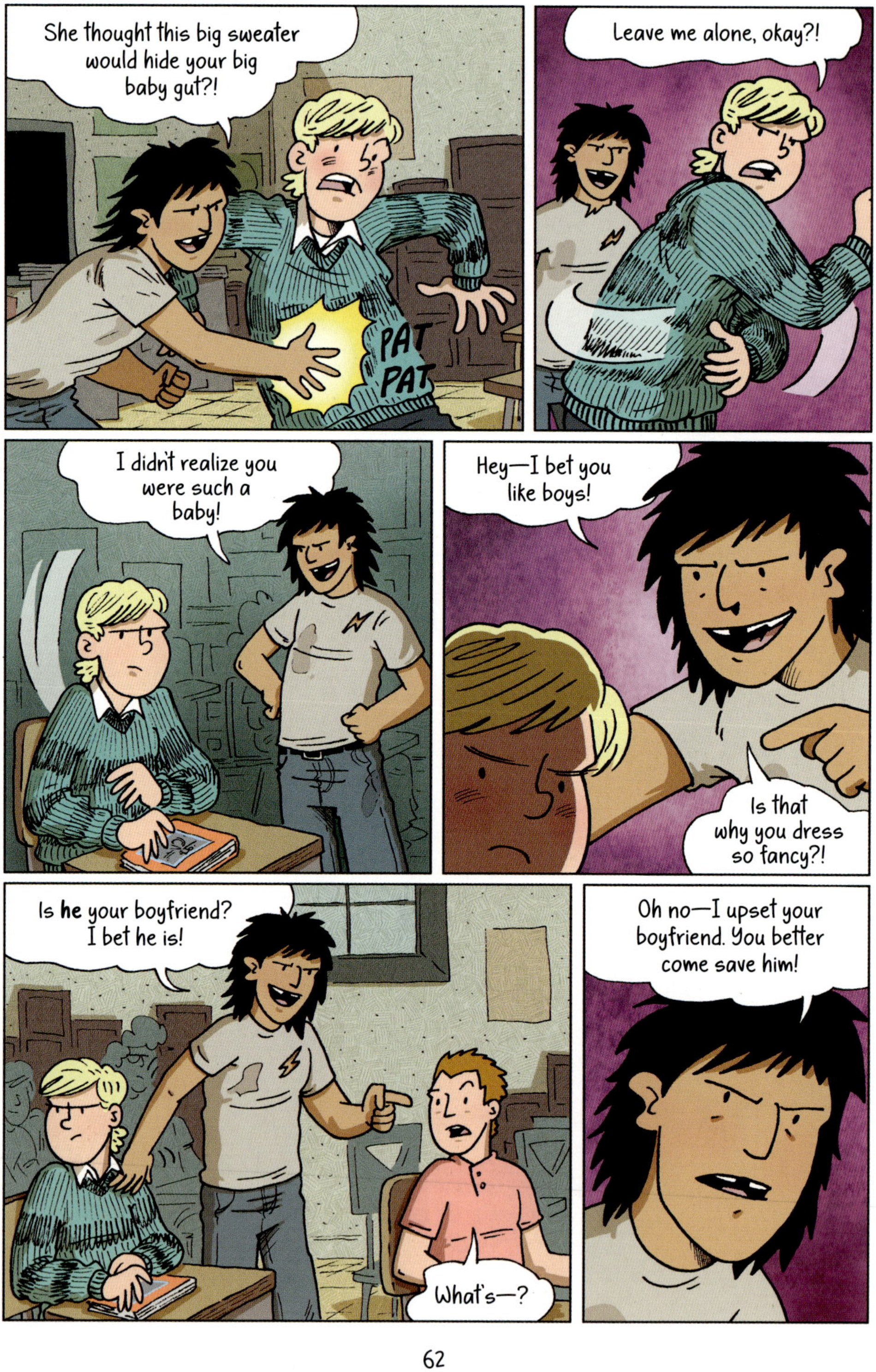

She thought this big sweater would hide your big baby gut?!
PAT PAT
Leave me alone, okay?!
I didn't realize you were such a baby!
Hey—I bet you like boys!
Is that why you dress so fancy?!
Is **he** your boyfriend? I bet he is!
What's—?
Oh no—I upset your boyfriend. You better come save him!

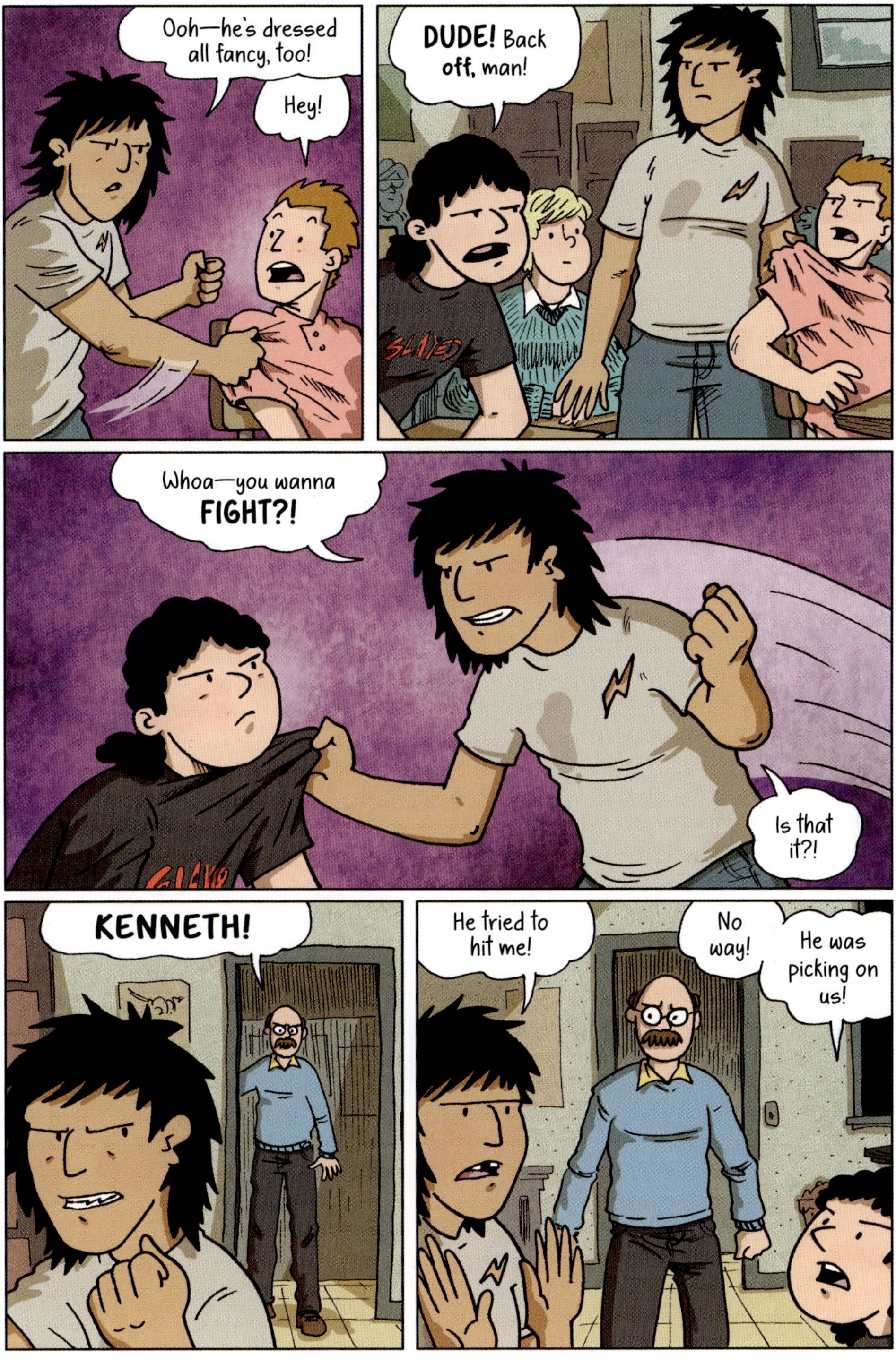
Ooh—he's dressed all fancy, too!
Hey!
DUDE! Back off, man!
SLAYED
Whoa—you wanna FIGHT?!
Is that it?!
KENNETH!
He tried to hit me!
No way!
He was picking on us!

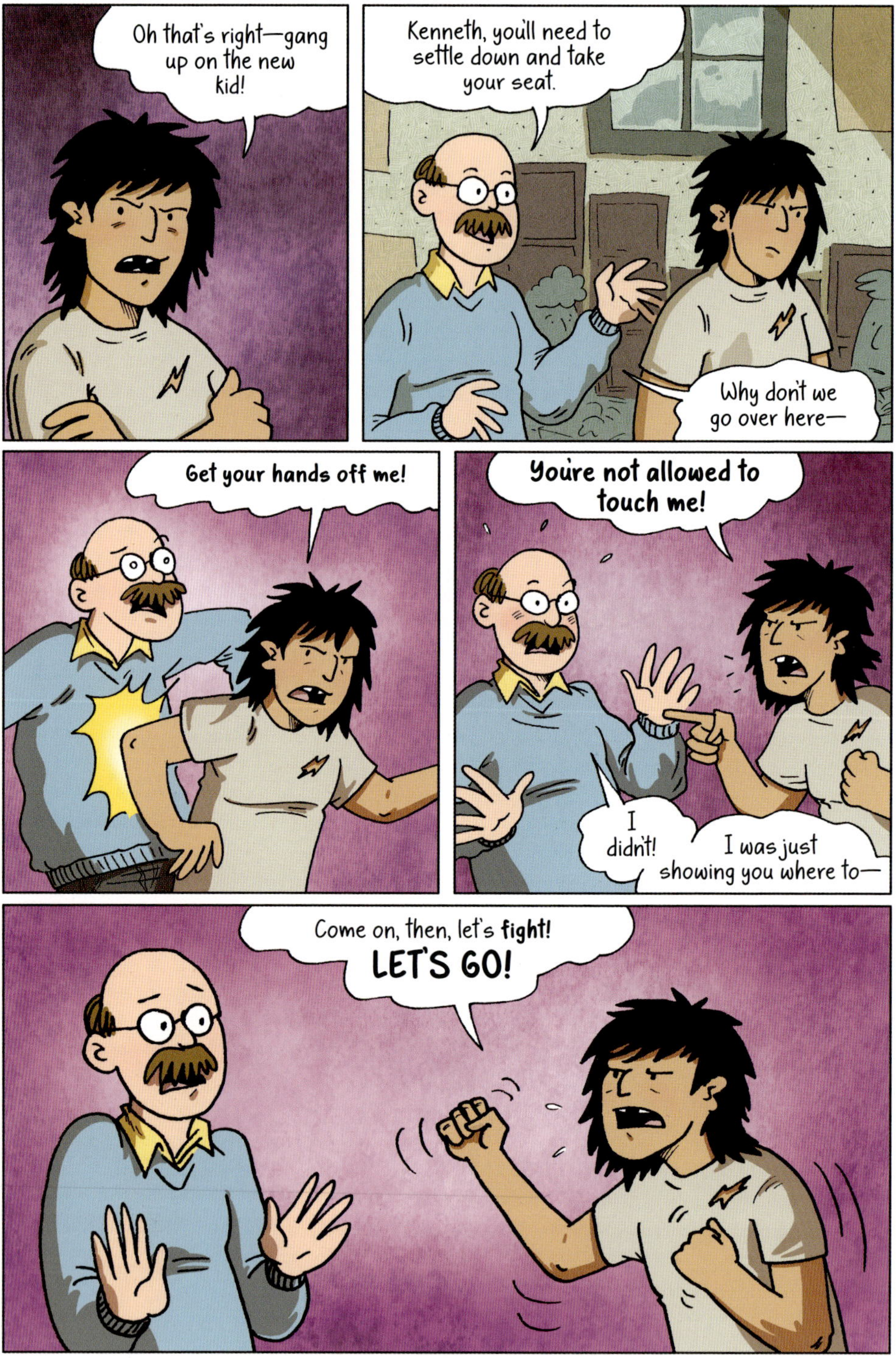
Oh that's right—gang up on the new kid!
Kenneth, you'll need to settle down and take your seat.
Why don't we go over here—
Get your hands off me!
You're not allowed to touch me!
I didn't!
I was just showing you where to—
Come on, then, let's fight!
LET'S GO!

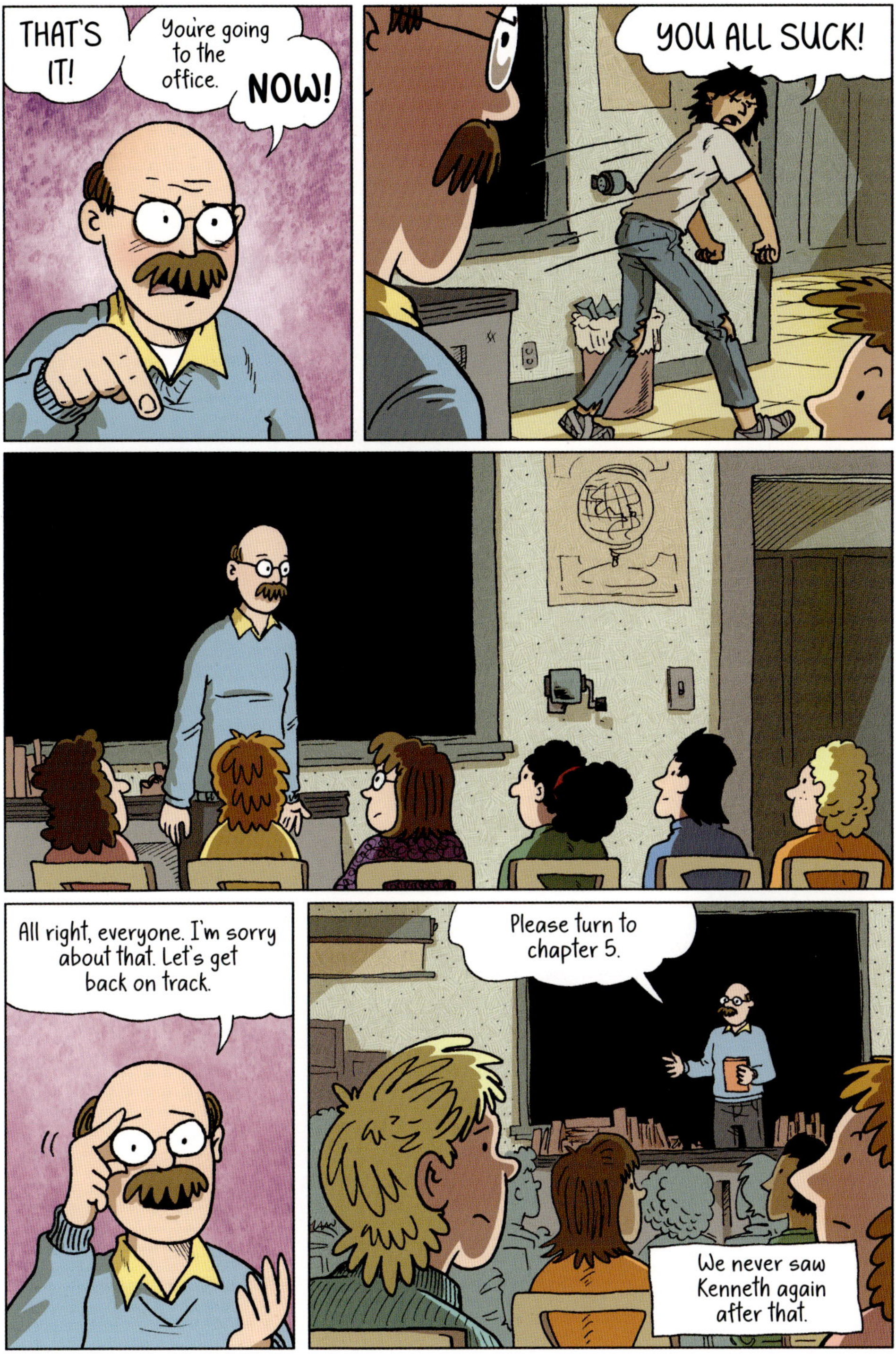
THAT'S IT!
You're going to the office.
NOW!
YOU ALL SUCK!
All right, everyone. I'm sorry about that. Let's get back on track.
Please turn to chapter 5.
We never saw Kenneth again after that.

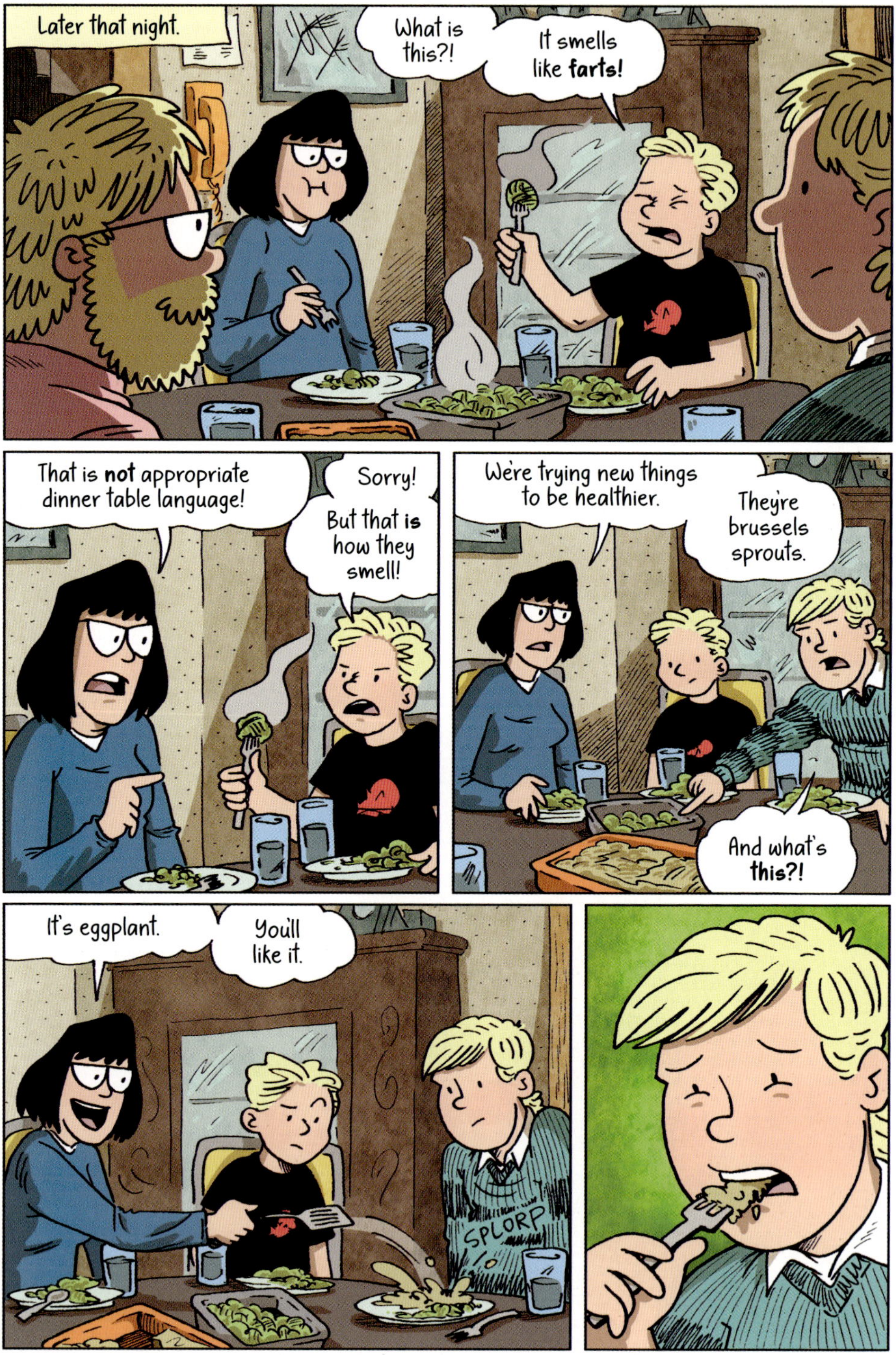

Later that night.
What is this?!
It smells like **farts!**
That is **not** appropriate dinner table language!
Sorry!
But that **is** how they smell!
We're trying new things to be healthier.
They're brussels sprouts.
And what's **this?!**
It's eggplant.
You'll like it.
SPLORP

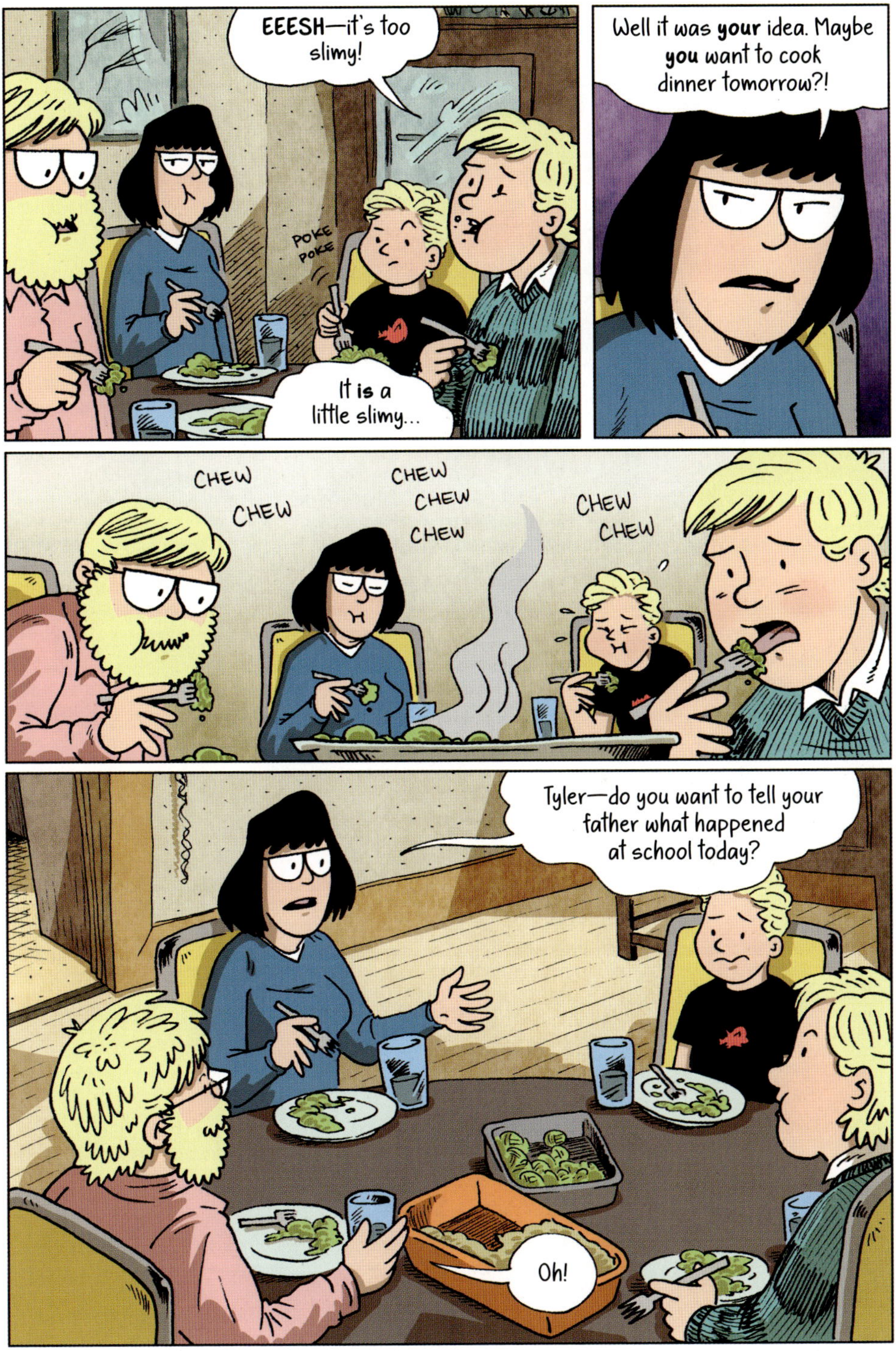
EEESH—it's too slimy!
POKE POKE
It is a little slimy...
Well it was your idea. Maybe you want to cook dinner tomorrow?!
CHEW
CHEW
CHEW
CHEW
CHEW
CHEW
CHEW
Tyler—do you want to tell your father what happened at school today?
Oh!

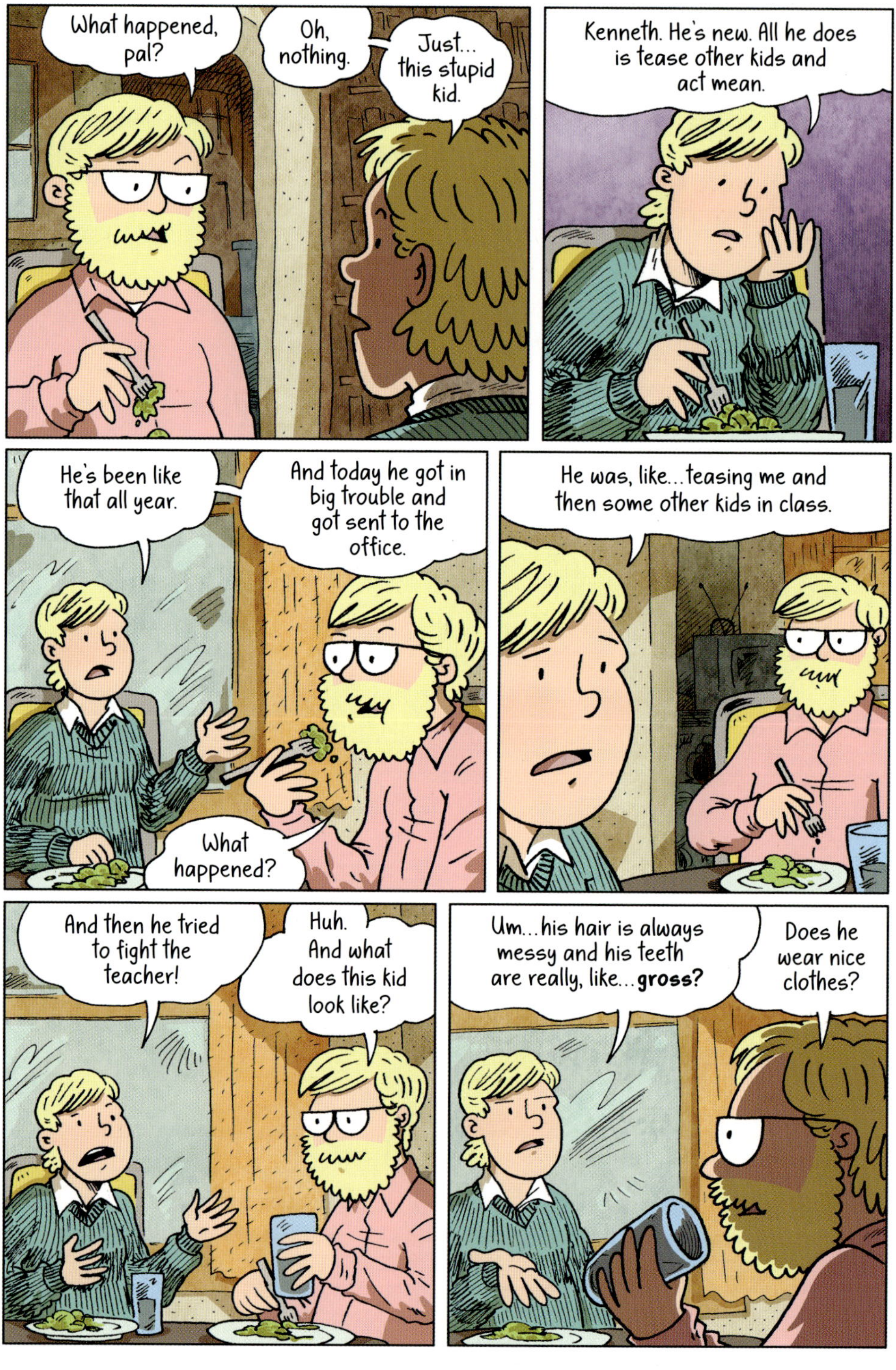
What happened, pal?
Oh, nothing.
Just... this stupid kid.
Kenneth. He's new. All he does is tease other kids and act mean.
He's been like that all year.
And today he got in big trouble and got sent to the office.
What happened?
He was, like...teasing me and then some other kids in class.
And then he tried to fight the teacher!
Huh. And what does this kid look like?
Um...his hair is always messy and his teeth are really, like...**gross?**
Does he wear nice clothes?

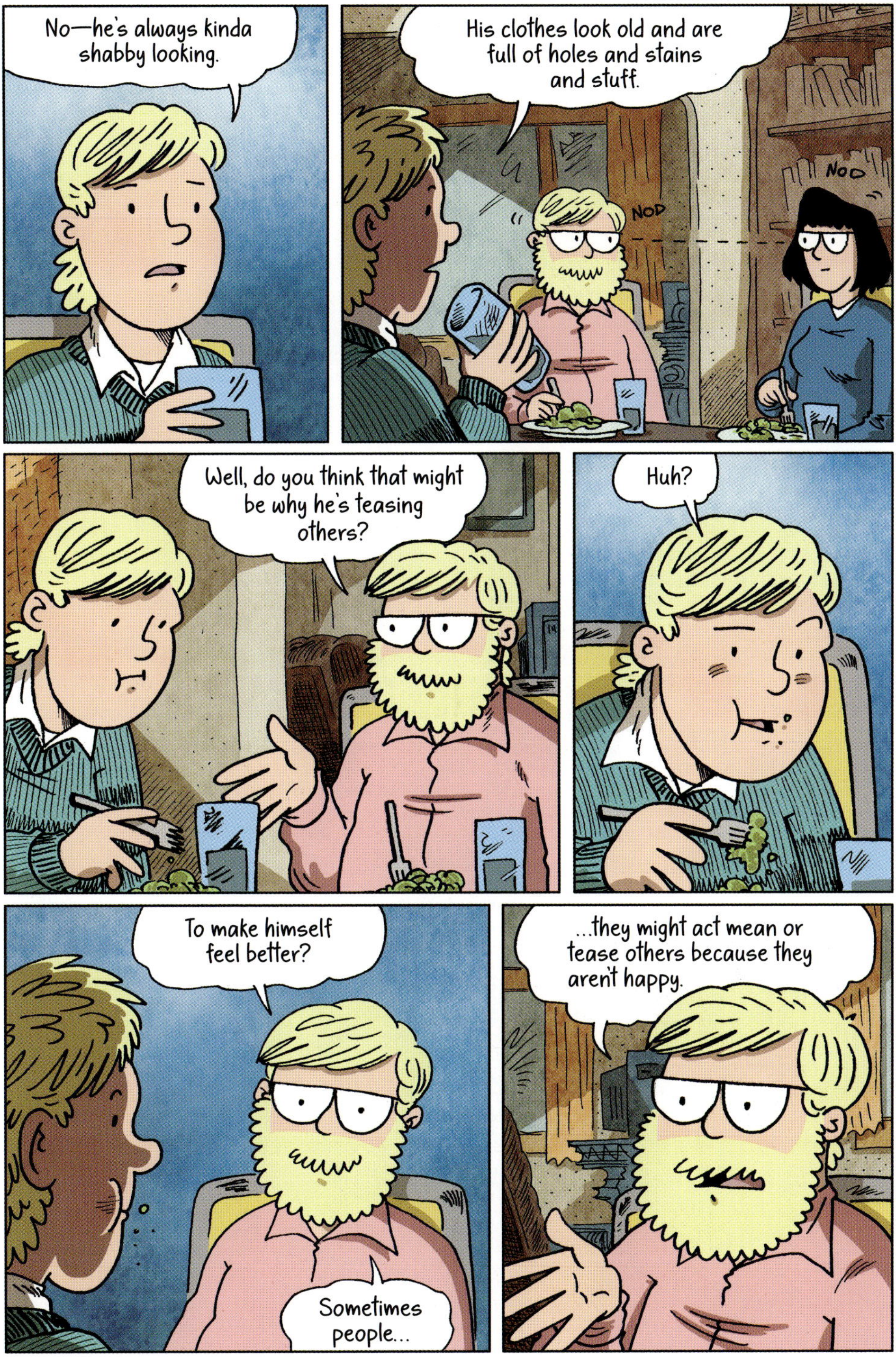
No—he's always kinda shabby looking.
His clothes look old and are full of holes and stains and stuff.
NOD
NOD
Well, do you think that might be why he's teasing others?
Huh?
To make himself feel better?
Sometimes people...
...they might act mean or tease others because they aren't happy.

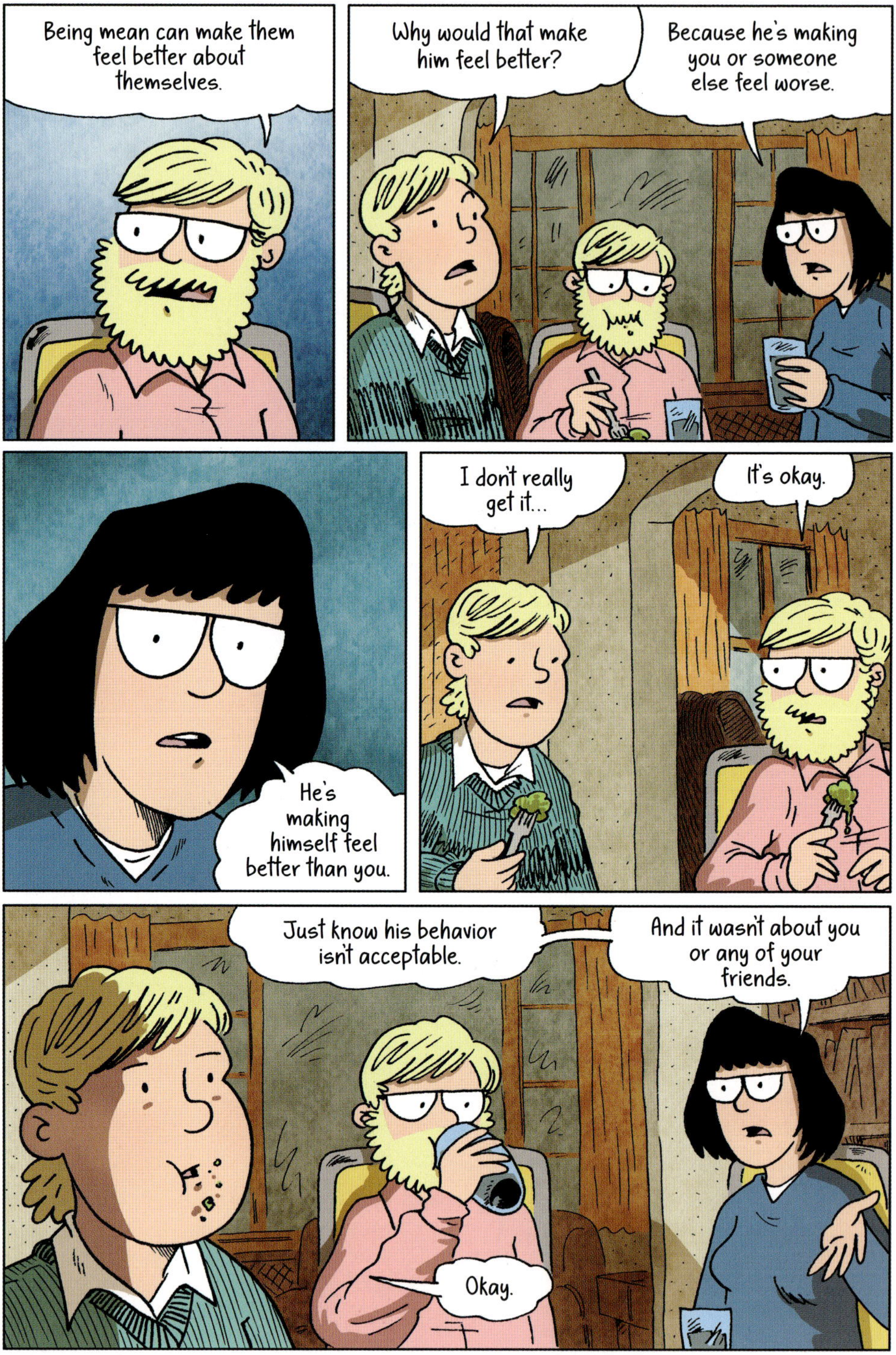

Being mean can make them feel better about themselves.
Why would that make him feel better?
Because he's making you or someone else feel worse.
He's making himself feel better than you.
I don't really get it...
It's okay.
Just know his behavior isn't acceptable.
And it wasn't about you or any of your friends.
Okay.

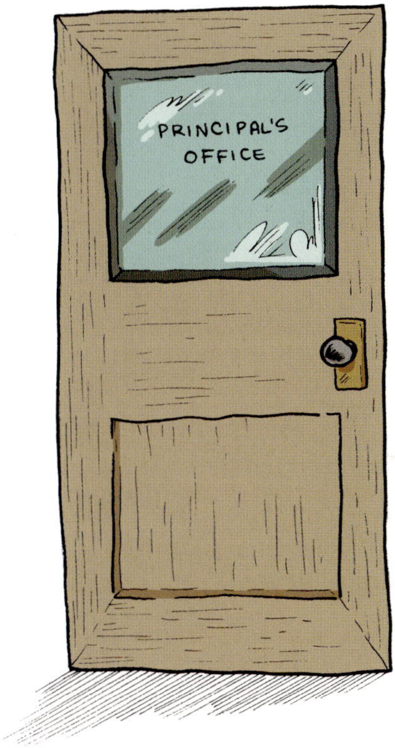
PRINCIPAL'S
OFFICE

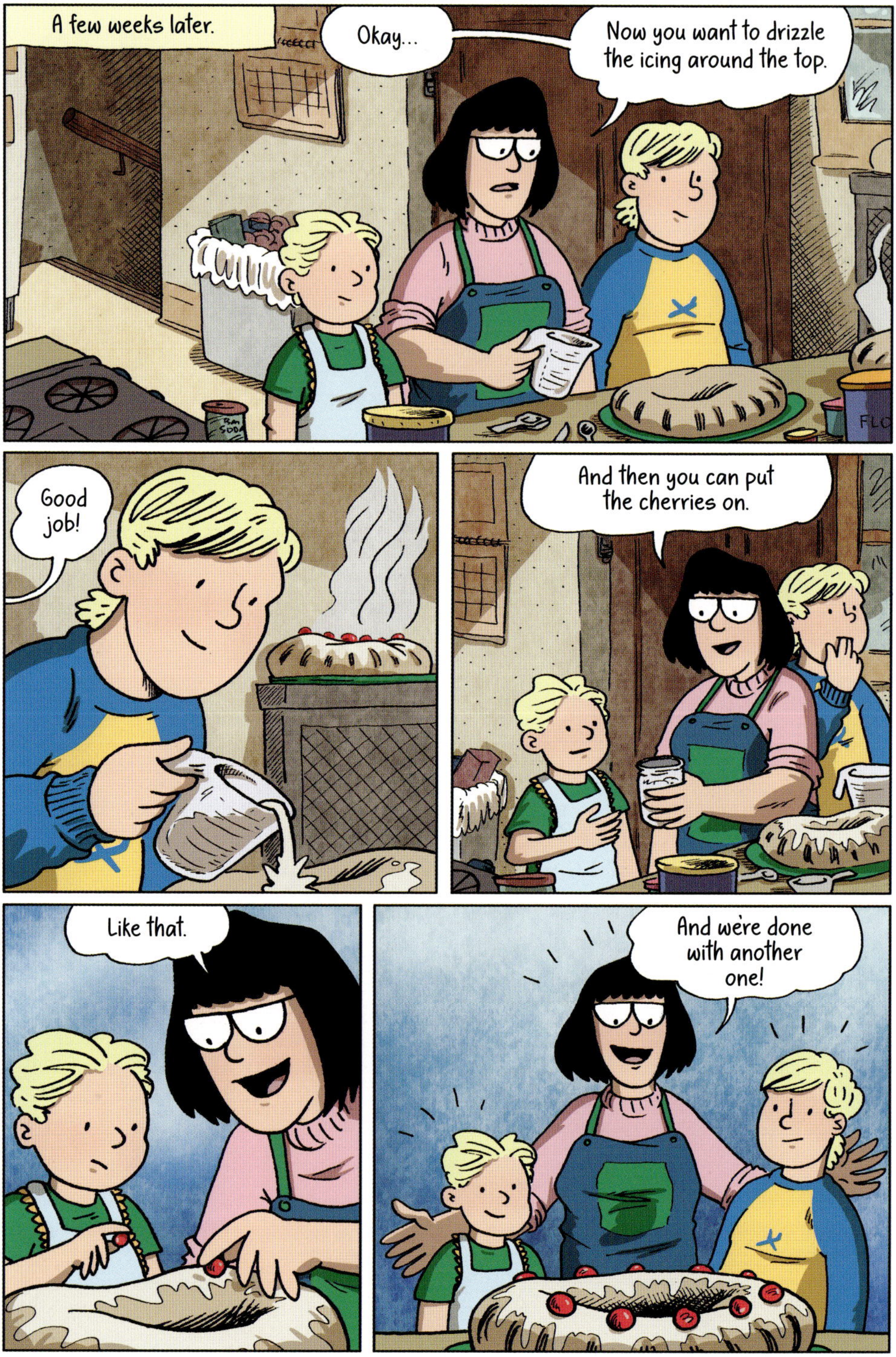
A few weeks later.
Okay...
Now you want to drizzle the icing around the top.
Good job!
And then you can put the cherries on.
Like that.
And we're done with another one!

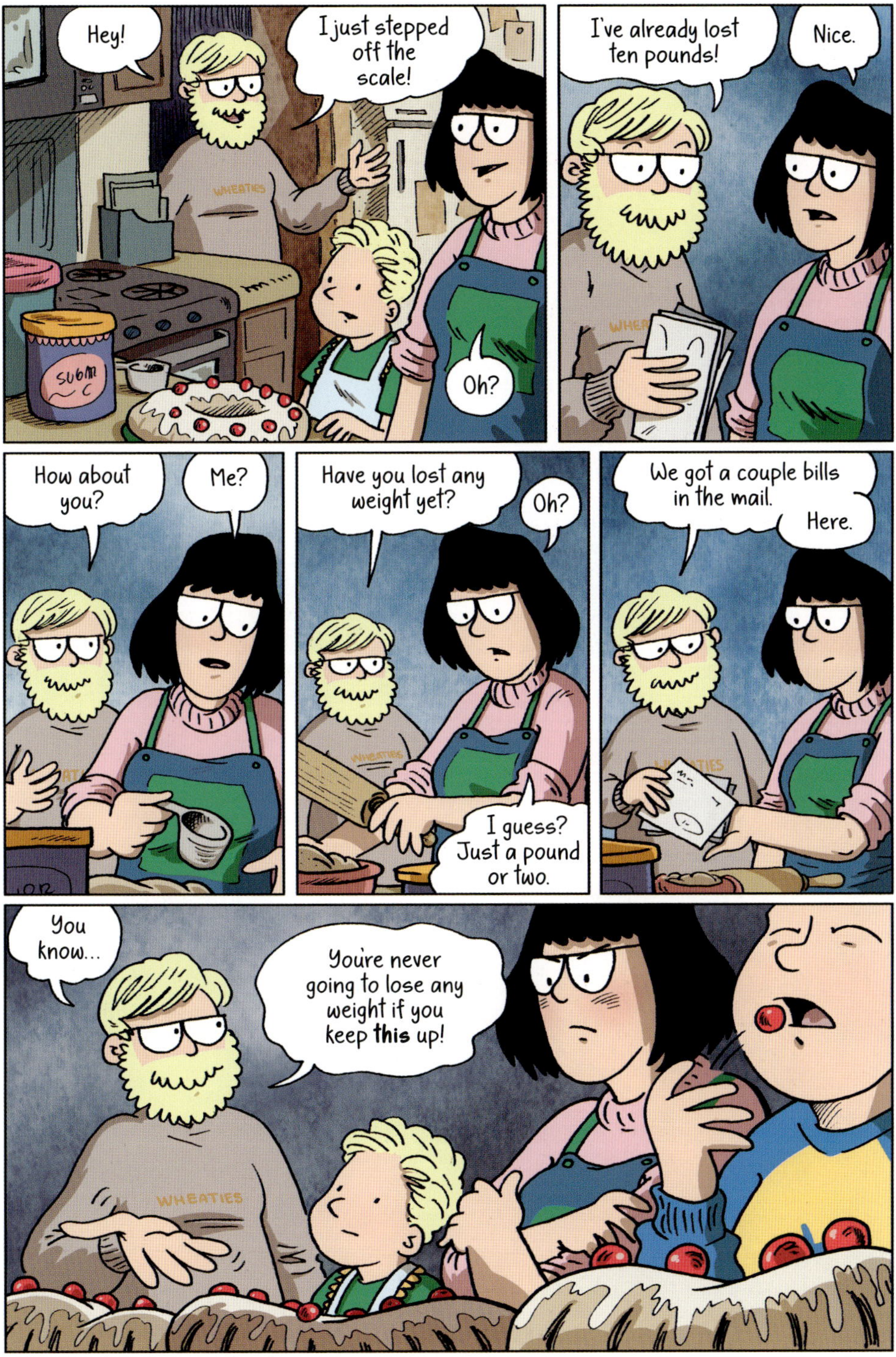
Hey!
I just stepped off the scale!
Oh?
I've already lost ten pounds!
Nice.
How about you?
Me?
Have you lost any weight yet?
Oh?
I guess? Just a pound or two.
We got a couple bills in the mail.
Here.
You know...
You're never going to lose any weight if you keep **this** up!

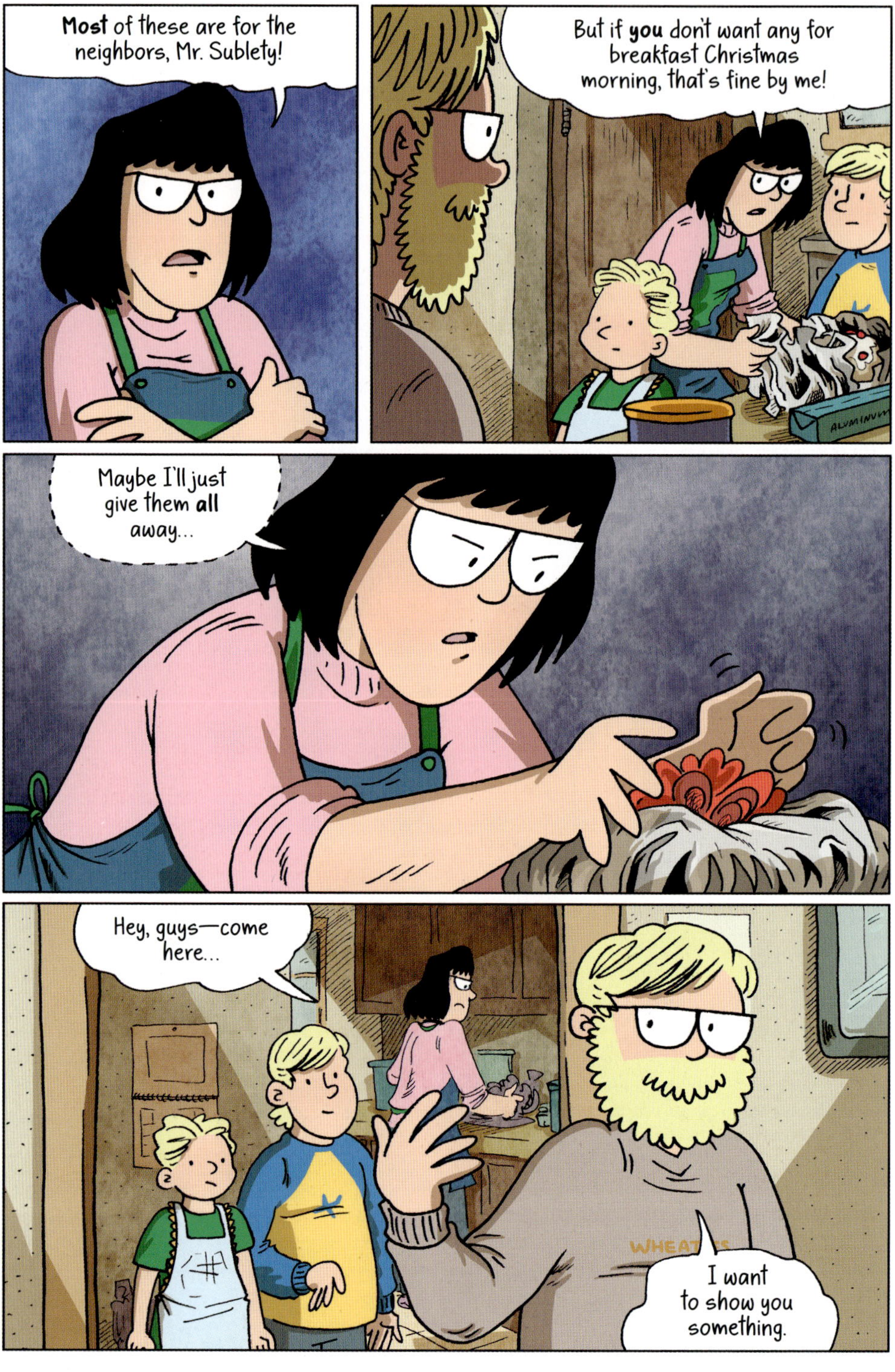
Most of these are for the neighbors, Mr. Sublety!
But if **you** don't want any for breakfast Christmas morning, that's fine by me!
ALUMINUM
Maybe I'll just give them **all** away...
Hey, guys—come here...
I want to show you something.

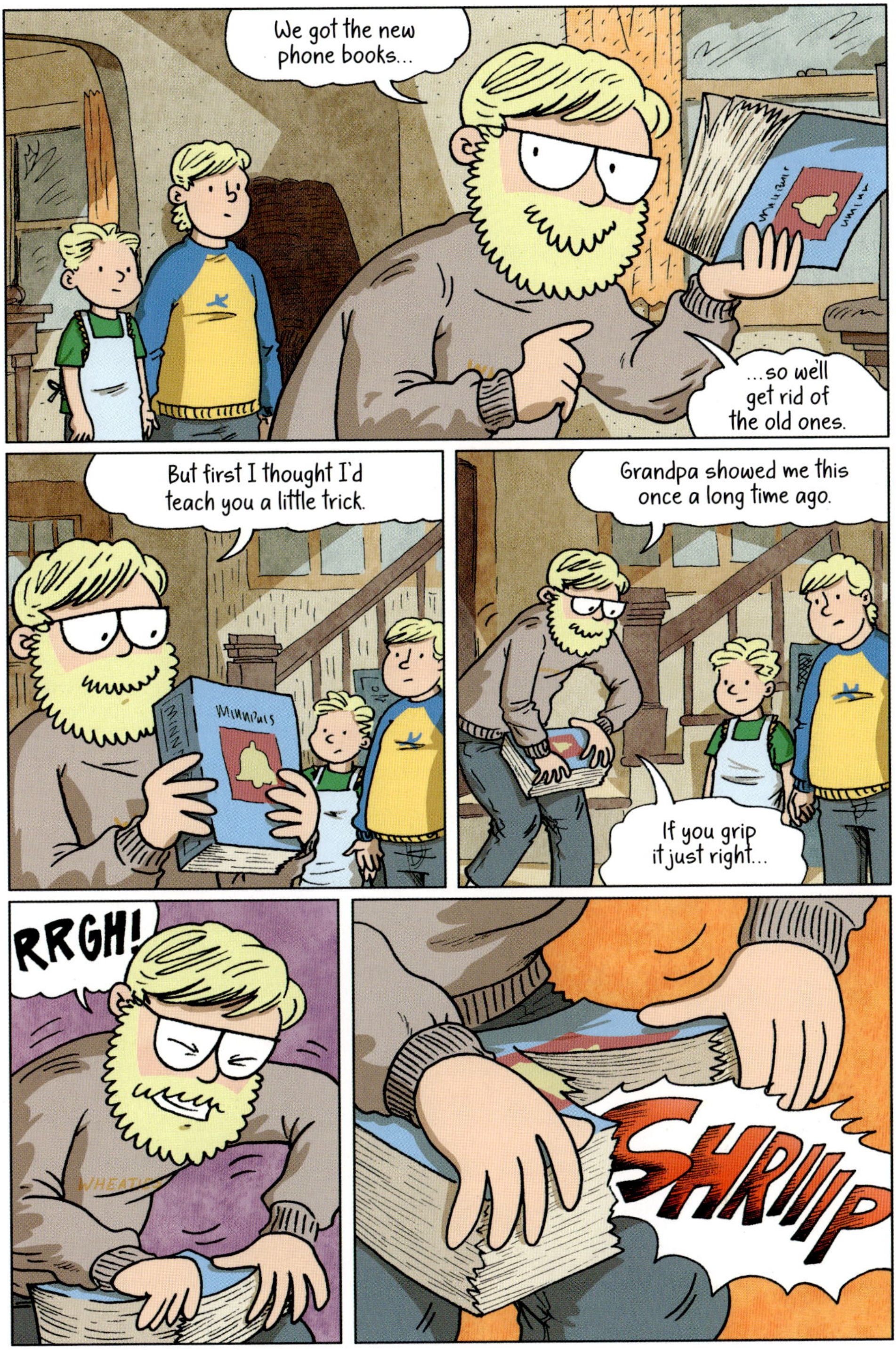
We got the new phone books...
...so we'll get rid of the old ones.
But first I thought I'd teach you a little trick.
Grandpa showed me this once a long time ago.
If you grip it just right...
RRGH!
SHRIIP

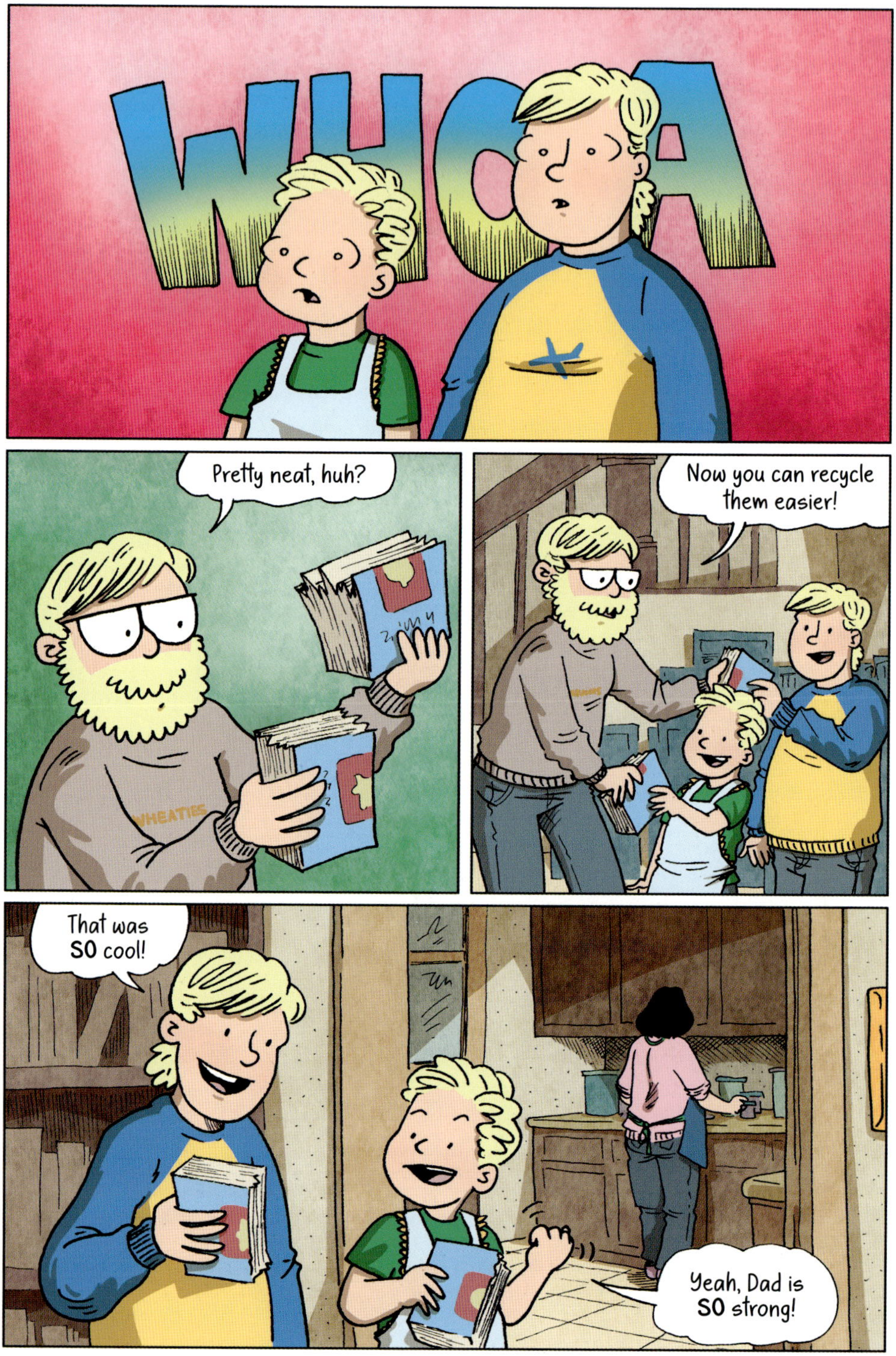
WHOA
Pretty neat, huh?
WHEATIES
Now you can recycle them easier!
That was SO cool!
Yeah, Dad is SO strong!

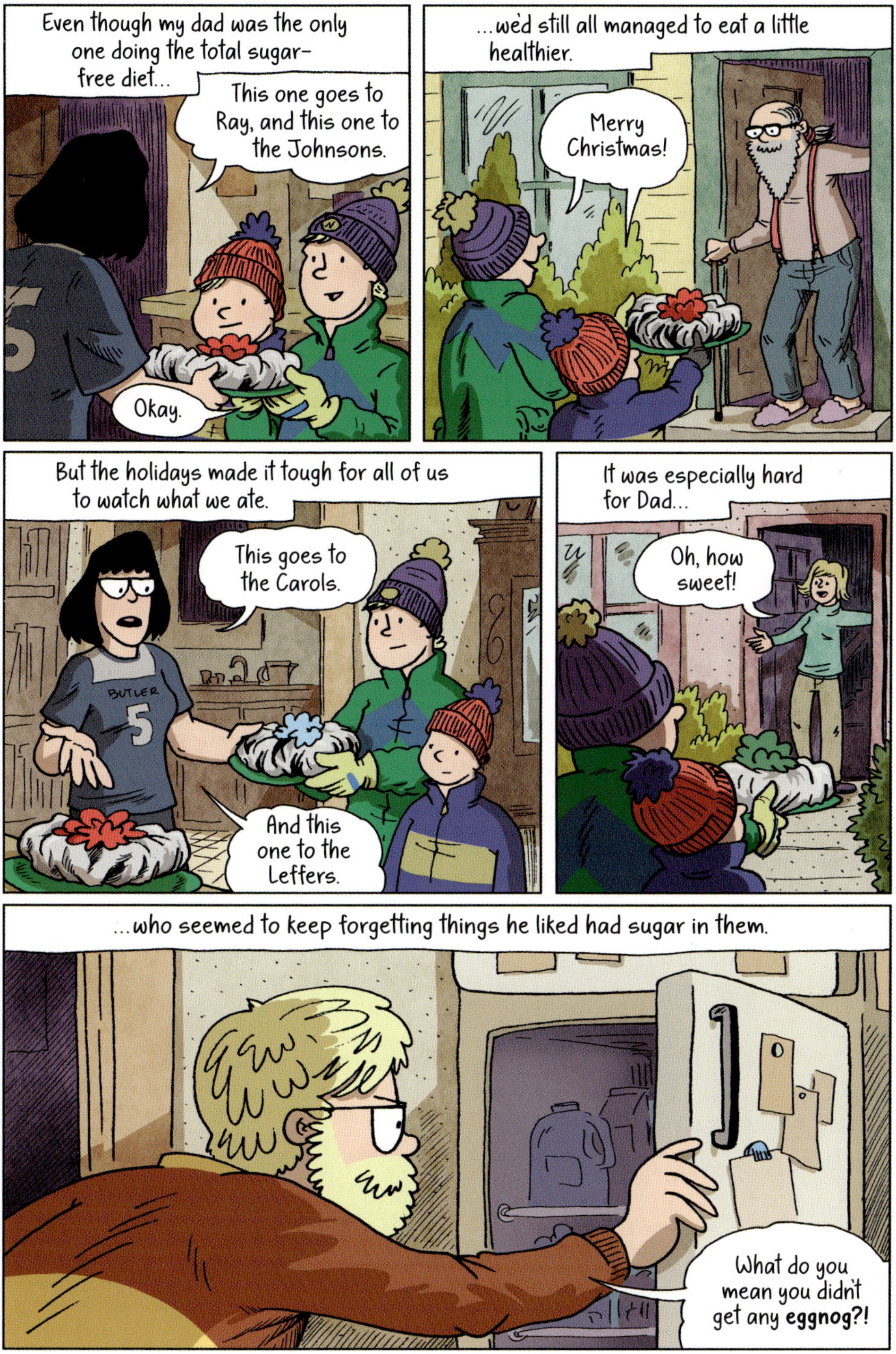
Even though my dad was the only one doing the total sugar-free diet...
This one goes to Ray, and this one to the Johnsons.
Okay.
...we'd still all managed to eat a little healthier.
Merry Christmas!
But the holidays made it tough for all of us to watch what we ate.
This goes to the Carols.
BUTLER
5
And this one to the Leffers.
It was especially hard for Dad...
Oh, how sweet!
...who seemed to keep forgetting things he liked had sugar in them.
What do you mean you didn't get any **eggnog**?!

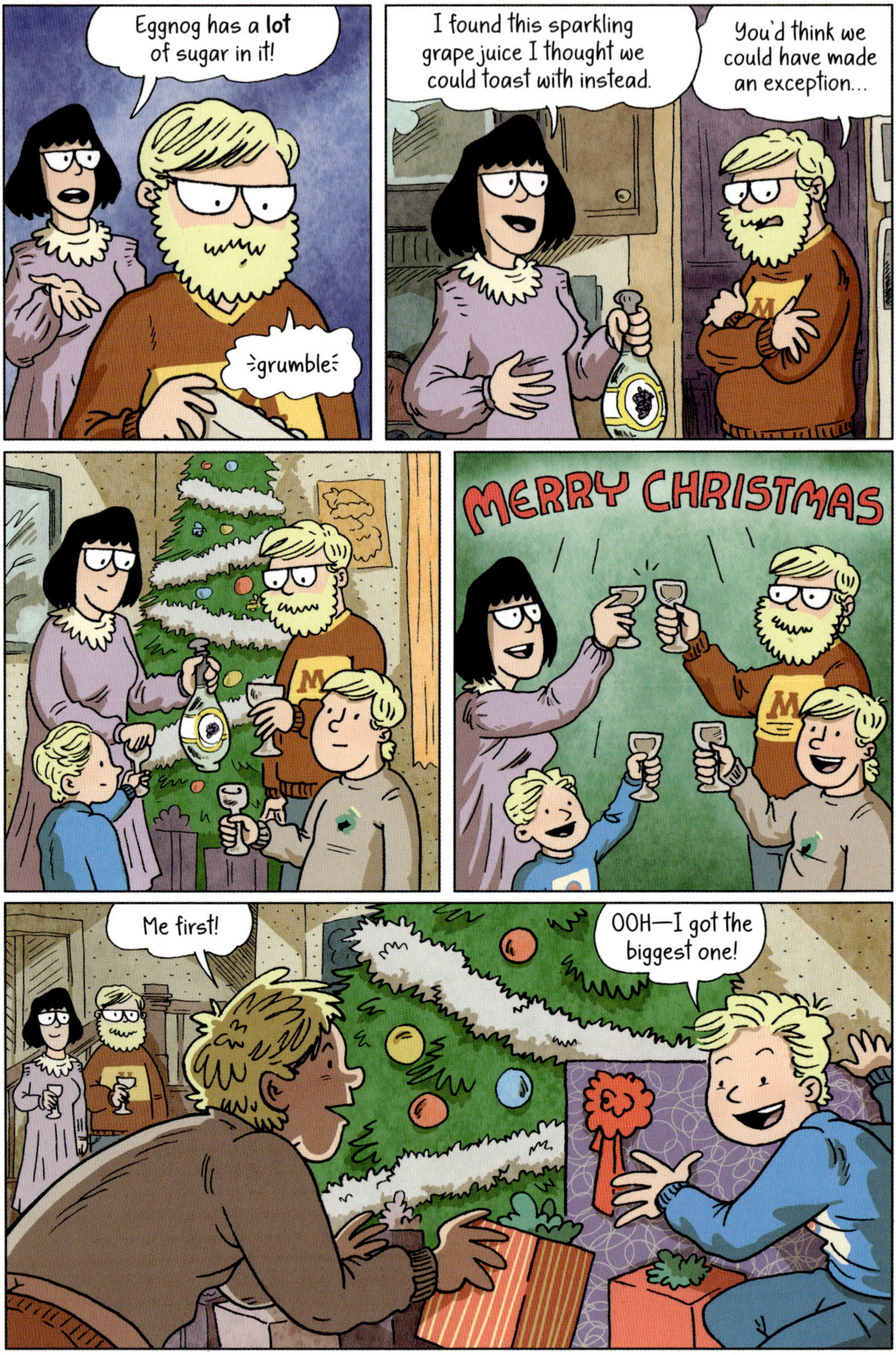
Eggnog has a **lot** of sugar in it!
grumble
I found this sparkling grape juice I thought we could toast with instead.
You'd think we could have made an exception...
MERRY CHRISTMAS
Me first!
OOH—I got the biggest one!

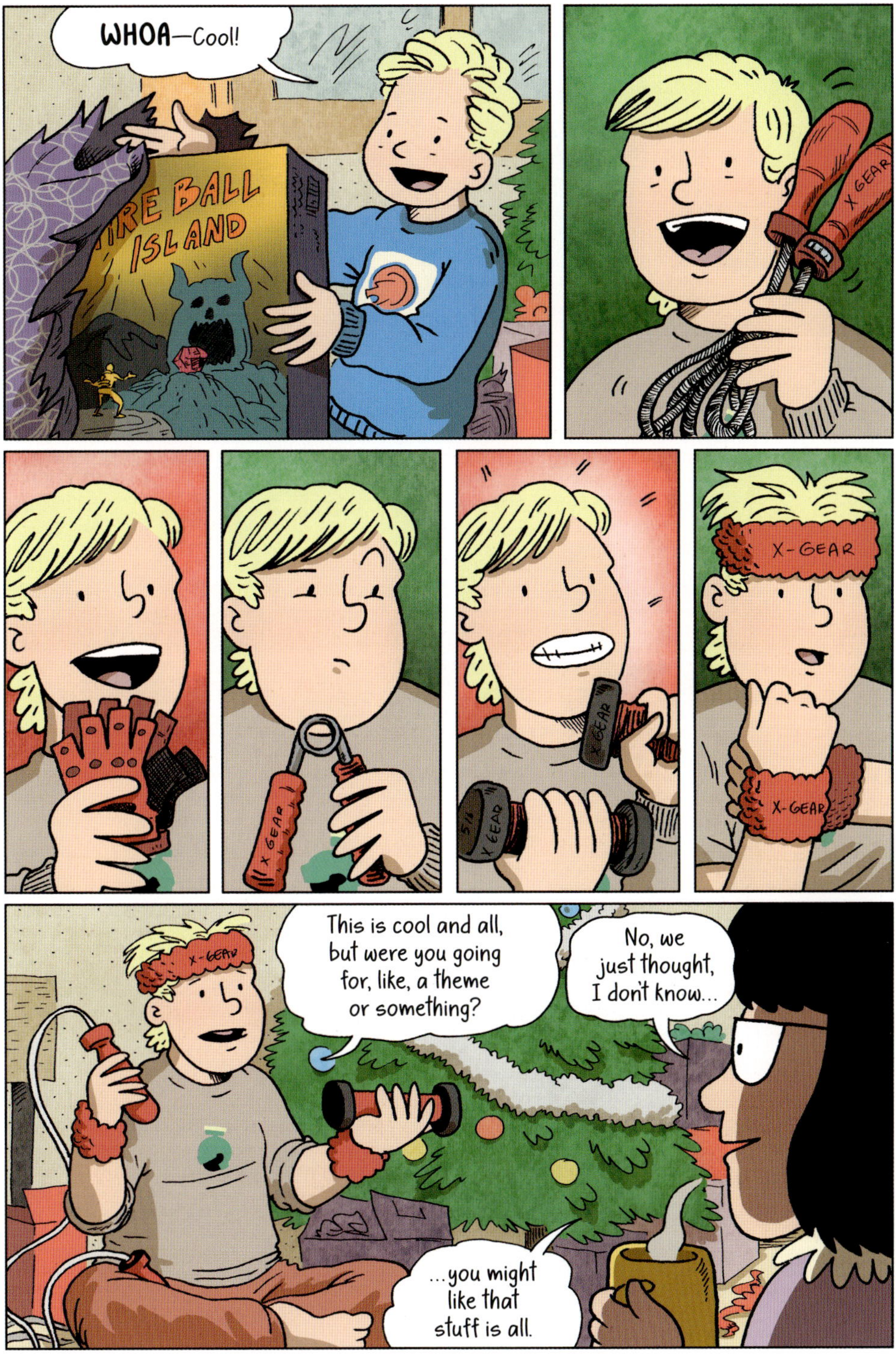
WHOA—Cool!
IRE BALL ISLAND
X GEAR
X-GEAR
X GEAR
X GEAR
X-GEAR
X-GEAR
This is cool and all, but were you going for, like, a theme or something?
No, we just thought, I don't know...
...you might like that stuff is all.

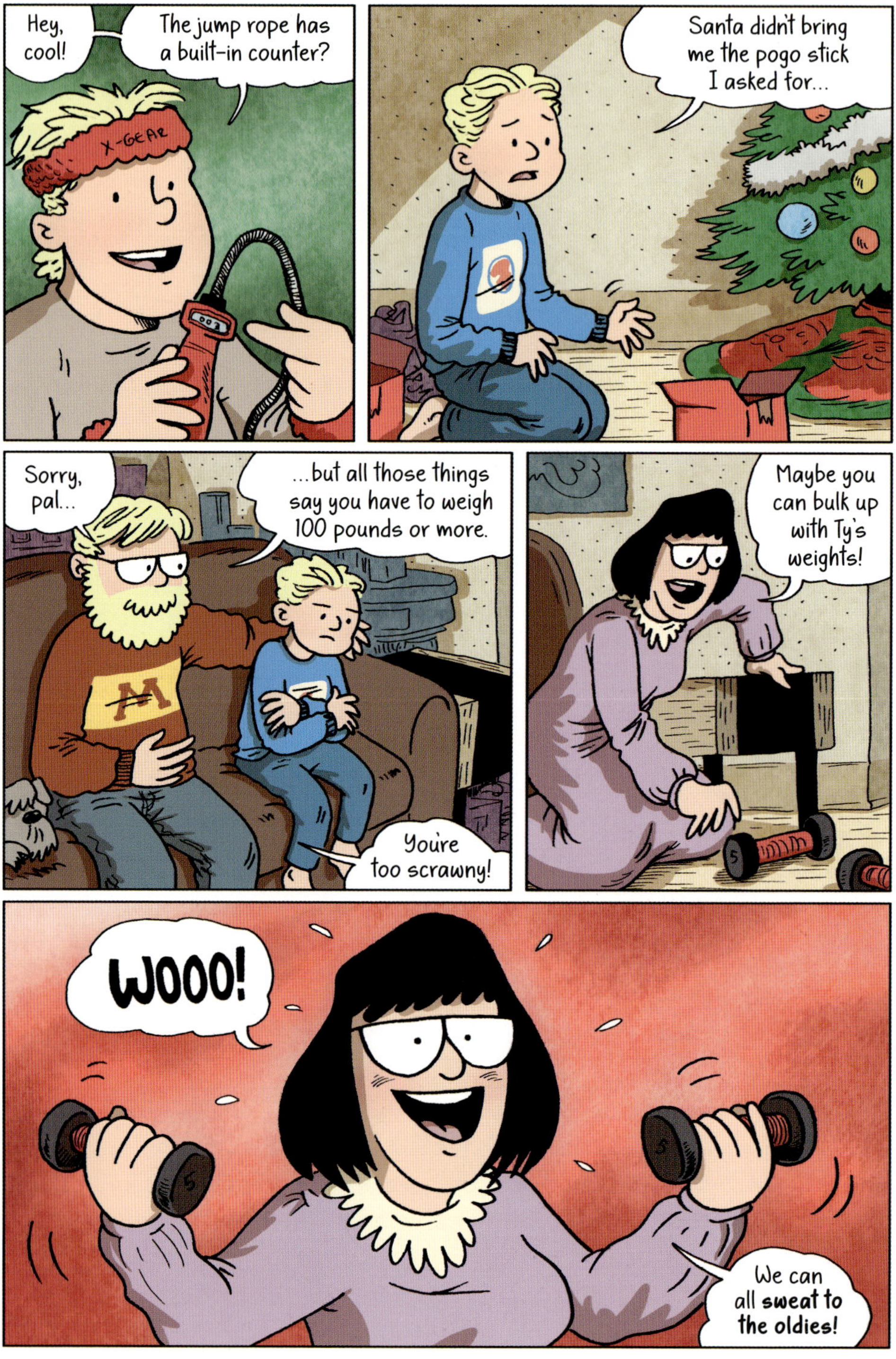

Hey, cool!
The jump rope has a built-in counter?
X-GEAR
Santa didn't bring me the pogo stick I asked for...
Sorry, pal...
...but all those things say you have to weigh 100 pounds or more.
You're too scrawny!
Maybe you can bulk up with Ty's weights!
WOOO!
We can all **sweat to the oldies!**

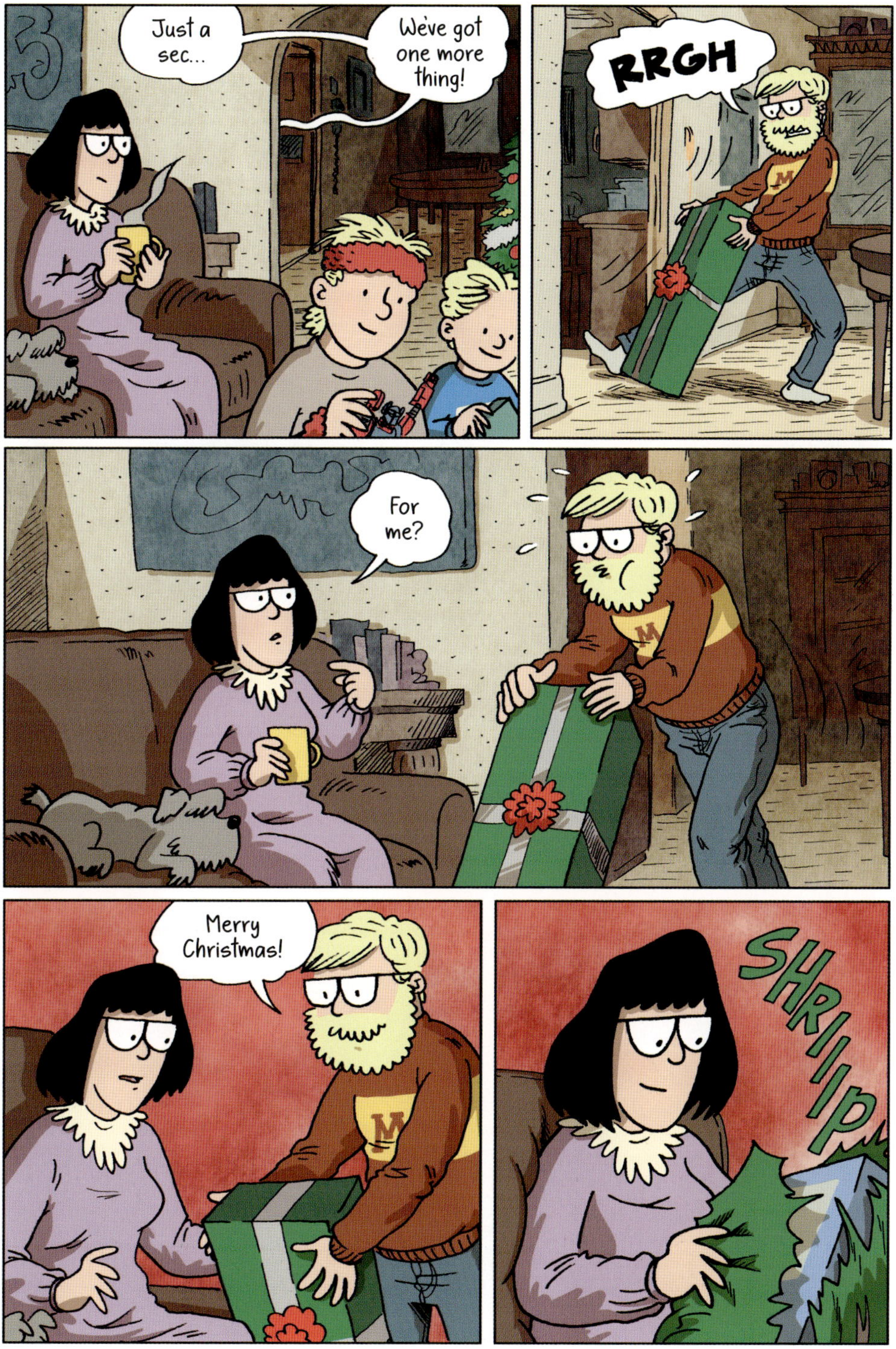
Just a sec...
We've got one more thing!
RRGH
For me?
Merry Christmas!
SHRIIIP!

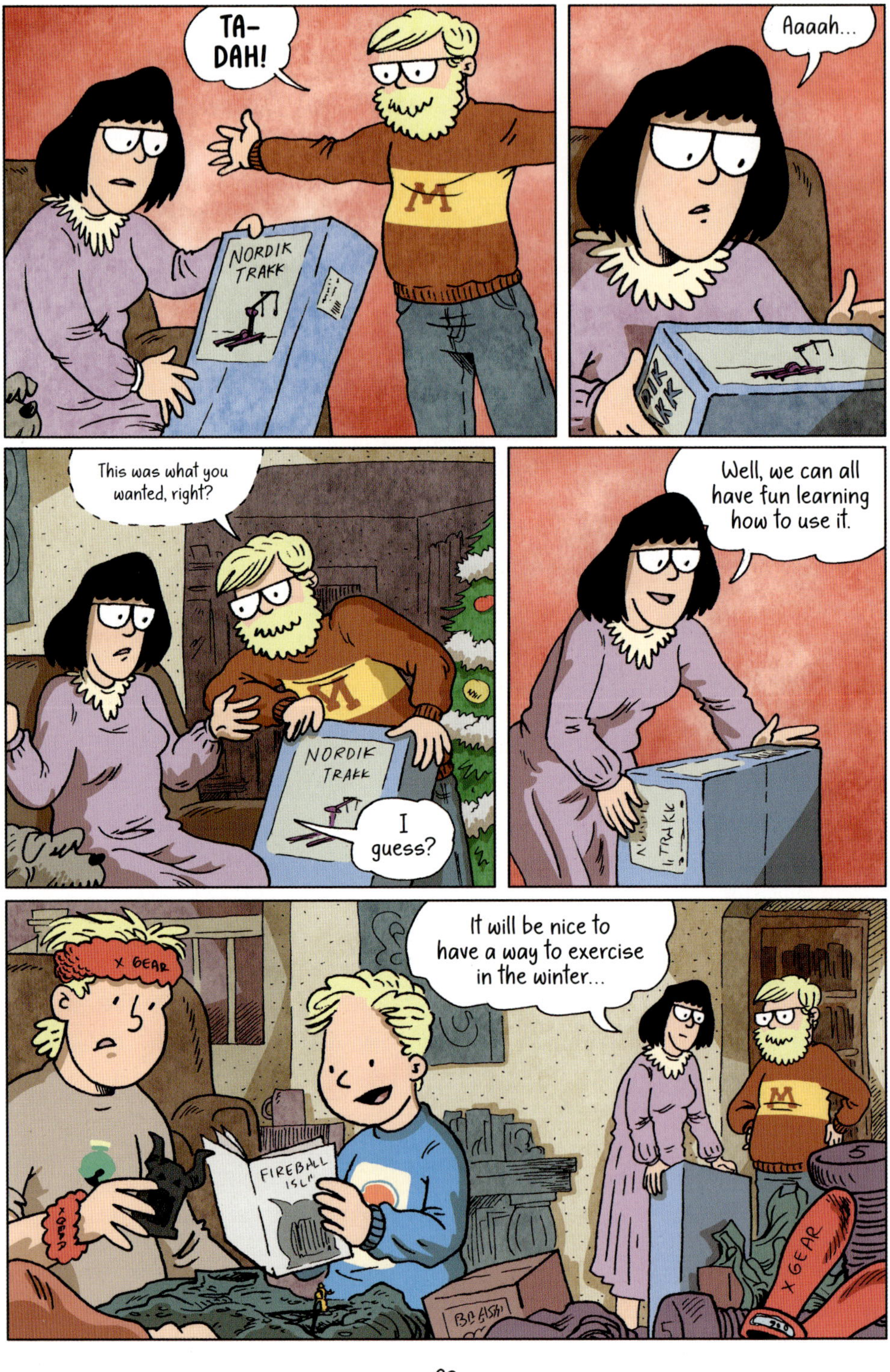
TA-DAH!
NORDIK TRAKK
Aaaah...
This was what you wanted, right?
NORDIK TRAKK
I guess?
Well, we can all have fun learning how to use it.
It will be nice to have a way to exercise in the winter...
X GEAR
FIREBALL ISL
M
X GEAR

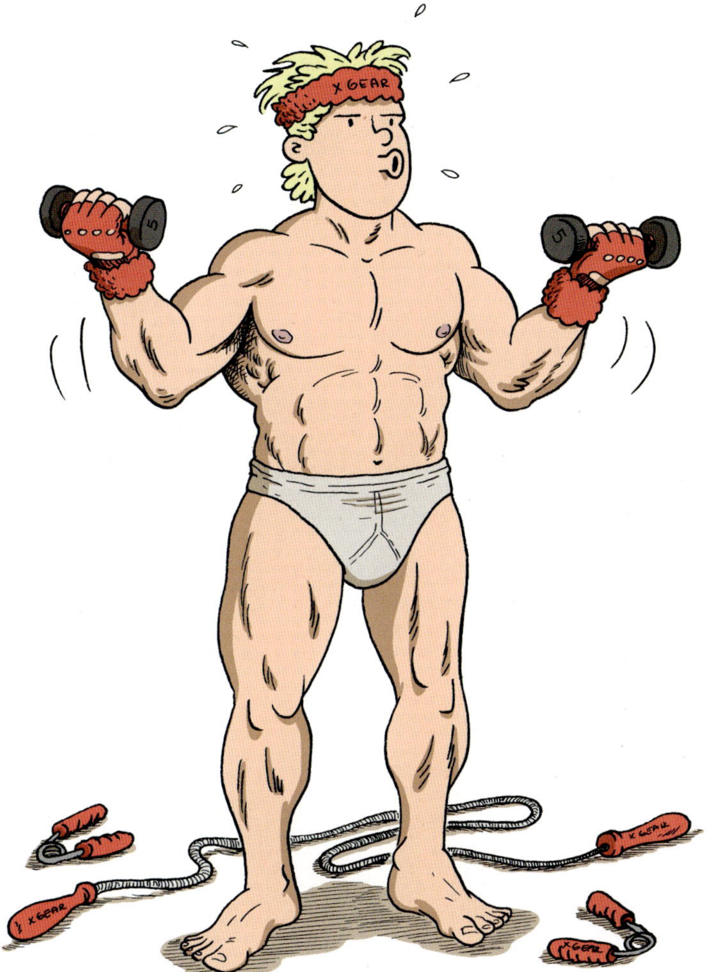
X GEAR
5
5
X GEAR
X GEAR
X GEAR

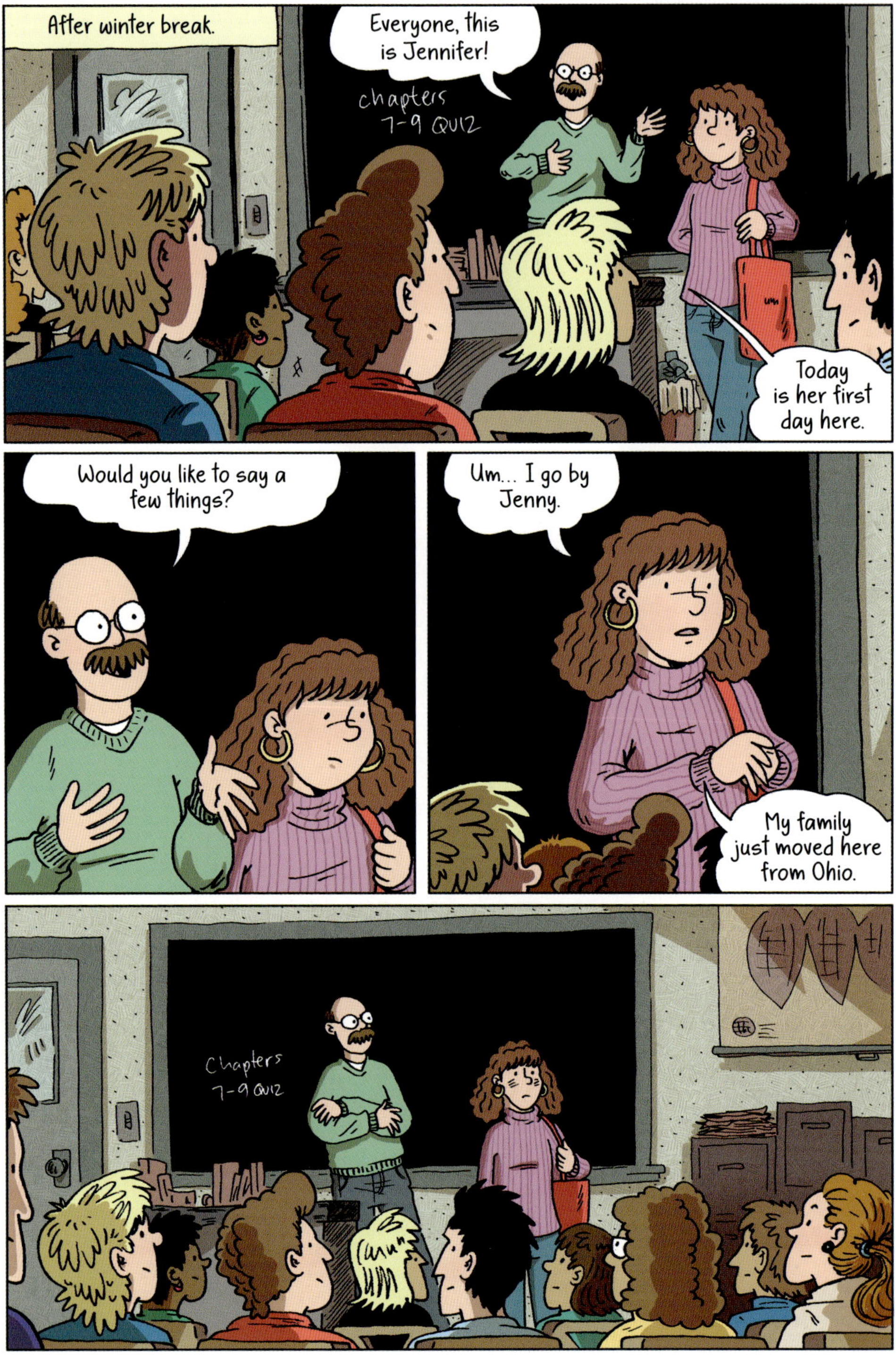
After winter break.
Everyone, this is Jennifer!
chapters 7-9 QUIZ
Today is her first day here.
Would you like to say a few things?
Um... I go by Jenny.
My family just moved here from Ohio.
Chapters 7-9 QUIZ

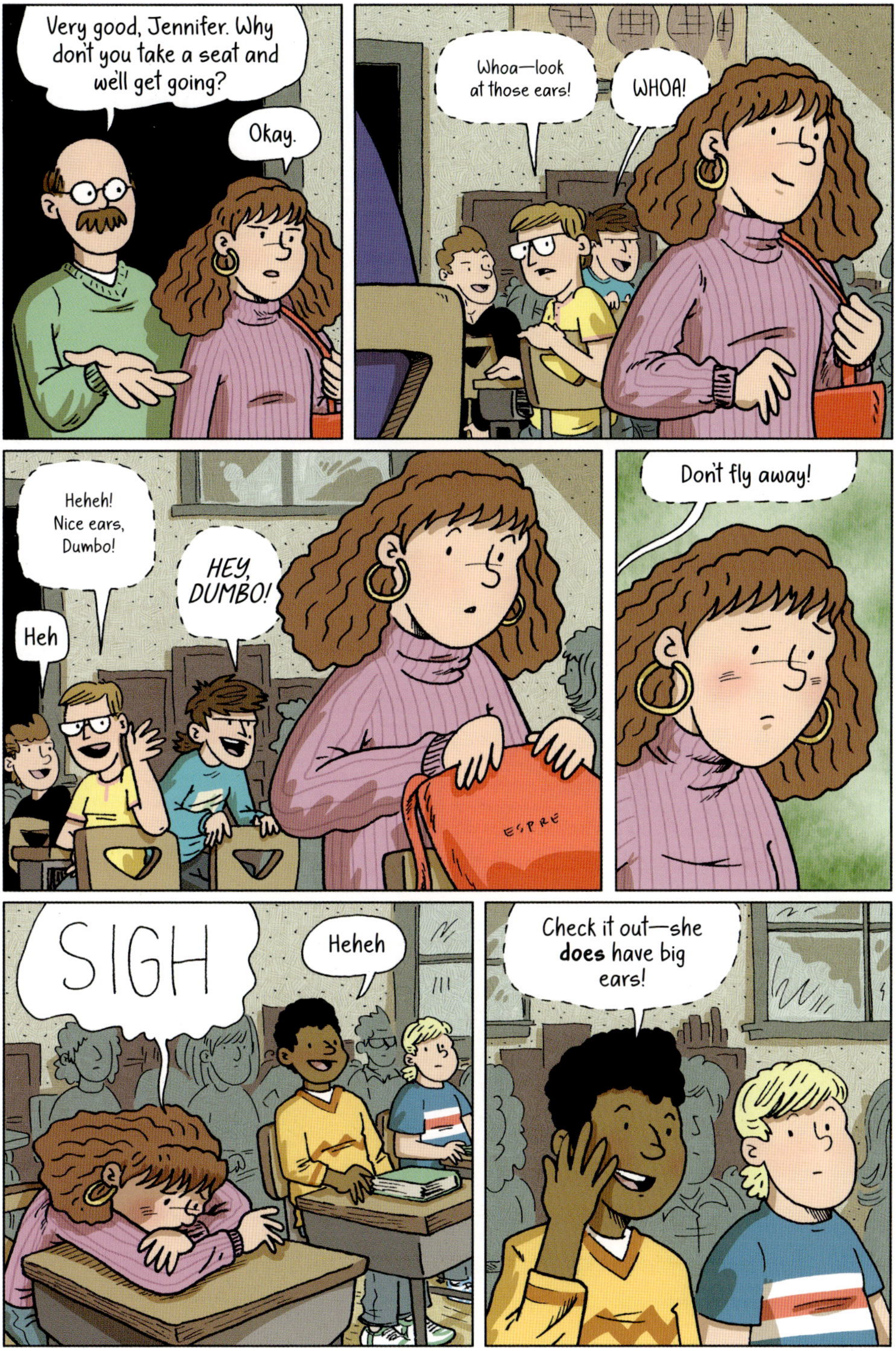
Very good, Jennifer. Why don't you take a seat and we'll get going?
Okay.
Whoa—look at those ears!
WHOA!
Heheh! Nice ears, Dumbo!
HEY, DUMBO!
Heh
ESPRE
Don't fly away!
SIGH
Heheh
Check it out—she **does** have big ears!

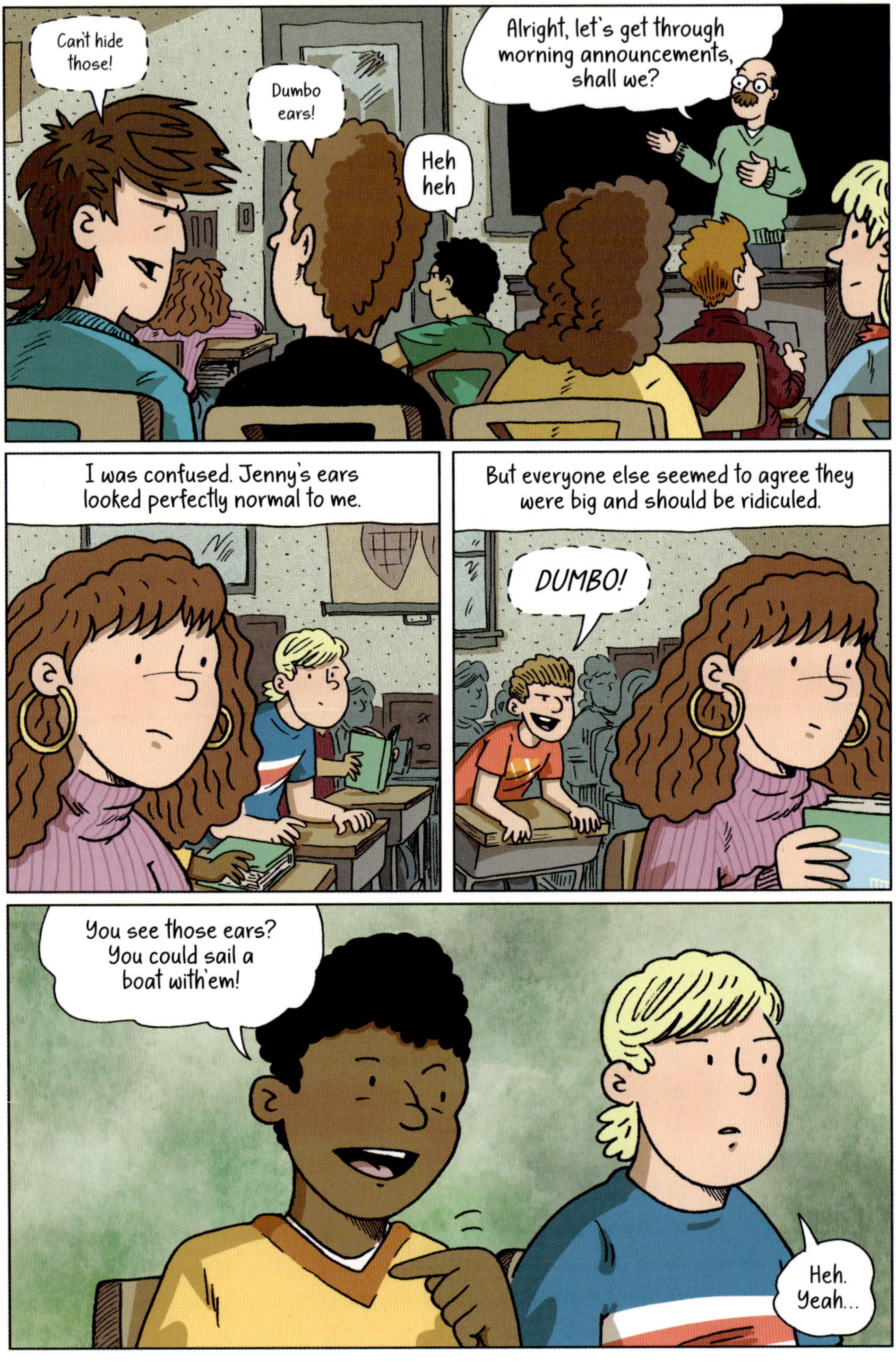
Can't hide those!
Dumbo ears!
Heh heh
Alright, let's get through morning announcements, shall we?
I was confused. Jenny's ears looked perfectly normal to me.
But everyone else seemed to agree they were big and should be ridiculed.
DUMBO!
You see those ears? You could sail a boat with'em!
Heh. Yeah...

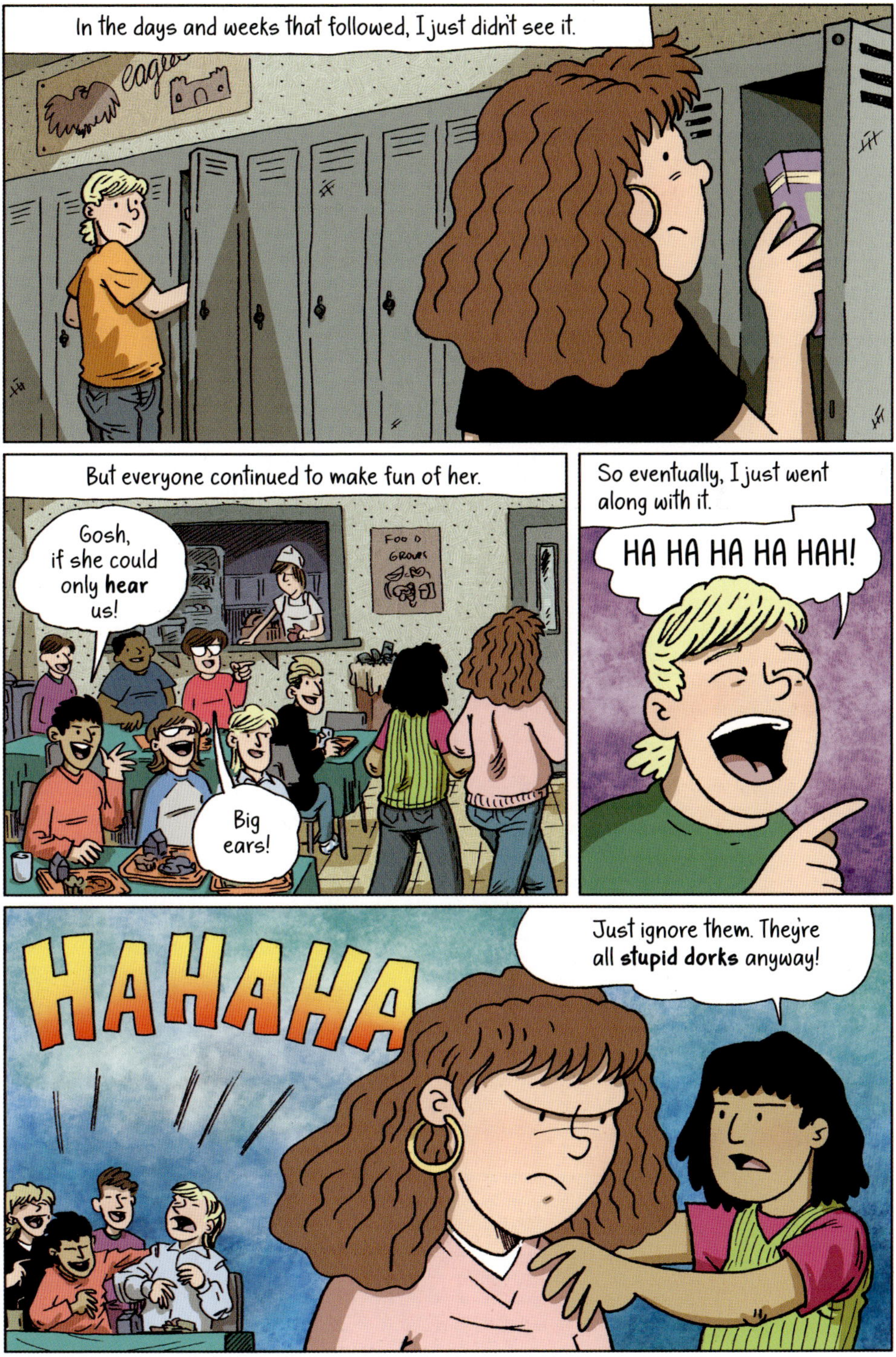
In the days and weeks that followed, I just didn't see it.
But everyone continued to make fun of her.
Gosh, if she could only **hear** us!
Big ears!
So eventually, I just went along with it.
HA HA HA HA HAH!
HAHAHA
Just ignore them. They're all **stupid dorks** anyway!

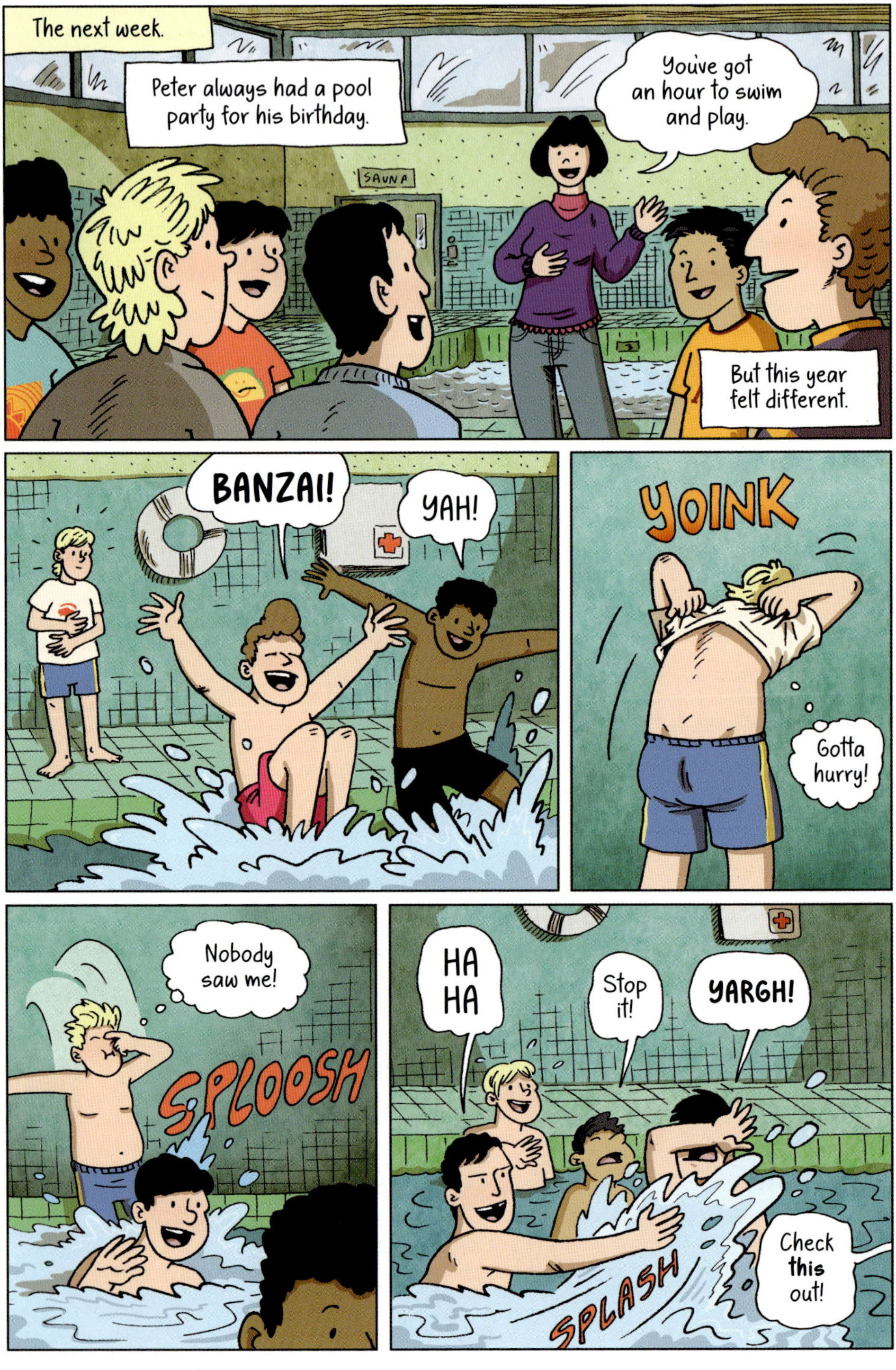
The next week.
Peter always had a pool party for his birthday.
You've got an hour to swim and play.
SAUNA
But this year felt different.
BANZAI!
YAH!
YOINK
Gotta hurry!
Nobody saw me!
SPLOOSH
HA HA
Stop it!
YARGH!
Check this out!
SPLASH

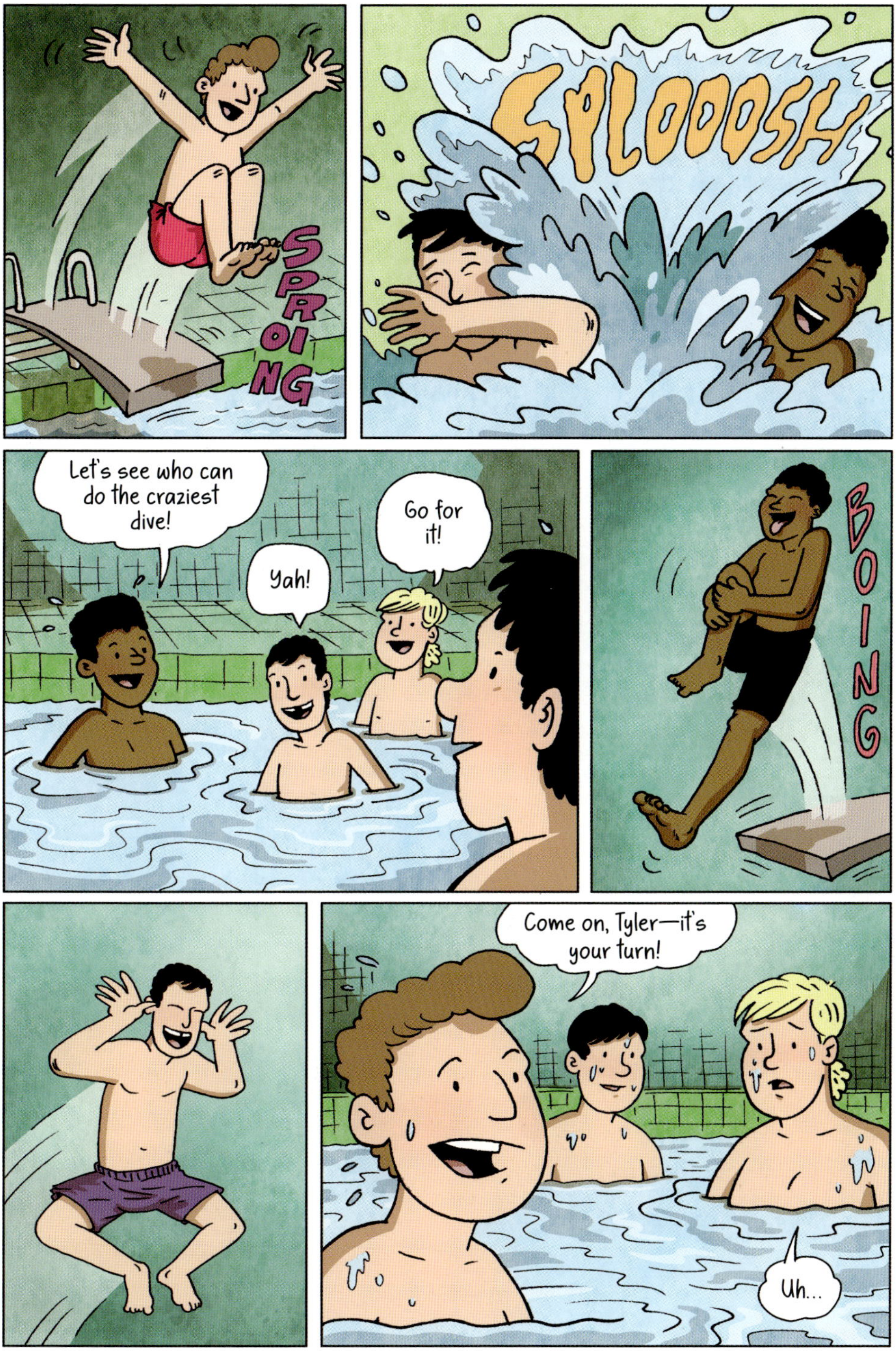
SPROING
SPLOOOSH
Let's see who can do the craziest dive!
Yah!
Go for it!
BOING
Come on, Tyler—it's your turn!
Uh...

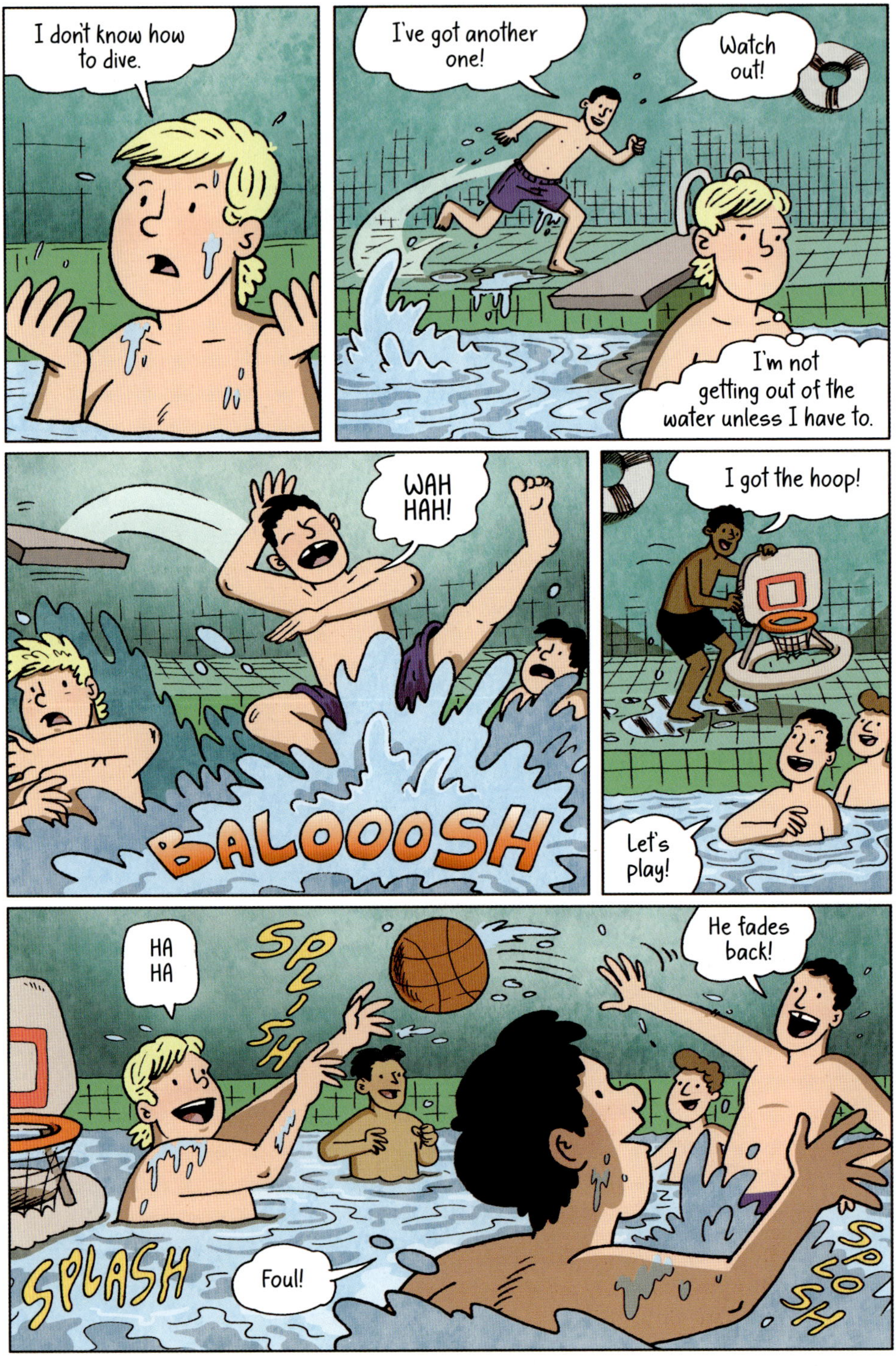

I don't know how to dive.
I've got another one!
Watch out!
I'm not getting out of the water unless I have to.
WAH HAH!
BALOOOSH
I got the hoop!
Let's play!
HA HA
SPLISH
He fades back!
SPLASH
Foul!
SPLOSH

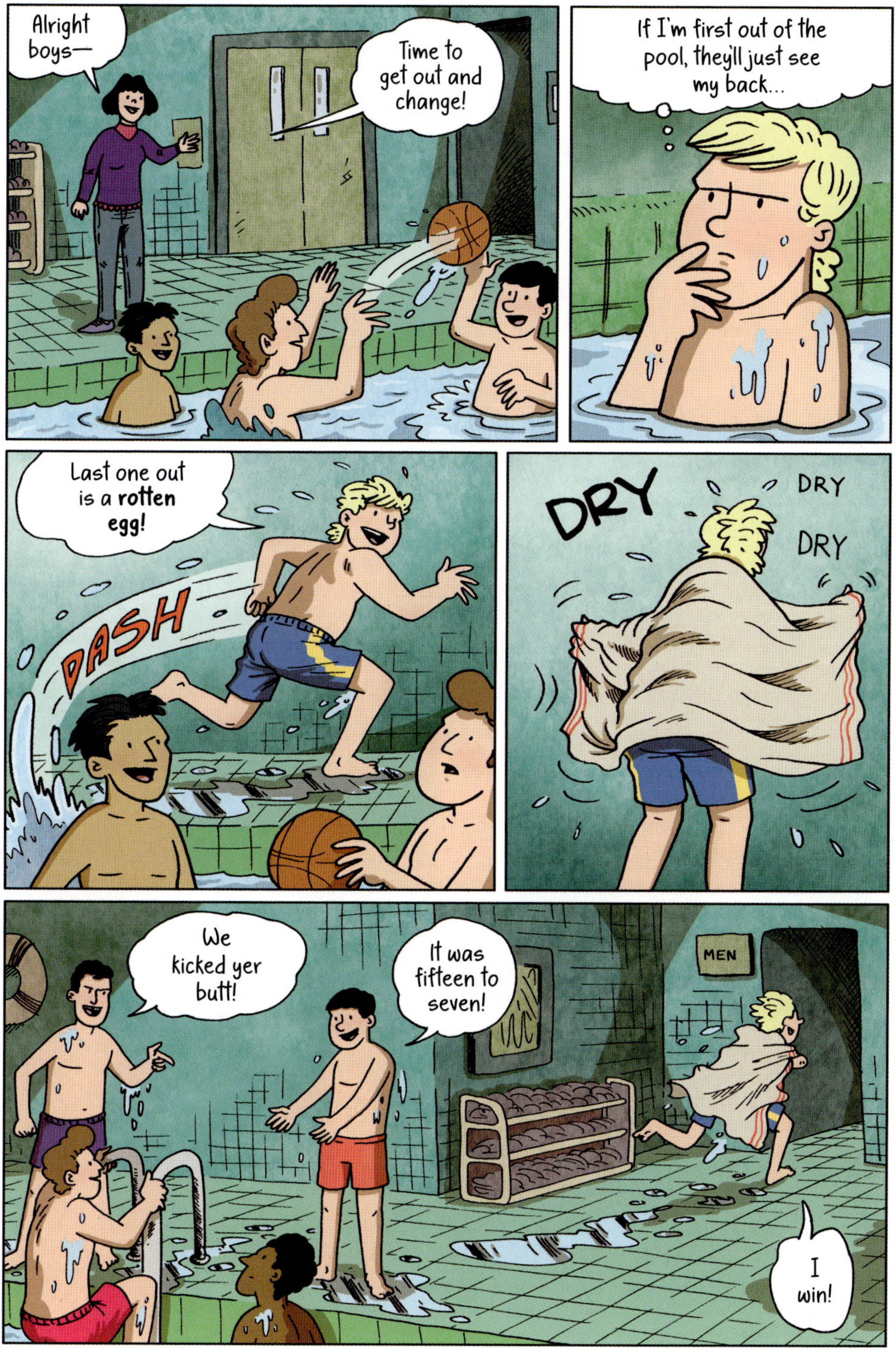

Alright boys—
Time to get out and change!
If I'm first out of the pool, they'll just see my back...
Last one out is a **rotten egg!**
DASH
DRY
DRY
DRY
We kicked yer butt!
It was fifteen to seven!
MEN
I win!

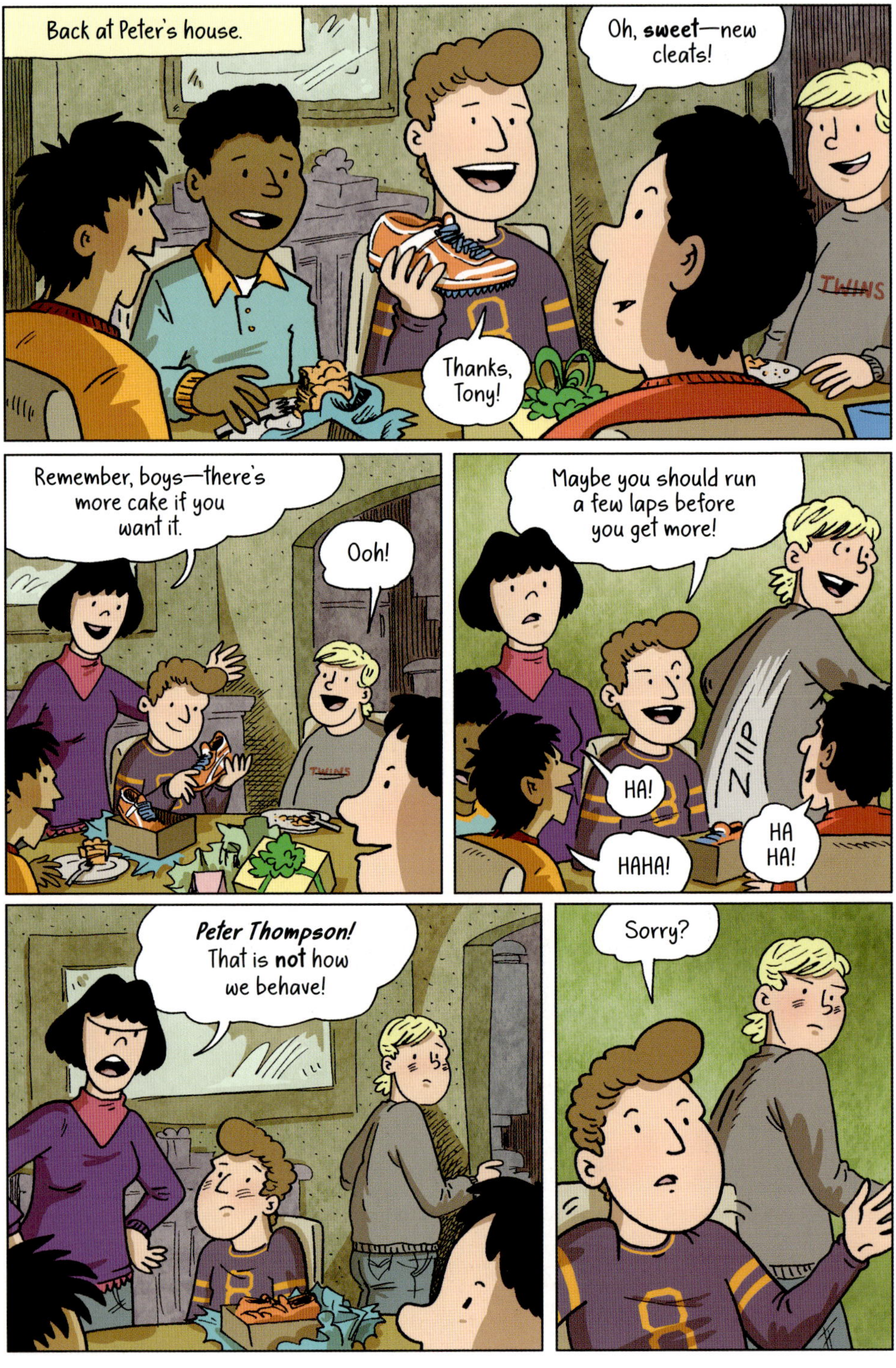
Back at Peter's house.
Oh, **sweet**—new cleats!
Thanks, Tony!
TWINS
Remember, boys—there's more cake if you want it.
Ooh!
TWINS
Maybe you should run a few laps before you get more!
ZIP
HA!
HAHA!
HA HA!
Peter Thompson! That is **not** how we behave!
Sorry?

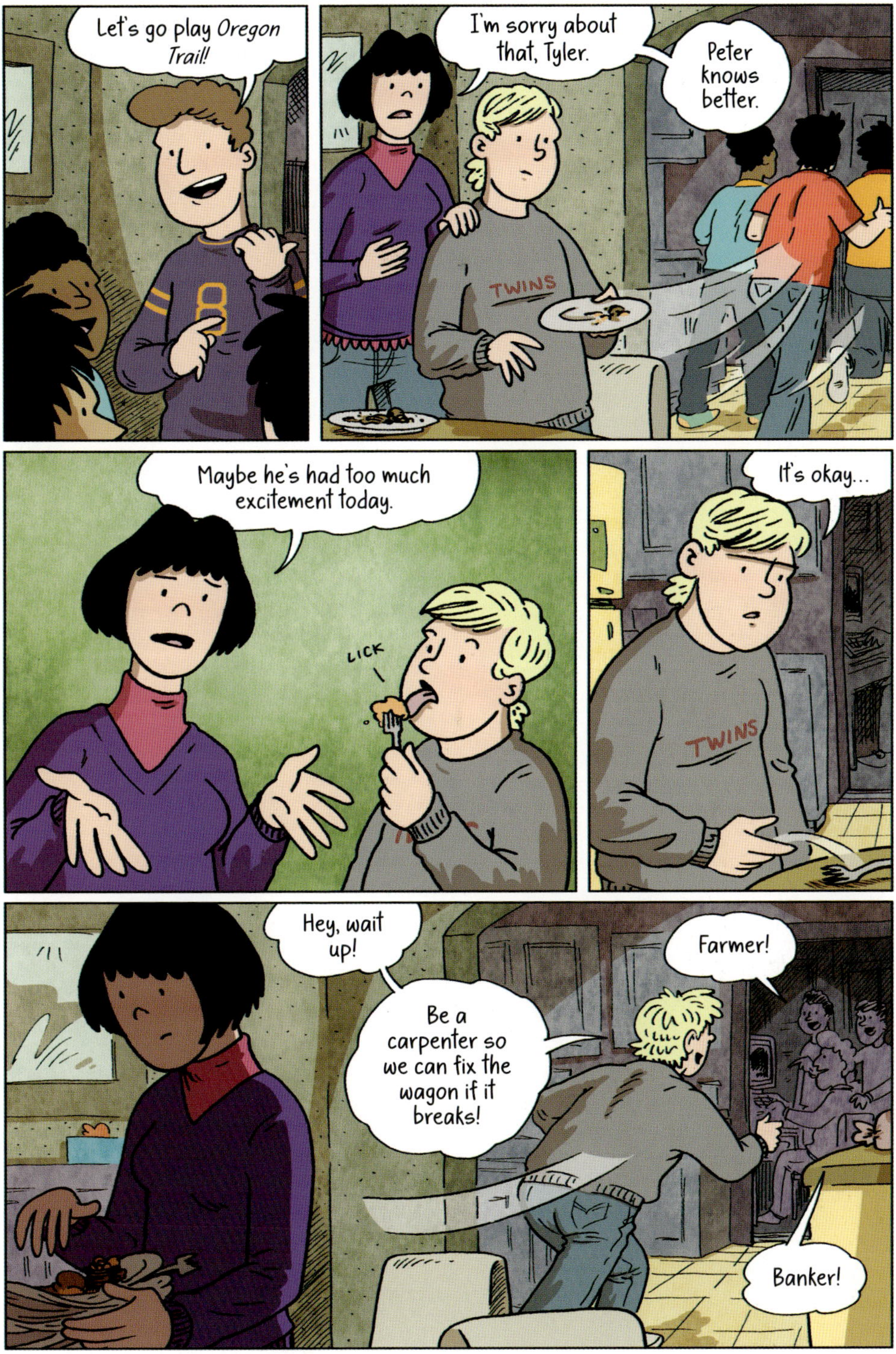
Let's go play *Oregon Trail!*
I'm sorry about that, Tyler.
Peter knows better.
Maybe he's had too much excitement today.
LICK
It's okay...
Hey, wait up!
Farmer!
Be a carpenter so we can fix the wagon if it breaks!
Banker!

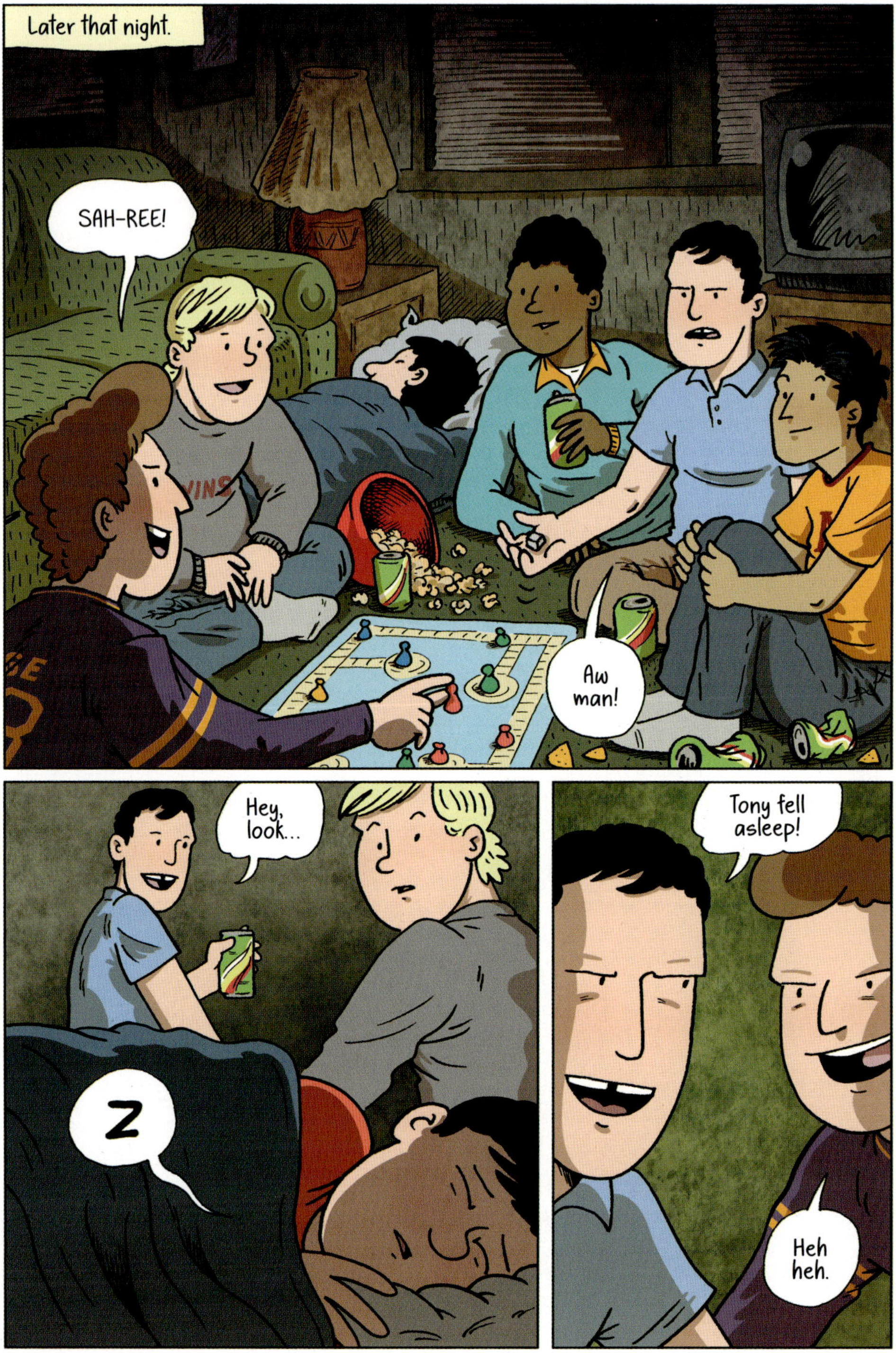
Later that night.
SAH-REE!
Aw man!
Hey, look...
Z
Tony fell asleep!
Heh heh.

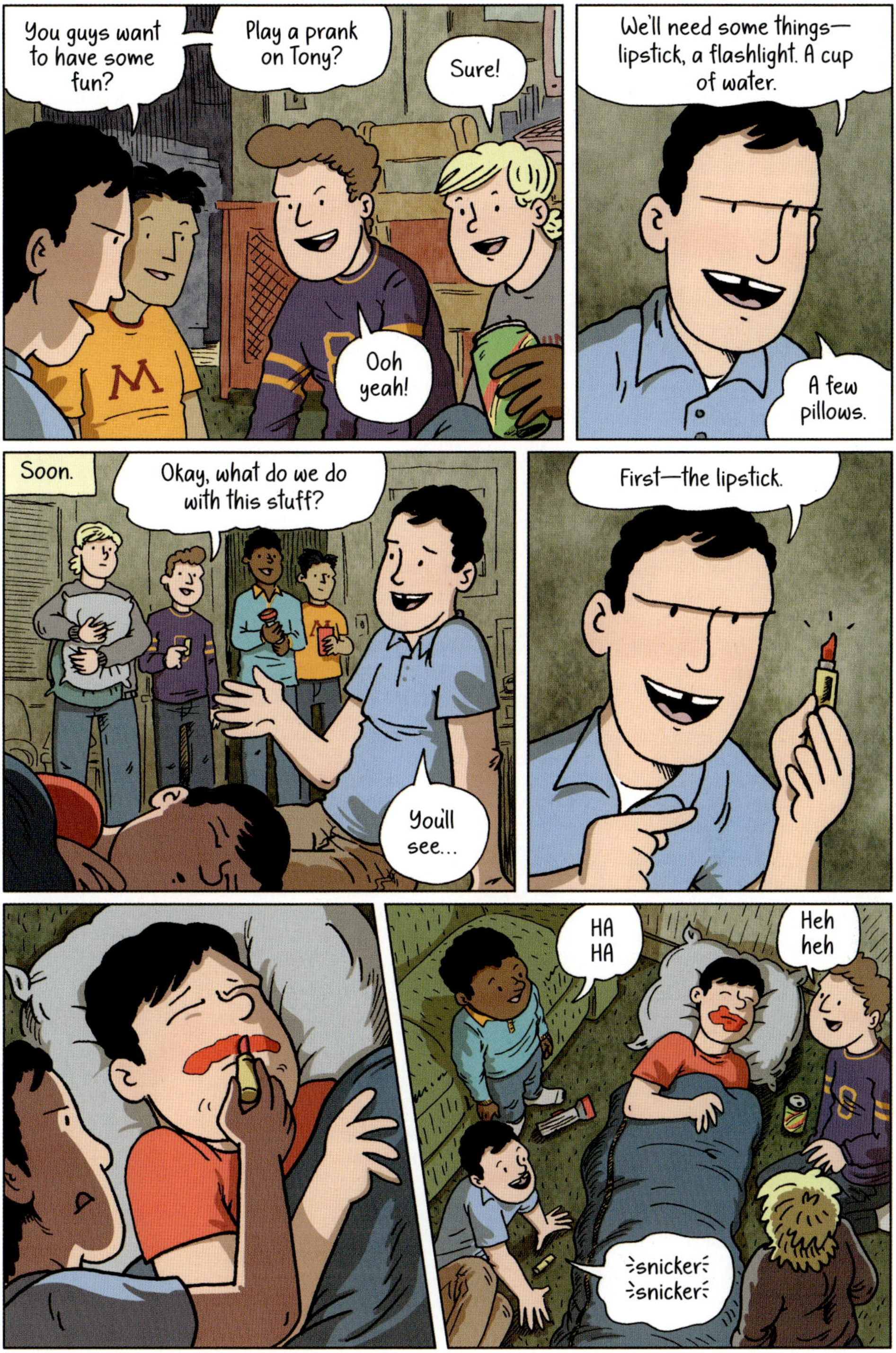
You guys want to have some fun?
Play a prank on Tony?
Sure!
Ooh yeah!
We'll need some things—lipstick, a flashlight. A cup of water.
A few pillows.
Soon.
Okay, what do we do with this stuff?
You'll see...
First—the lipstick.
HA HA
Heh heh
snicker snicker

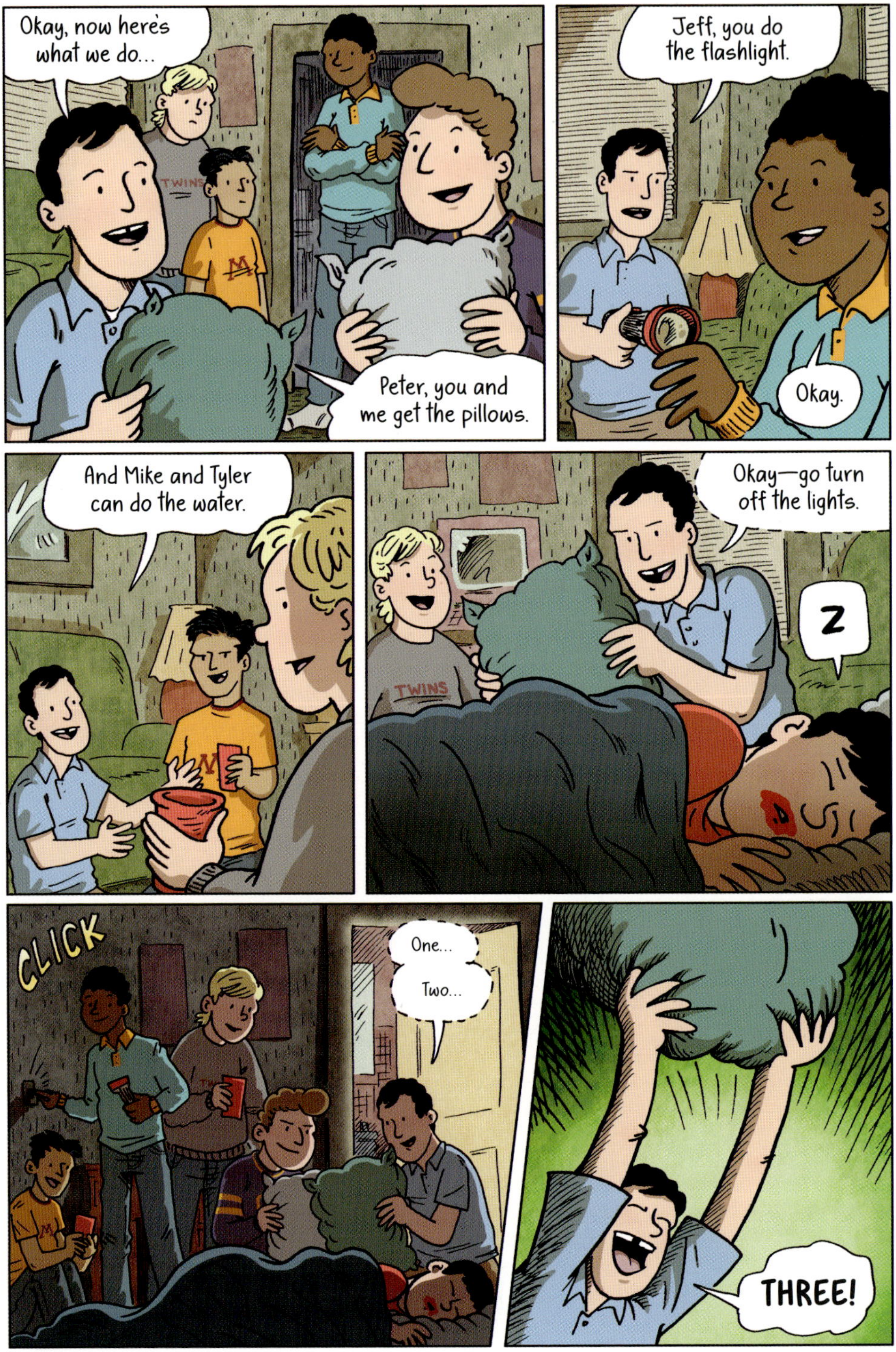
Okay, now here's what we do...
Peter, you and me get the pillows.
Jeff, you do the flashlight.
Okay.
And Mike and Tyler can do the water.
Okay—go turn off the lights.
Z
CLICK
One...
Two...
THREE!

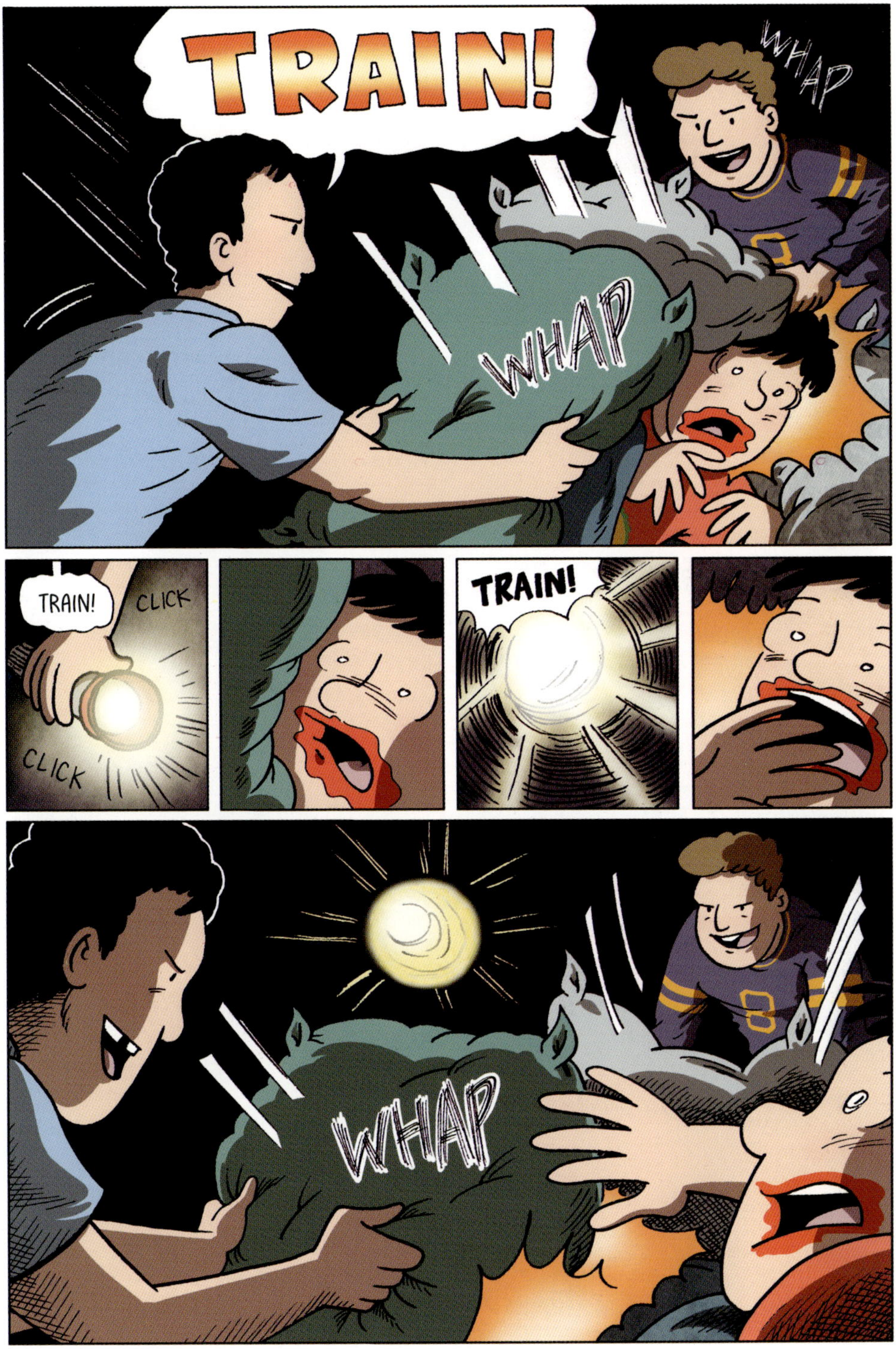
TRAIN!
WHAP
WHAP
TRAIN!
CLICK
CLICK
TRAIN!
WHAP

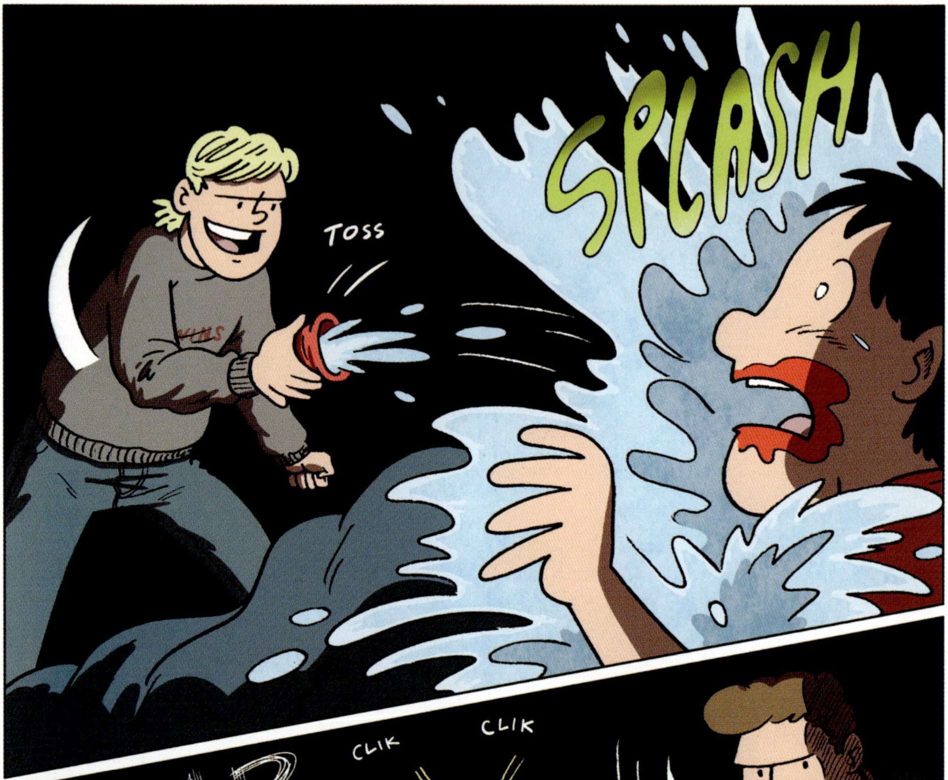
TOSS
SPLASH

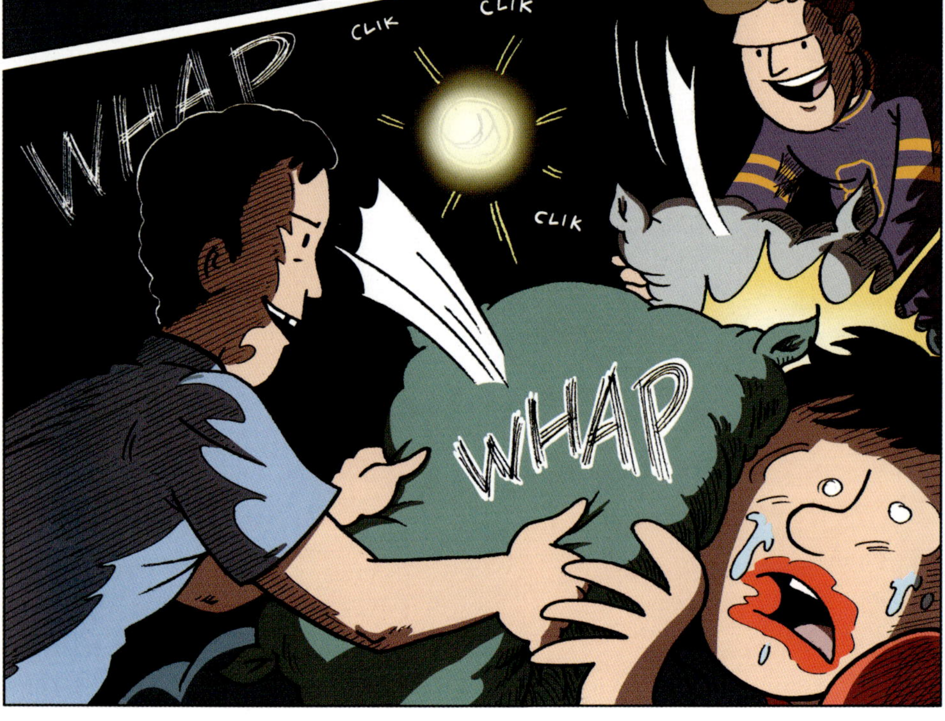
WHAP
CLIK
CLIK
CLIK
WHAP

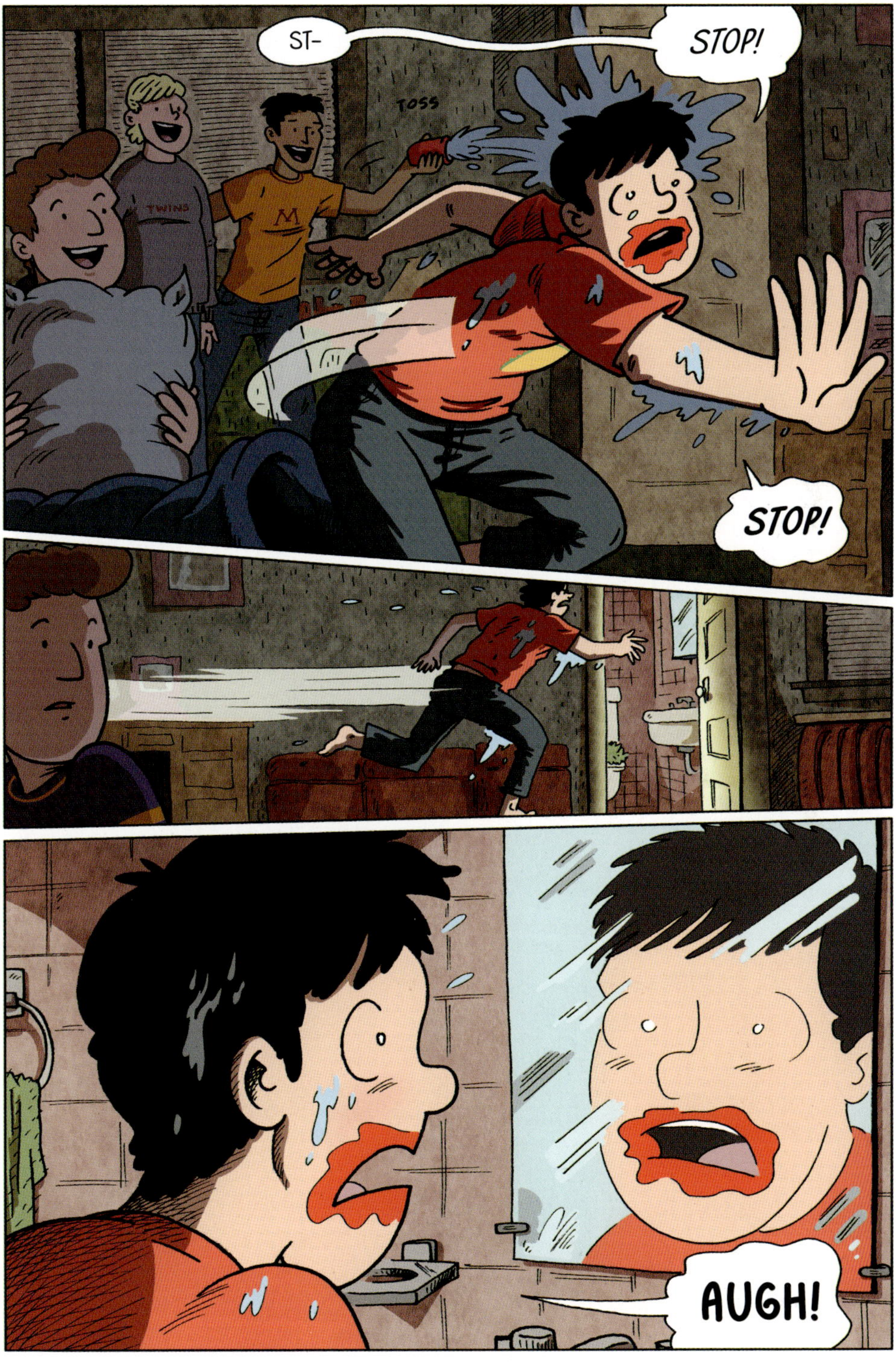
ST-
STOP!
TOSS
TWINS
M
STOP!
AUGH!

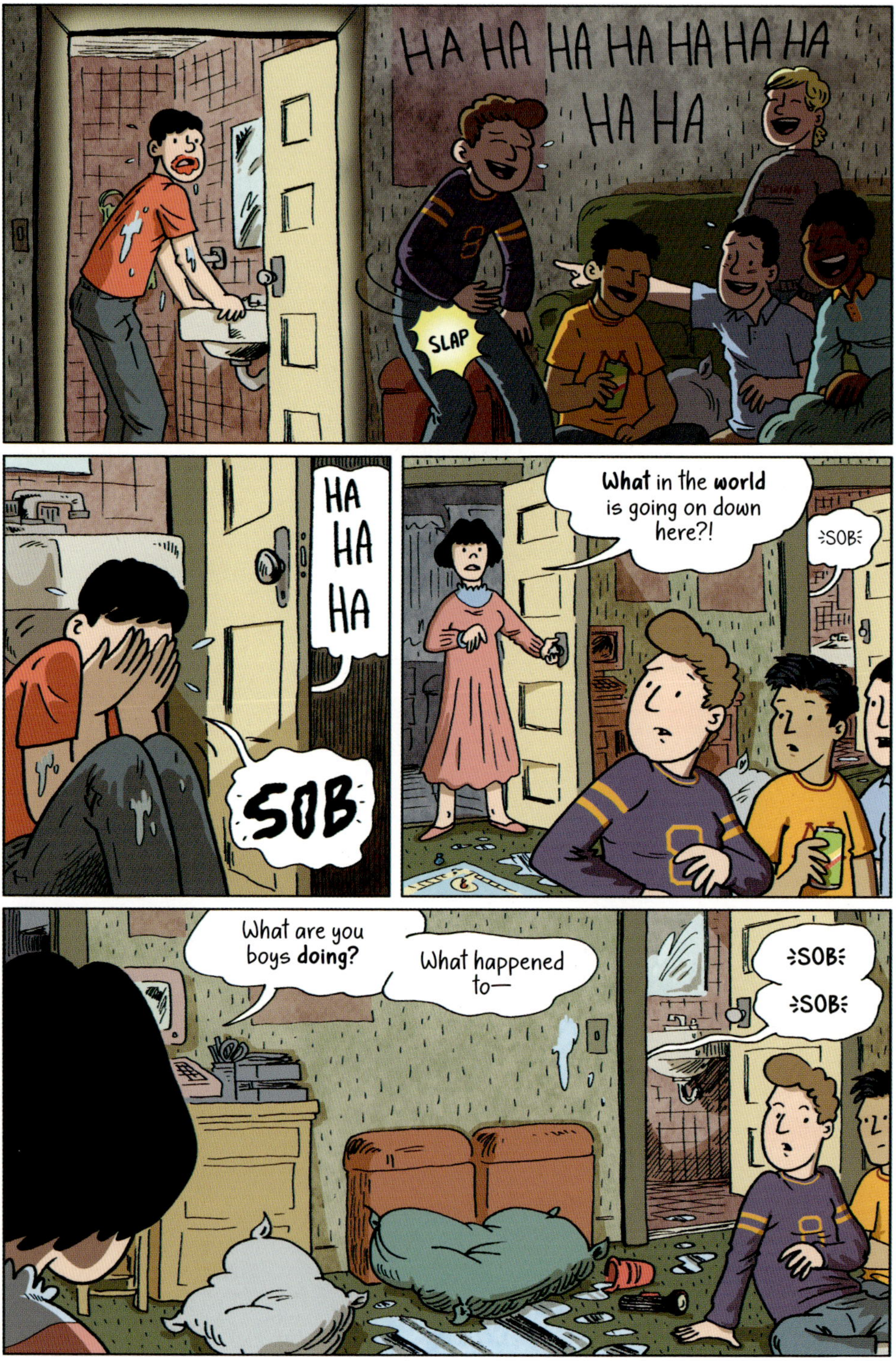
HA HA HA HA HA HA HA
HA HA
SLAP
HA
HA
HA
SOB
What in the world is going on down here?!
SOB
What are you boys doing?
What happened to—
SOB
SOB

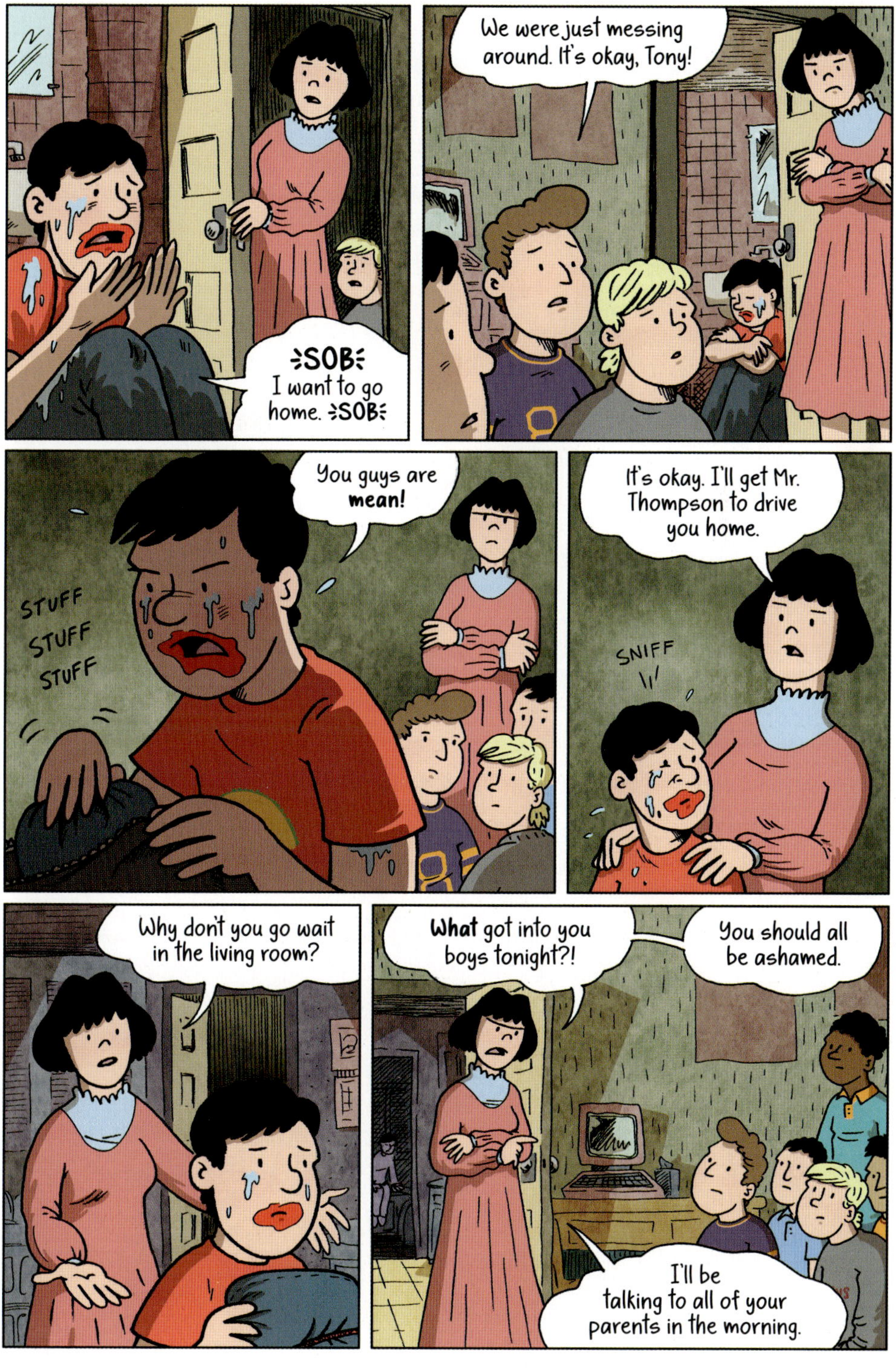

≈SOB≈ I want to go home. ≈SOB≈
We were just messing around. It's okay, Tony!
You guys are **mean!**
STUFF STUFF STUFF
It's okay. I'll get Mr. Thompson to drive you home.
SNIFF
Why don't you go wait in the living room?
What got into you boys tonight?!
You should all be ashamed.
I'll be talking to all of your parents in the morning.

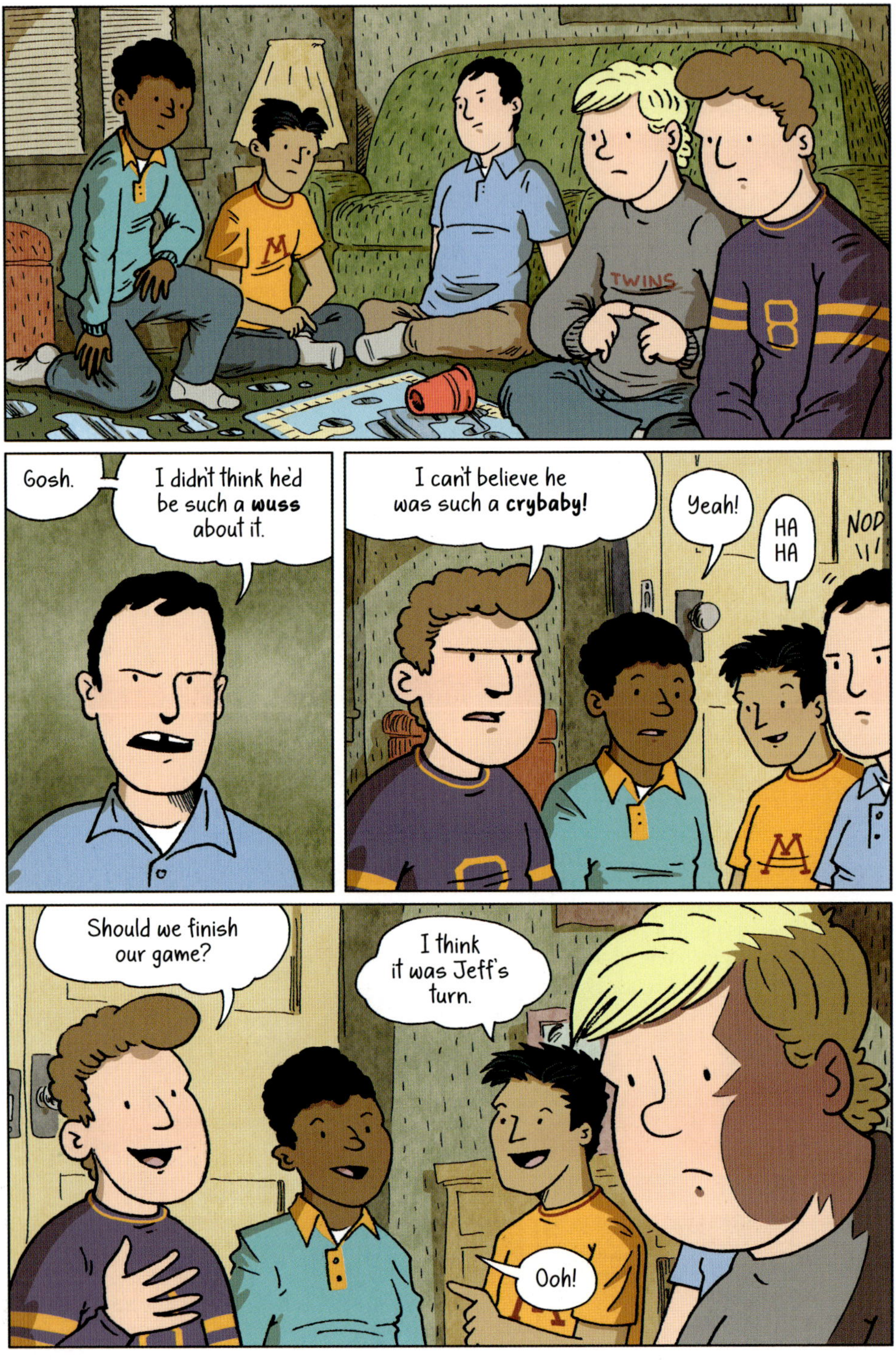
Gosh.
I didn't think he'd be such a **wuss** about it.
I can't believe he was such a **crybaby!**
Yeah!
HA HA
NOD
Should we finish our game?
I think it was Jeff's turn.
Ooh!

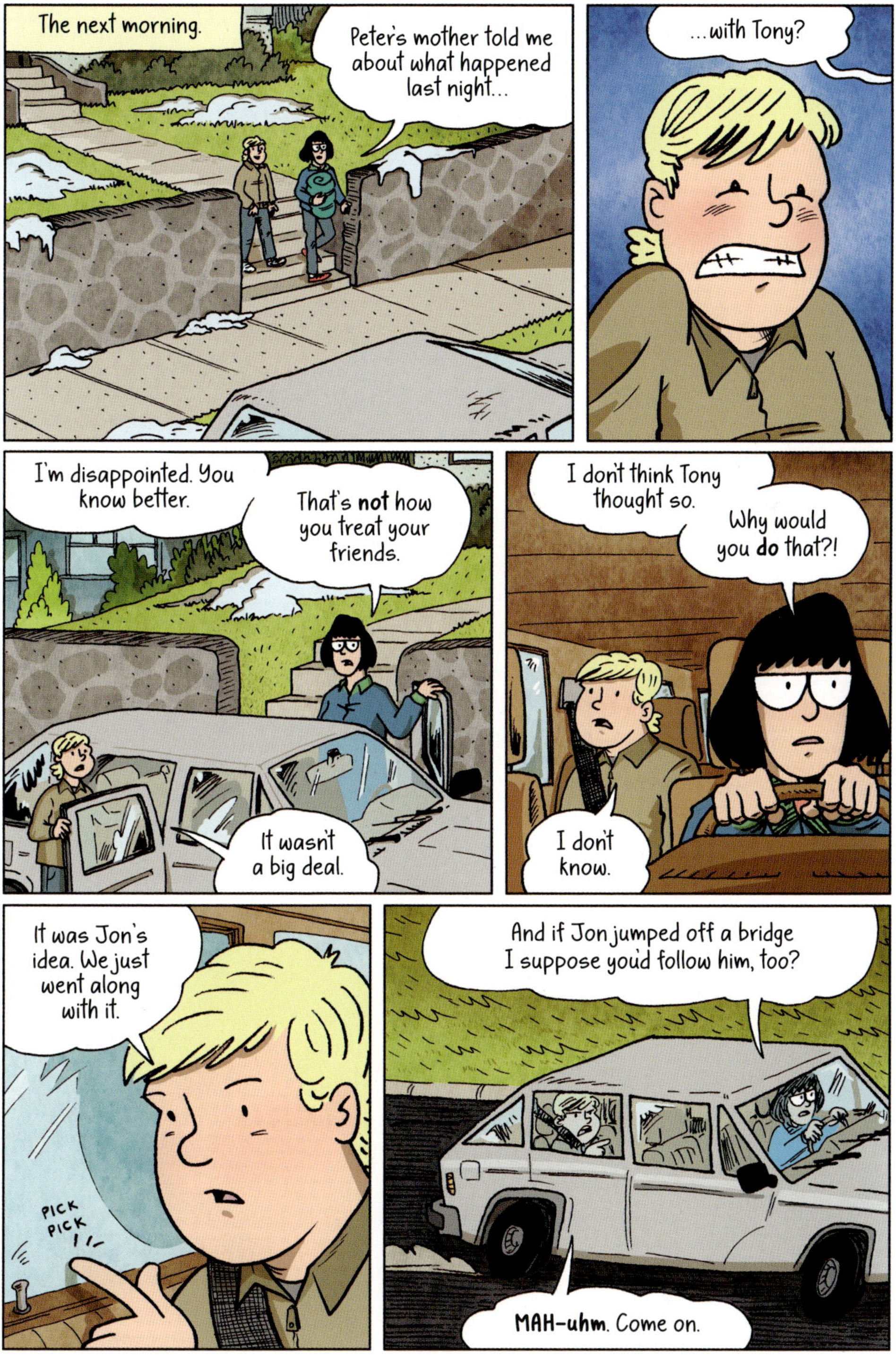

The next morning.
Peter's mother told me about what happened last night...
...with Tony?
I'm disappointed. You know better.
That's **not** how you treat your friends.
It wasn't a big deal.
I don't think Tony thought so.
Why would you **do** that?!
I don't know.
It was Jon's idea. We just went along with it.
PICK PICK
And if Jon jumped off a bridge I suppose you'd follow him, too?
MAH-uhm. Come on.

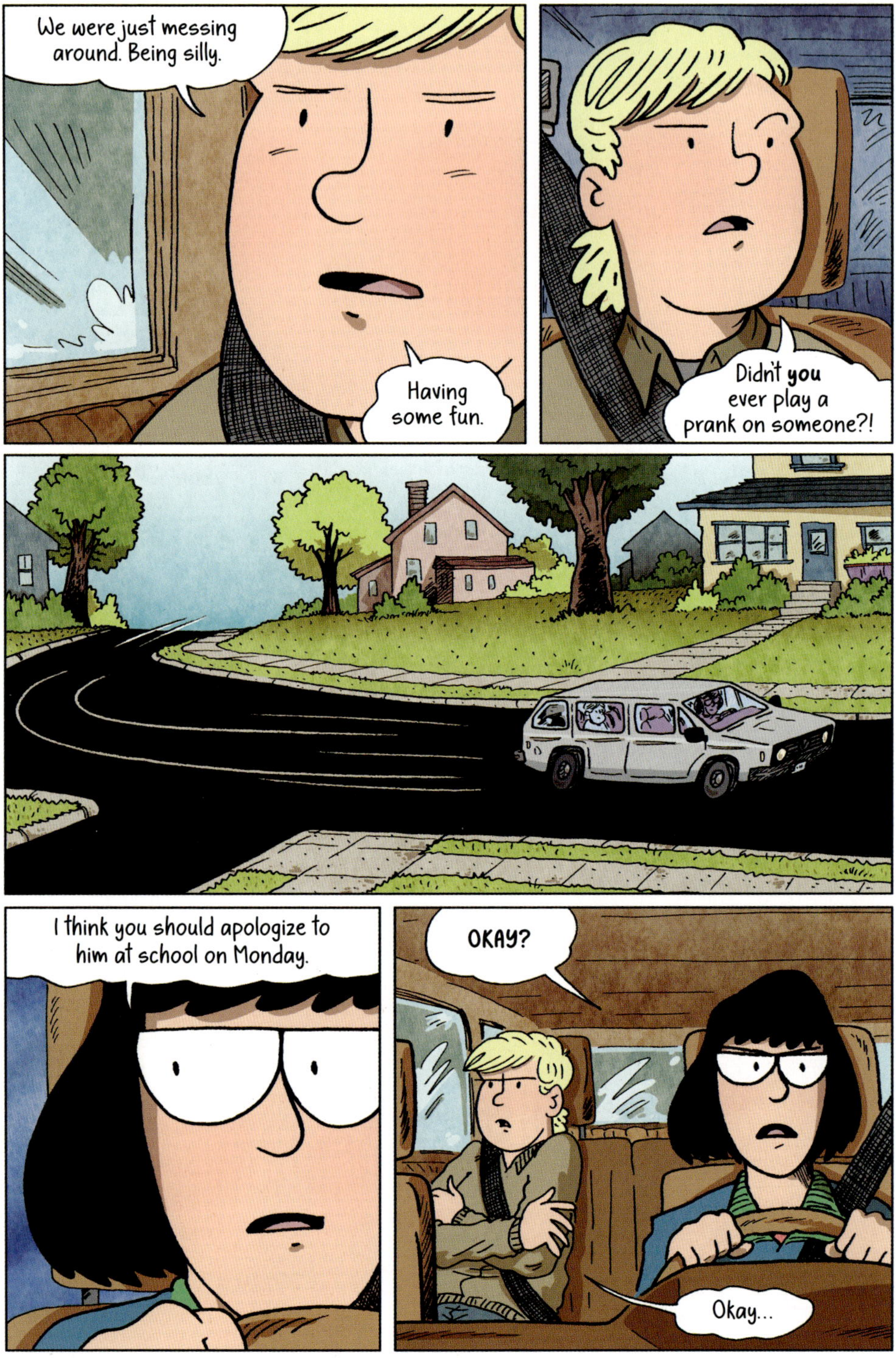

We were just messing around. Being silly.
Having some fun.
Didn't **you** ever play a prank on someone?!
I think you should apologize to him at school on Monday.
OKAY?
Okay...

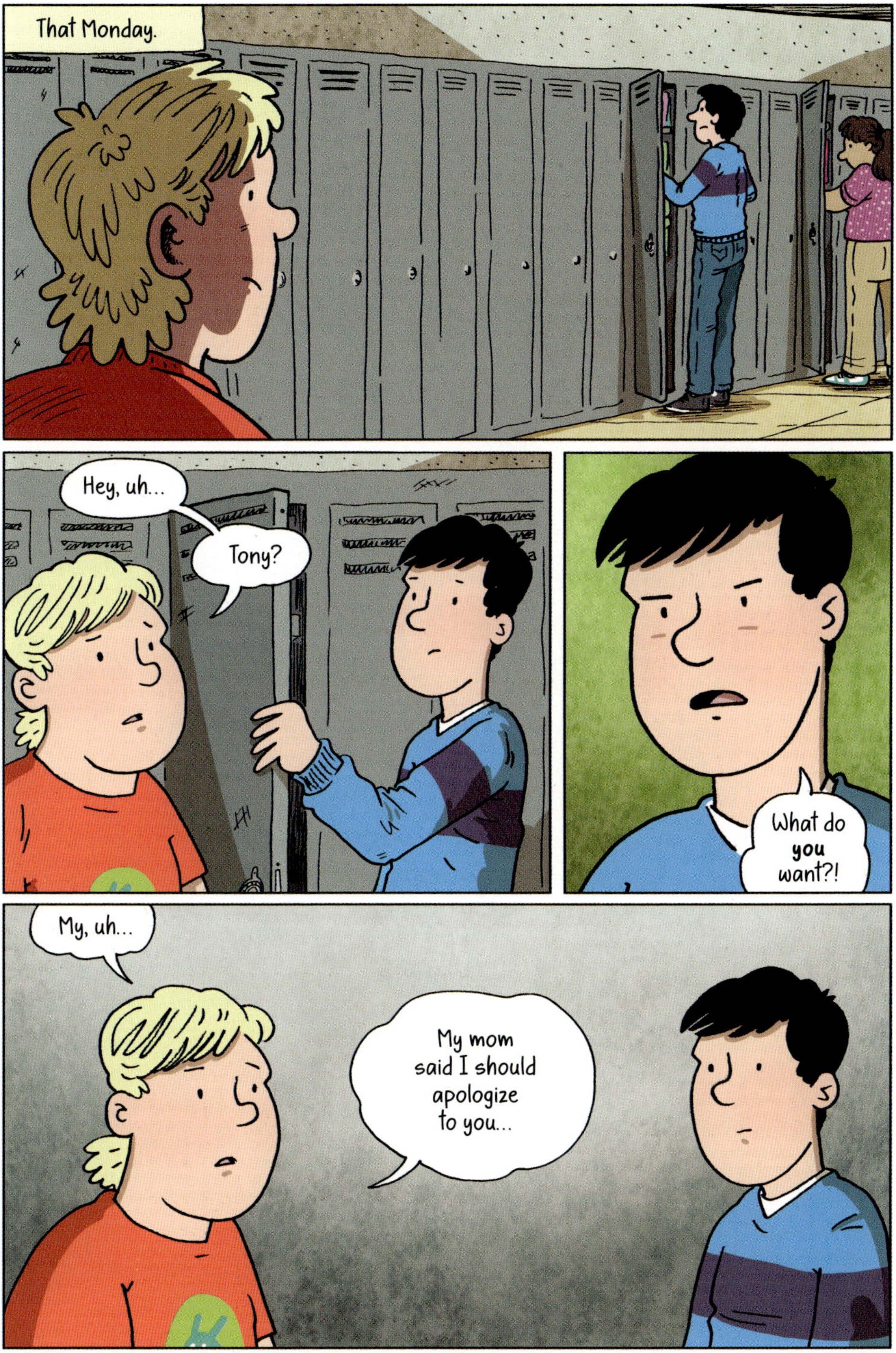
That Monday.
Hey, uh...
Tony?
What do **you** want?!
My, uh...
My mom said I should apologize to you...

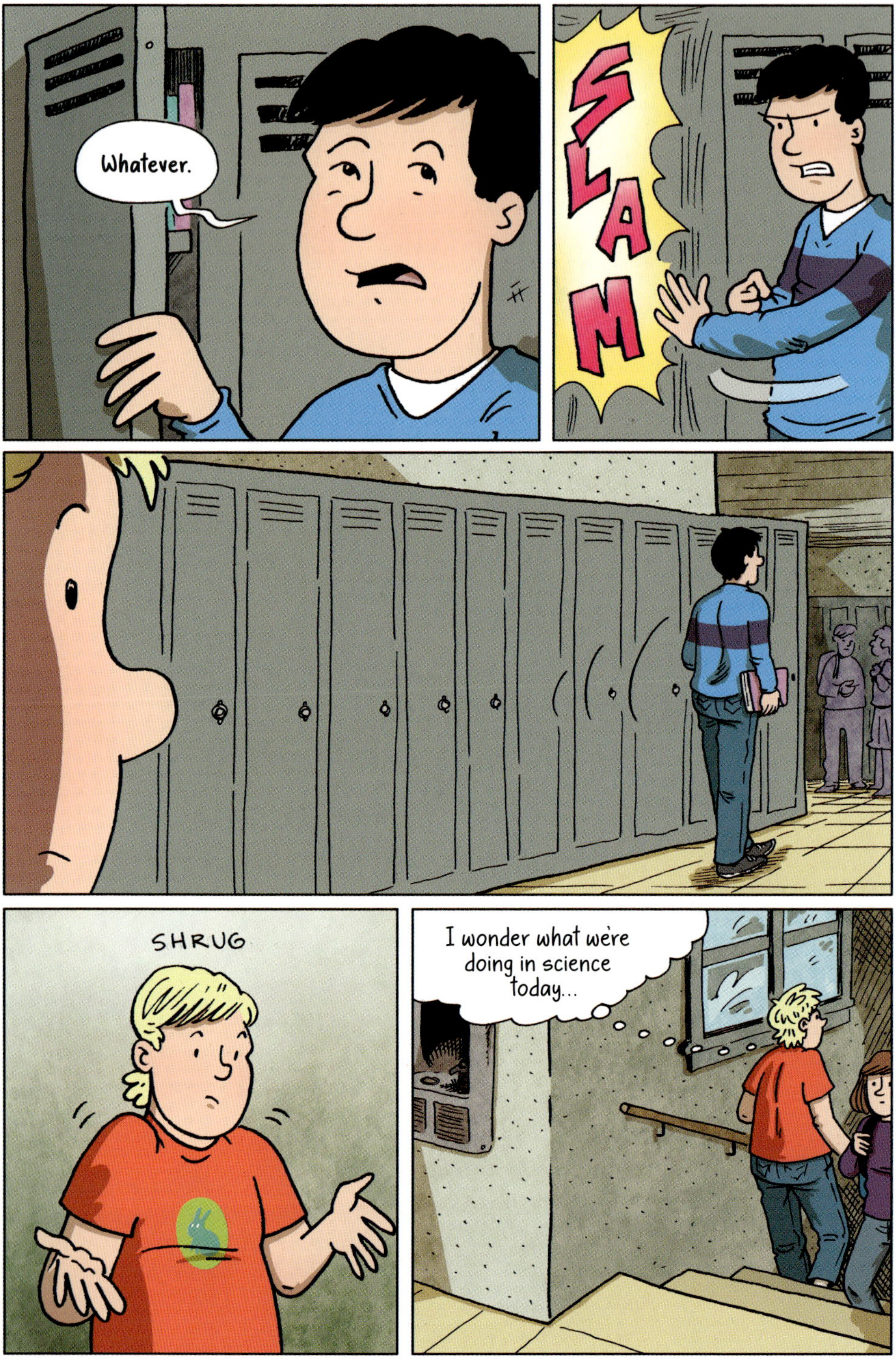
Whatever.
SLAM
SHRUG
I wonder what we're doing in science today...

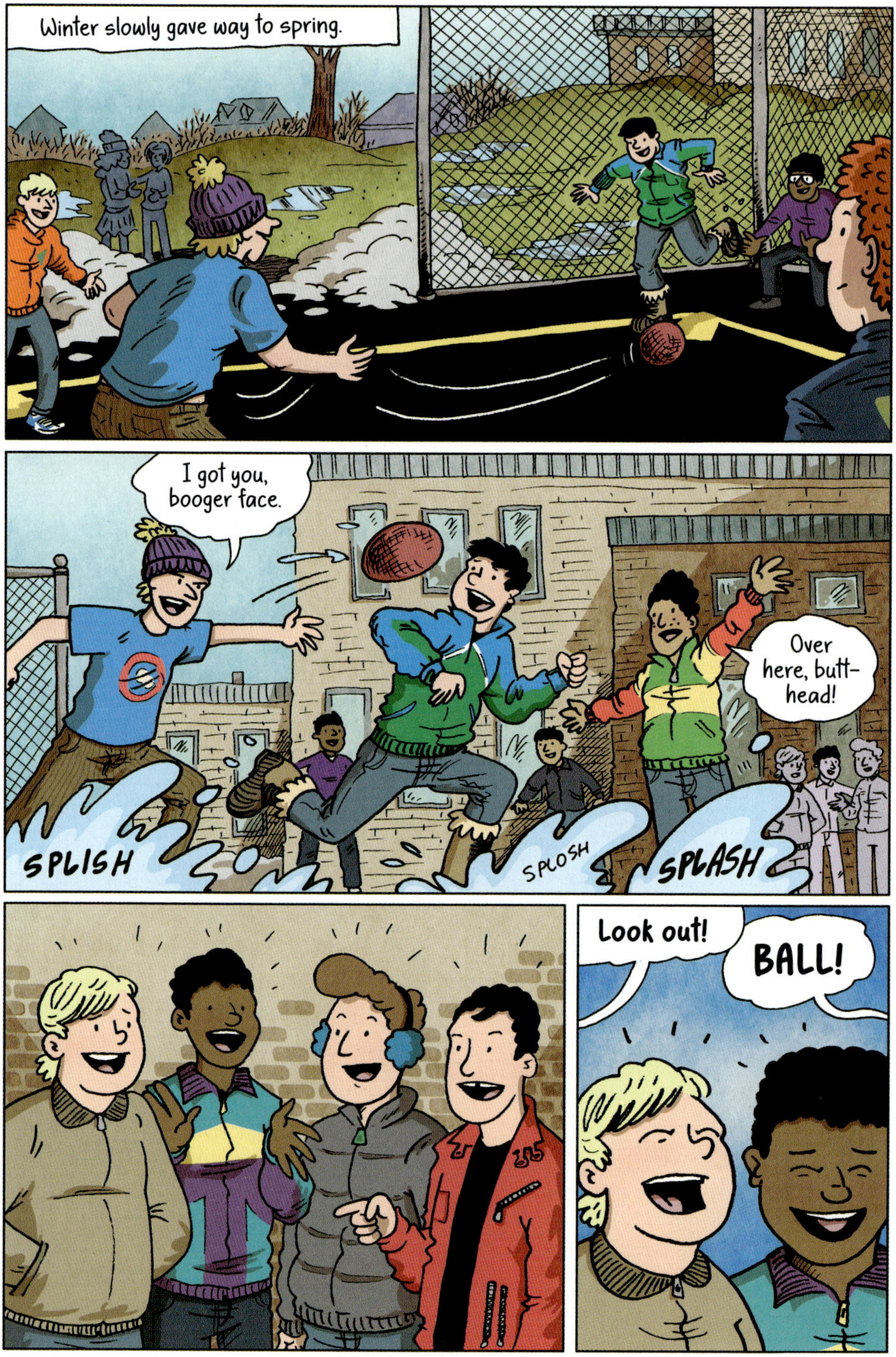
Winter slowly gave way to spring.
I got you, booger face.
Over here, butt-head!
SPLISH
SPLOSH
SPLASH
Look out!
BALL!

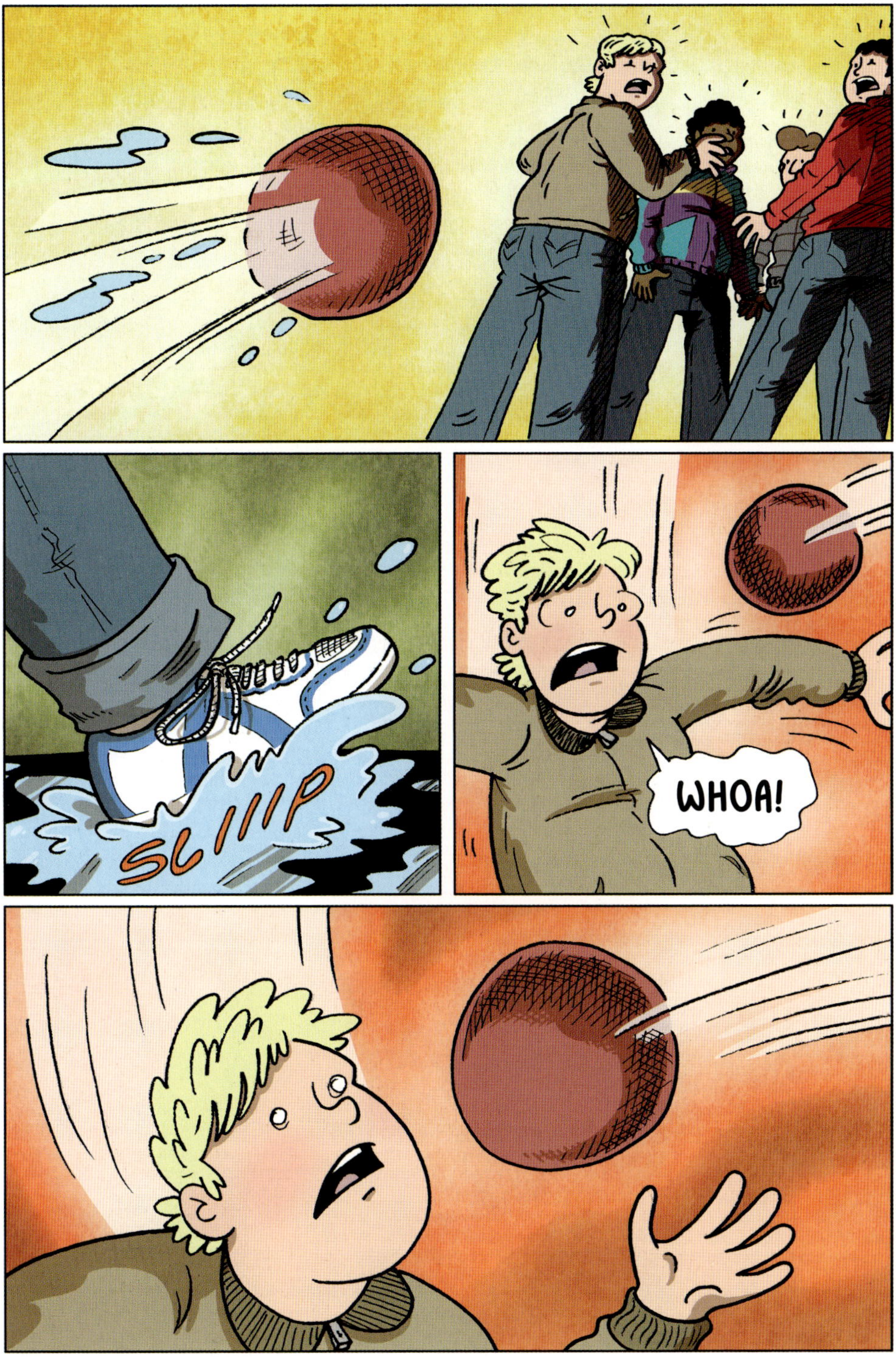
SLIIIP
WHOA!

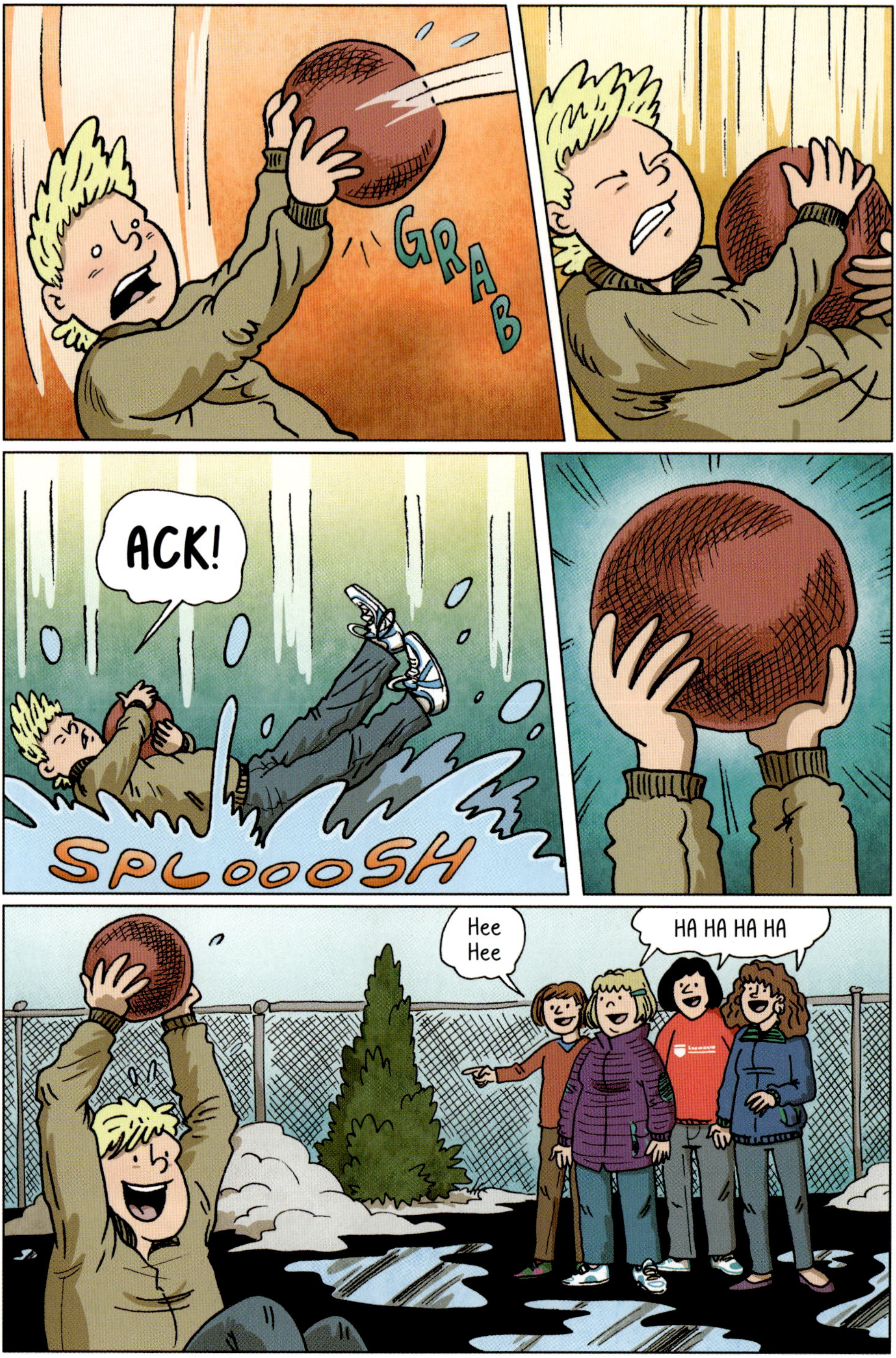
GRAB
ACK!
SPLOOOSH
Hee
Hee
HA HA HA HA

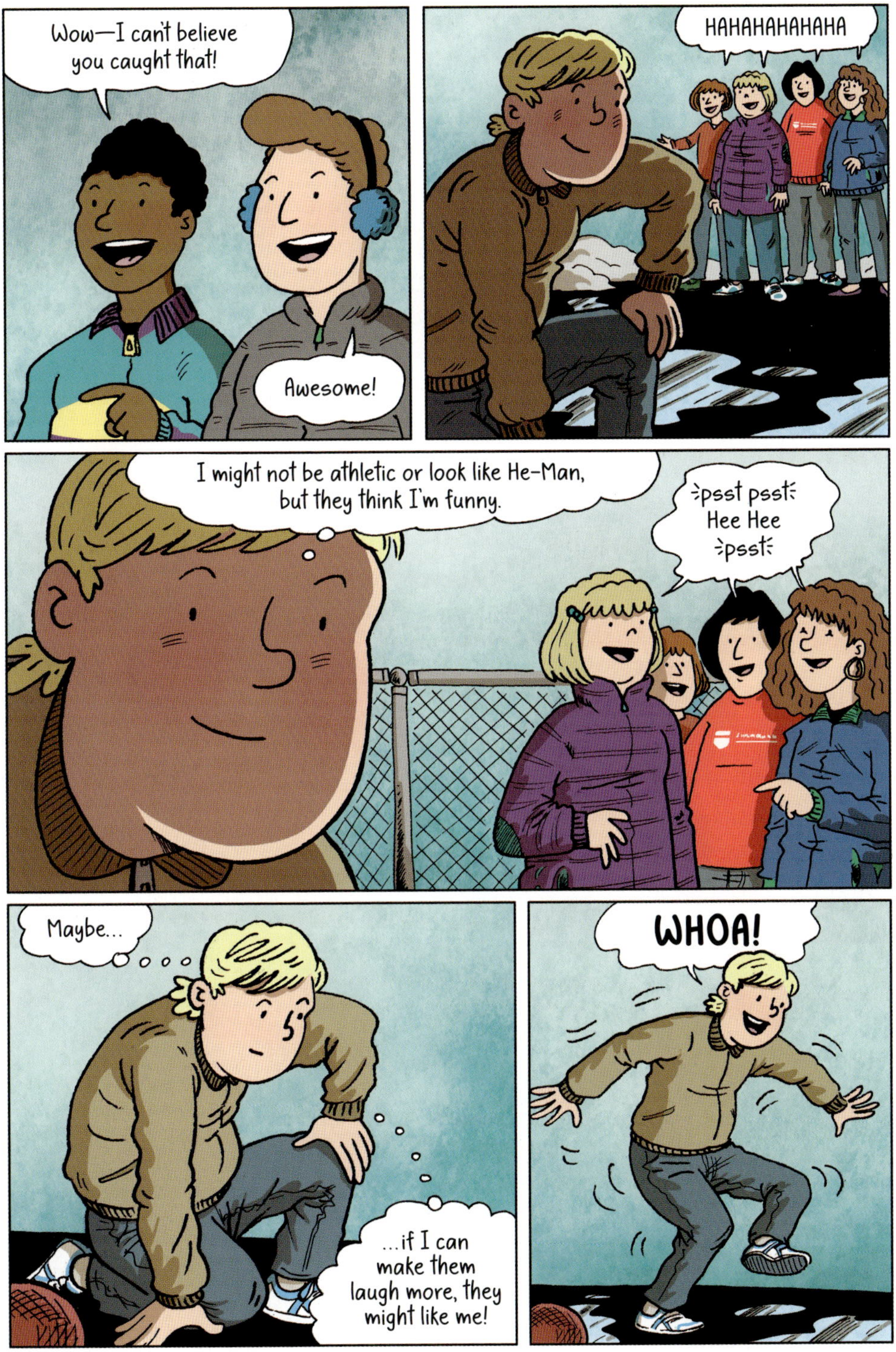
Wow—I can't believe you caught that!
Awesome!
HAHAHAHAHAHA
I might not be athletic or look like He-Man, but they think I'm funny.
psst psst Hee Hee psst
Maybe...
...if I can make them laugh more, they might like me!
WHOA!

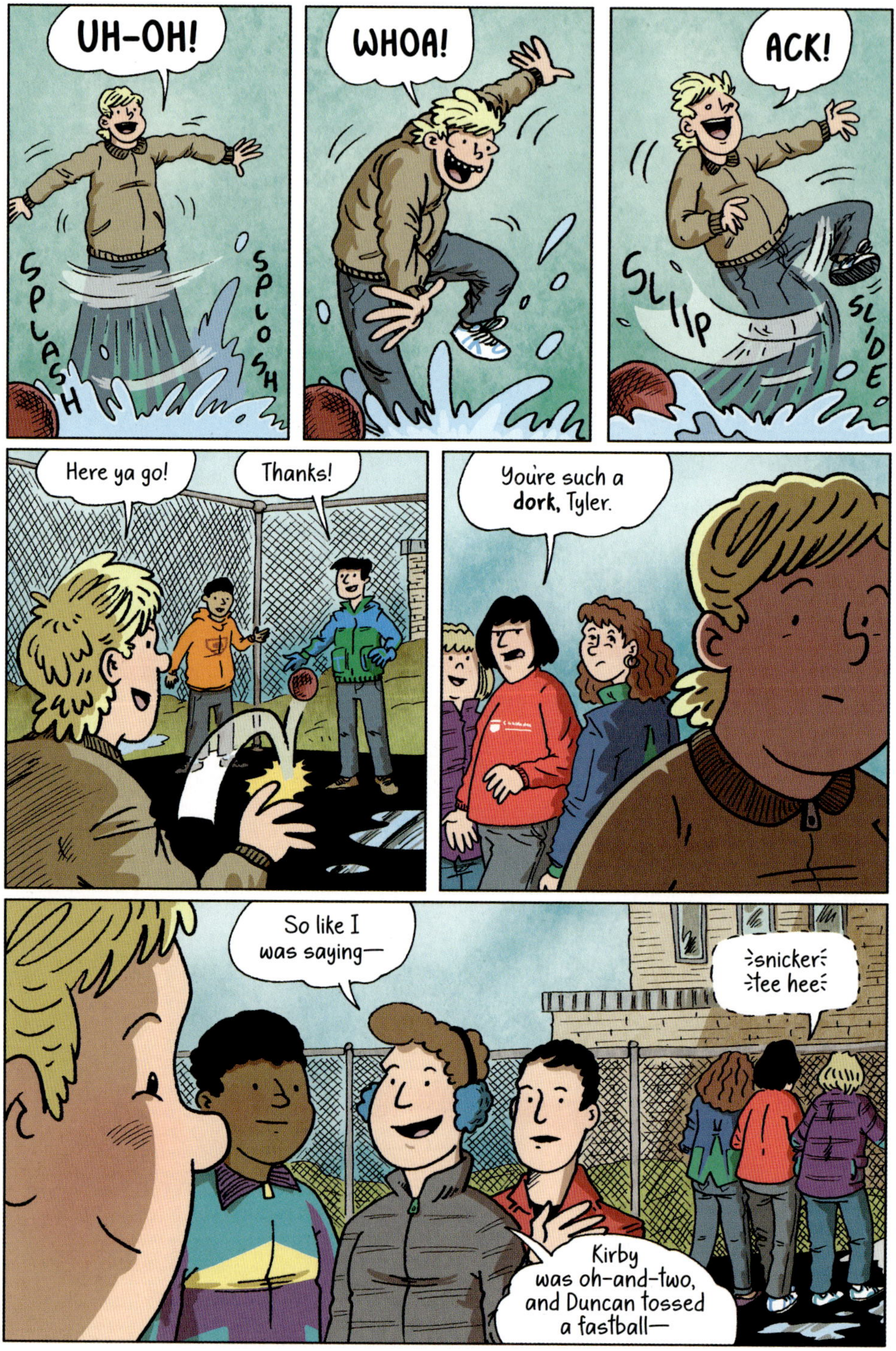
UH-OH!
SPLASH
SPLOSH
WHOA!
ACK!
SLIIP
SLIDE
Here ya go!
Thanks!
You're such a **dork,** Tyler.
So like I was saying—
snicker
tee hee
Kirby was oh-and-two, and Duncan tossed a fastball—

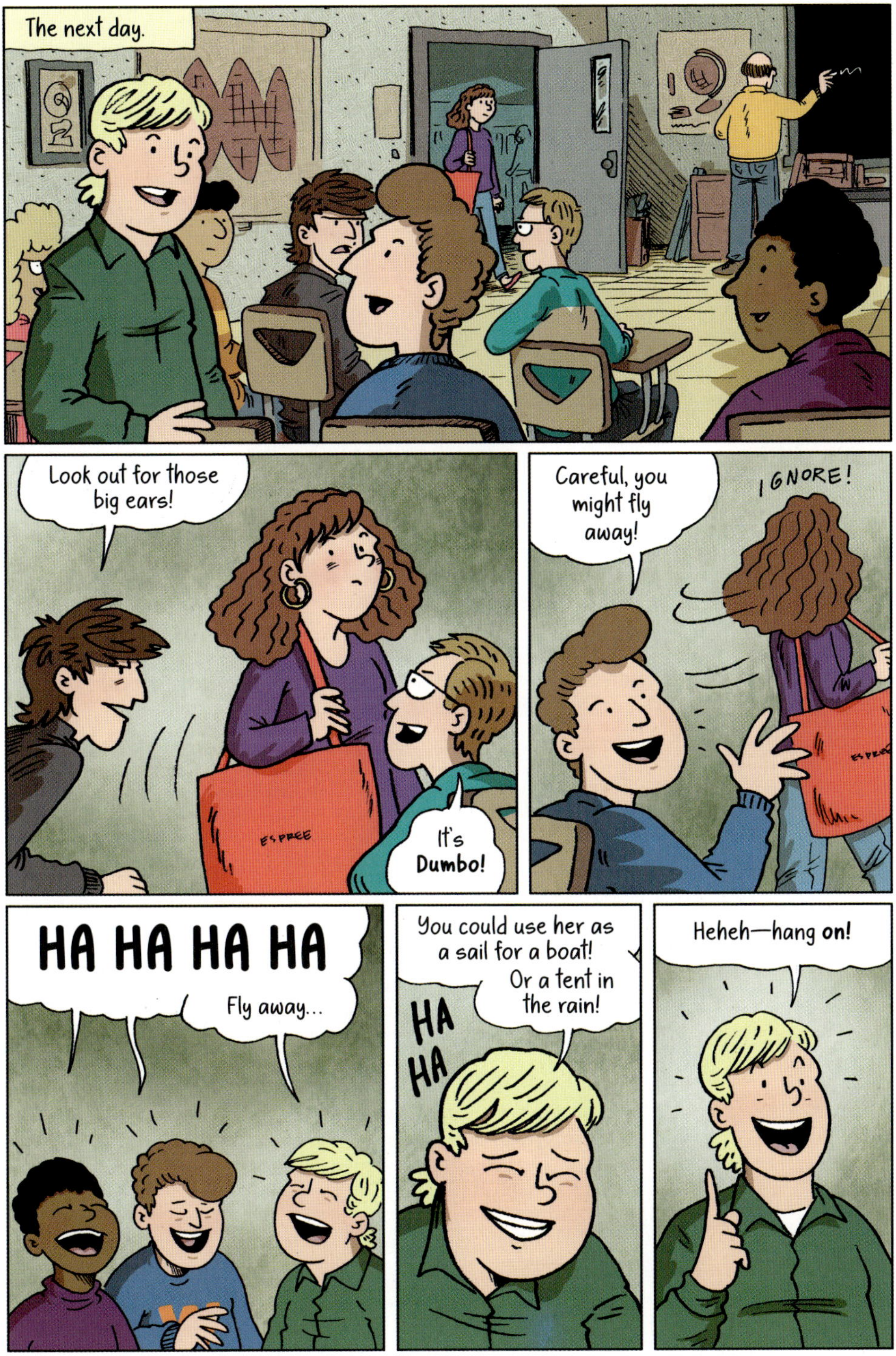
The next day.
Look out for those big ears!
It's **Dumbo!**
Careful, you might fly away!
IGNORE!
HA HA HA HA
Fly away...
You could use her as a sail for a boat!
Or a tent in the rain!
HA HA
Heheh—hang **on!**

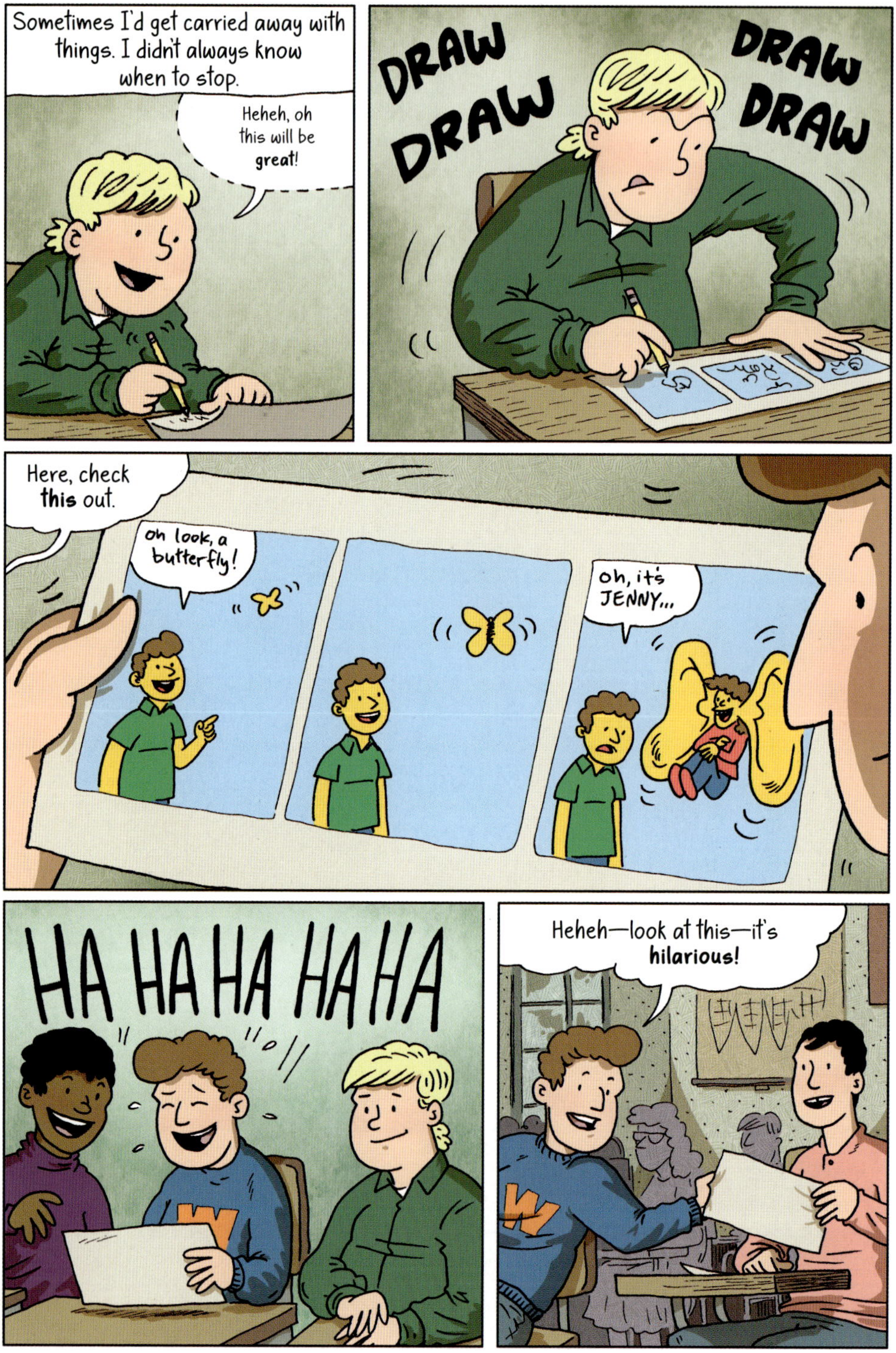

Sometimes I'd get carried away with things. I didn't always know when to stop.
Heheh, oh this will be **great**!
DRAW
DRAW
DRAW
DRAW
Here, check **this** out.
oh look, a butterfly!
Oh, it's JENNY...
HA HA HA HA HA HA
Heheh—look at this—it's **hilarious**!

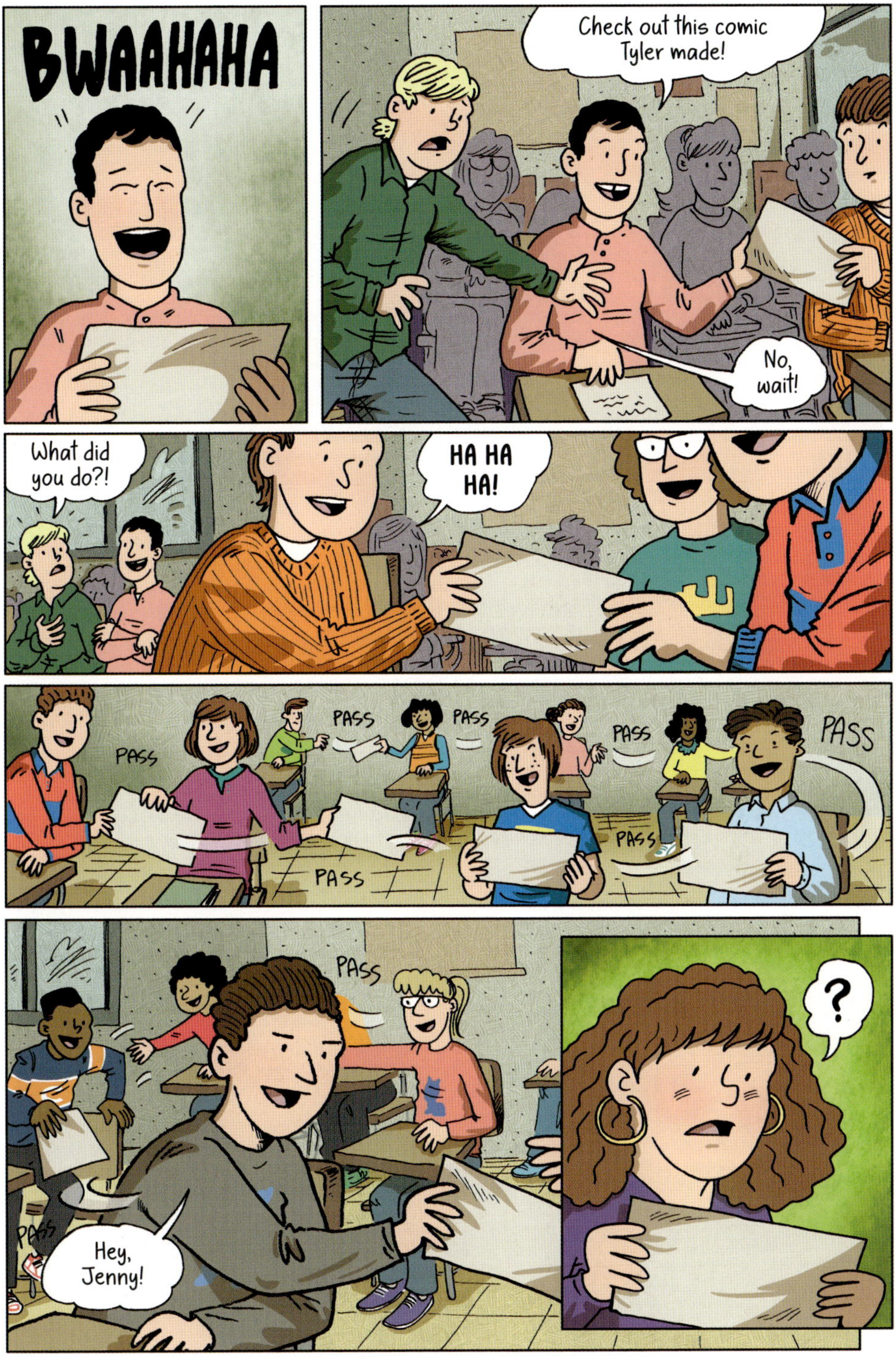
BWAAHAHA
Check out this comic Tyler made!
No, wait!
What did you do?!
HA HA HA!
PASS
PASS
PASS
PASS
PASS
PASS
PASS
PASS
PASS
Hey, Jenny!
?

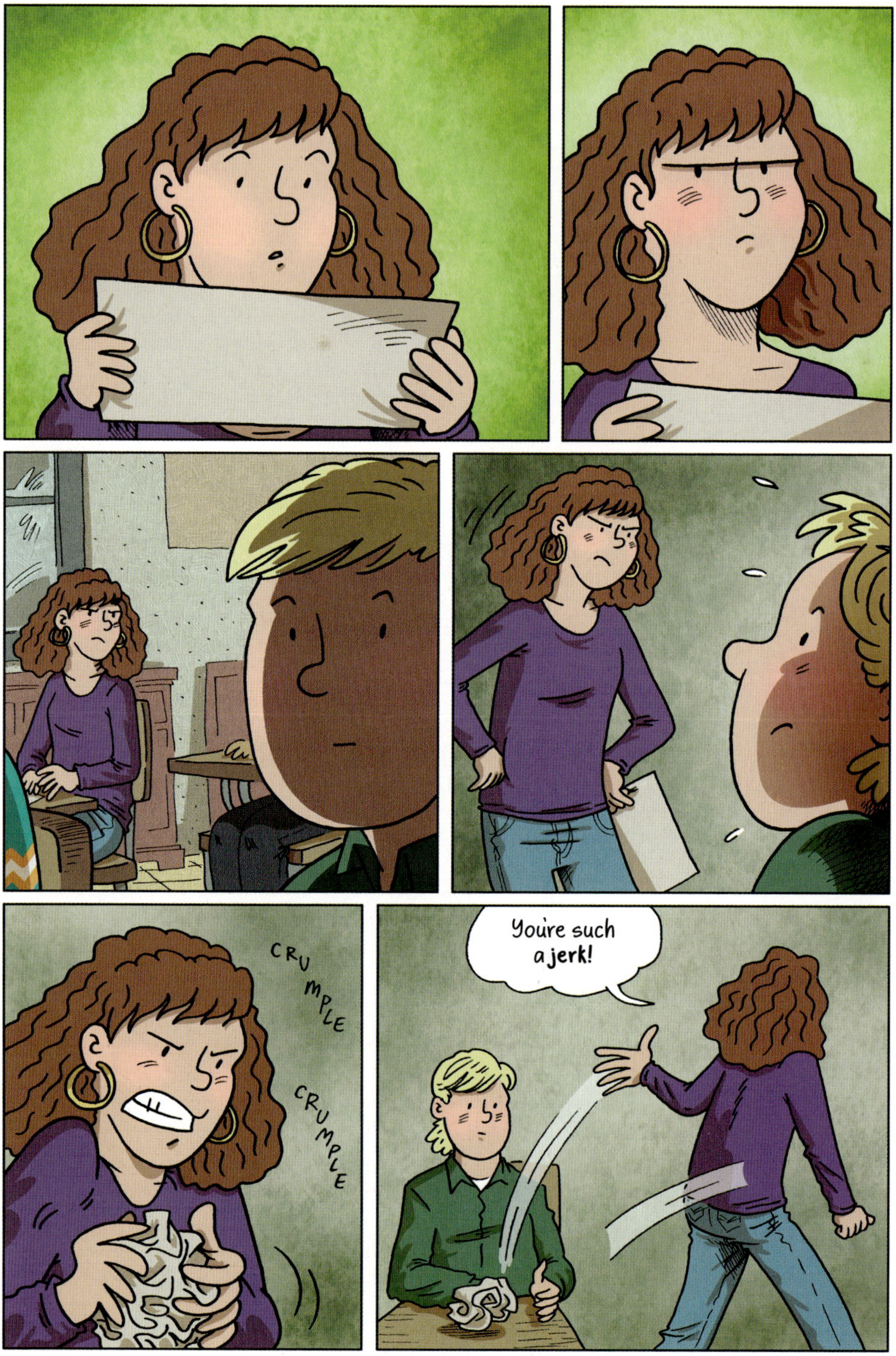
CRUMPLE
CRUMPLE
You're such a jerk!

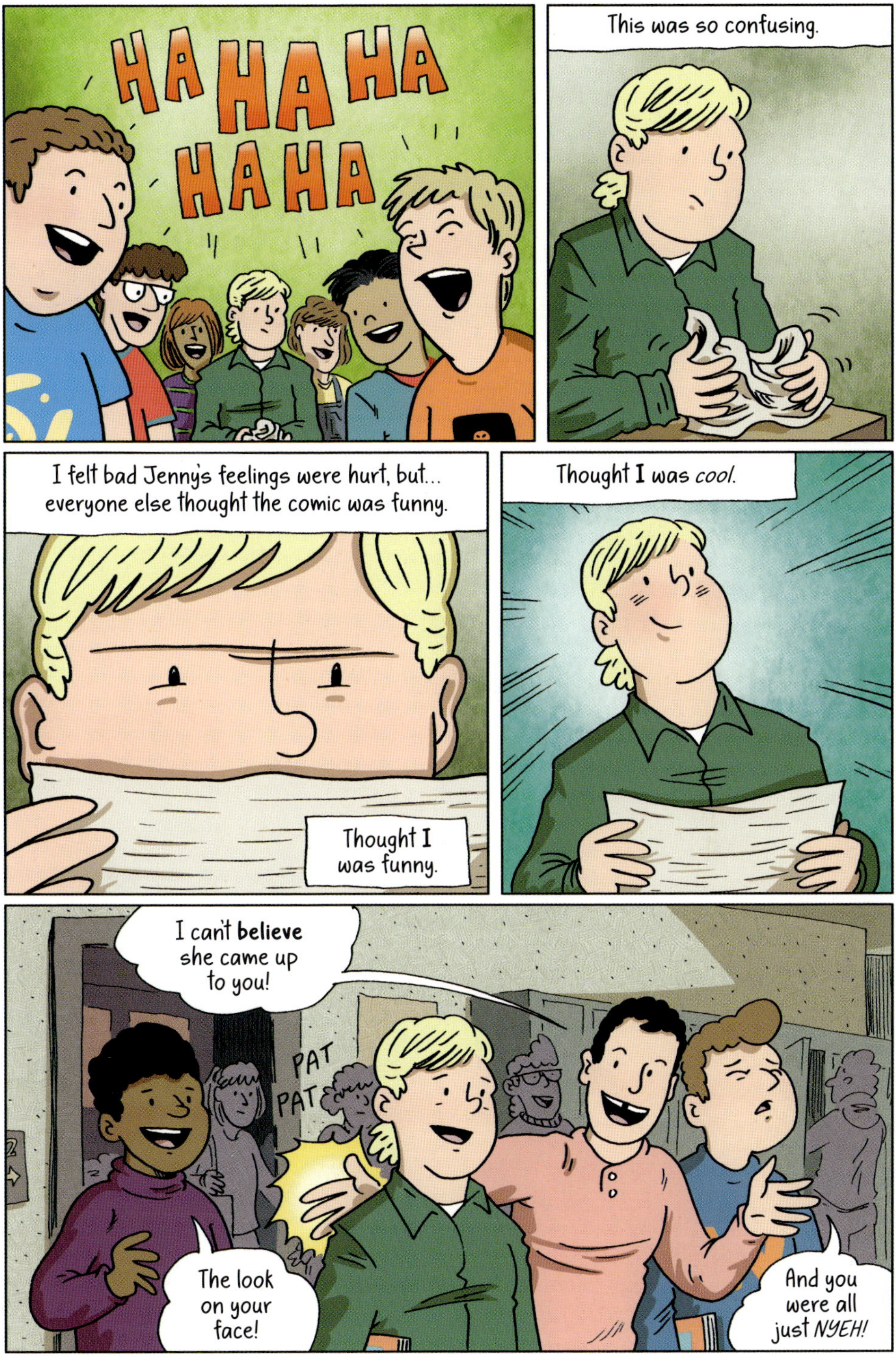
HA HA HA HA HA
HA HA HA
This was so confusing.
I felt bad Jenny's feelings were hurt, but... everyone else thought the comic was funny.
Thought **I** was funny.
Thought **I** was *cool.*
I can't **believe** she came up to you!
PAT PAT
The look on your face!
And you were all just *NYEH!*

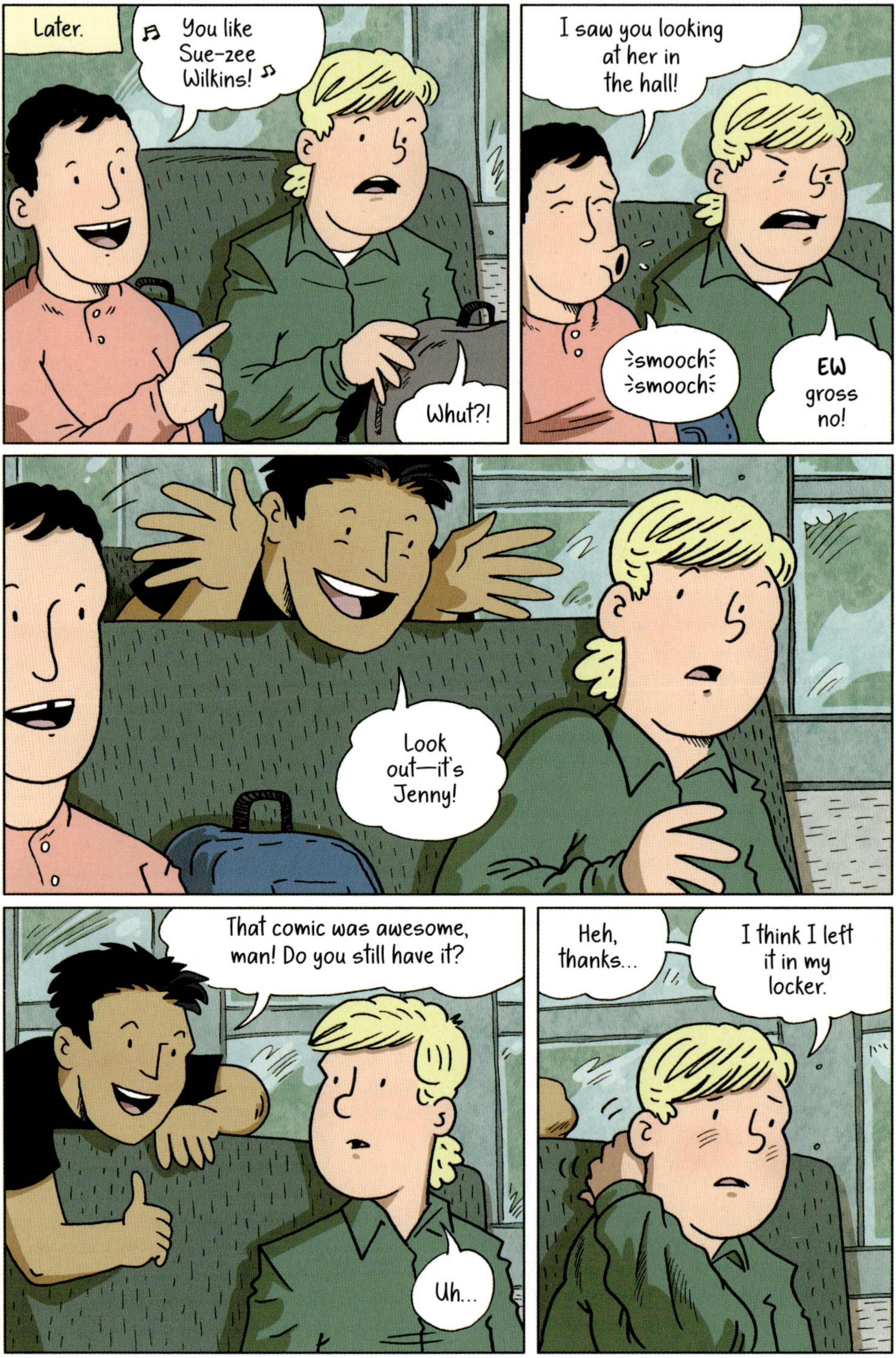
Later.
♫ You like Sue-zee Wilkins! ♫
Whut?!
I saw you looking at her in the hall!
smooch smooch
EW gross no!
Look out—it's Jenny!
That comic was awesome, man! Do you still have it?
Uh...
Heh, thanks...
I think I left it in my locker.

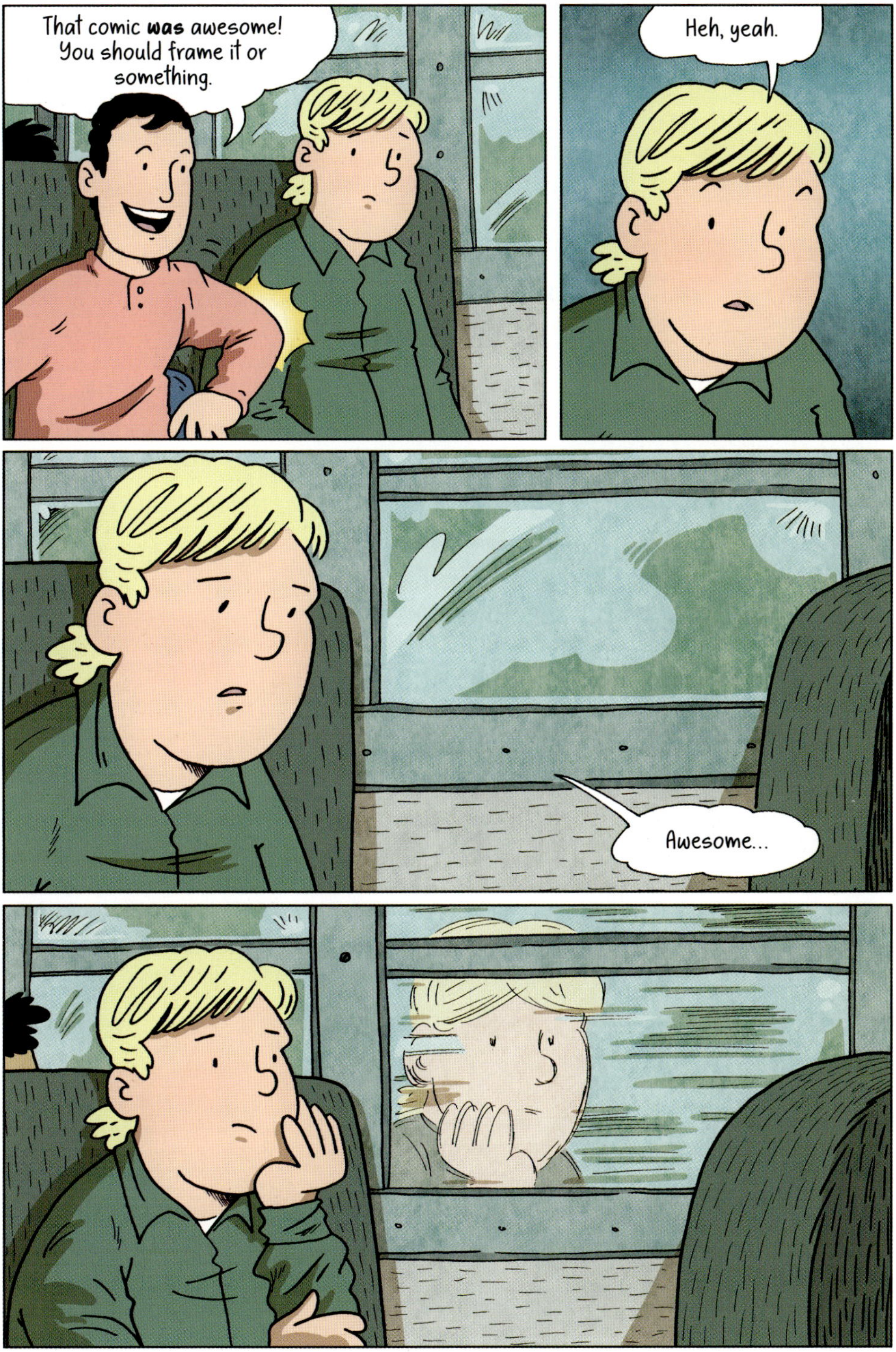
That comic **was** awesome! You should frame it or something.
Heh, yeah.
Awesome...

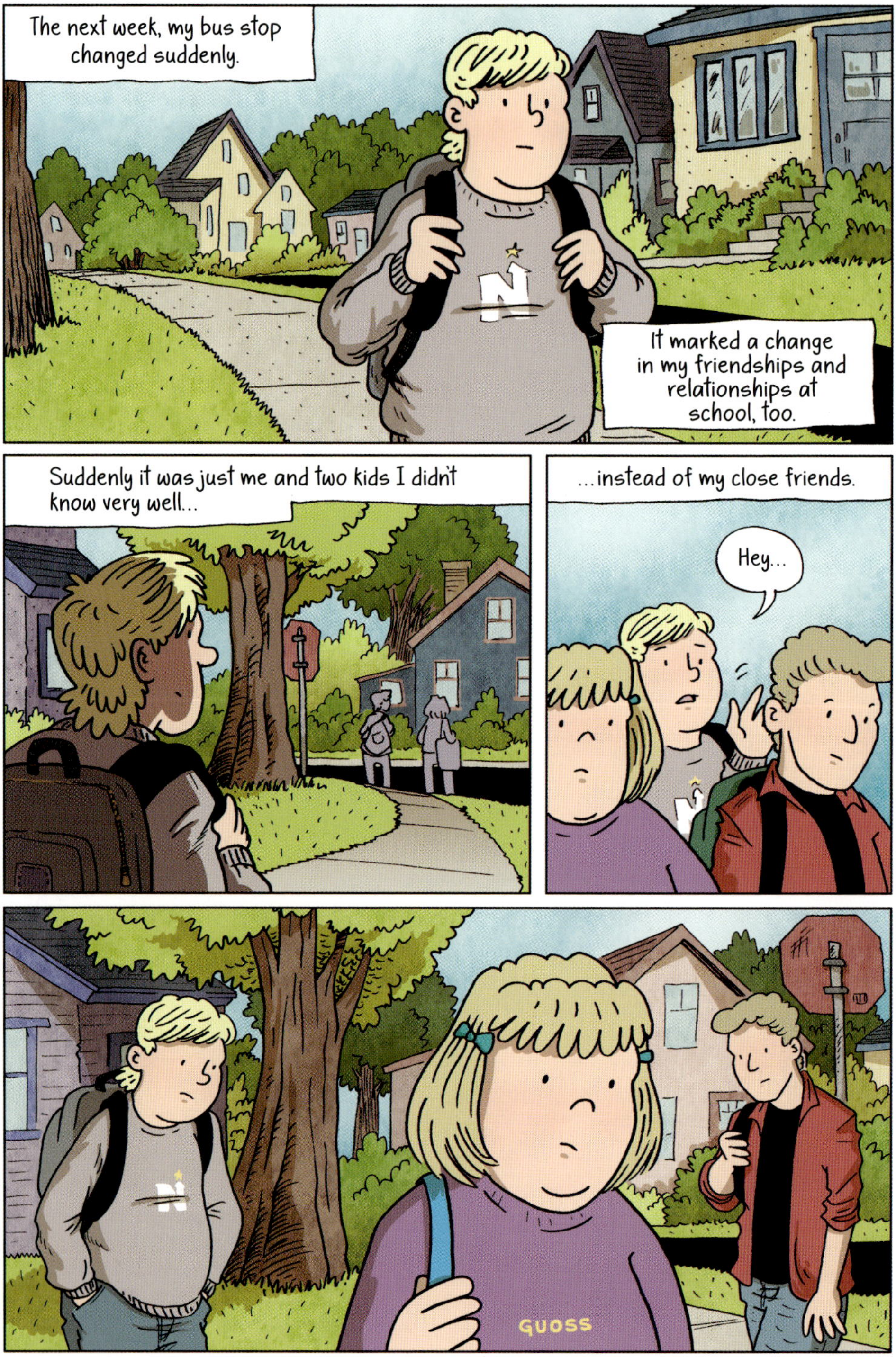
The next week, my bus stop changed suddenly.
It marked a change in my friendships and relationships at school, too.
Suddenly it was just me and two kids I didn't know very well...
...instead of my close friends.
Hey...
GUOSS

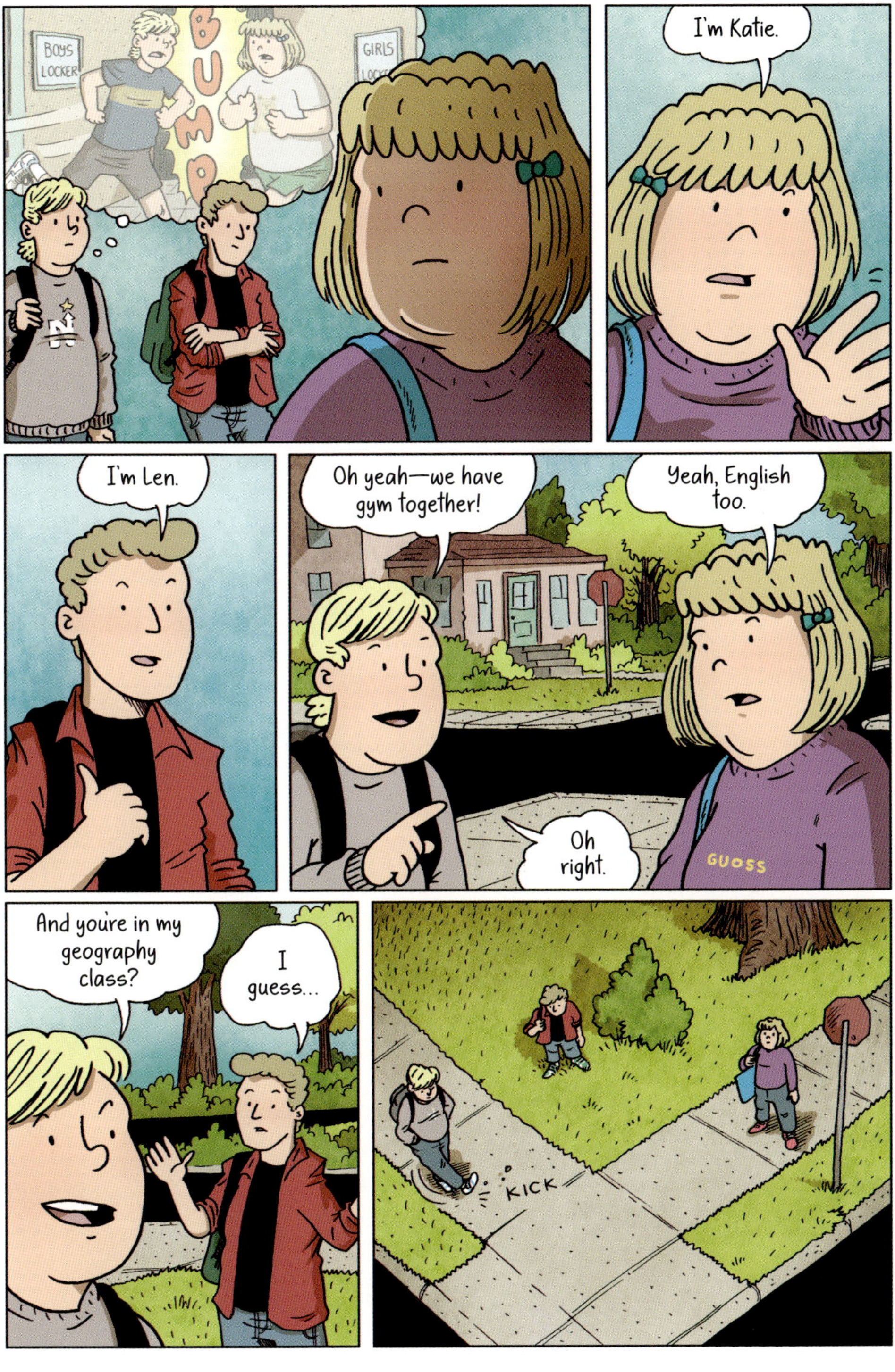
BOYS LOCKER
BUMP
GIRLS LOCKER
I'm Katie.
I'm Len.
Oh yeah—we have gym together!
Yeah, English too.
Oh right.
GUOSS
And you're in my geography class?
I guess...
KICK

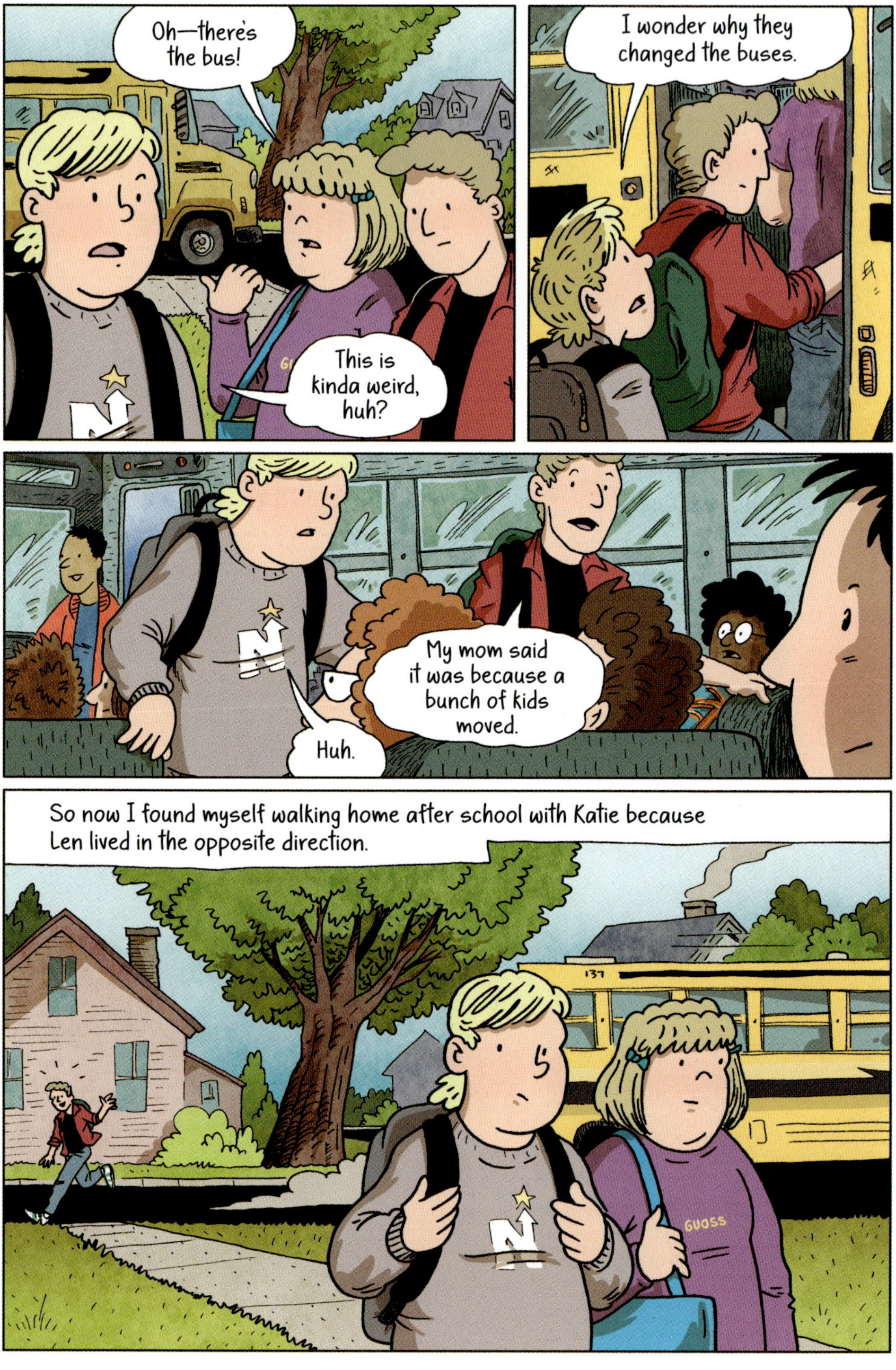
Oh—there's the bus!
This is kinda weird, huh?
I wonder why they changed the buses.
My mom said it was because a bunch of kids moved.
Huh.
So now I found myself walking home after school with Katie because Len lived in the opposite direction.
137
GUOSS

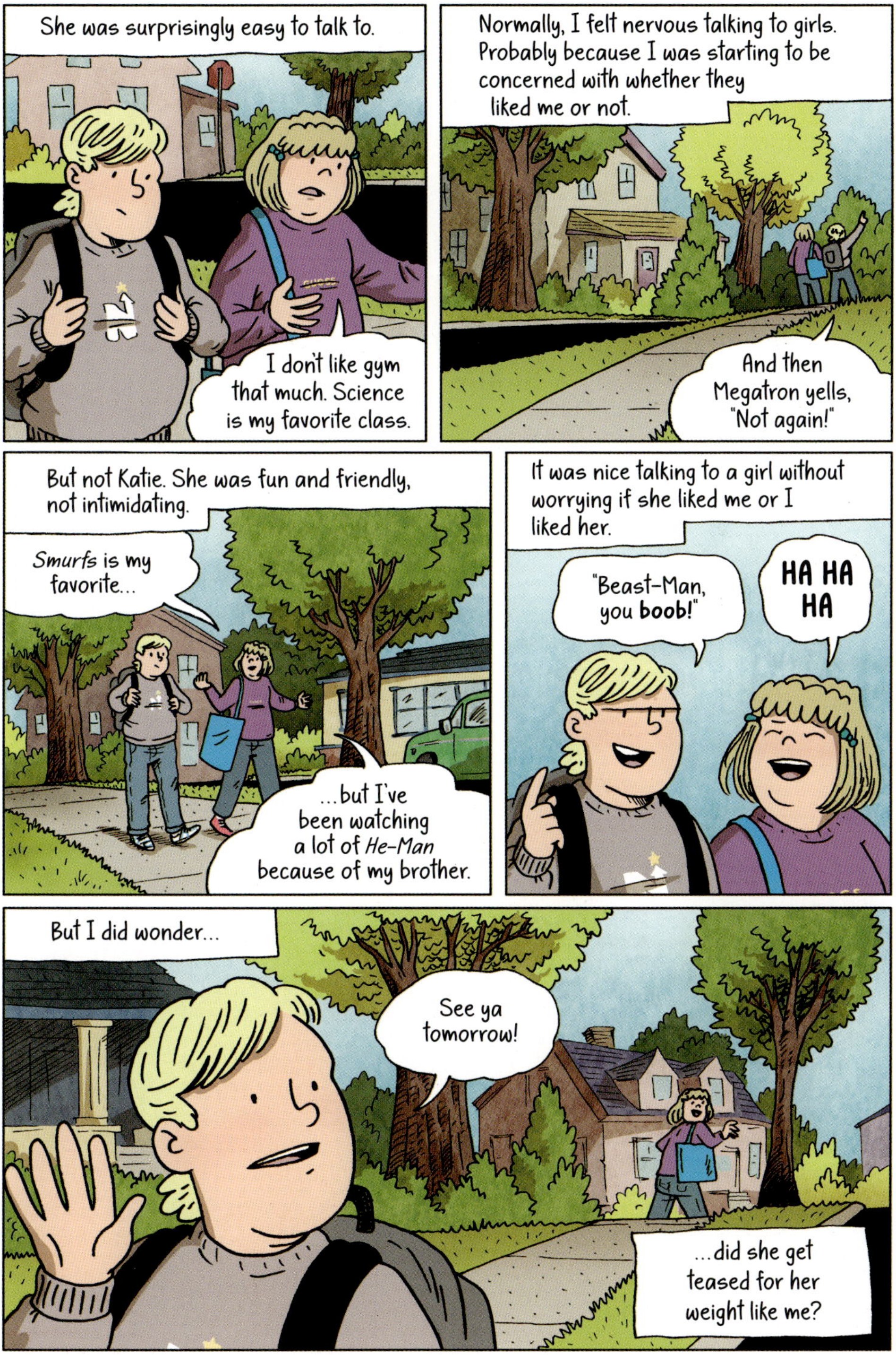

She was surprisingly easy to talk to.
I don't like gym that much. Science is my favorite class.
Normally, I felt nervous talking to girls. Probably because I was starting to be concerned with whether they liked me or not.
And then Megatron yells, "Not again!"
But not Katie. She was fun and friendly, not intimidating.
Smurfs is my favorite...
...but I've been watching a lot of *He-Man* because of my brother.
It was nice talking to a girl without worrying if she liked me or I liked her.
"Beast-Man, you **boob!**"
HA HA HA
But I did wonder...
See ya tomorrow!
...did she get teased for her weight like me?

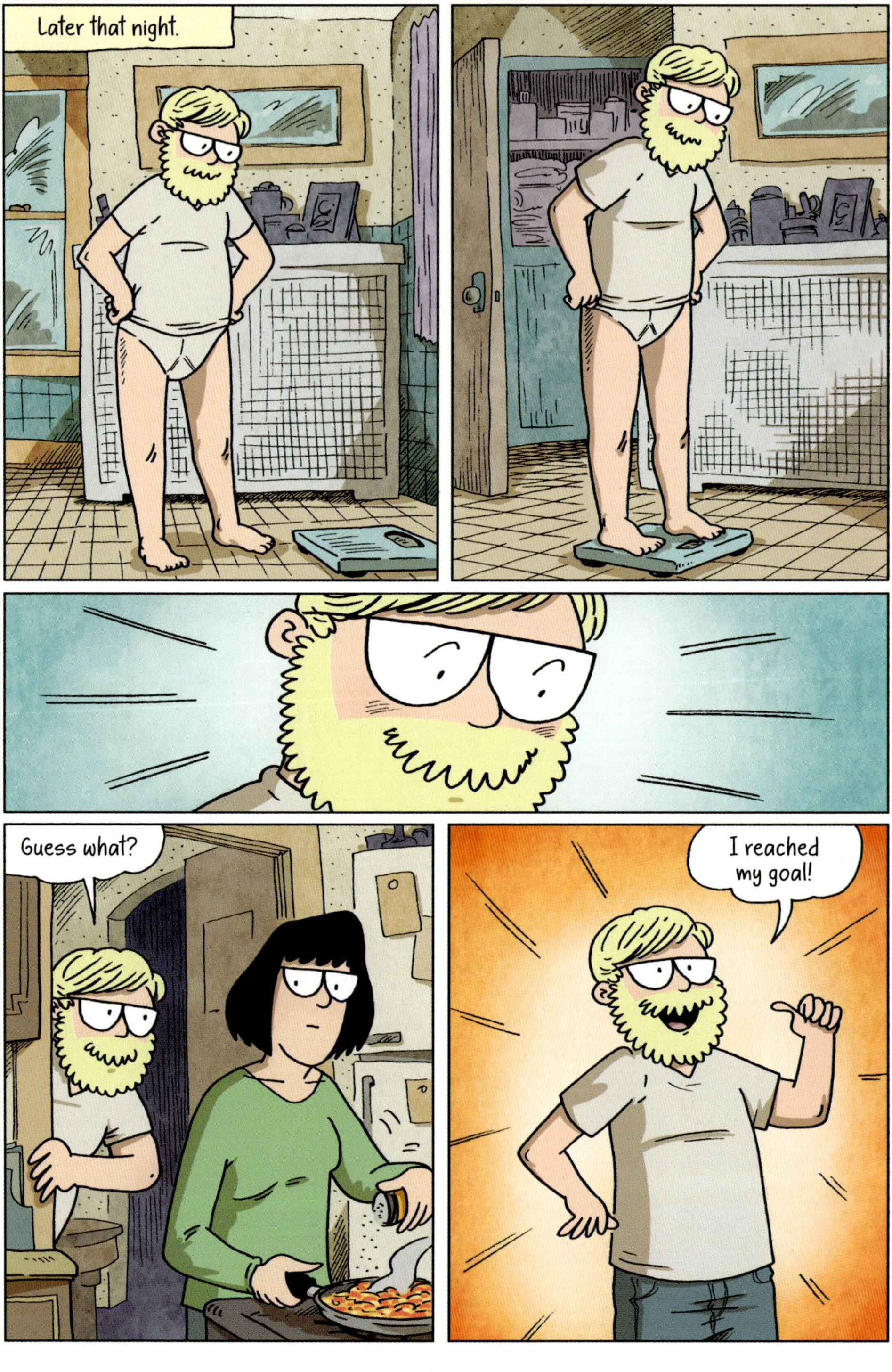
Later that night.
Guess what?
I reached my goal!

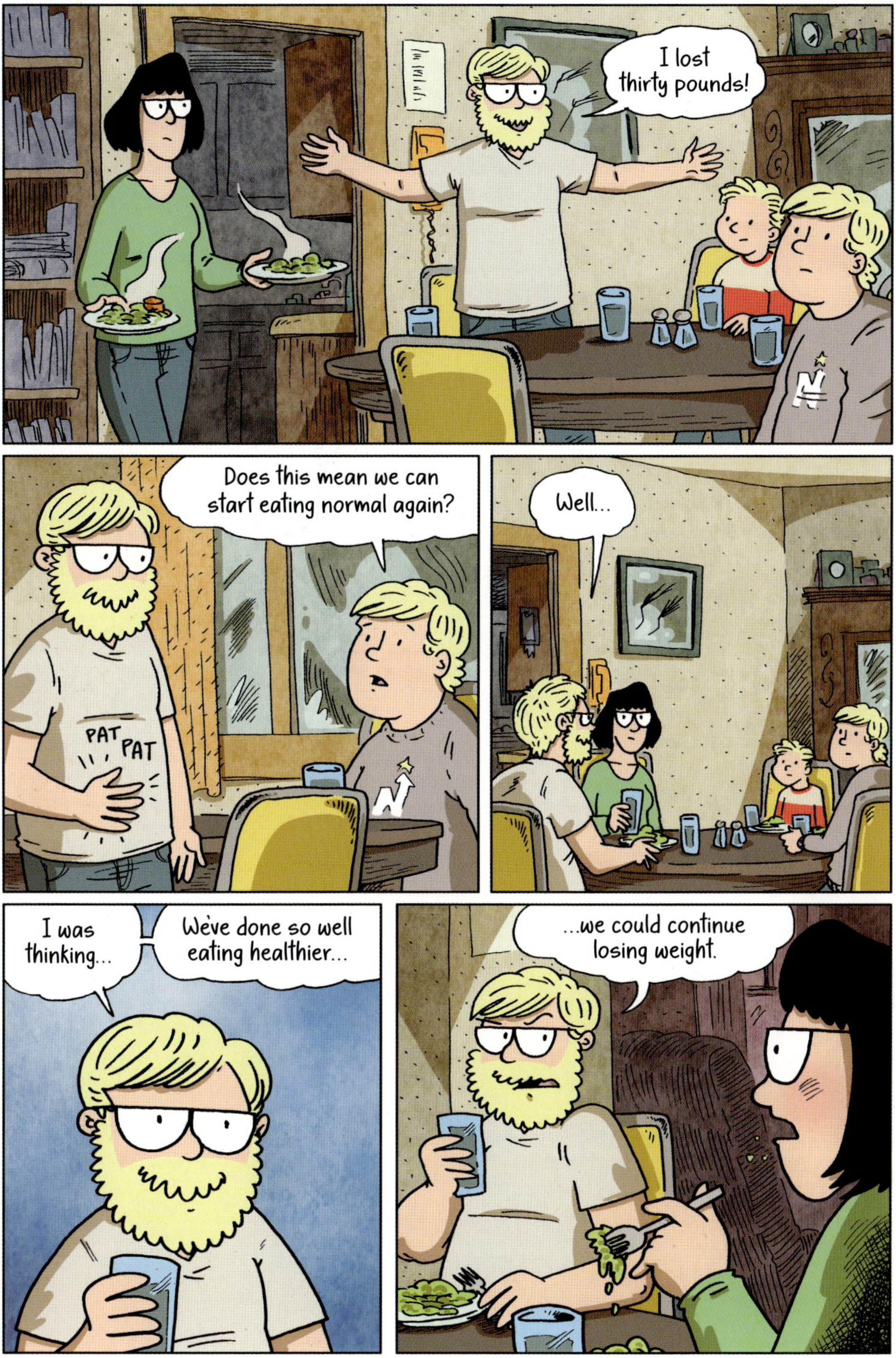

I lost thirty pounds!
Does this mean we can start eating normal again?
PAT PAT
Well...
I was thinking...
We've done so well eating healthier...
...we could continue losing weight.

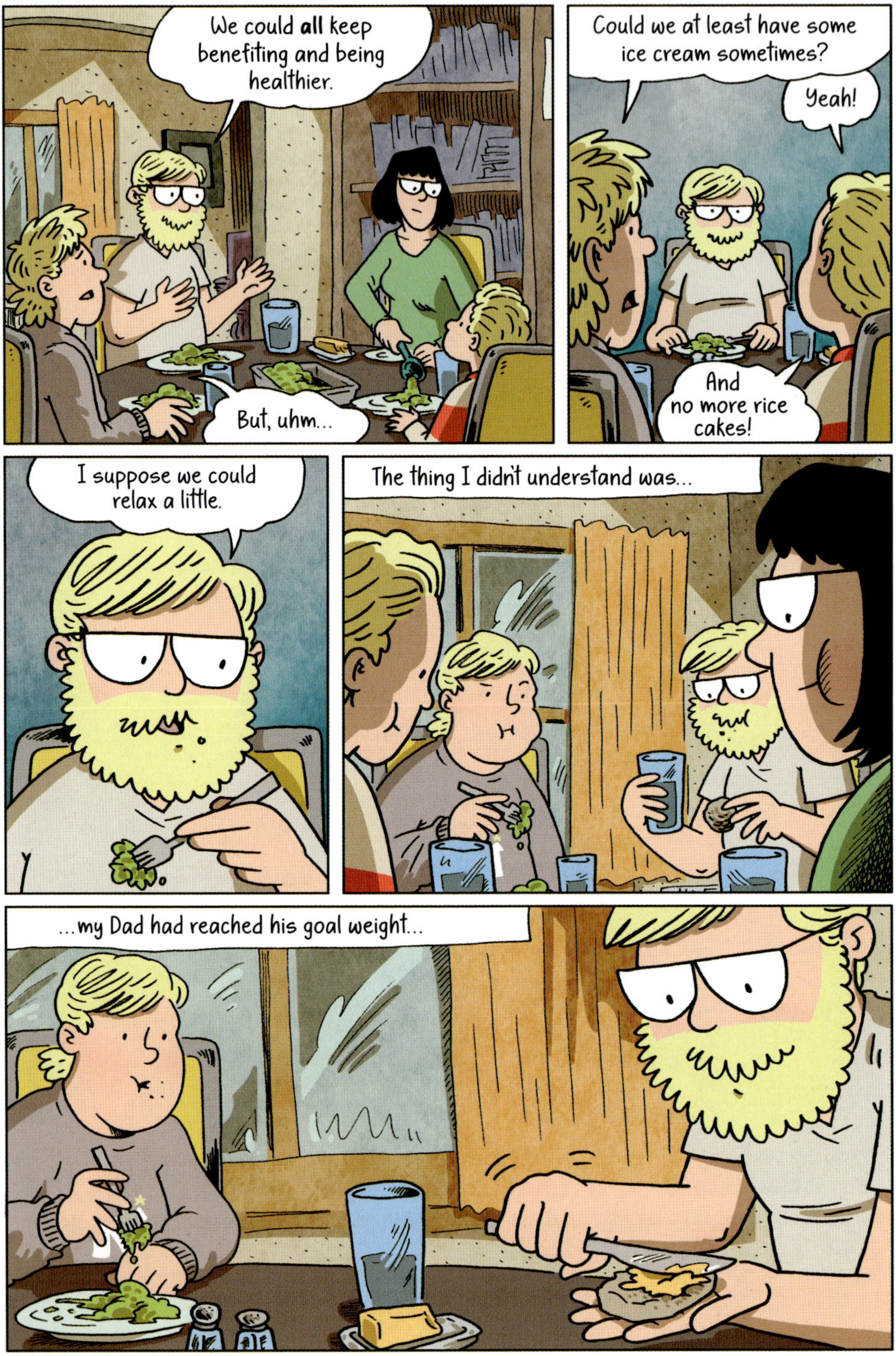

We could **all** keep benefiting and being healthier.
But, uhm...
Could we at least have some ice cream sometimes?
Yeah!
And no more rice cakes!
I suppose we could relax a little.
The thing I didn't understand was...
...my Dad had reached his goal weight...

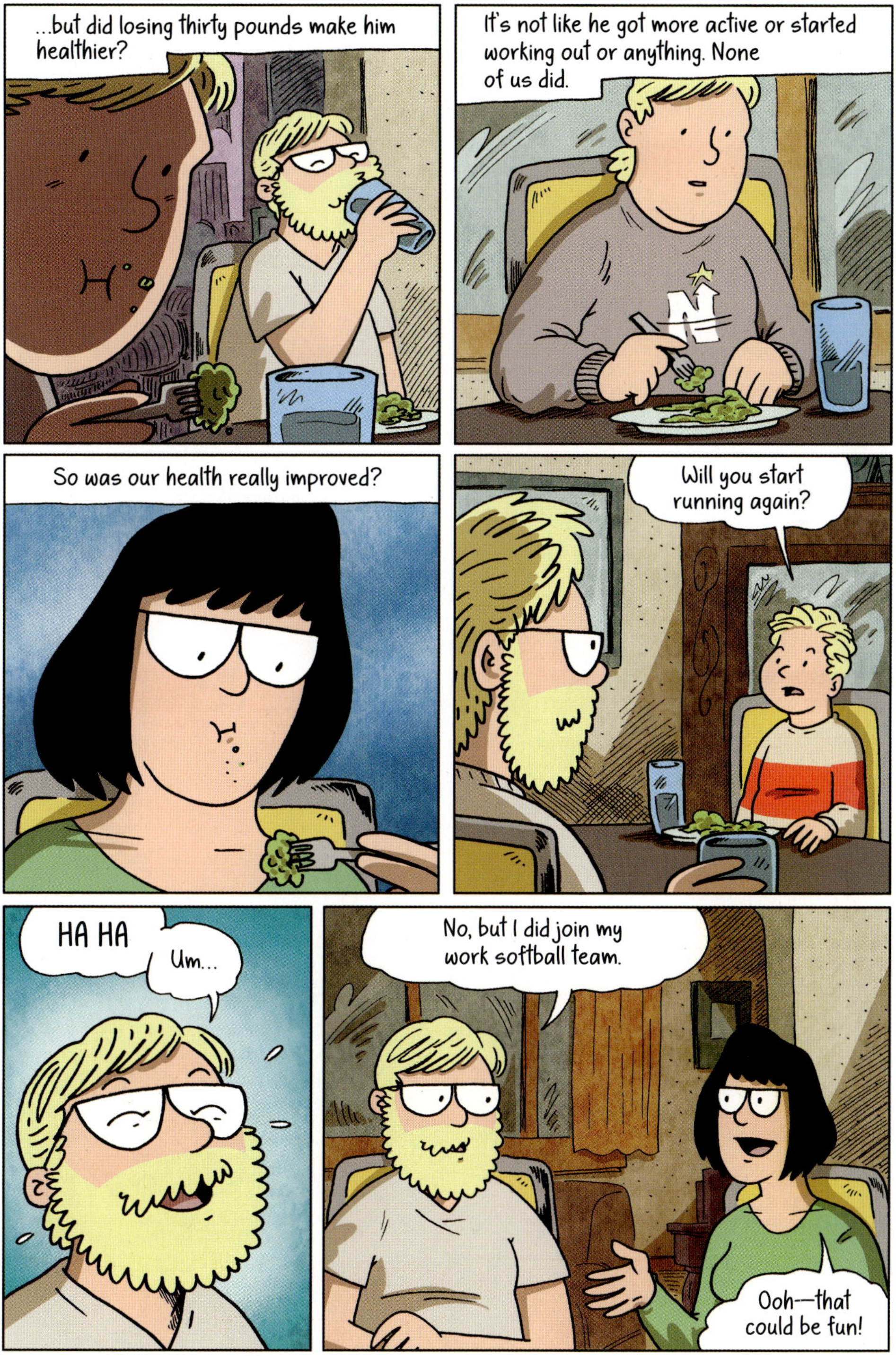
...but did losing thirty pounds make him healthier?
It's not like he got more active or started working out or anything. None of us did.
So was our health really improved?
Will you start running again?
HA HA
Um...
No, but I did join my work softball team.
Ooh—that could be fun!

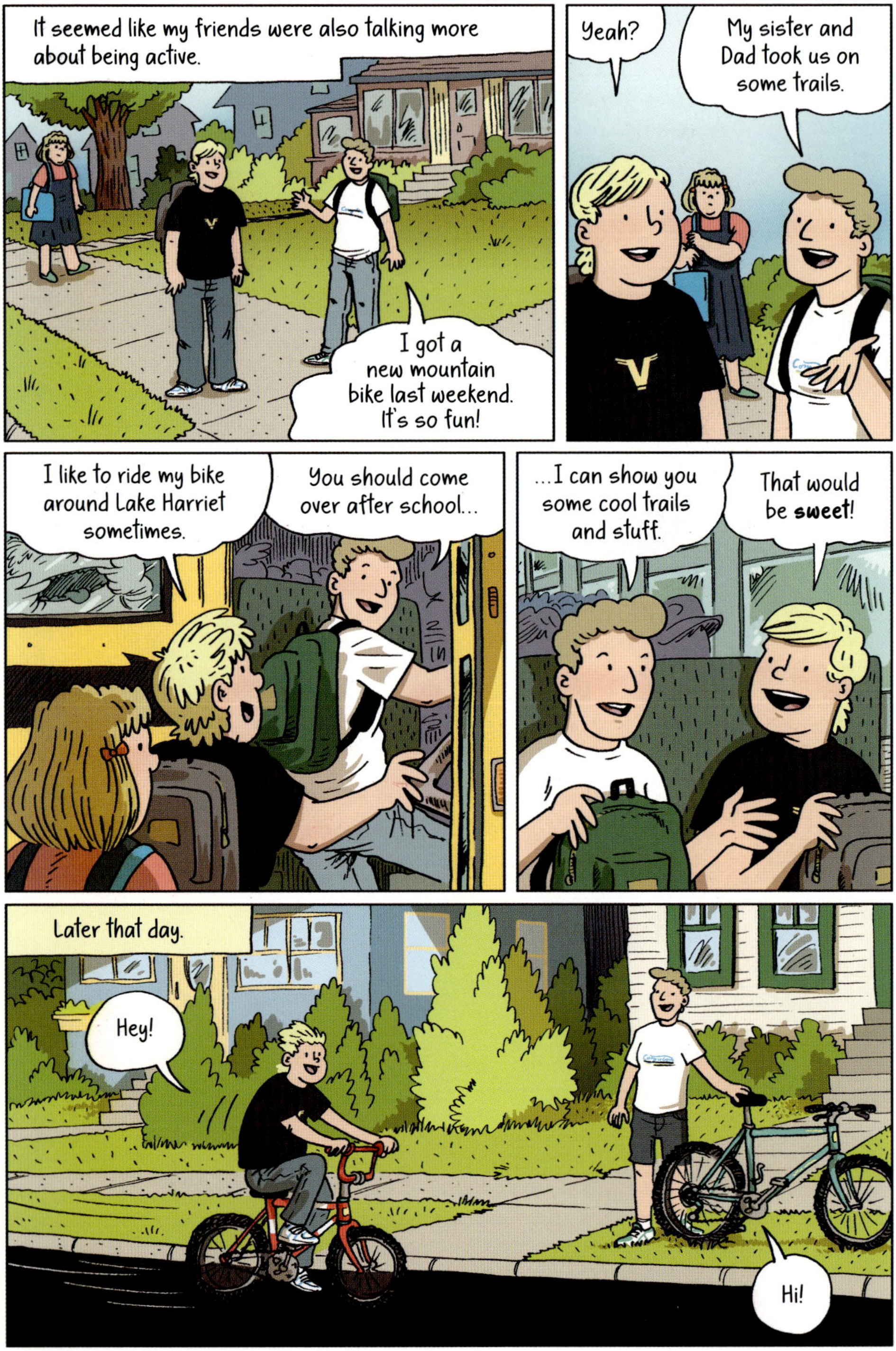
It seemed like my friends were also talking more about being active.
I got a new mountain bike last weekend. It's so fun!
Yeah?
My sister and Dad took us on some trails.
I like to ride my bike around Lake Harriet sometimes.
You should come over after school...
...I can show you some cool trails and stuff.
That would be **sweet**!
Later that day.
Hey!
Hi!

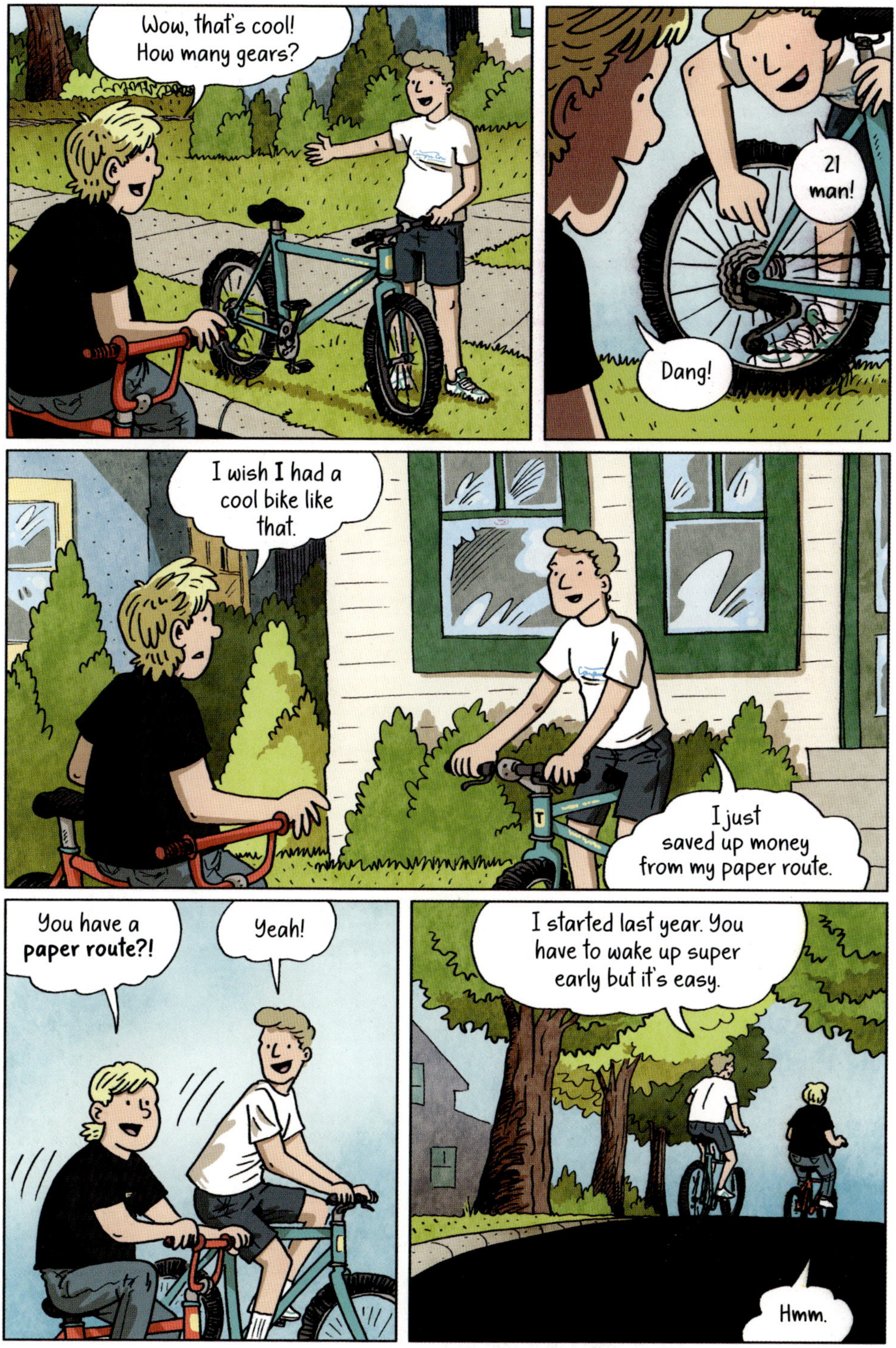

Wow, that's cool! How many gears?
21 man!
Dang!
I wish I had a cool bike like that.
I just saved up money from my paper route.
You have a paper route?!
Yeah!
I started last year. You have to wake up super early but it's easy.
Hmm.

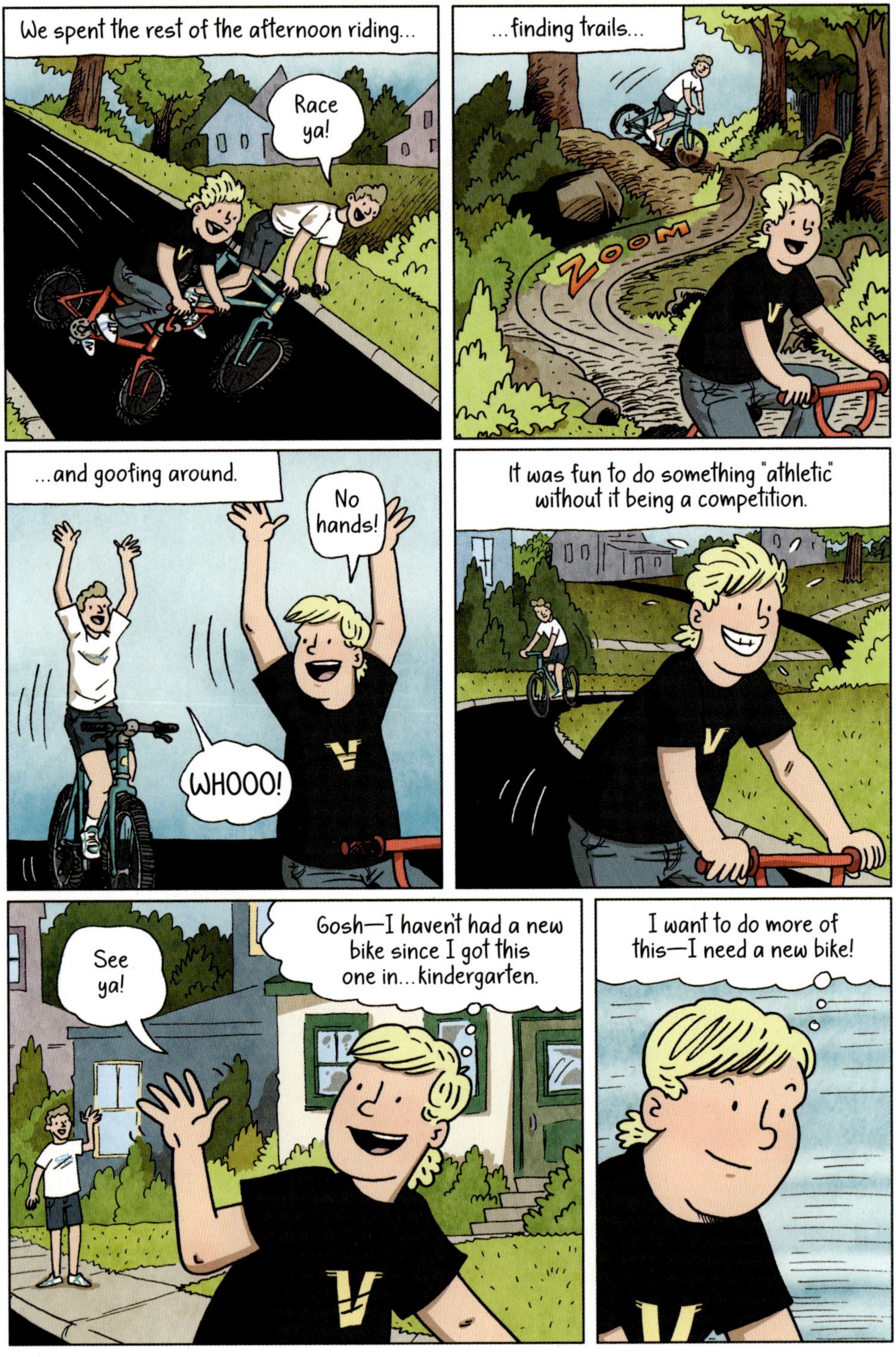
We spent the rest of the afternoon riding...
Race ya!
...finding trails...
ZOOM
...and goofing around.
No hands!
WHOOO!
It was fun to do something "athletic" without it being a competition.
See ya!
Gosh—I haven't had a new bike since I got this one in... kindergarten.
I want to do more of this—I need a new bike!

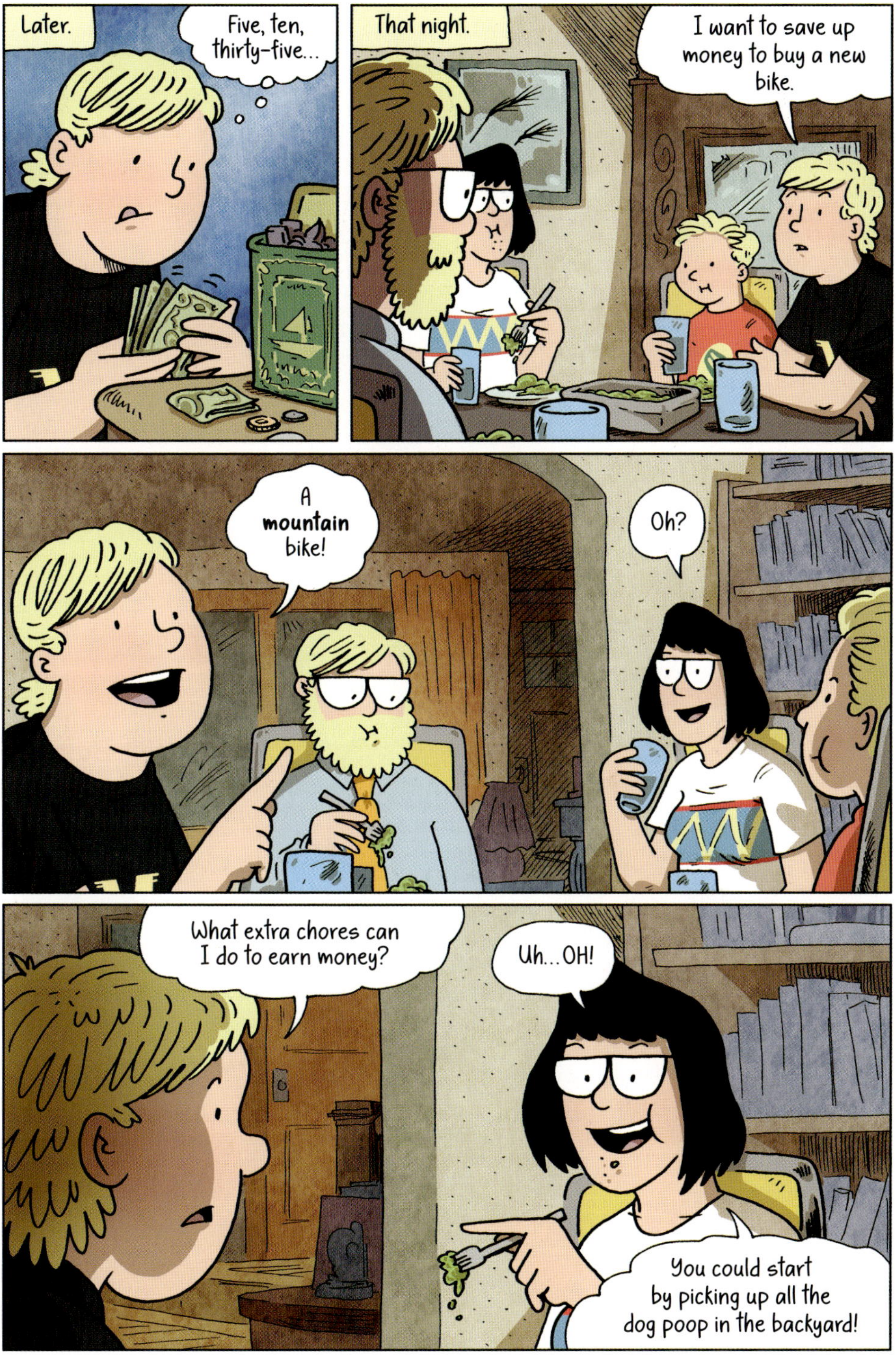
Later.
Five, ten, thirty-five...
That night.
I want to save up money to buy a new bike.
A **mountain** bike!
Oh?
What extra chores can I do to earn money?
Uh...OH!
You could start by picking up all the dog poop in the backyard!

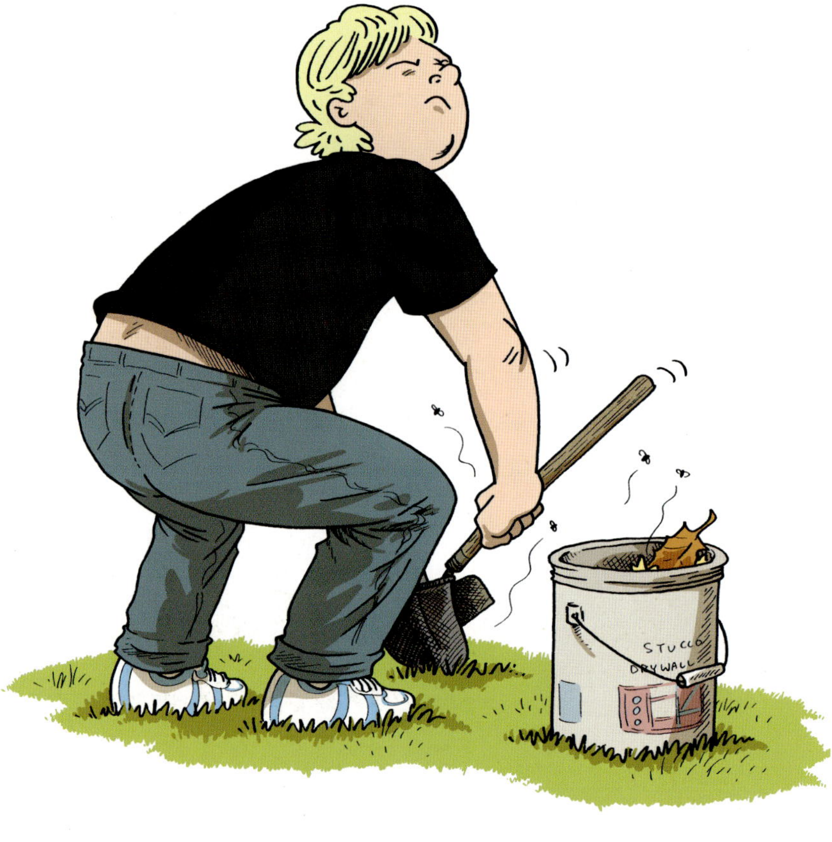
STUCCO
DRYWALL

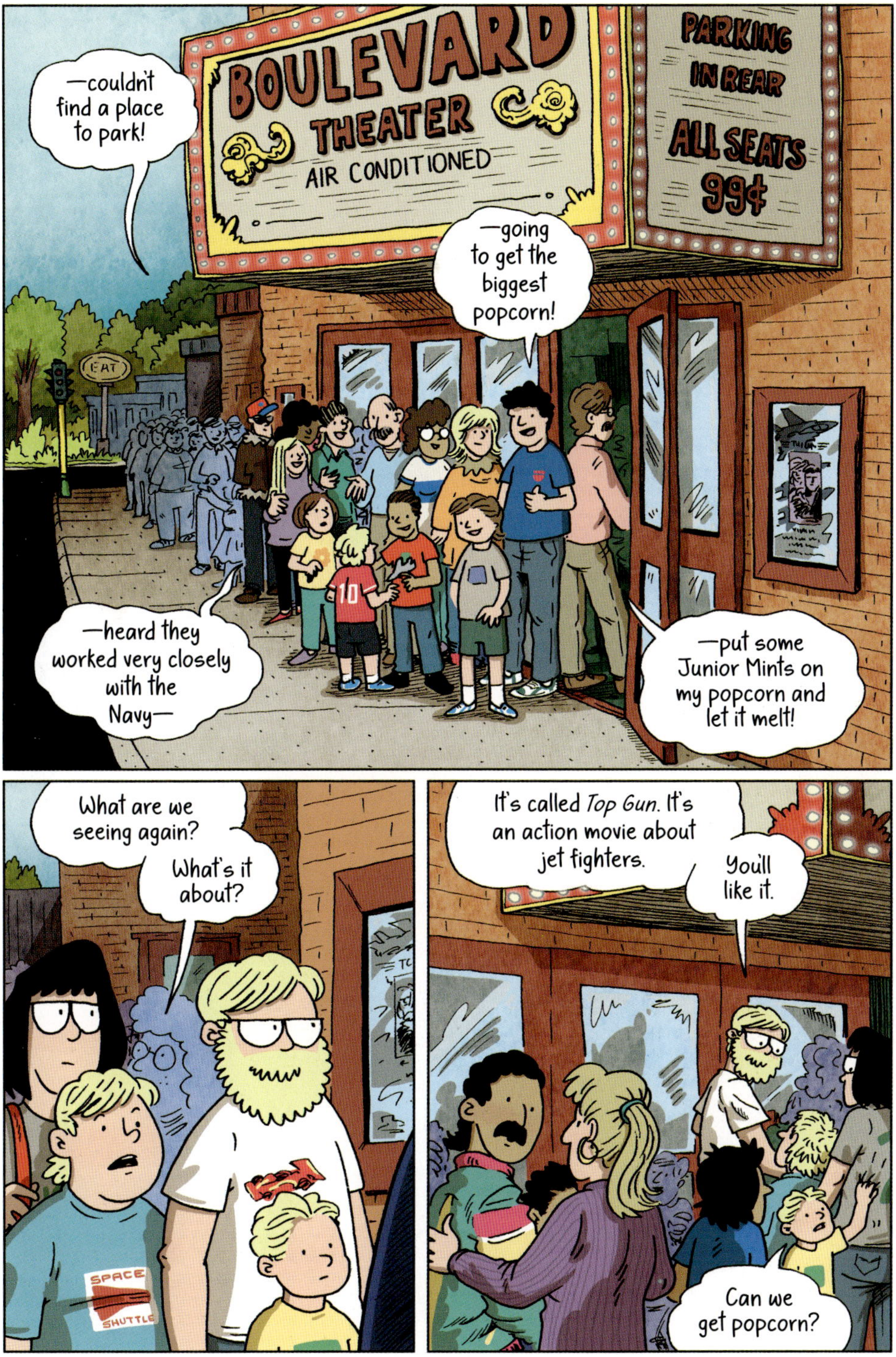
BOULEVARD THEATER
AIR CONDITIONED
PARKING IN REAR
ALL SEATS 99¢
—couldn't find a place to park!
—going to get the biggest popcorn!
—heard they worked very closely with the Navy—
—put some Junior Mints on my popcorn and let it melt!
What are we seeing again?
What's it about?
SPACE SHUTTLE
It's called *Top Gun*. It's an action movie about jet fighters.
You'll like it.
Can we get popcorn?

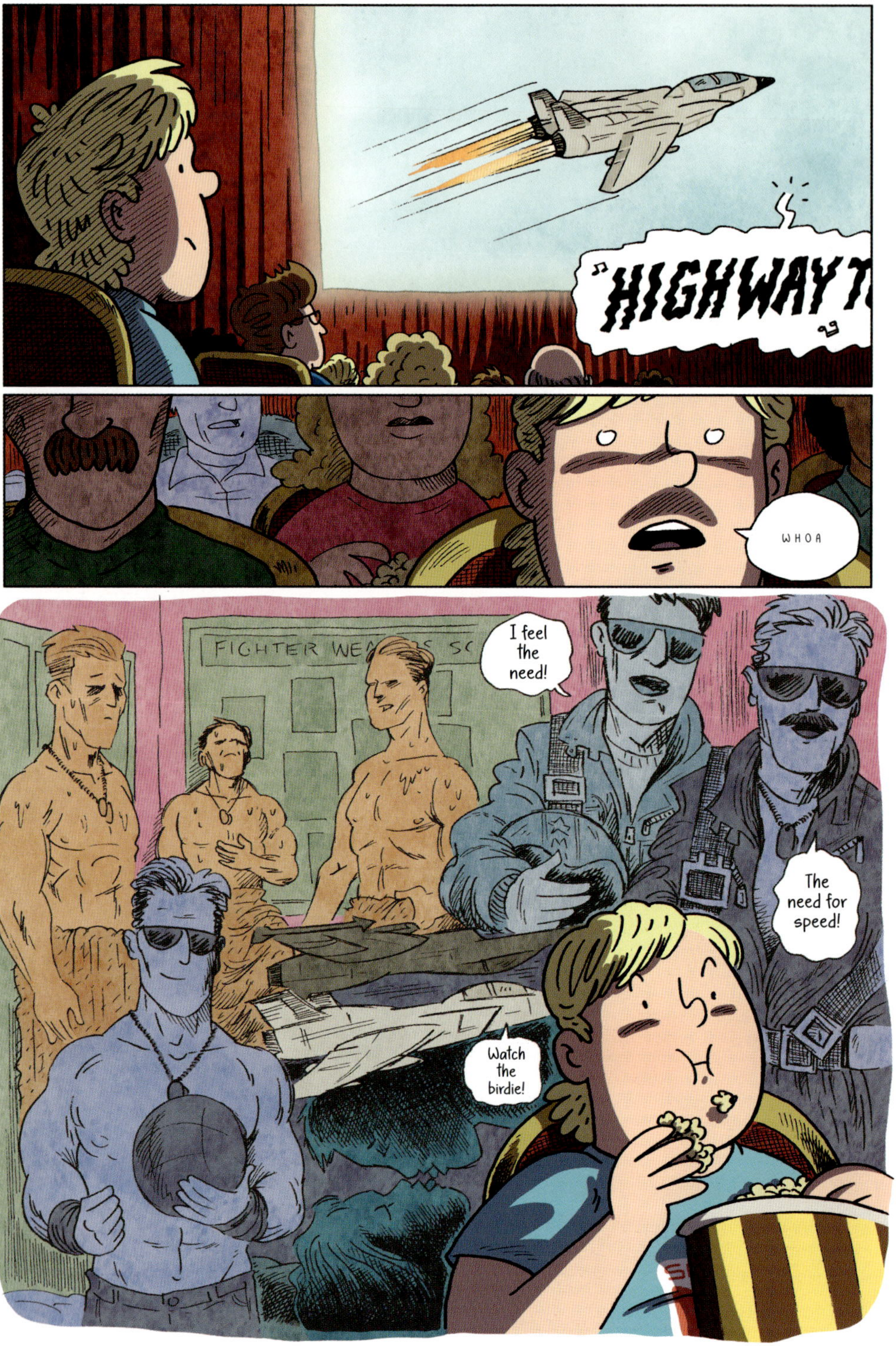
HIGHWAY T
WHOA
FIGHTER WEA S SC
I feel the need!
The need for speed!
Watch the birdie!

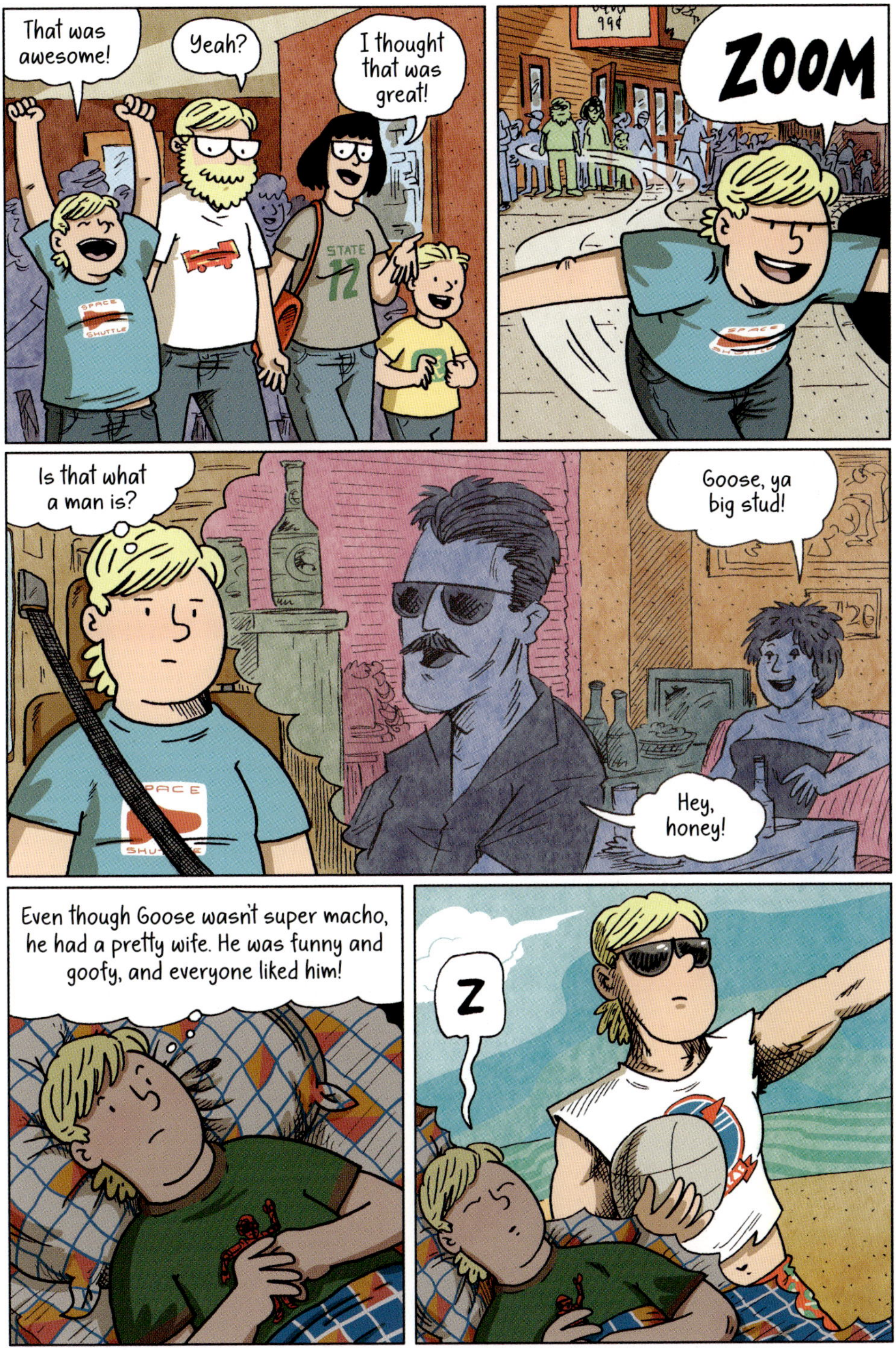
That was awesome!
Yeah?
I thought that was great!
ZOOM
Is that what a man is?
Goose, ya big stud!
Hey, honey!
Even though Goose wasn't super macho, he had a pretty wife. He was funny and goofy, and everyone liked him!
Z

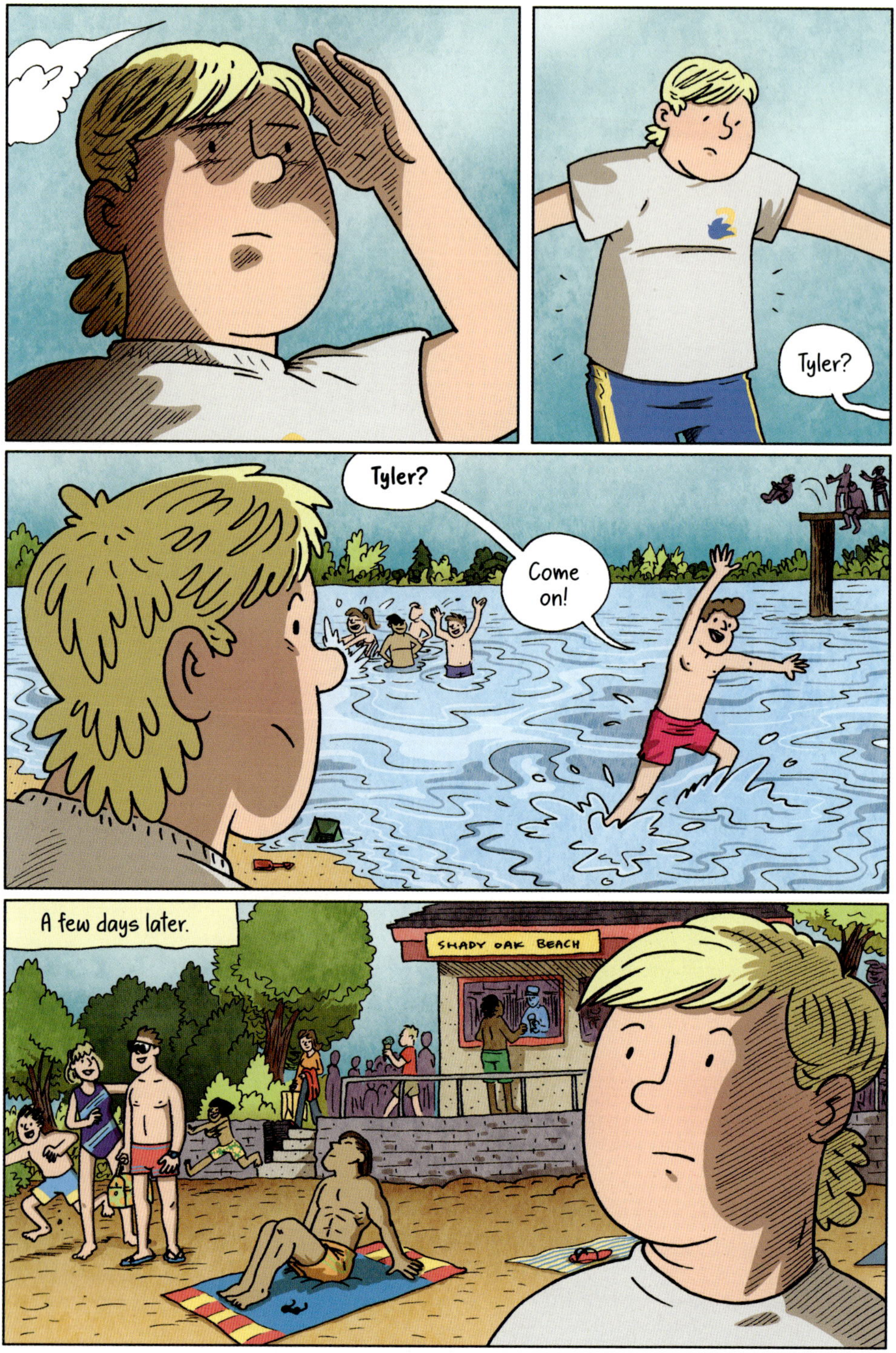
Tyler?
Tyler?
Come on!
A few days later.
SHADY OAK BEACH

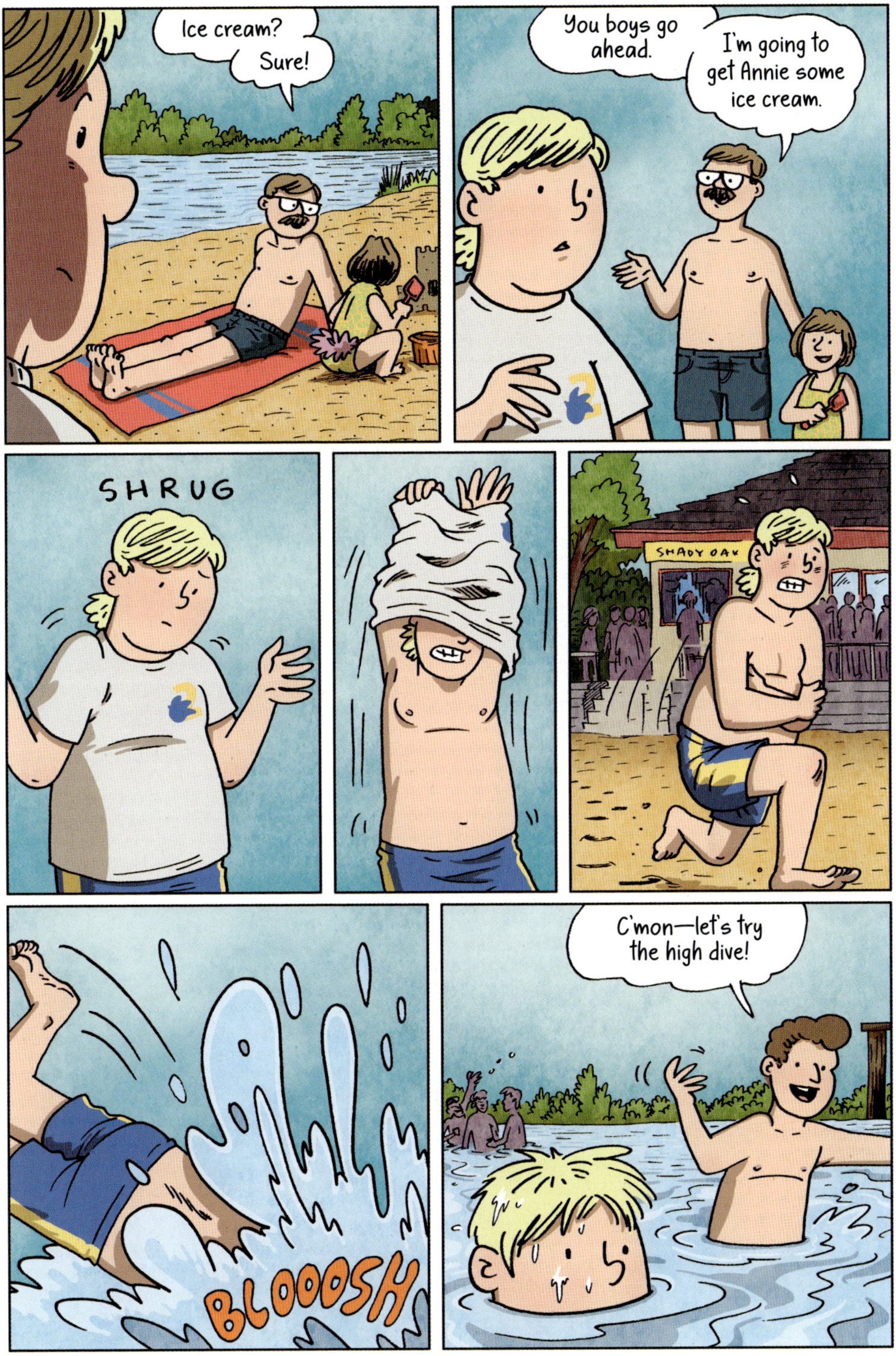
Ice cream?
Sure!
You boys go ahead.
I'm going to get Annie some ice cream.
SHRUG
SHADY OAK
BLOOOSH
C'mon—let's try the high dive!

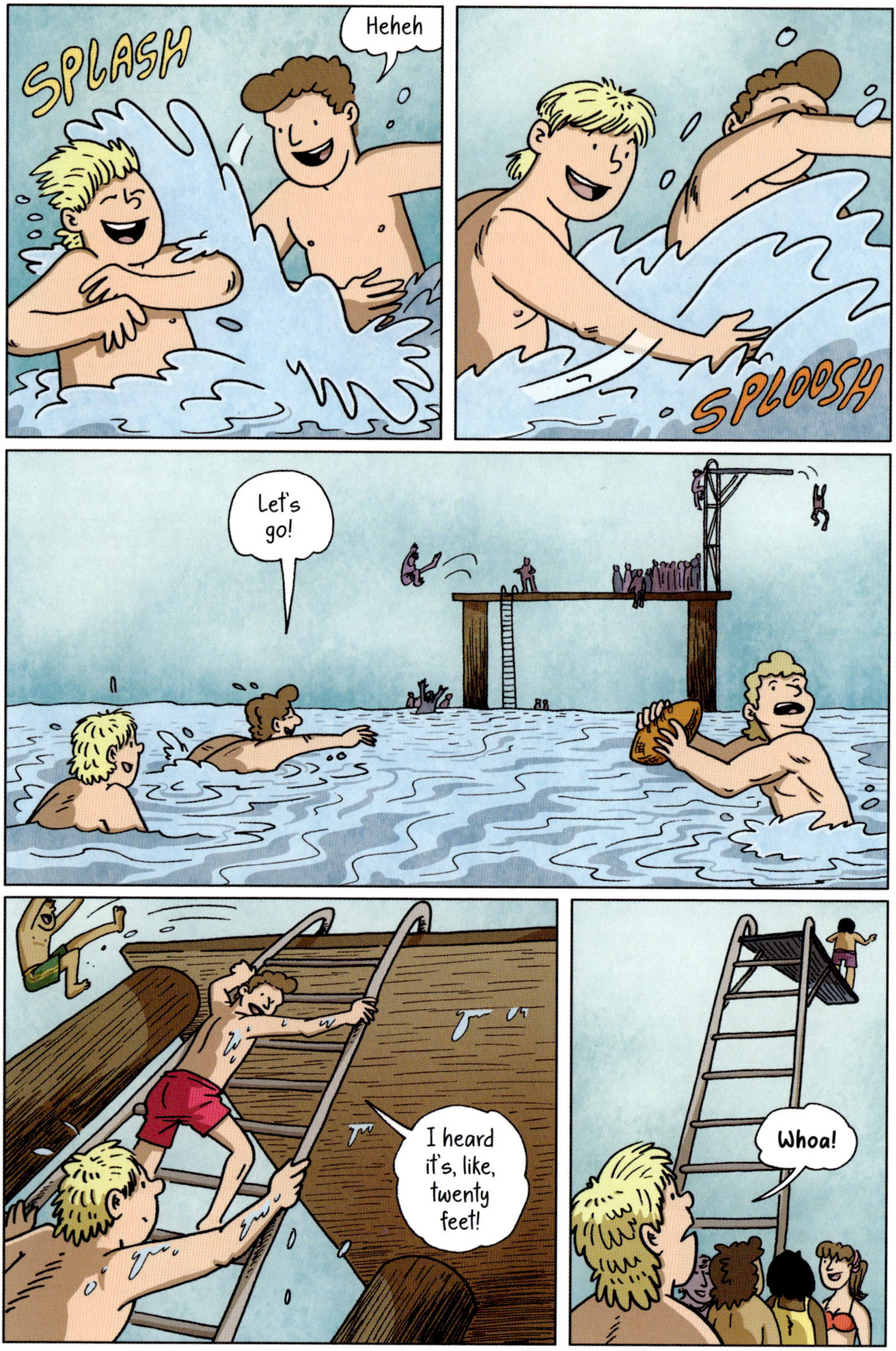
SPLASH
Heheh
SPLOOSH
Let's go!
I heard it's, like, twenty feet!
Whoa!

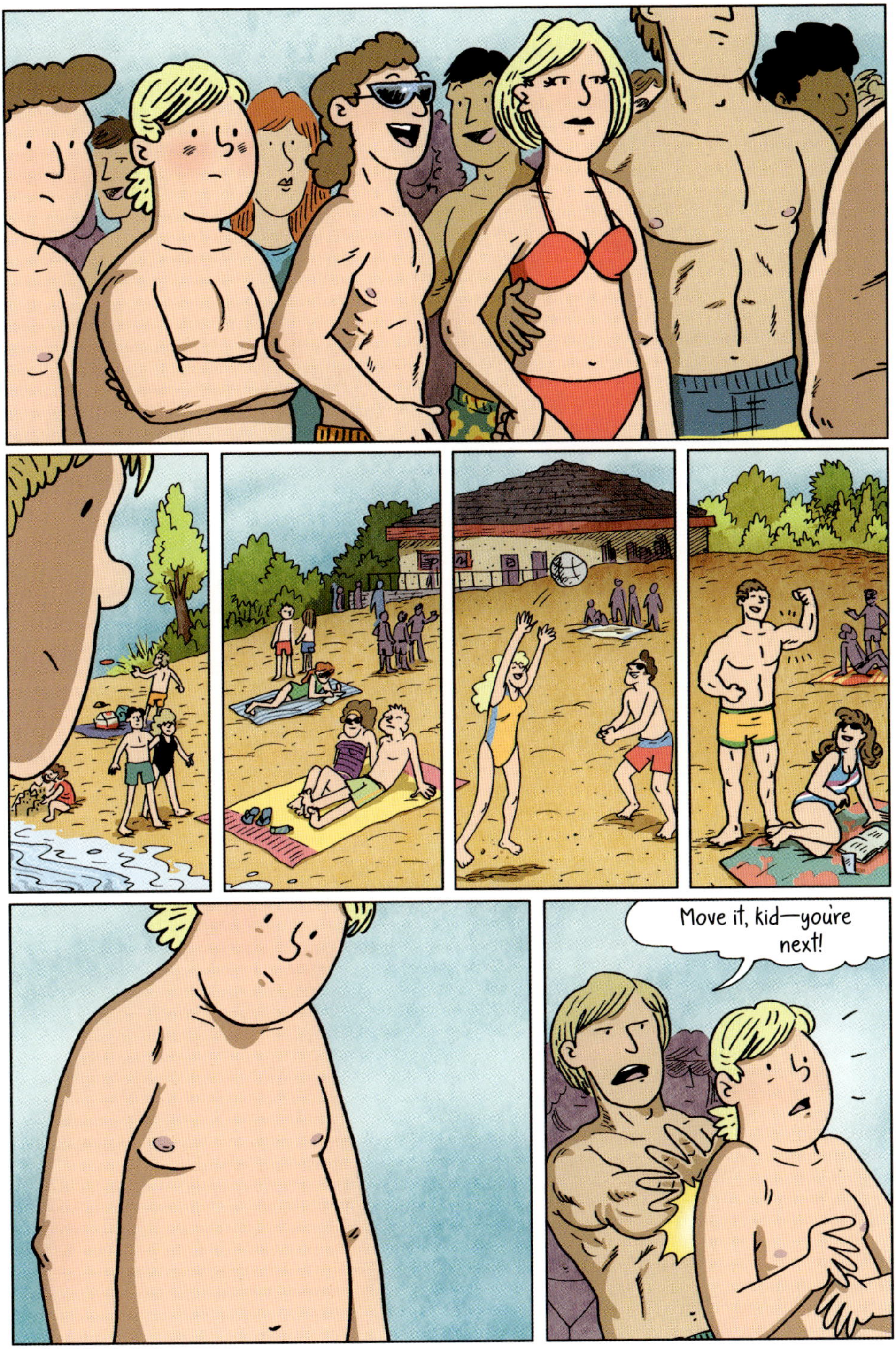
Move it, kid—you're next!

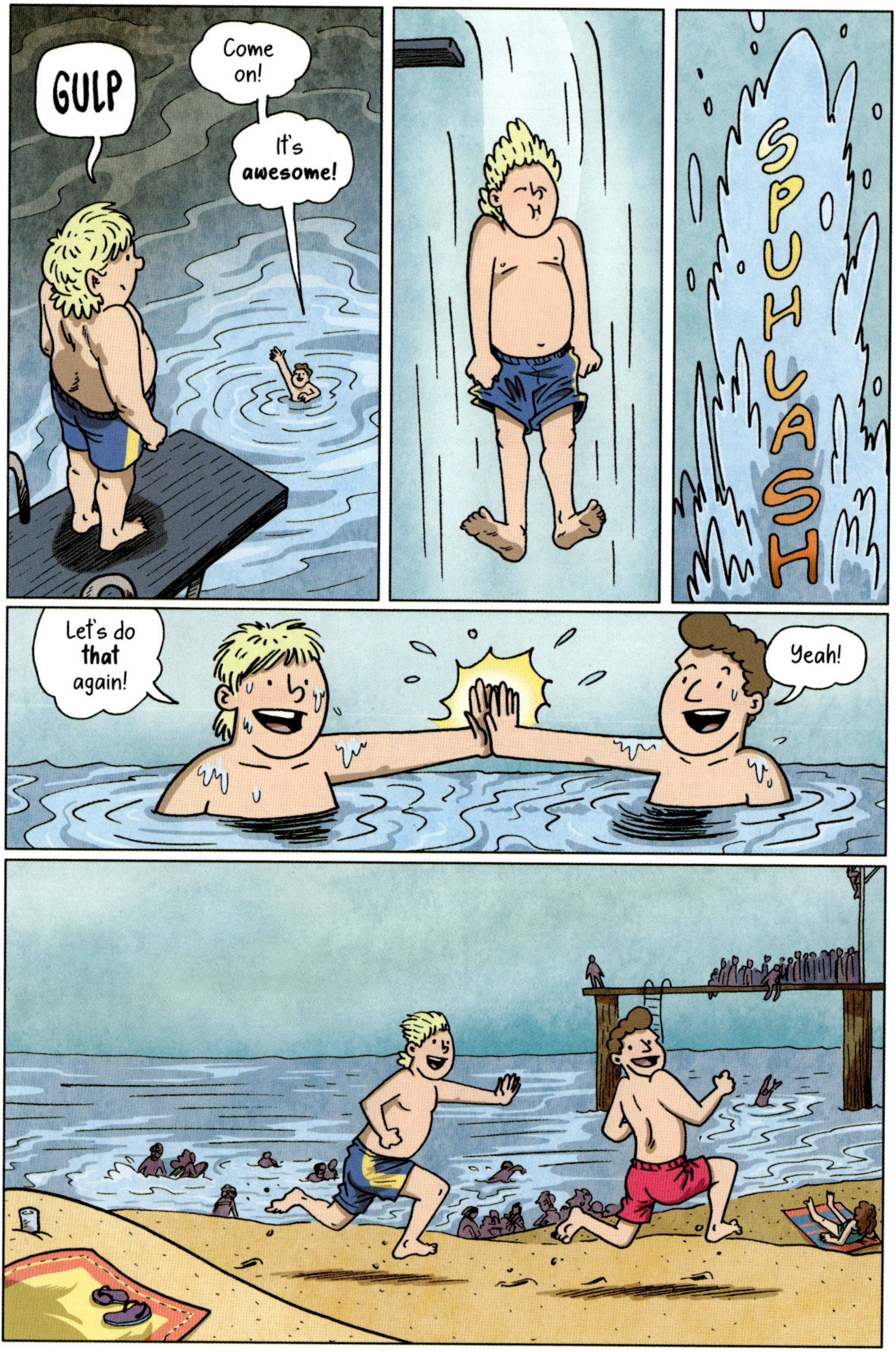

GULP
Come on!
It's **awesome!**
SPUHLASH
Let's do **that** again!
Yeah!

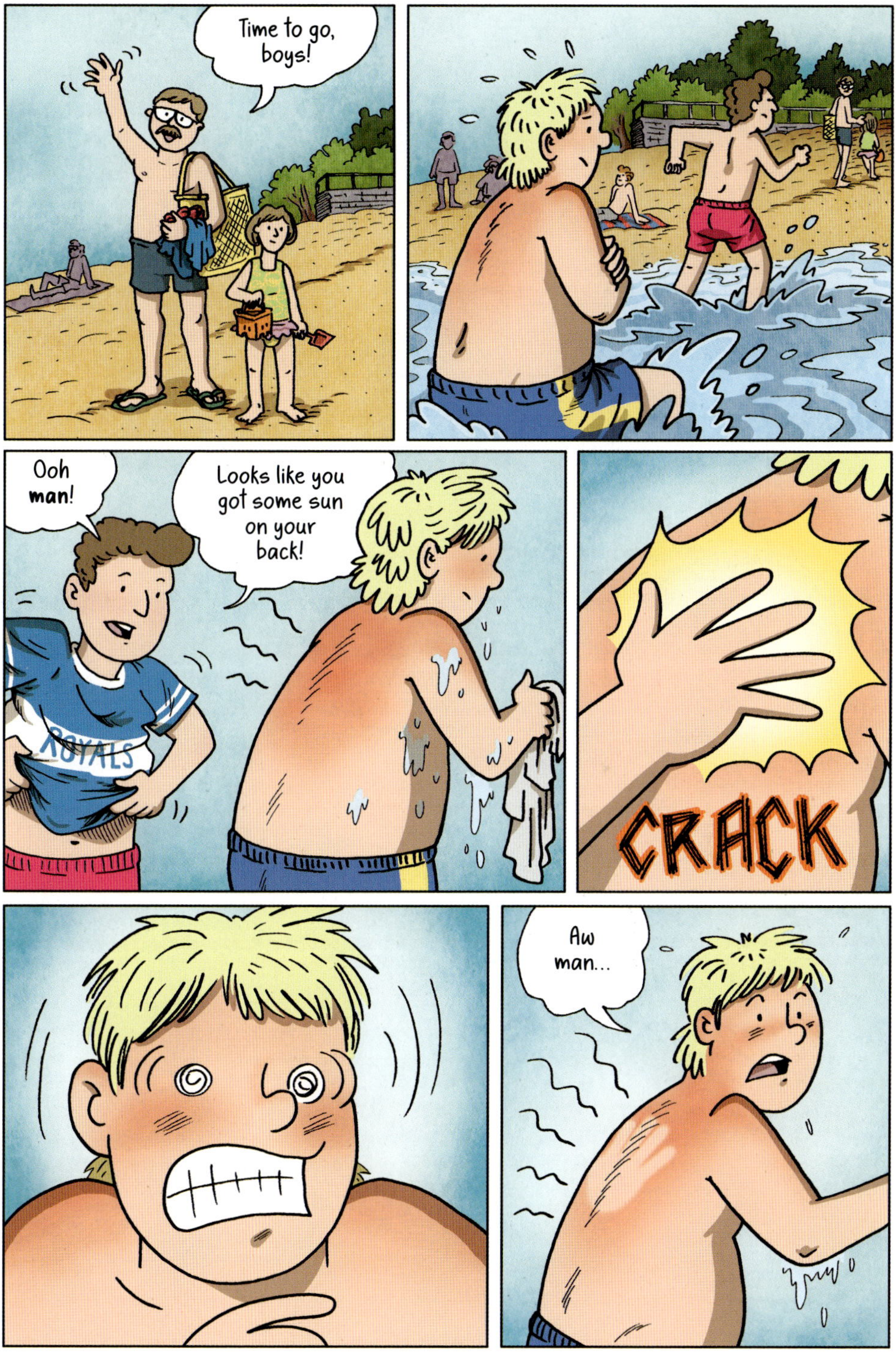
Time to go, boys!
Ooh man!
Looks like you got some sun on your back!
ROYALS
CRACK
Aw man...

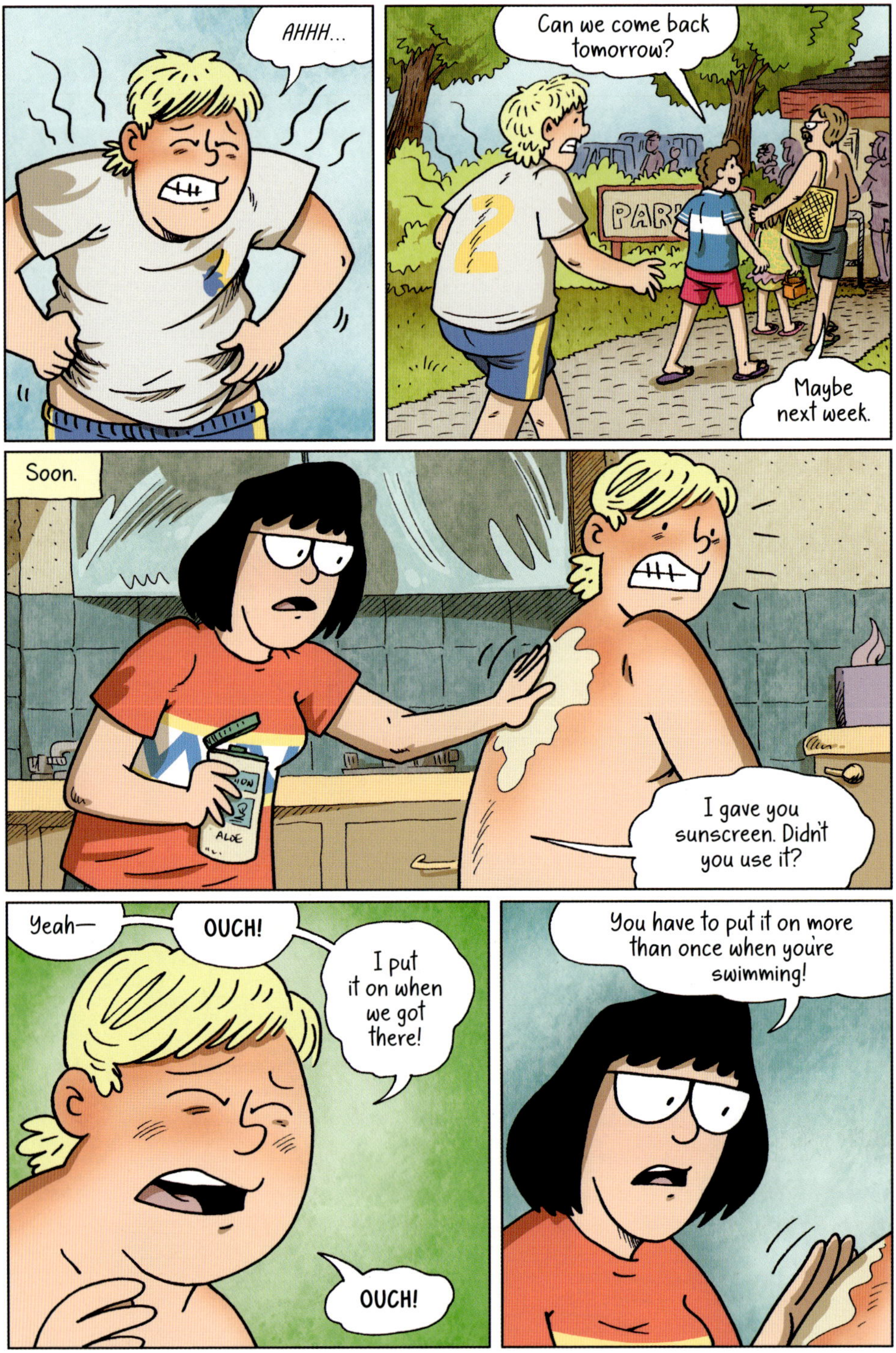
AHHH...
Can we come back tomorrow?
PARK
Maybe next week.
Soon.
ALOE
I gave you sunscreen. Didn't you use it?
Yeah—
OUCH!
I put it on when we got there!
OUCH!
You have to put it on more than once when you're swimming!

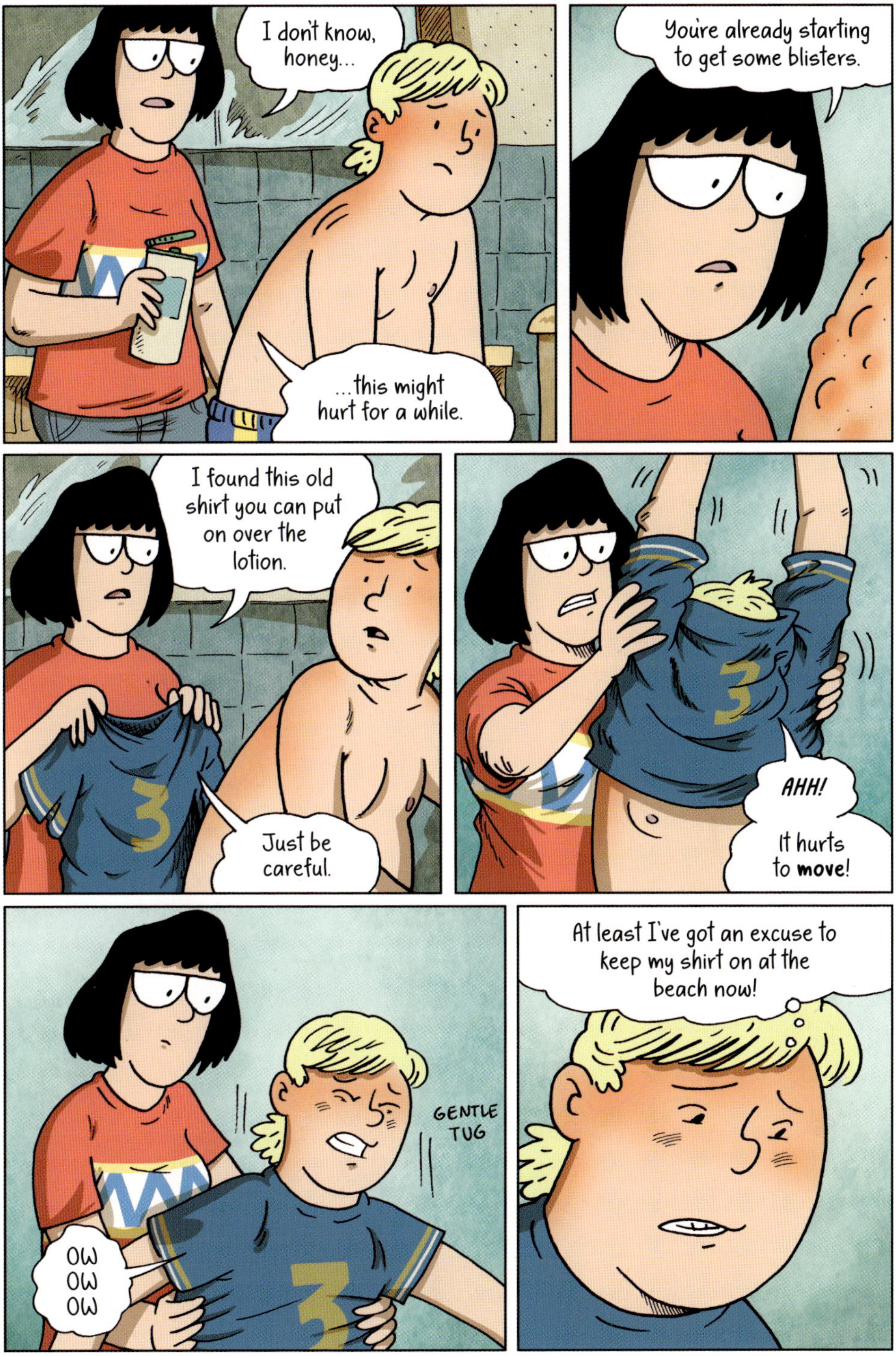
I don't know, honey...
...this might hurt for a while.
You're already starting to get some blisters.
I found this old shirt you can put on over the lotion.
Just be careful.
AHH!
It hurts to **move**!
GENTLE TUG
OW OW OW
At least I've got an excuse to keep my shirt on at the beach now!

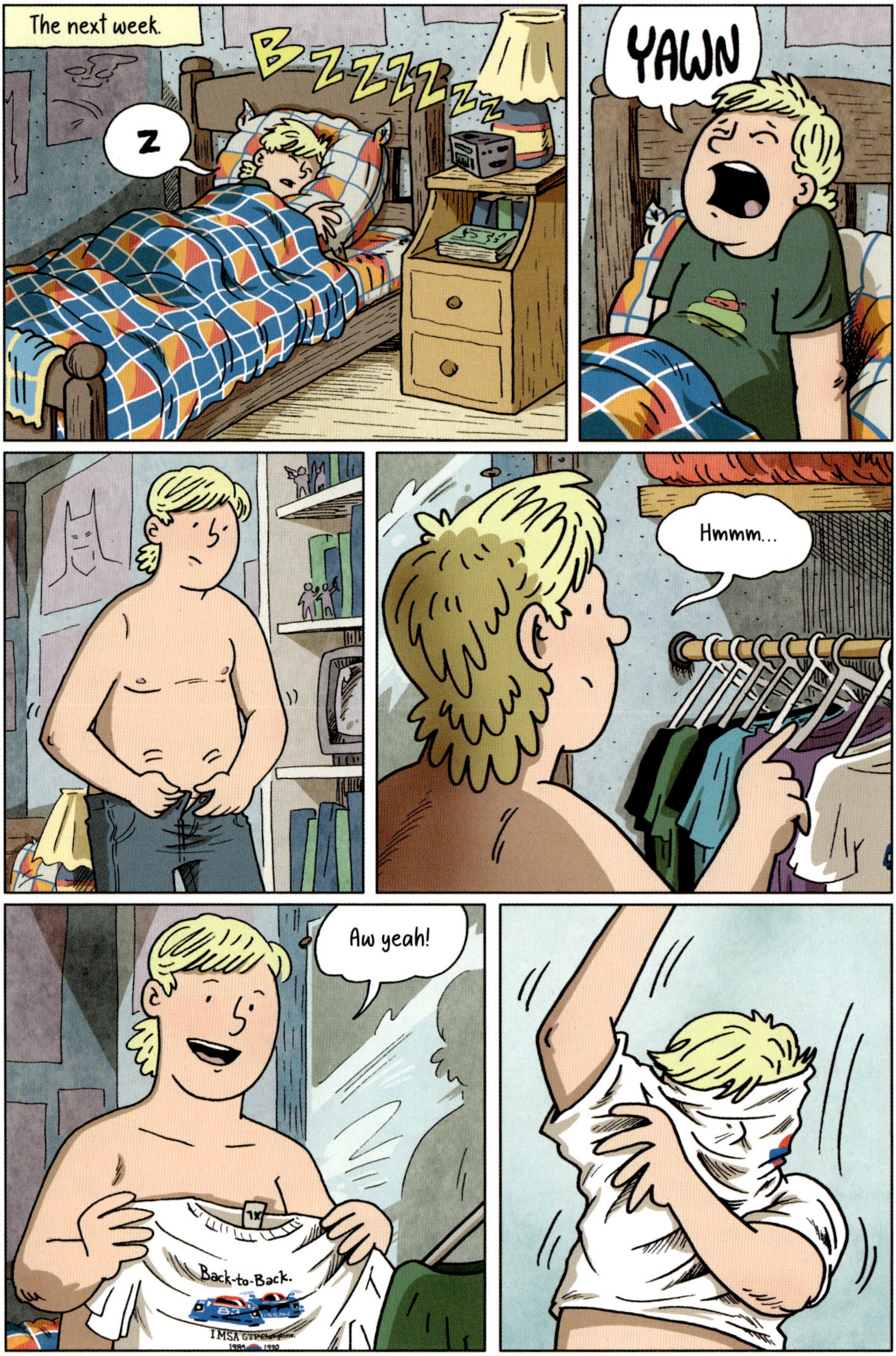
The next week.
BZZZZZzz
Z
YAWN
Hmmm...
Aw yeah!
Back-to-Back.

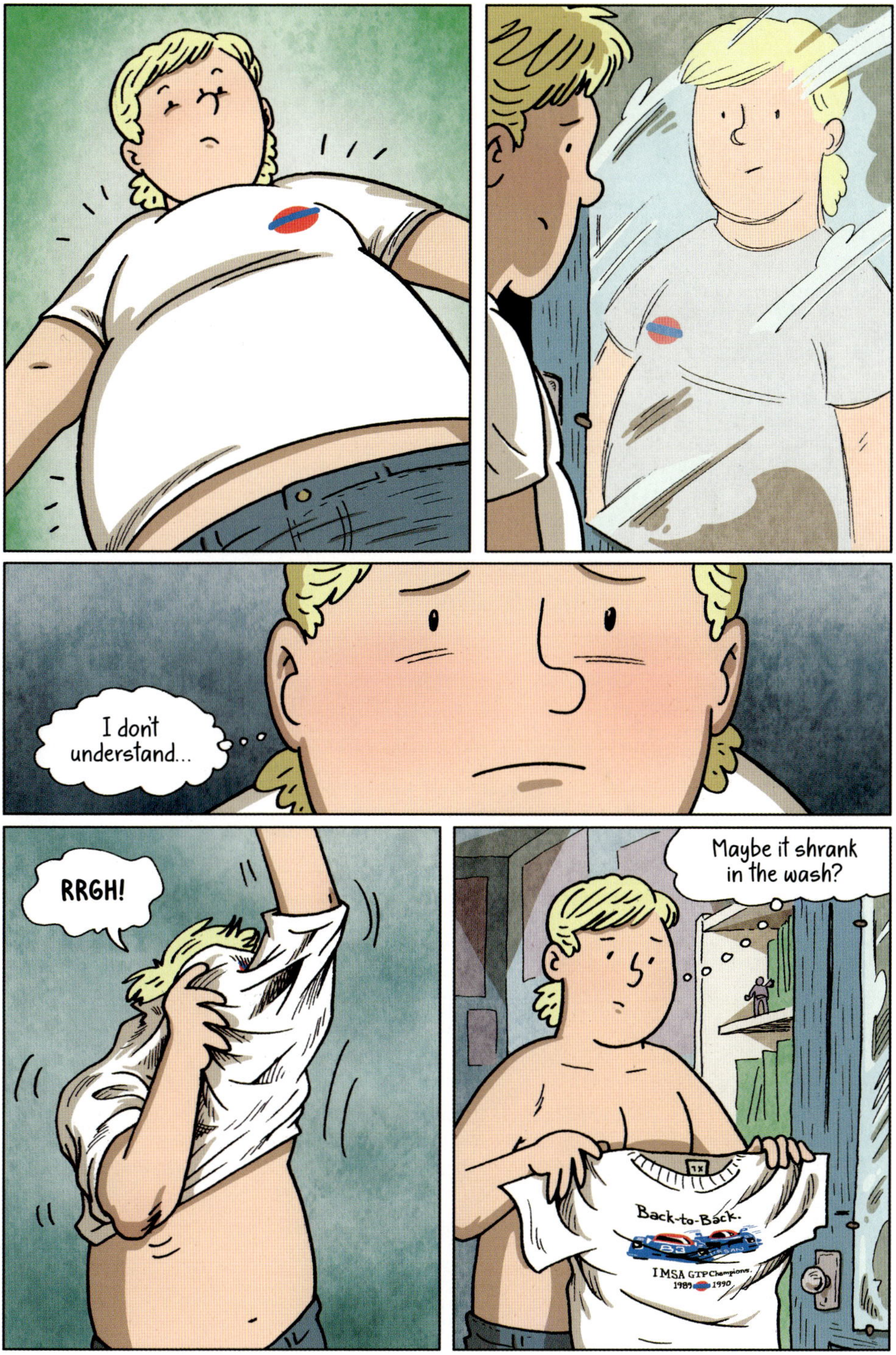
I don't understand...
RRGH!
Maybe it shrank in the wash?
1X
Back-to-Back.
83
IMSA GTP Champions.
1989 1990

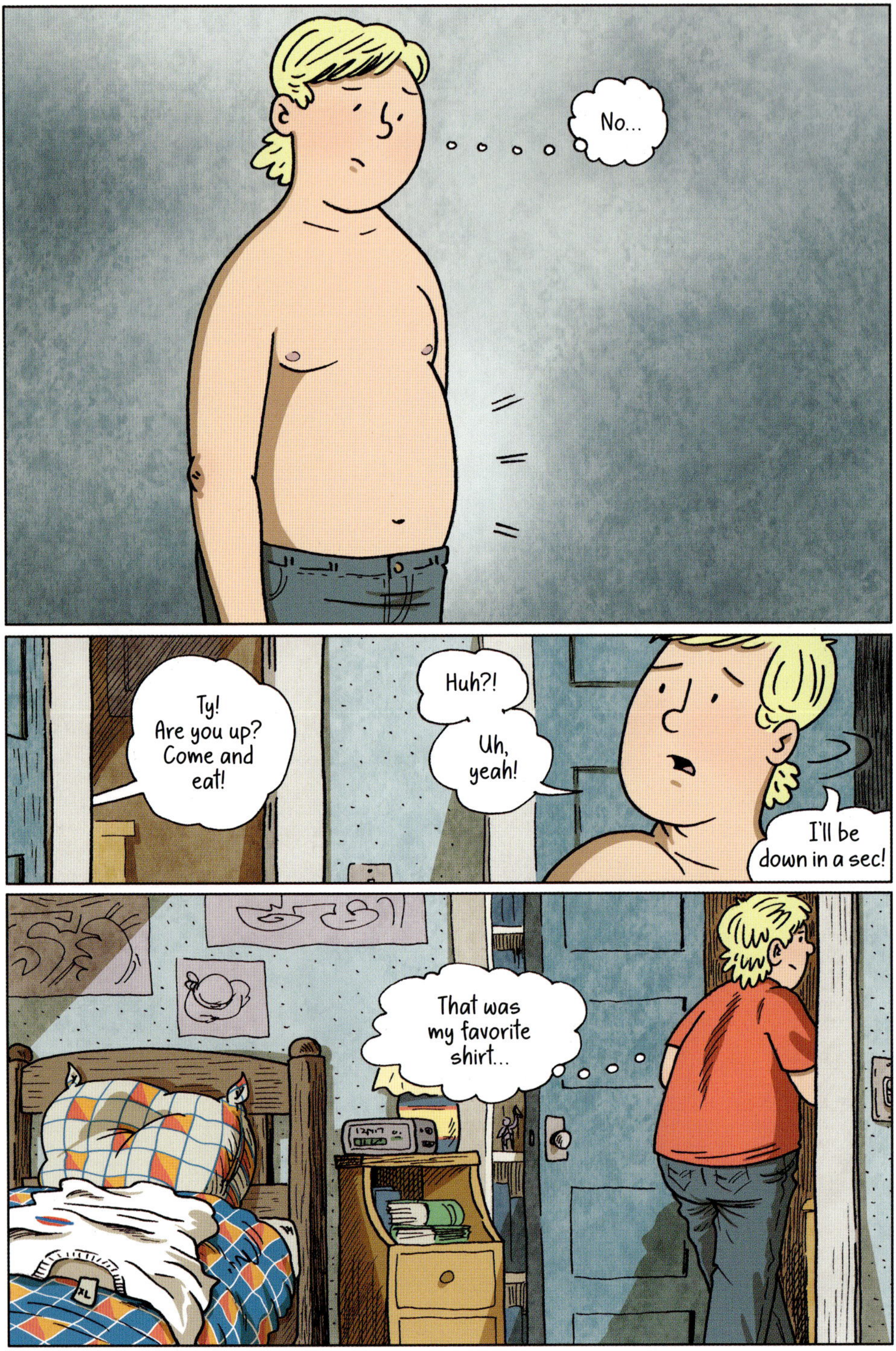
No...
Ty! Are you up? Come and eat!
Huh?!
Uh, yeah!
I'll be down in a sec!
That was my favorite shirt...

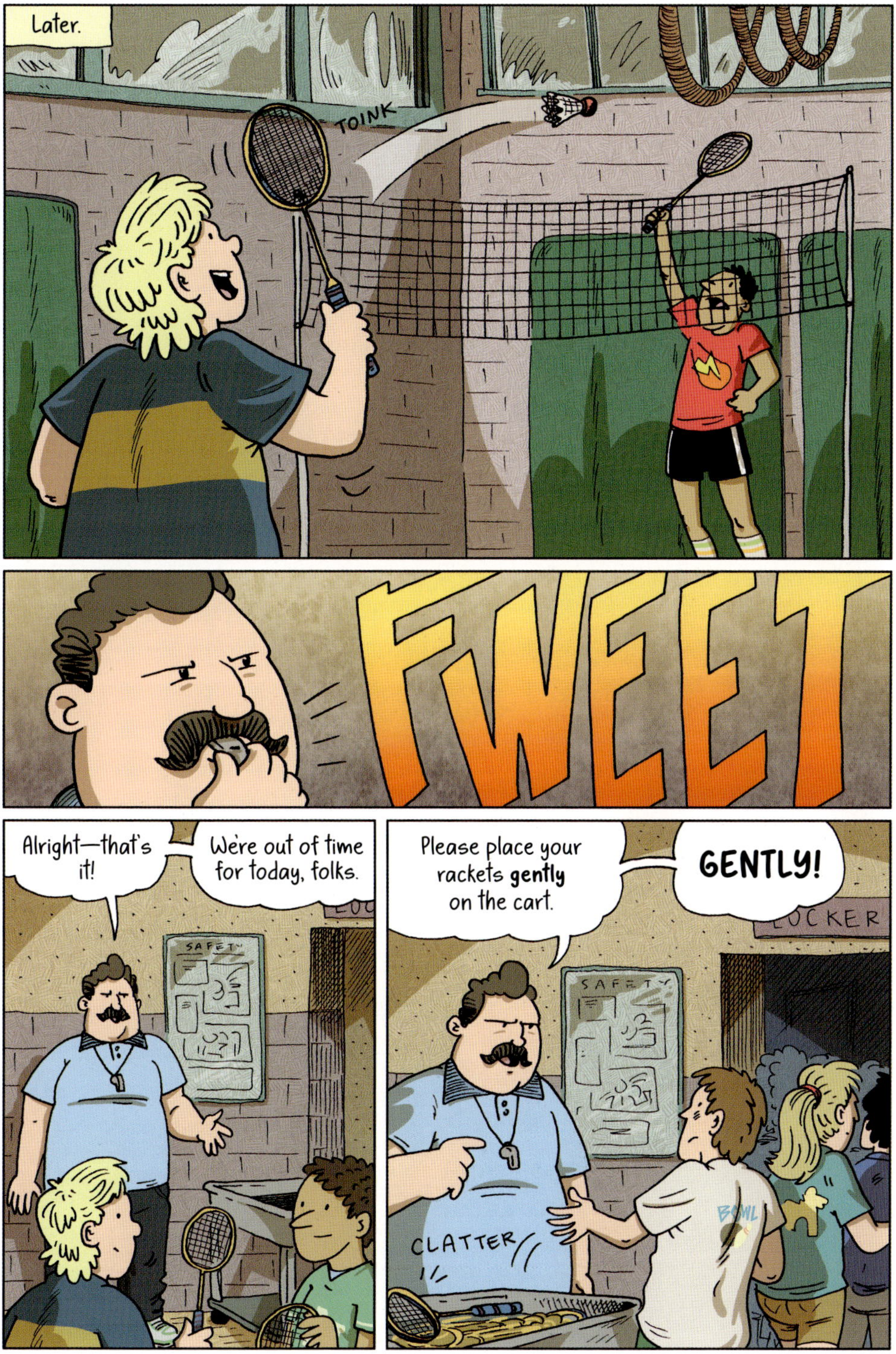
Later.
TOINK
FWEET
Alright—that's it!
We're out of time for today, folks.
SAFETY
Please place your rackets **gently** on the cart.
GENTLY!
LOCKER
SAFETY
CLATTER
BOWL

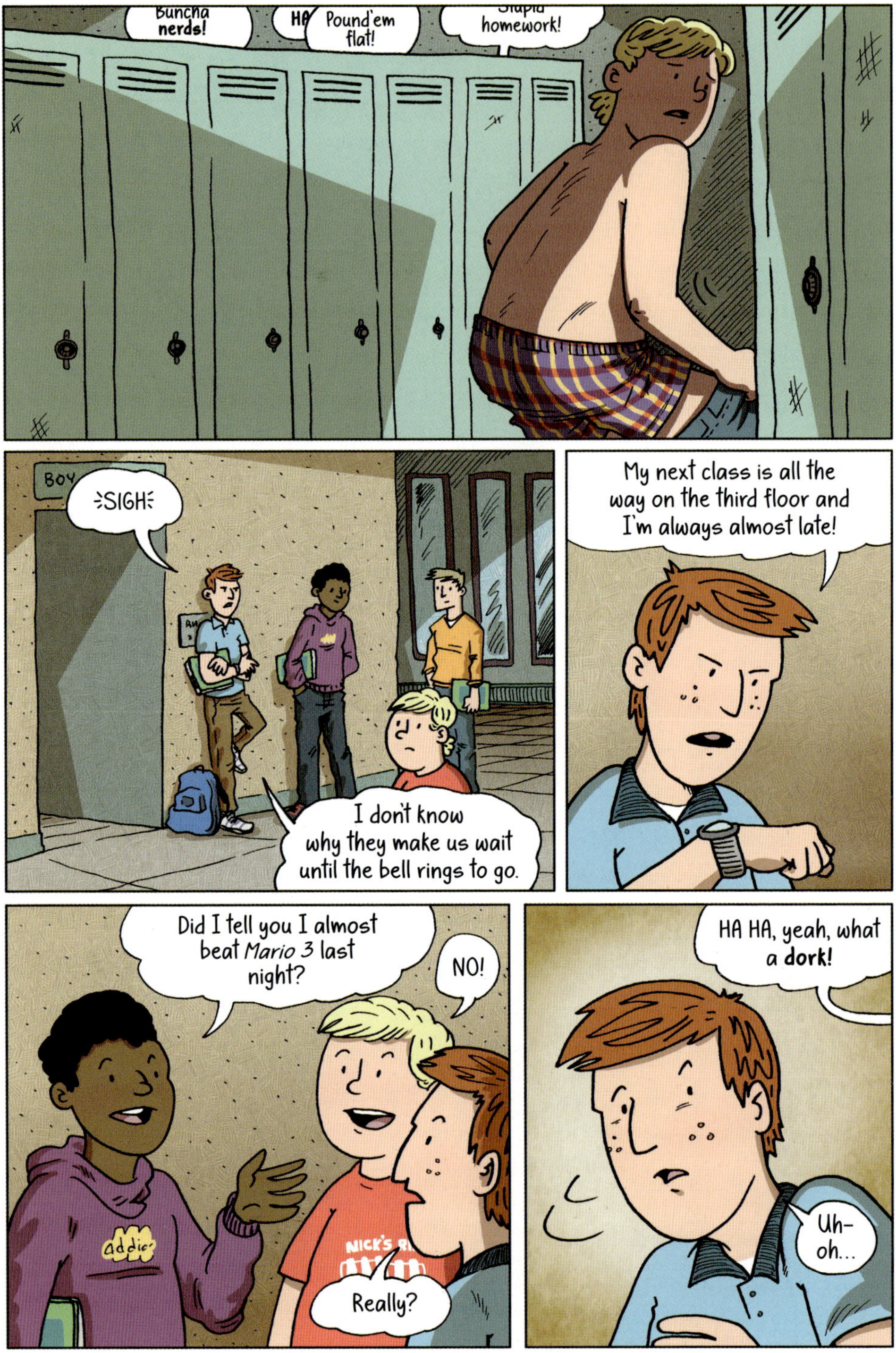
Buncha nerds!
HA
Pound'em flat!
homework!
BOY
SIGH
I don't know why they make us wait until the bell rings to go.
My next class is all the way on the third floor and I'm always almost late!
Did I tell you I almost beat *Mario 3* last night?
NO!
Really?
HA HA, yeah, what a **dork!**
Uh-oh...

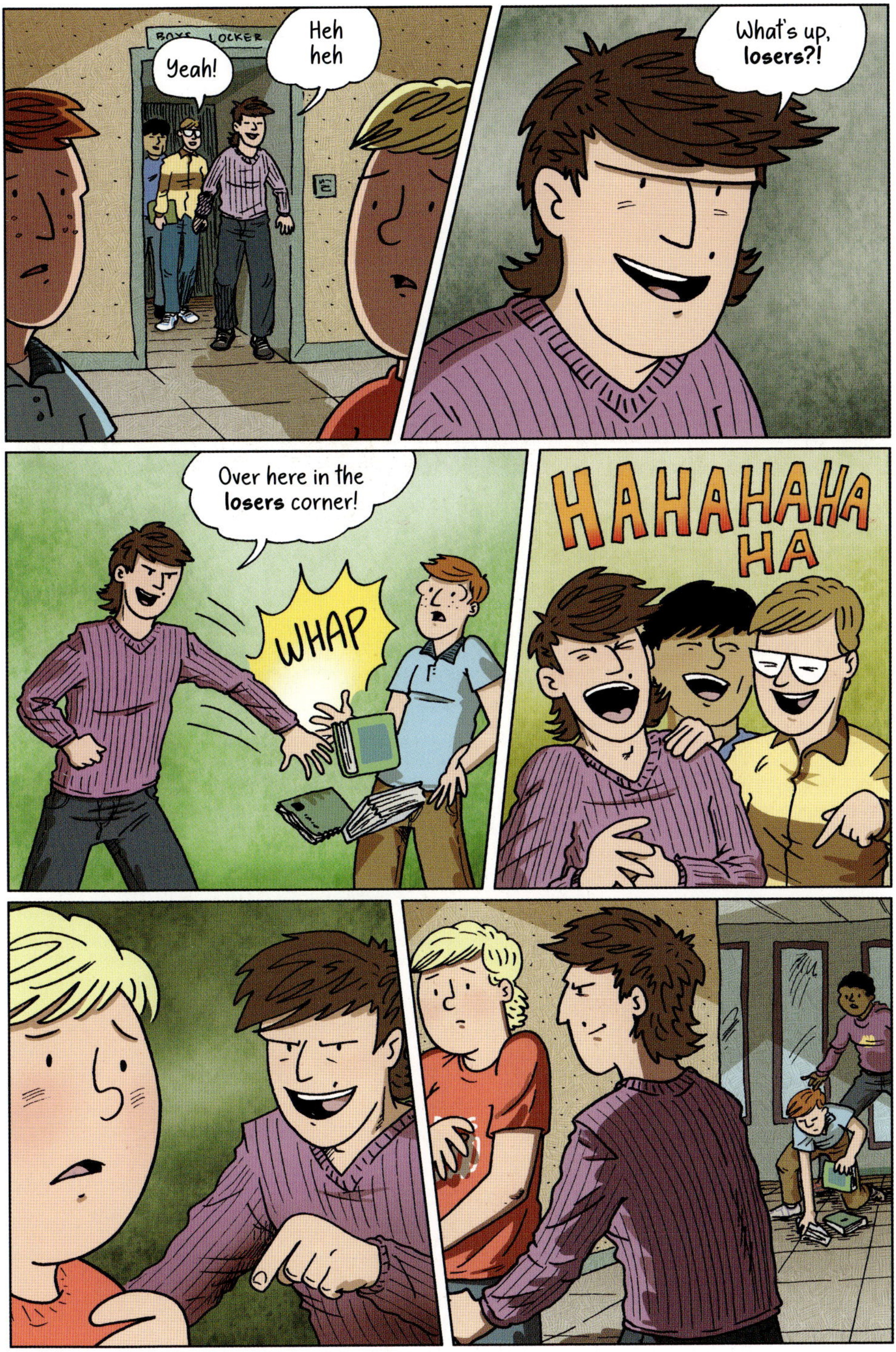
BOYS LOCKER
Yeah!
Heh heh
What's up, **losers?!**
Over here in the **losers** corner!
WHAP
HAHAHAHA HA

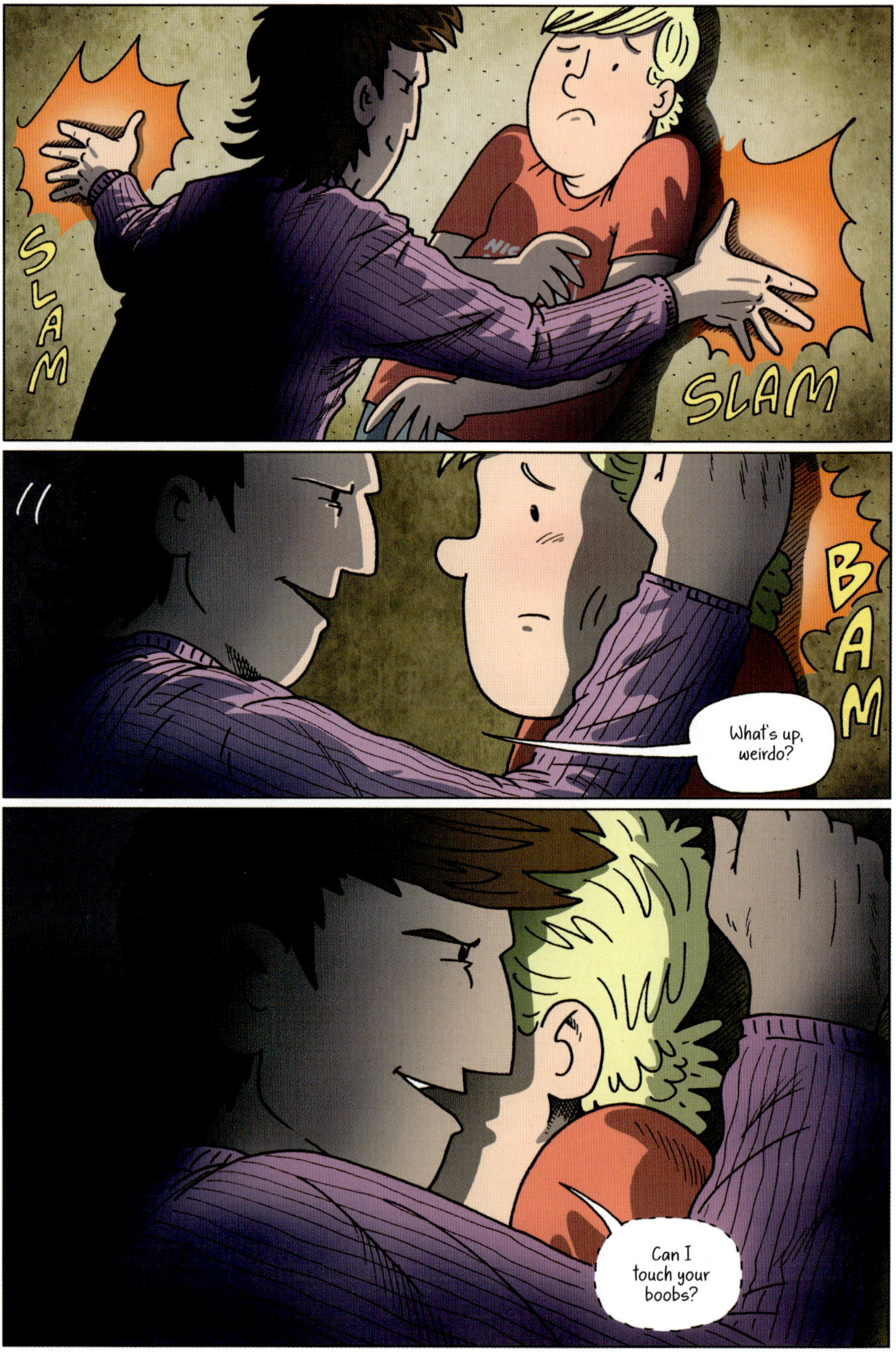
SLAM
SLAM
BAM
What's up, weirdo?
Can I touch your boobs?

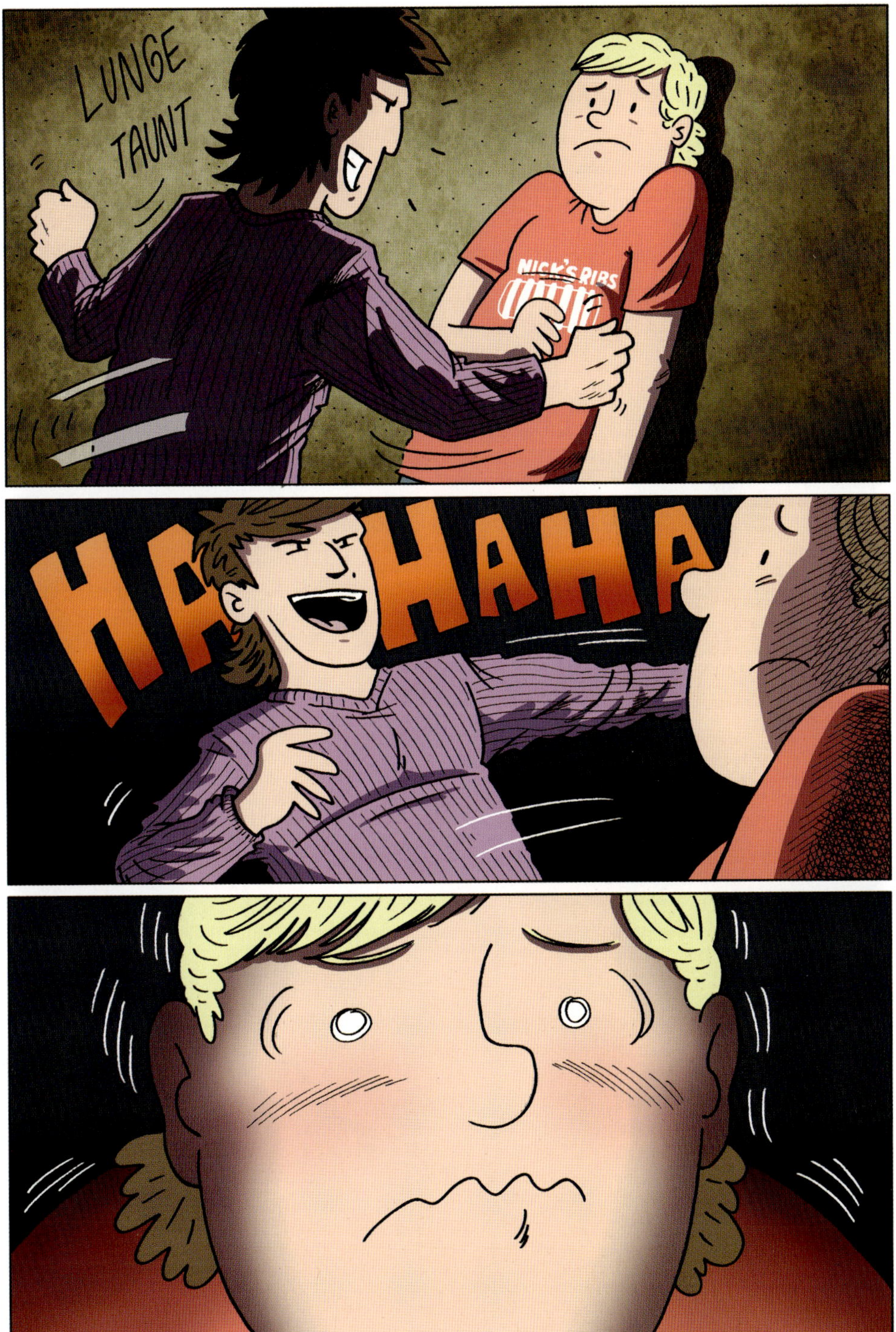

LUNGE
TAUNT
NICK'S RIBS
HAHAHA

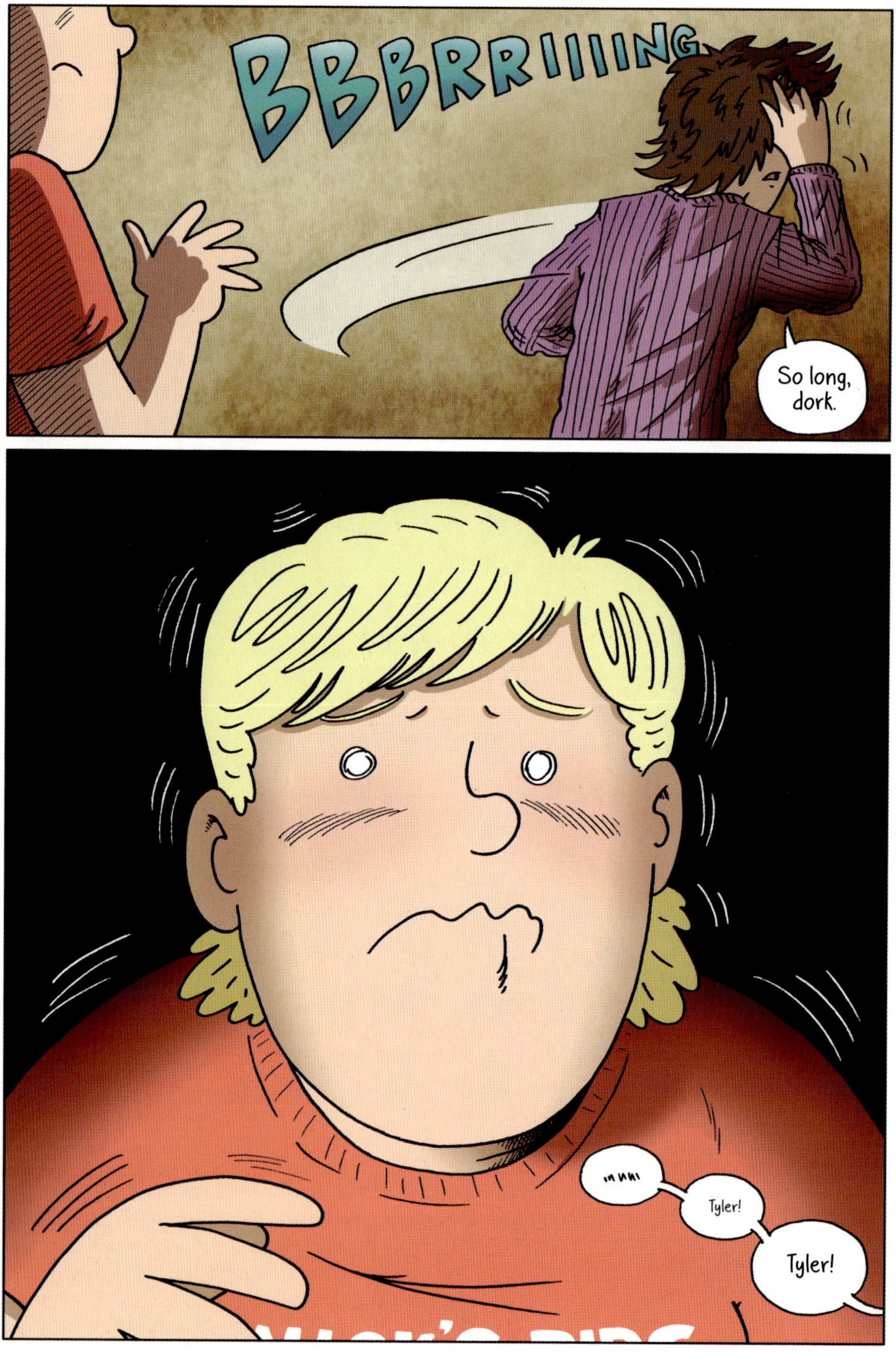
BBBRRIIIING
So long, dork.
Tyler!
Tyler!

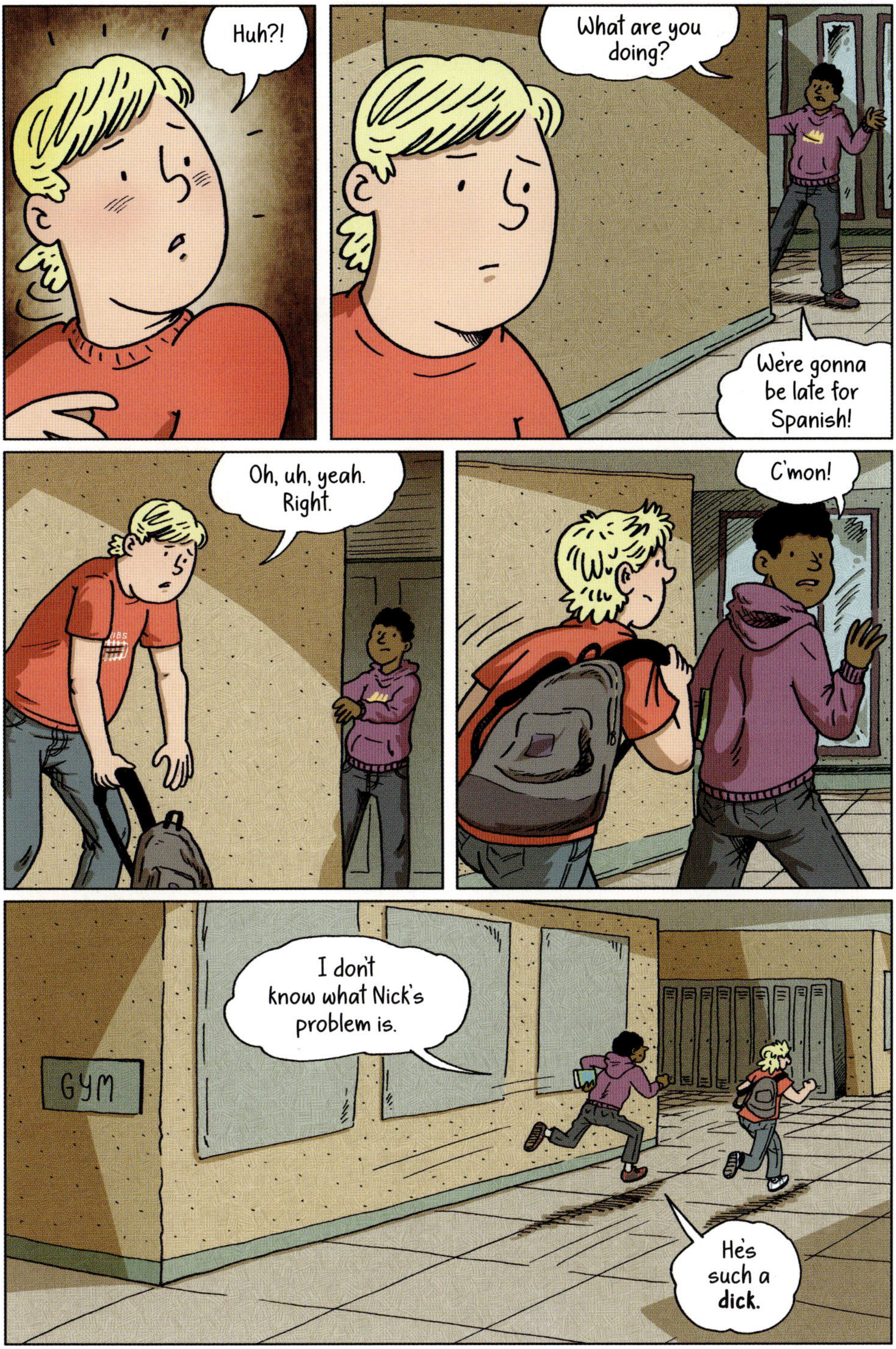
Huh?!
What are you doing?
We're gonna be late for Spanish!
Oh, uh, yeah. Right.
C'mon!
GYM
I don't know what Nick's problem is.
He's such a **dick.**

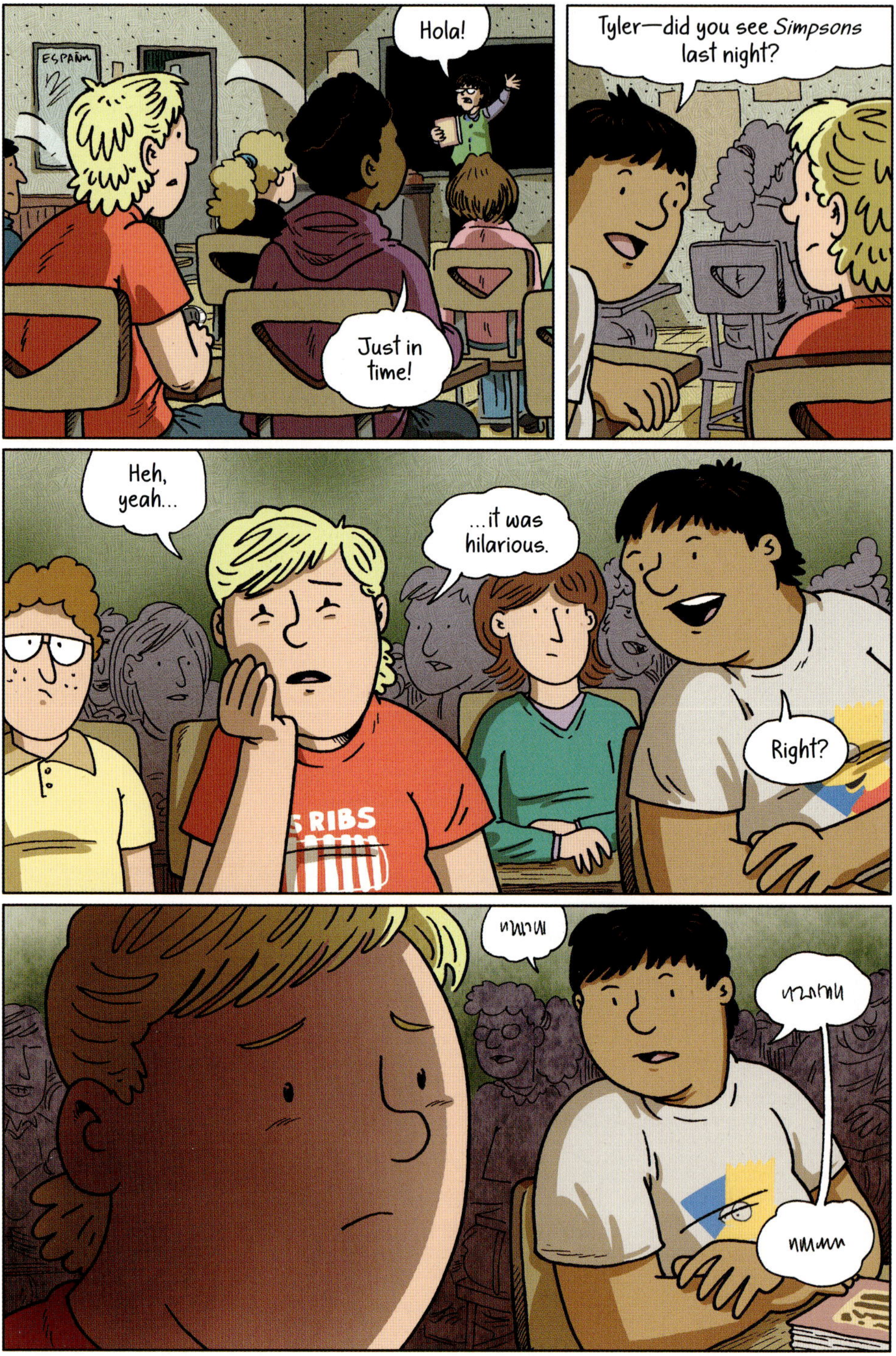
ESPAÑA
Hola!
Just in time!
Tyler—did you see *Simpsons* last night?
Heh, yeah...
...it was hilarious.
S RIBS
Right?

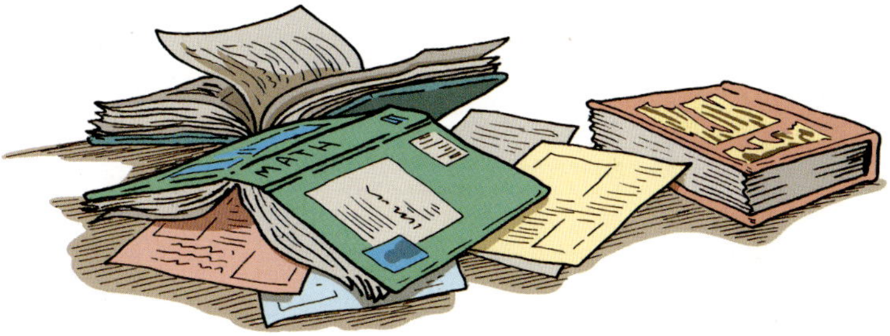
MATH

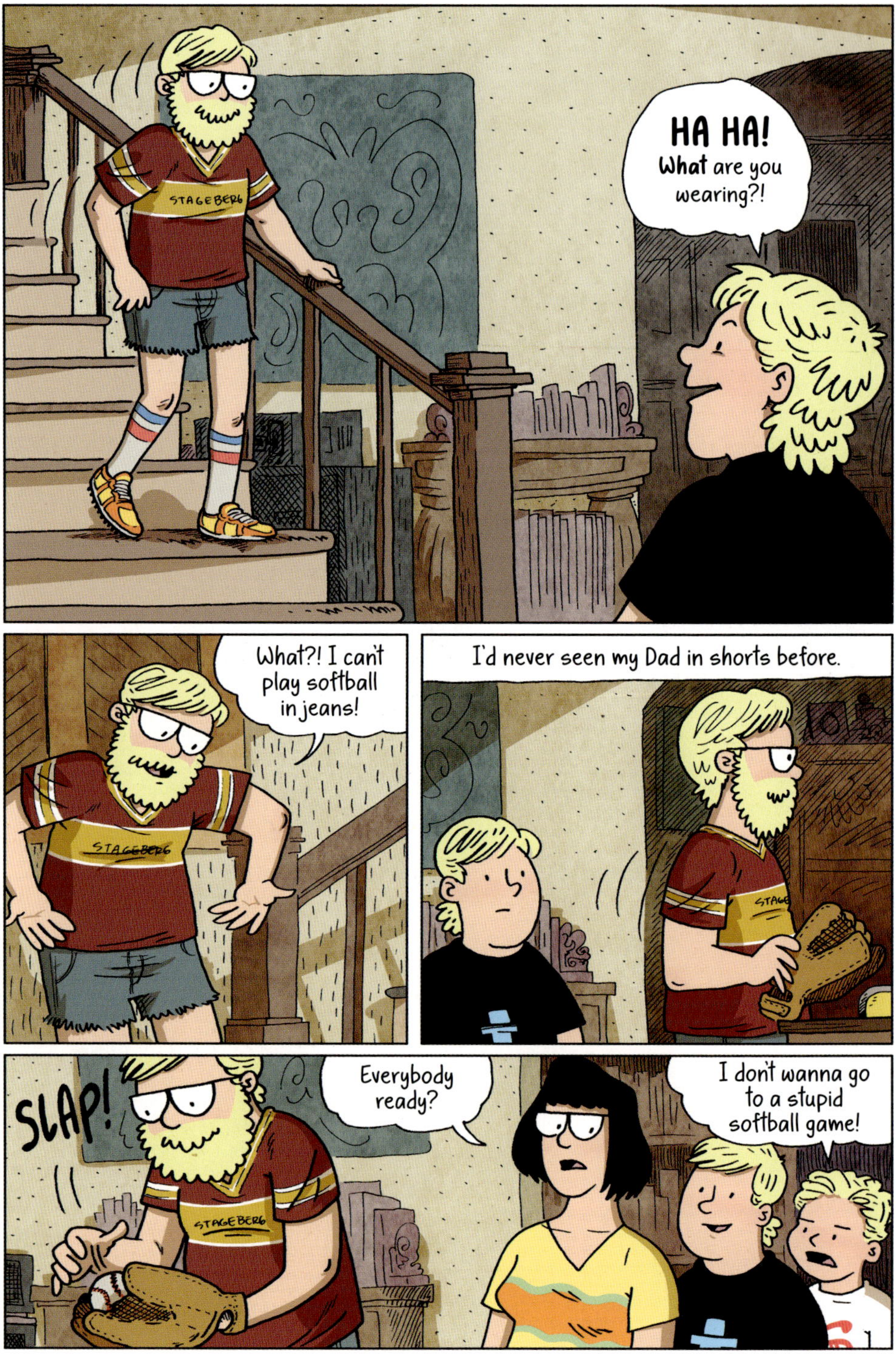
HA HA!
What are you wearing?!
STAGEBERG
What?! I can't play softball in jeans!
STAGEBERG
I'd never seen my Dad in shorts before.
SLAP!
Everybody ready?
STAGEBERG
I don't wanna go to a stupid softball game!

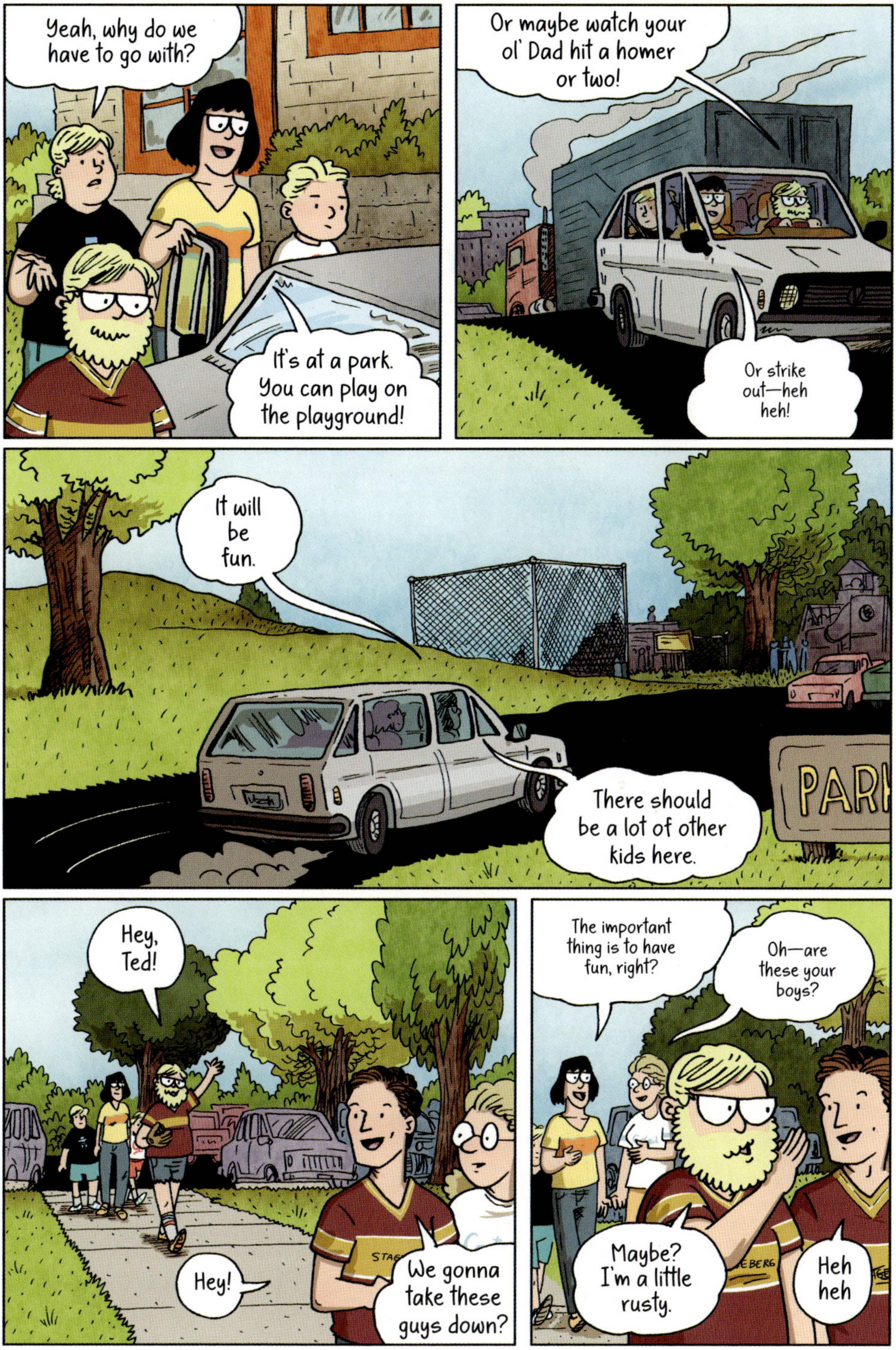
Yeah, why do we have to go with?
It's at a park. You can play on the playground!
Or maybe watch your ol' Dad hit a homer or two!
Or strike out—heh heh!
It will be fun.
There should be a lot of other kids here.
PARK
Hey, Ted!
Hey!
We gonna take these guys down?
The important thing is to have fun, right?
Oh—are these your boys?
Maybe? I'm a little rusty.
Heh heh

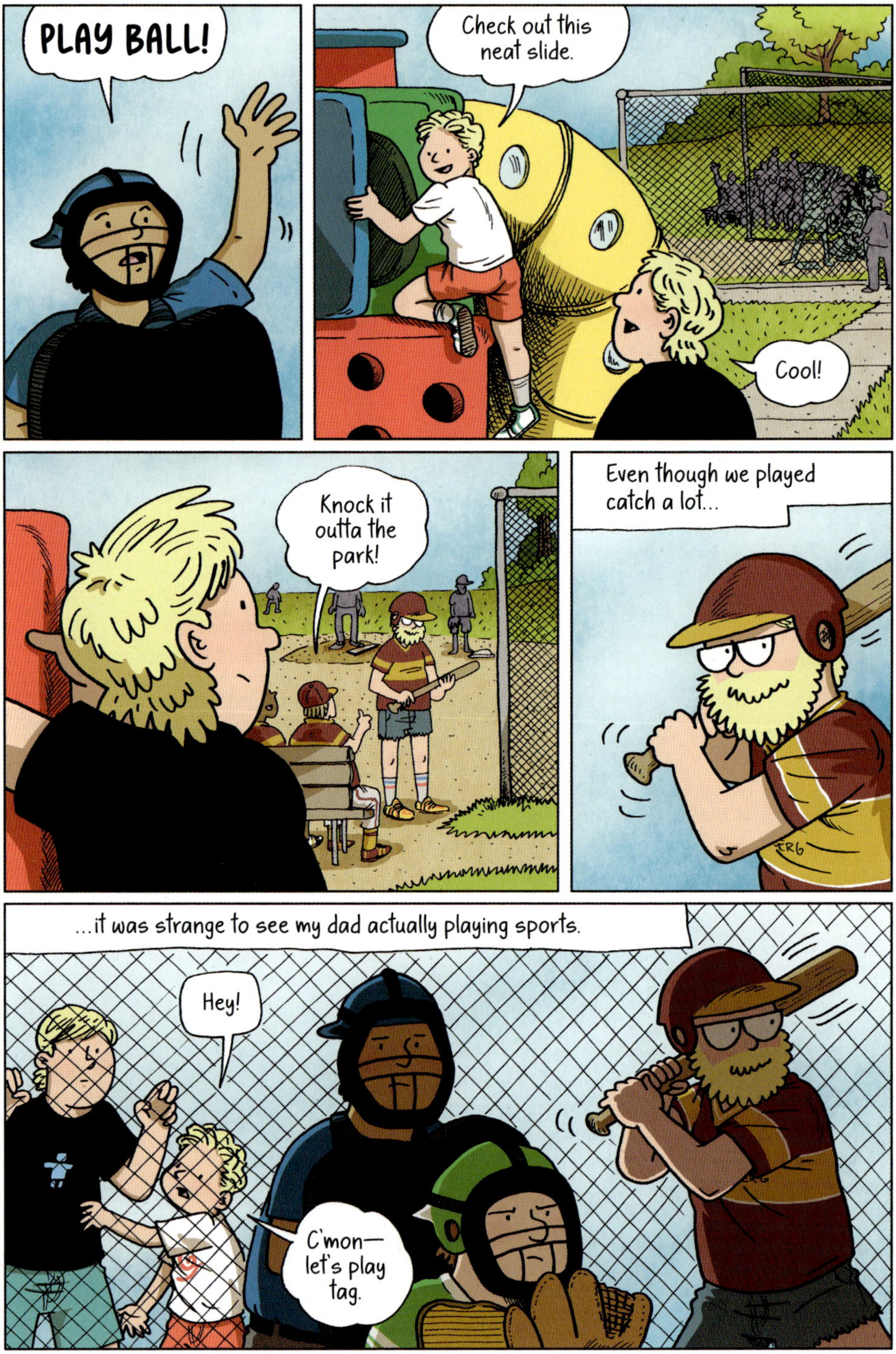
PLAY BALL!
Check out this neat slide.
Cool!
Knock it outta the park!
Even though we played catch a lot...
...it was strange to see my dad actually playing sports.
Hey!
C'mon— let's play tag.

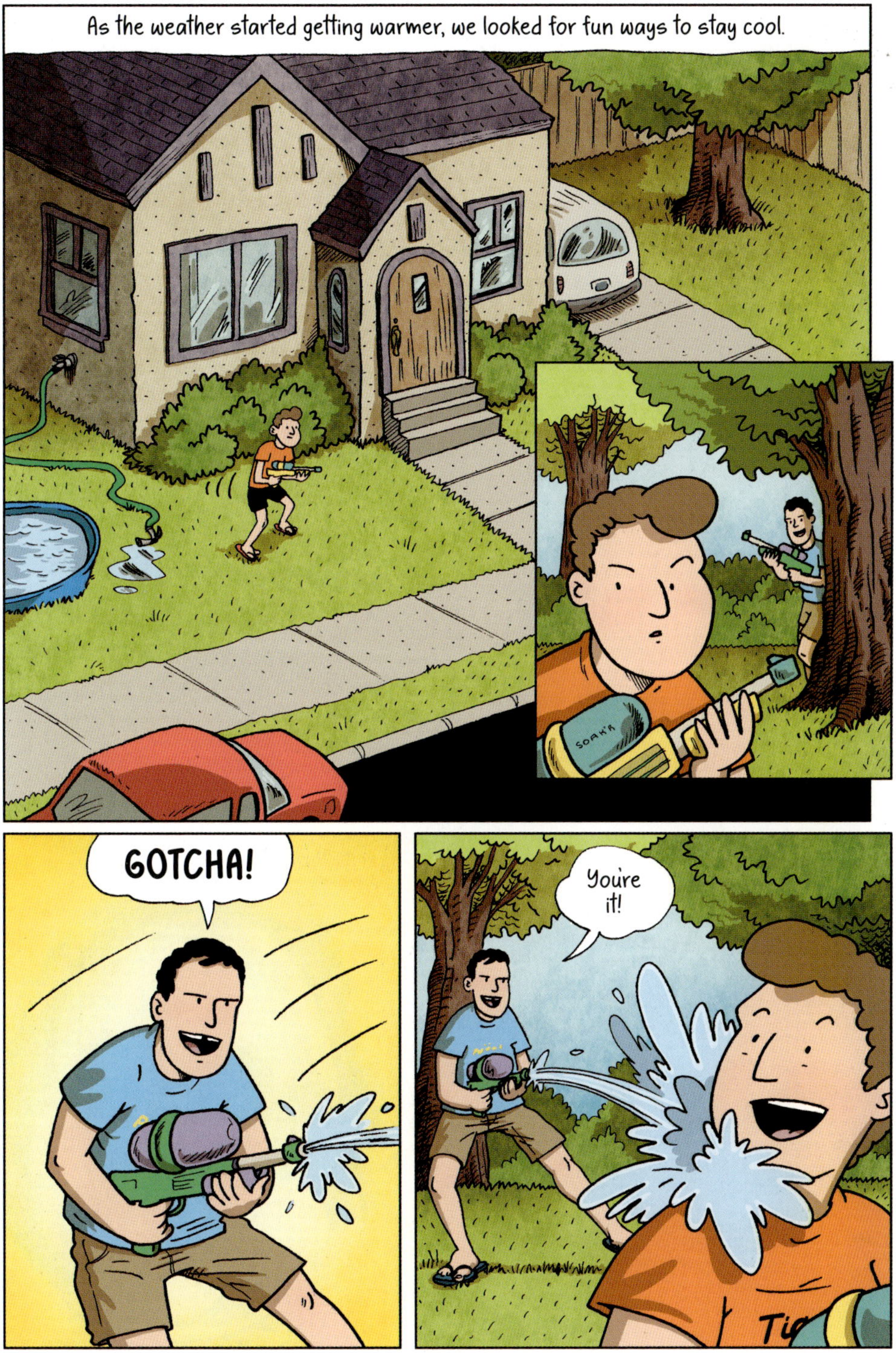
As the weather started getting warmer, we looked for fun ways to stay cool.
SOAK'R
GOTCHA!
You're it!

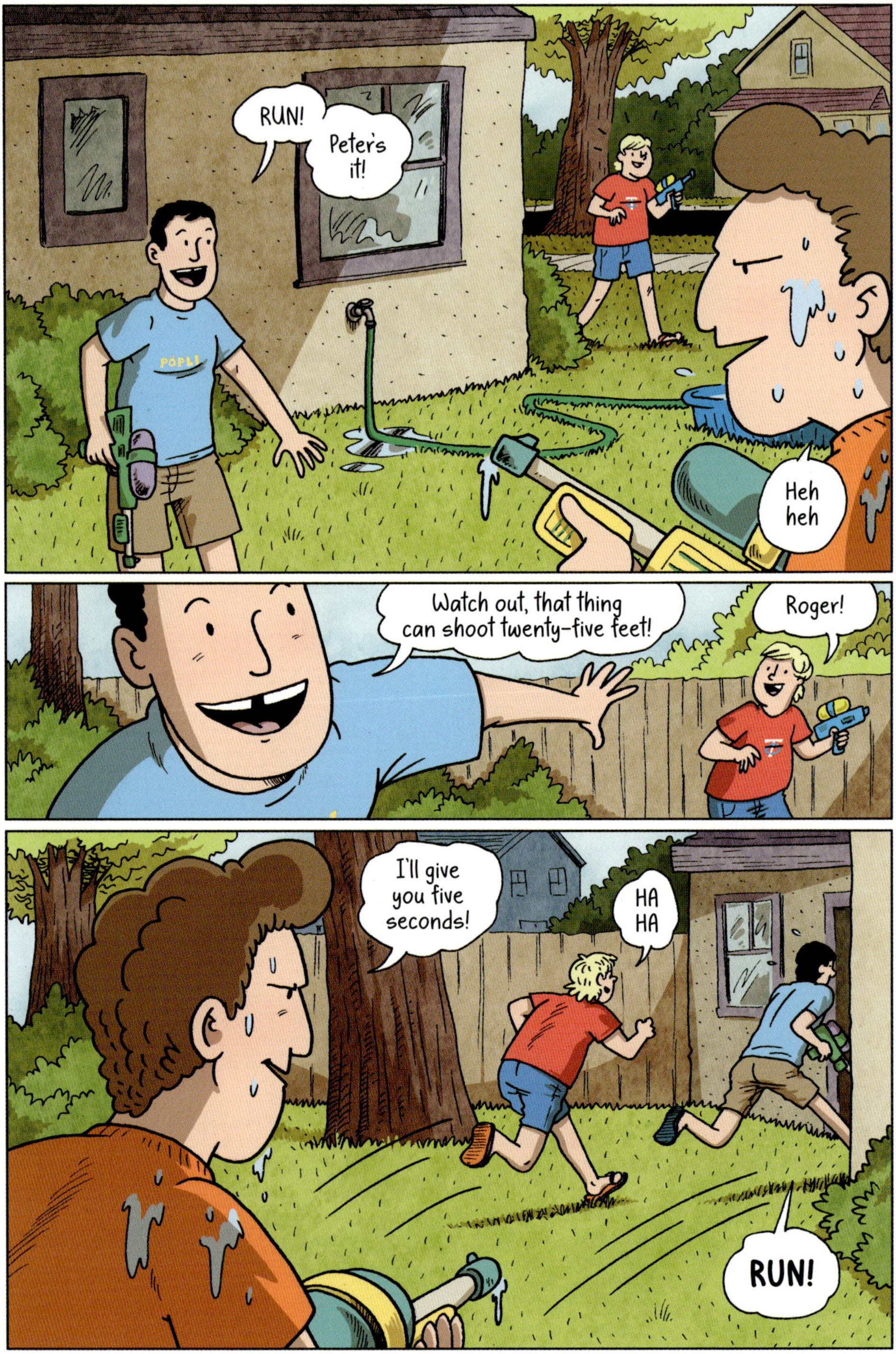
RUN!
Peter's it!
PÖPLI
Heh heh
Watch out, that thing can shoot twenty-five feet!
Roger!
I'll give you five seconds!
HA HA
RUN!

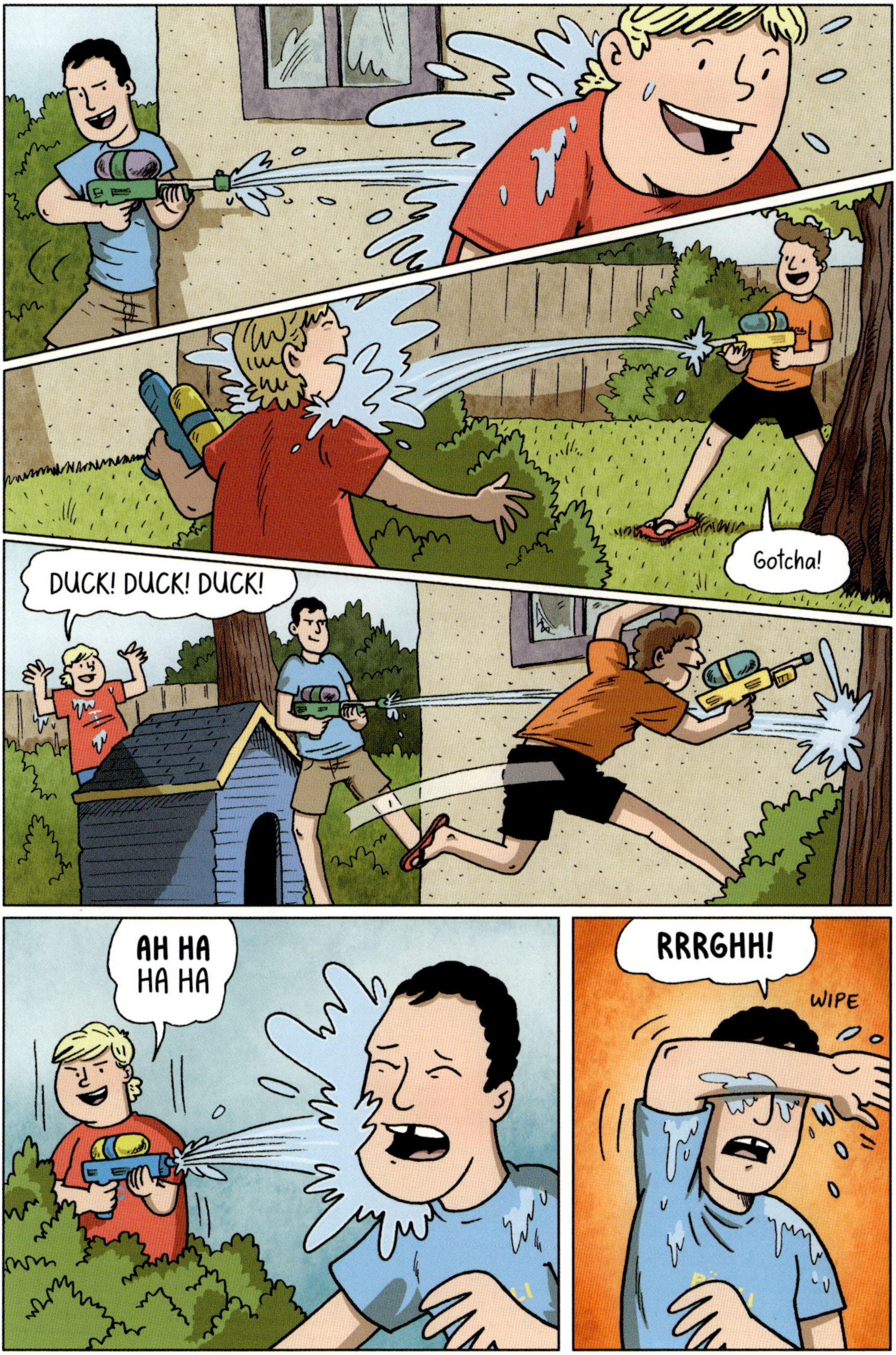
Gotcha!
DUCK! DUCK! DUCK!
AH HA HA HA
RRRGHH!
WIPE

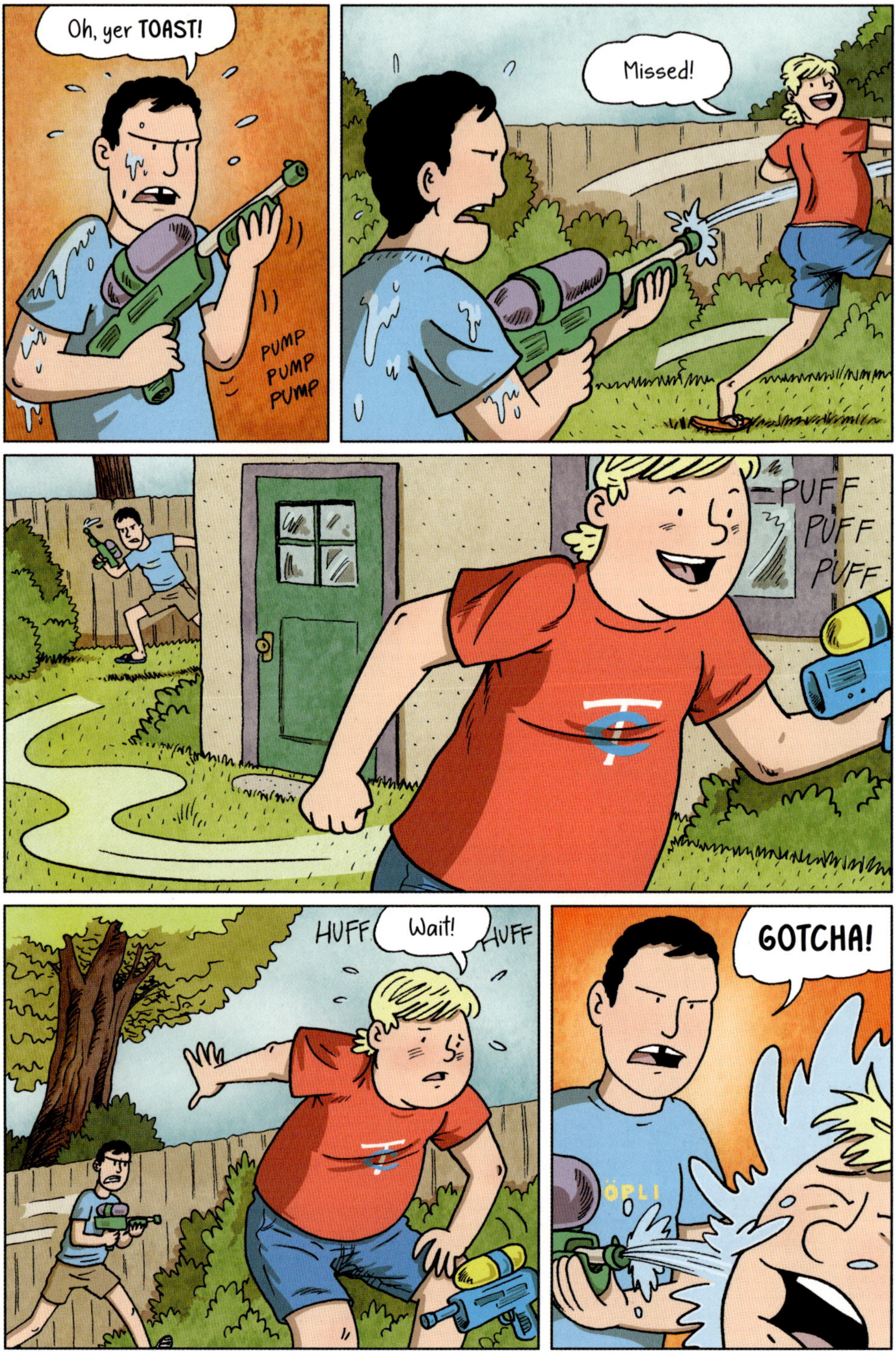
Oh, yer TOAST!
PUMP
PUMP
PUMP
Missed!
PUFF
PUFF
PUFF
HUFF
Wait!
HUFF
GOTCHA!
ÖPLI

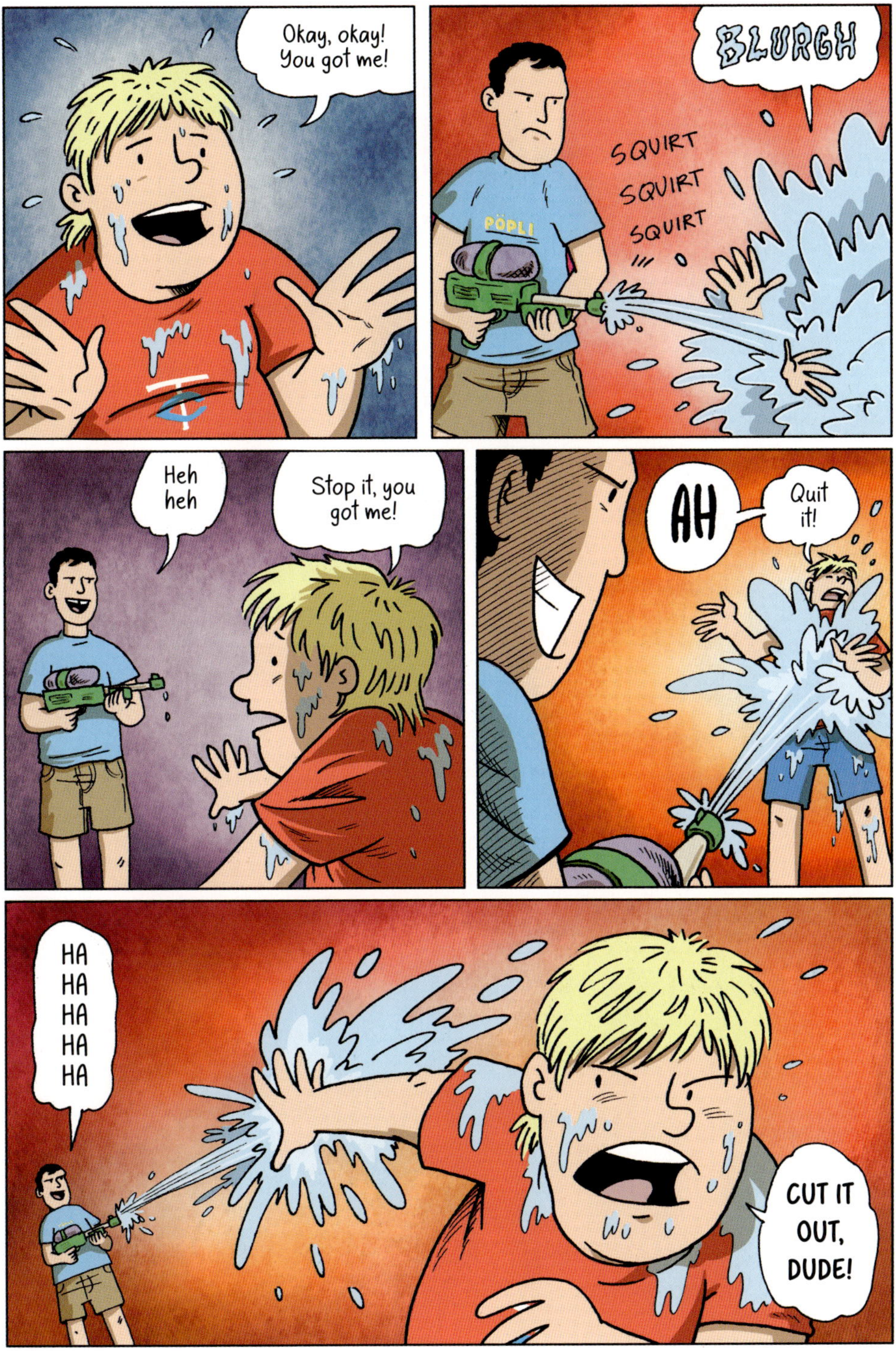
Okay, okay! You got me!
BLURGH
SQUIRT
SQUIRT
SQUIRT
PÖPLI
Heh heh
Stop it, you got me!
AH
Quit it!
HA HA HA HA HA
CUT IT OUT, DUDE!

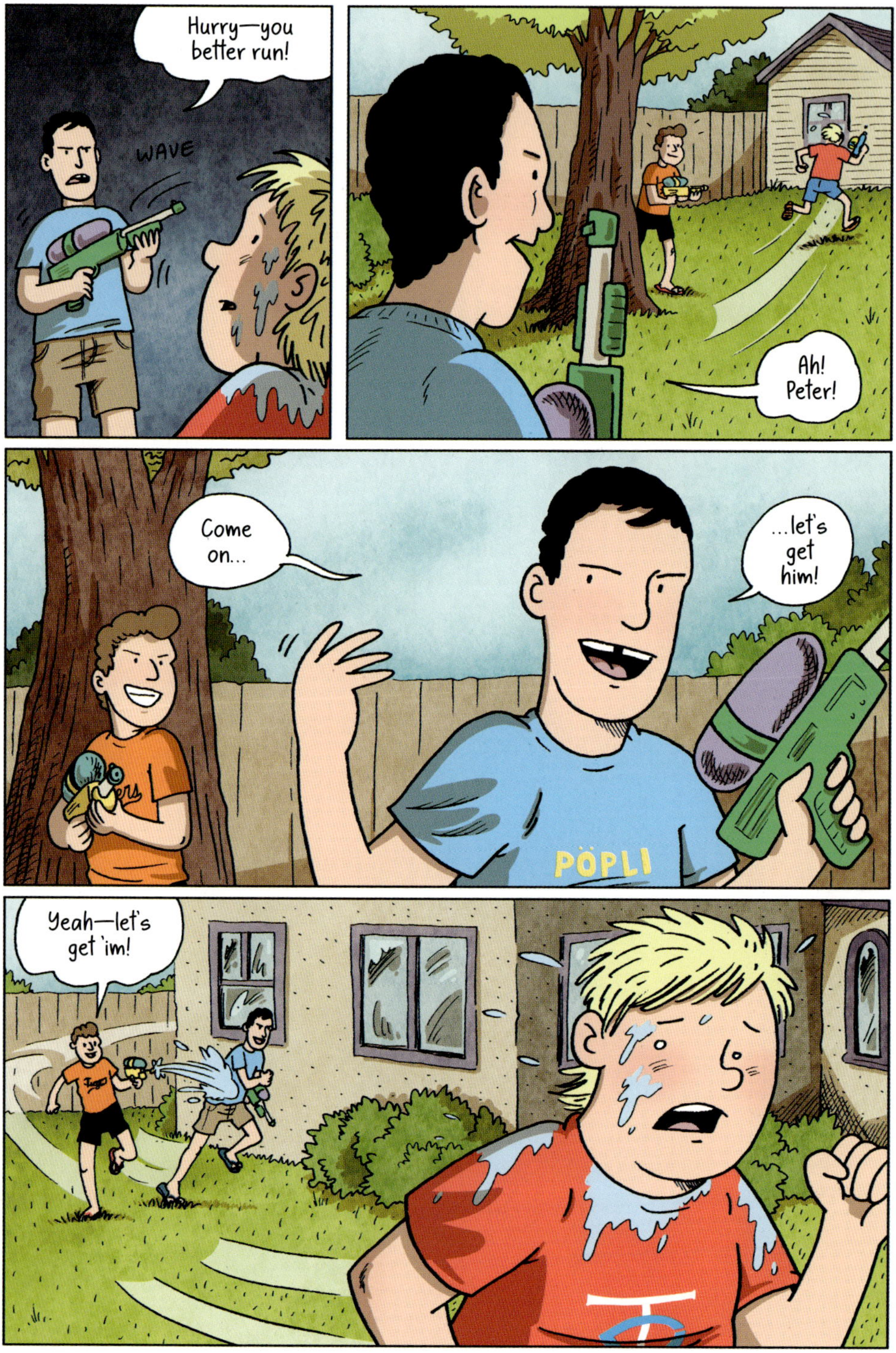
Hurry—you better run!
WAVE
Ah! Peter!
Come on...
...let's get him!
PÖPLI
Yeah—let's get 'im!

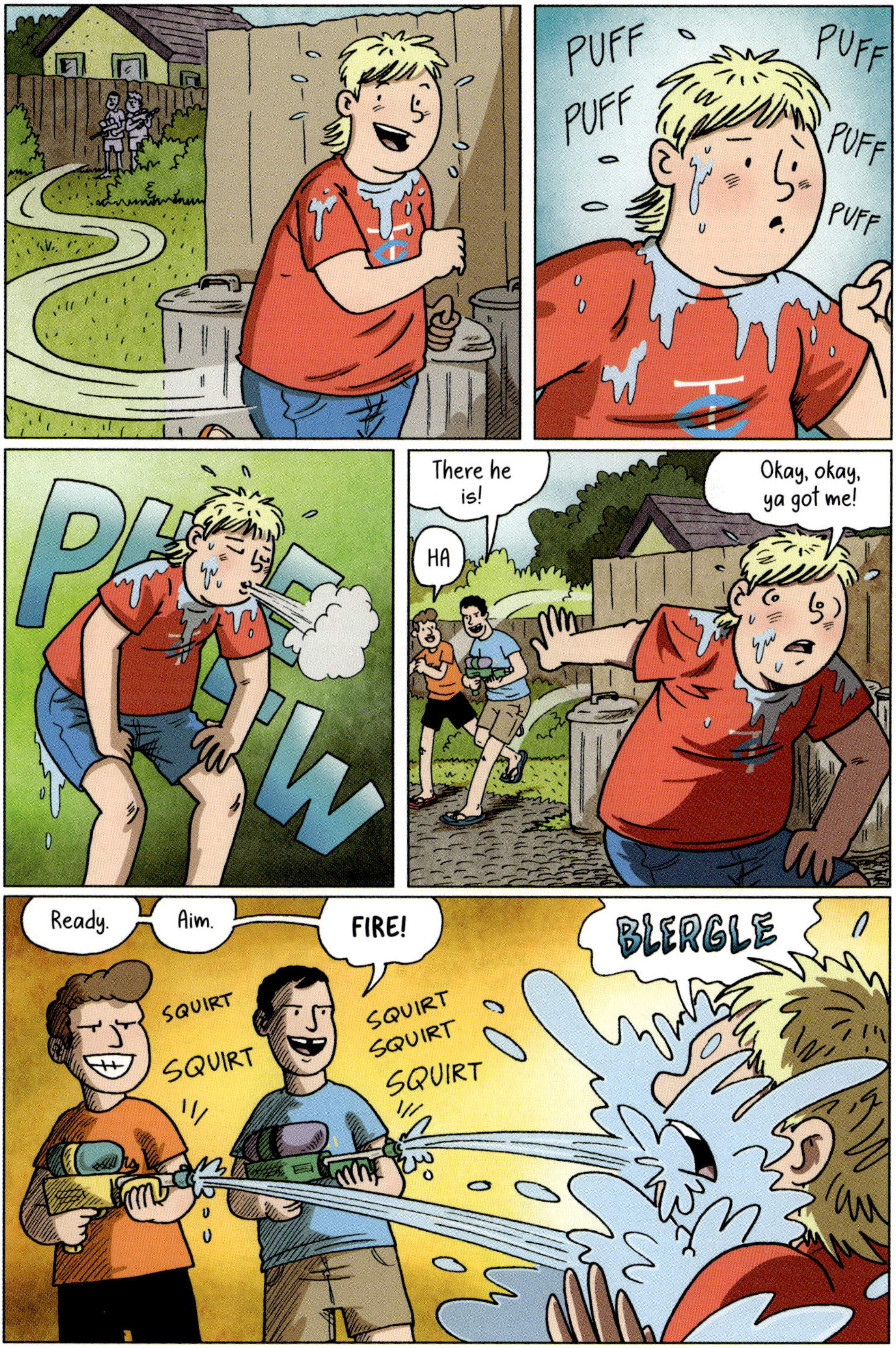
PUFF
PUFF
PUFF
PUFF
PUFF
PHEW
There he is!
HA
Okay, okay, ya got me!
Ready.
Aim.
FIRE!
SQUIRT
SQUIRT
SQUIRT
SQUIRT
SQUIRT
BLERGLE

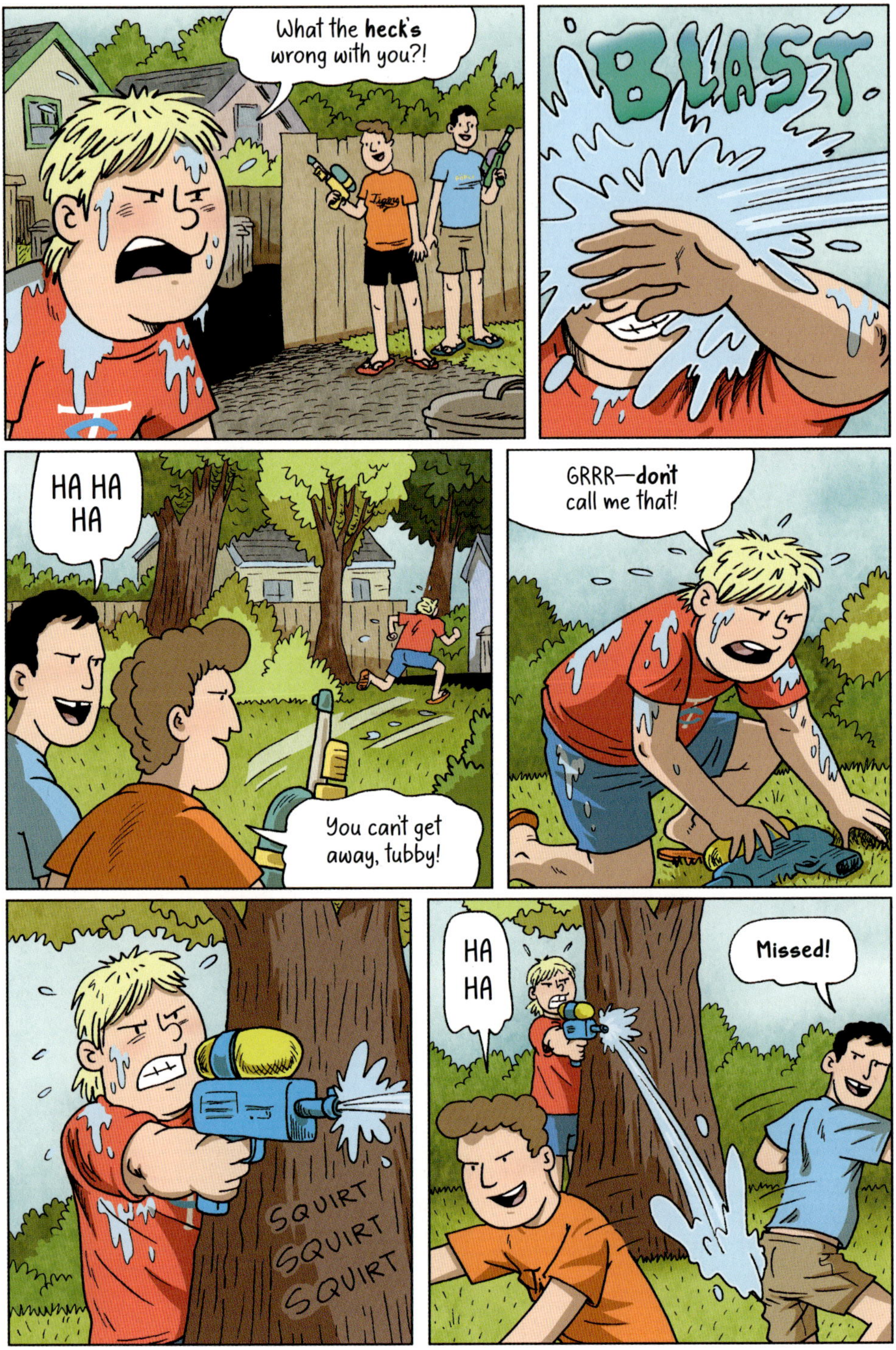
What the **heck's** wrong with you?!
BLAST
HA HA HA
You can't get away, tubby!
GRRR—**don't** call me that!
SQUIRT SQUIRT SQUIRT
HA HA
Missed!

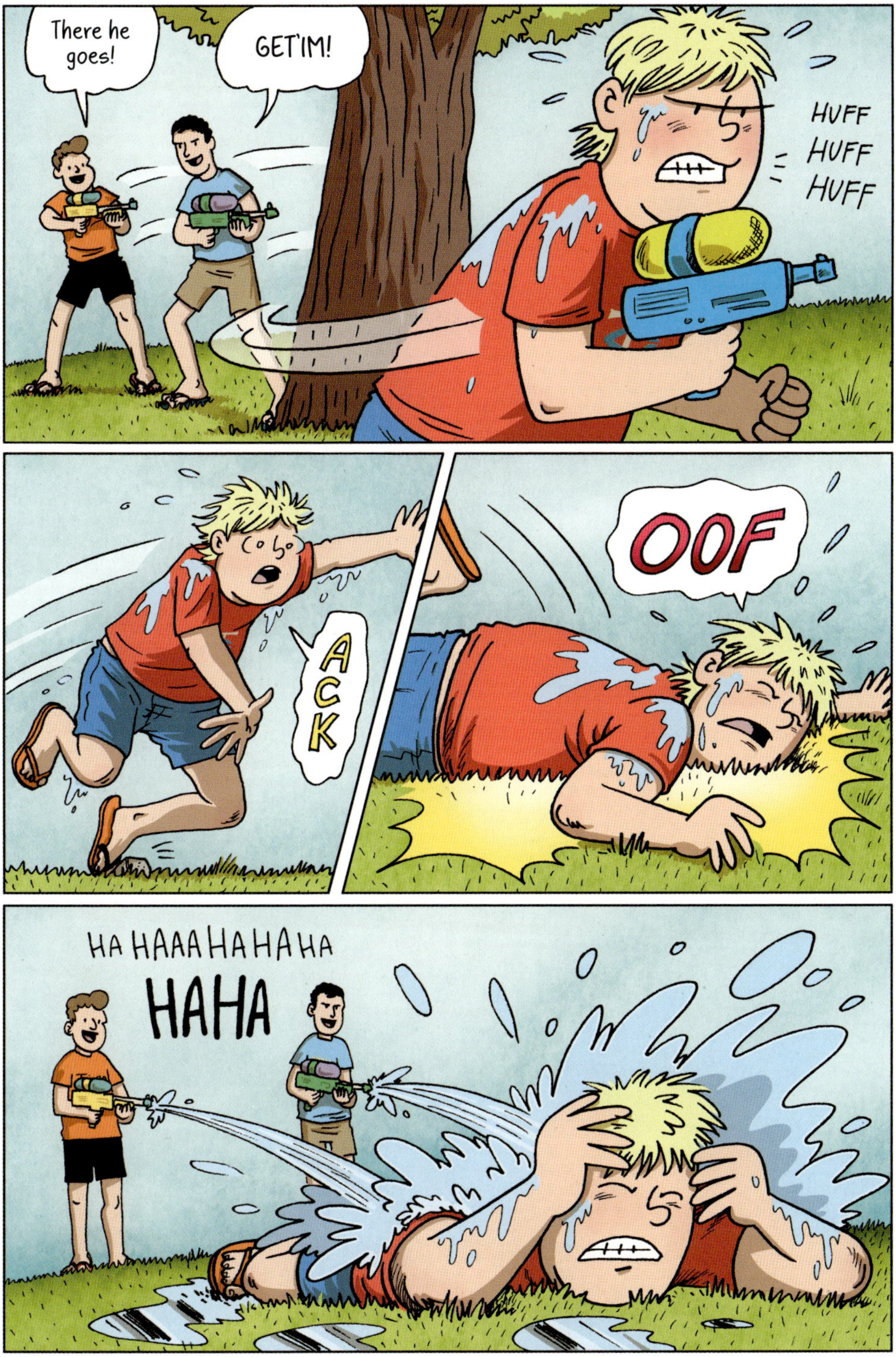
There he goes!
GET'IM!
HUFF
HUFF
HUFF
ACK
OOF
HA HAAA HA HA HA HA
HAHA

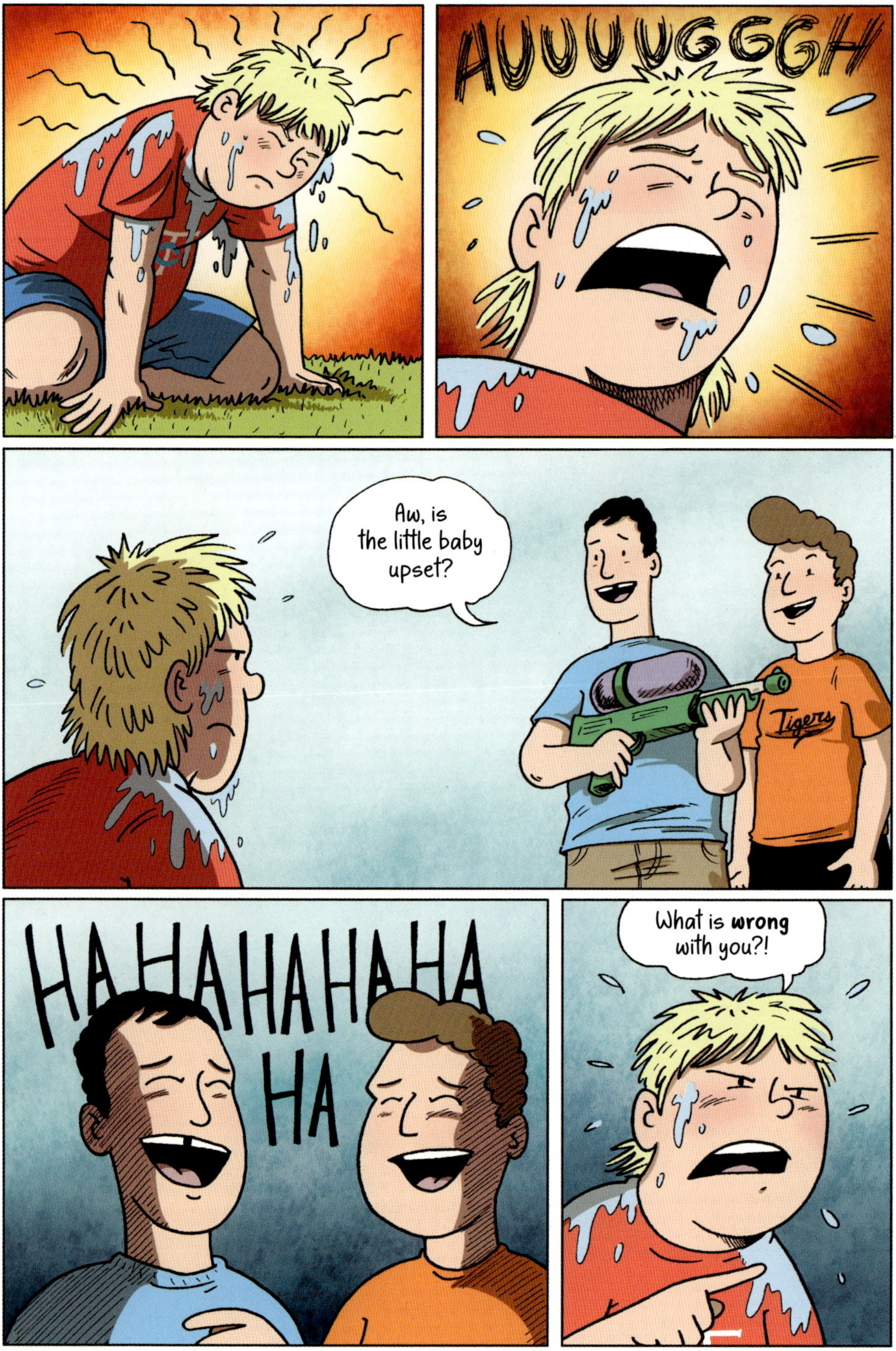
AUUUUGGGH
Aw, is the little baby upset?
Tigers
HAHAHAHAHAHA HA
What is **wrong** with you?!

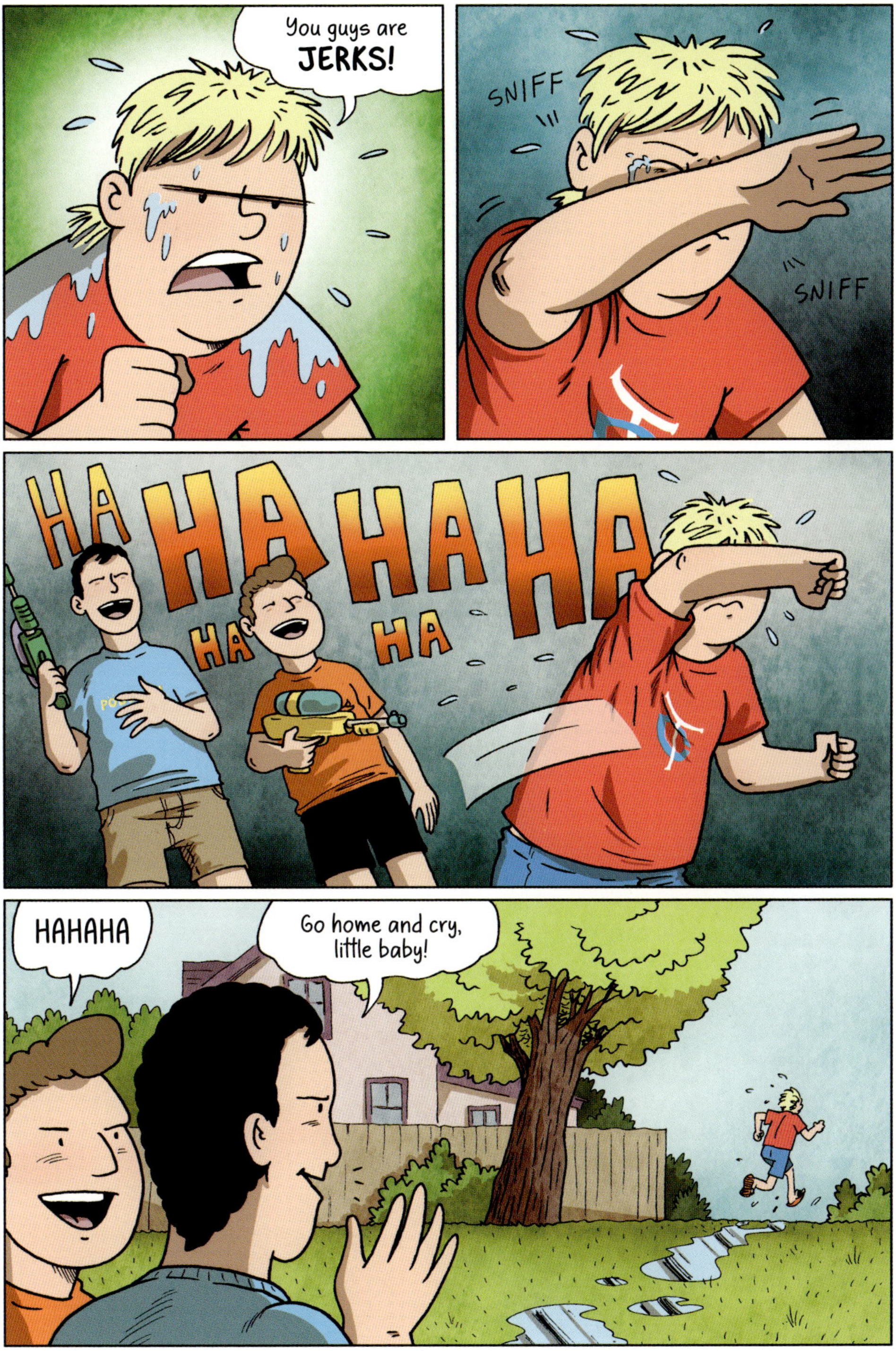
You guys are JERKS!
SNIFF
SNIFF
HA HA HA HA HA HA
HA
HA
HAHAHA
Go home and cry, little baby!

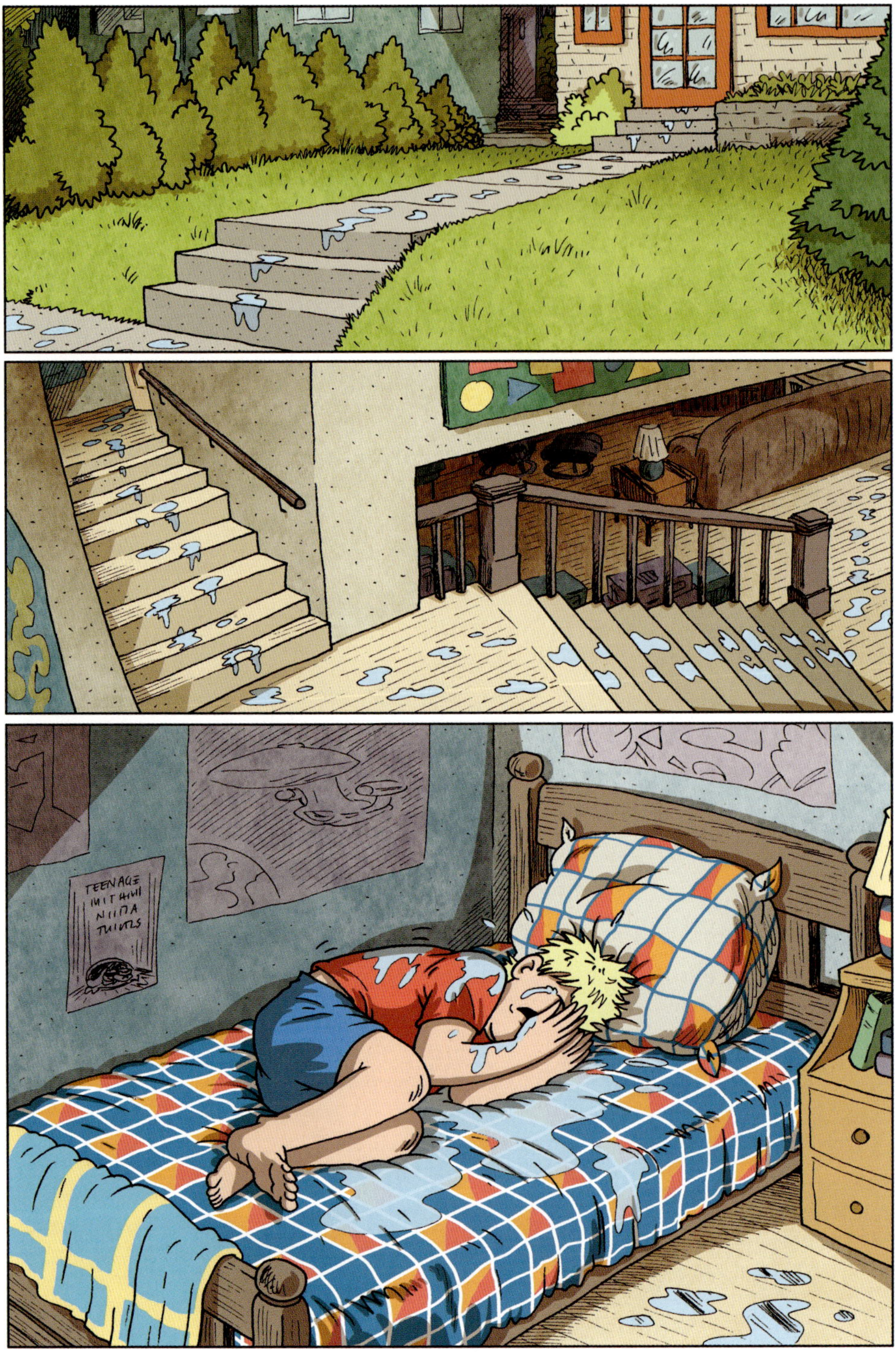
TEENAGE

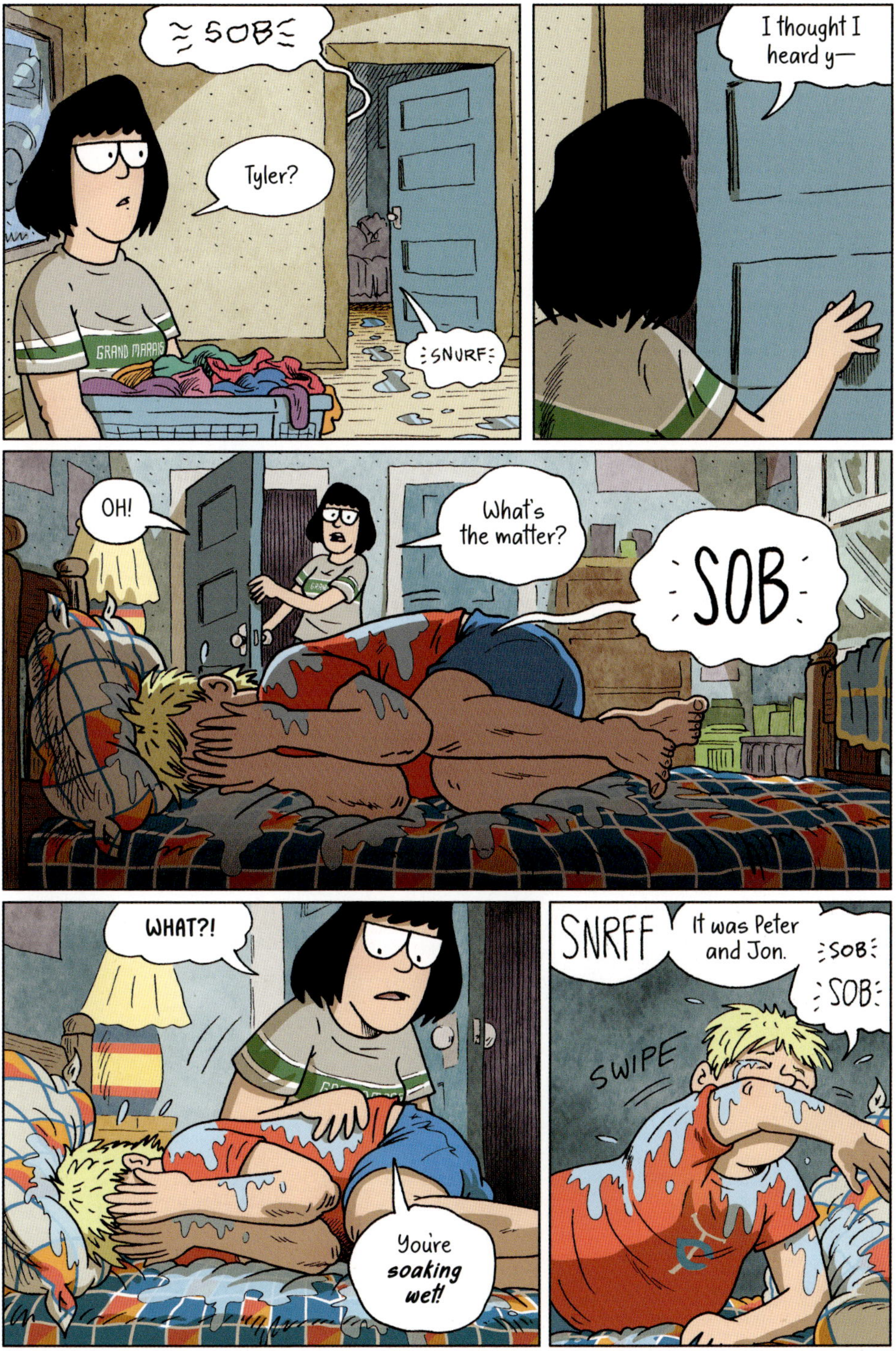
SOB
Tyler?
SNURF
I thought I heard y—
OH!
What's the matter?
SOB
WHAT?!
You're *soaking wet!*
SNRFF
It was Peter and Jon.
SOB
SOB
SWIPE

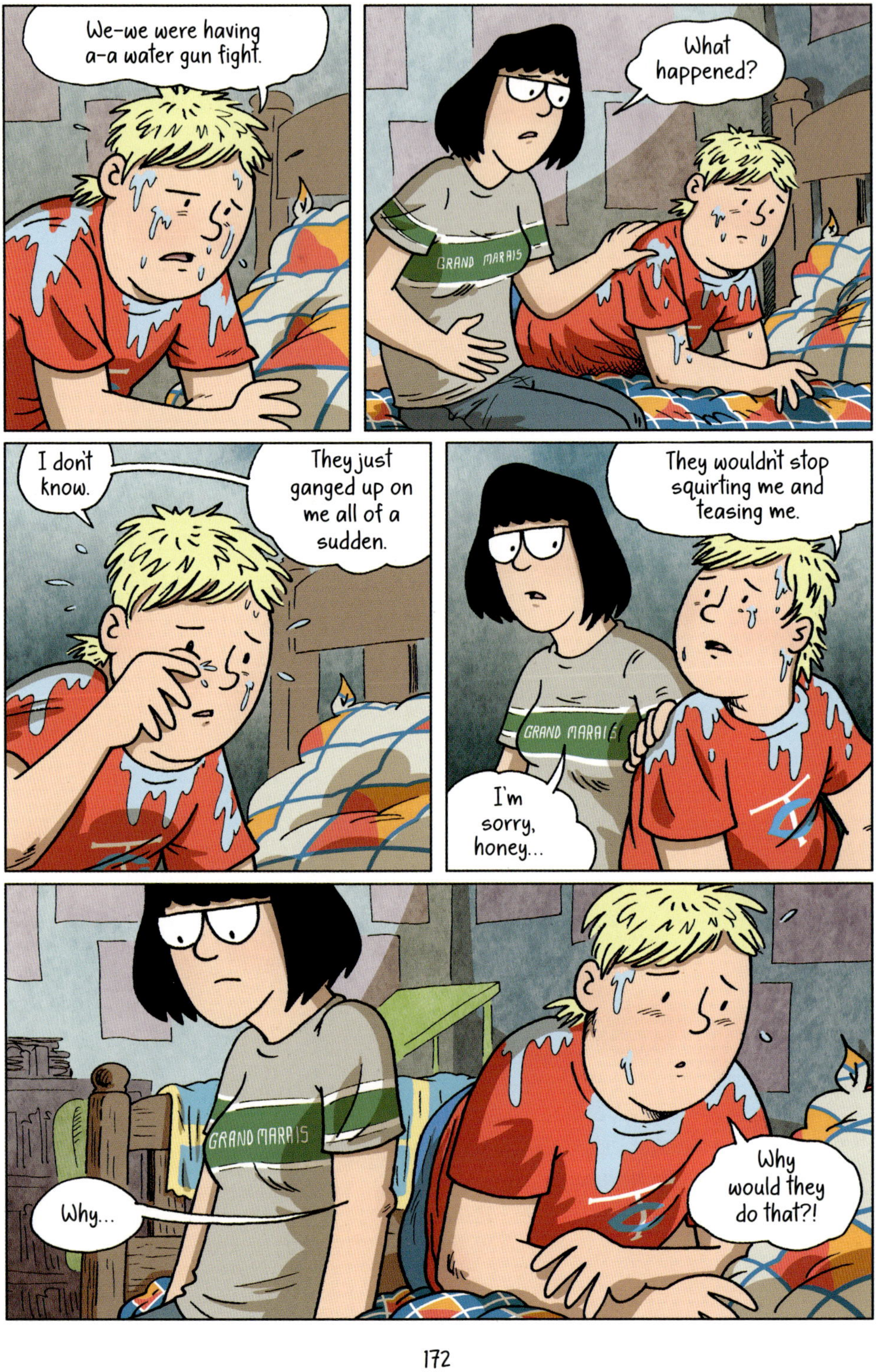
We-we were having a-a water gun fight.
What happened?
GRAND MARAIS
I don't know.
They just ganged up on me all of a sudden.
They wouldn't stop squirting me and teasing me.
GRAND MARAIS
I'm sorry, honey...
GRAND MARAIS
Why...
Why would they do that?!

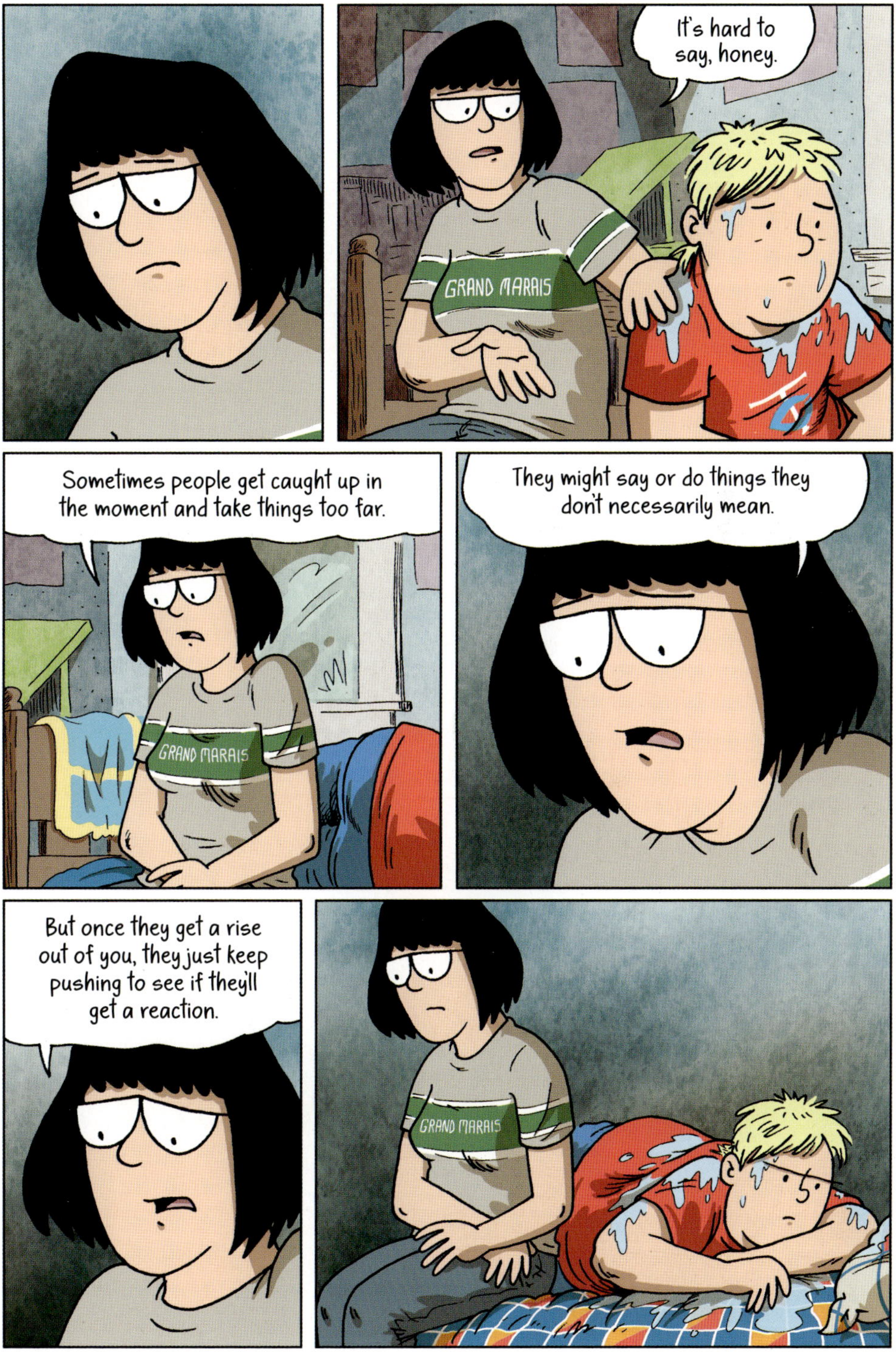
It's hard to say, honey.
GRAND MARAIS
Sometimes people get caught up in the moment and take things too far.
GRAND MARAIS
They might say or do things they don't necessarily mean.
But once they get a rise out of you, they just keep pushing to see if they'll get a reaction.
GRAND MARAIS

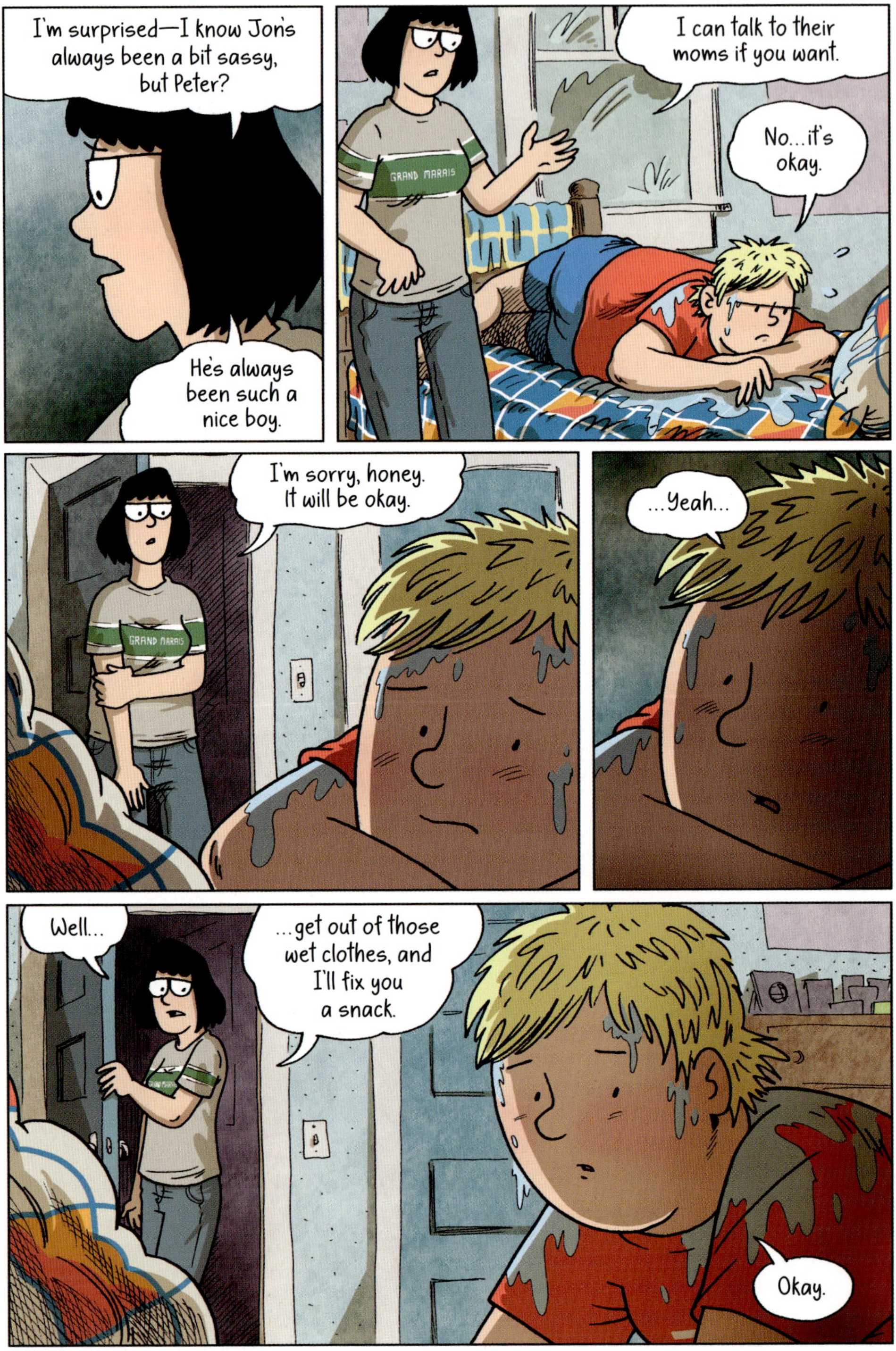
I'm surprised—I know Jon's always been a bit sassy, but Peter?
He's always been such a nice boy.
I can talk to their moms if you want.
GRAND MARAIS
No...it's okay.
I'm sorry, honey. It will be okay.
GRAND MARAIS
...Yeah...
Well...
...get out of those wet clothes, and I'll fix you a snack.
Okay.

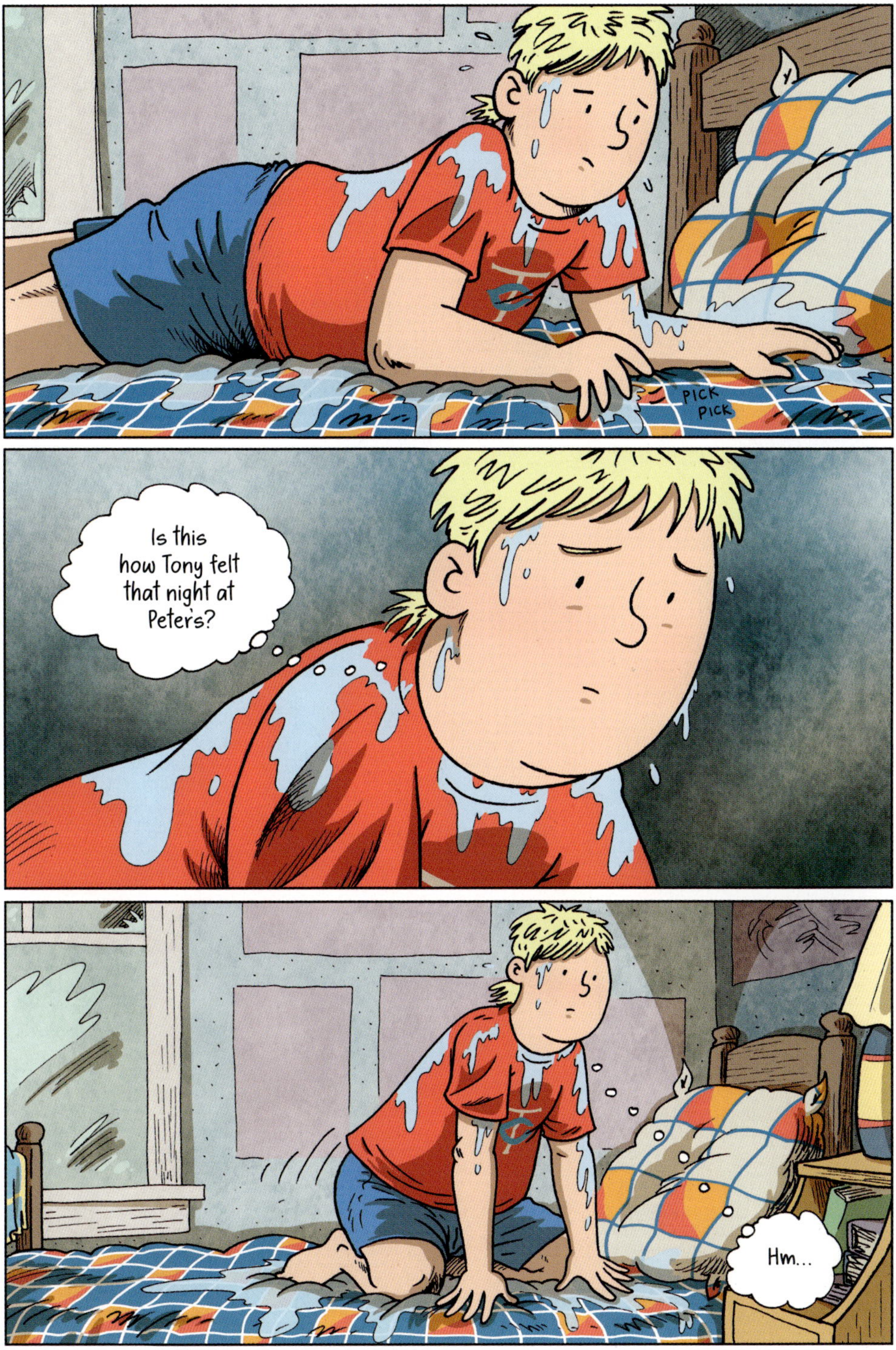
PICK
PICK
Is this how Tony felt that night at Peter's?
Hm...

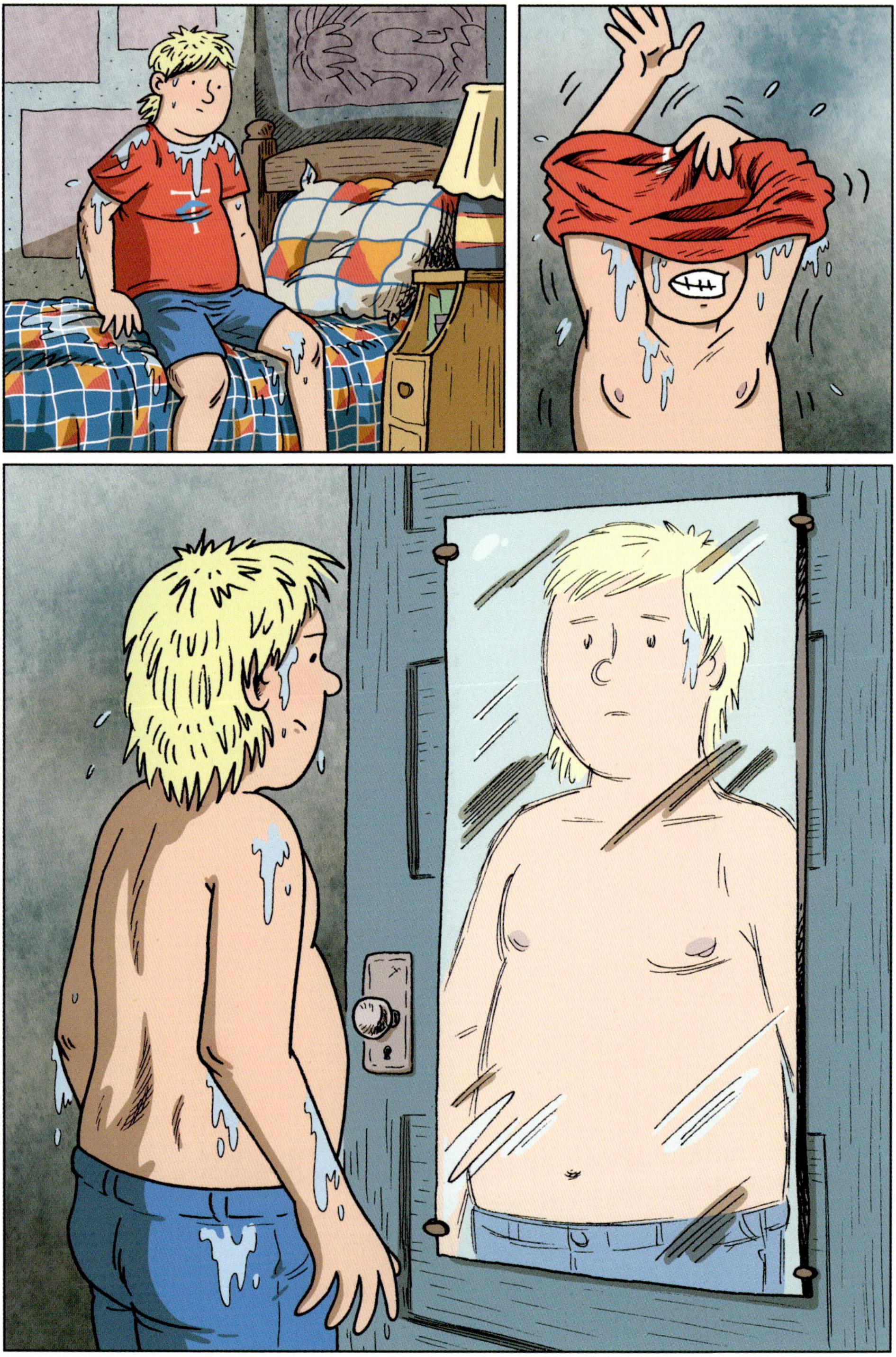

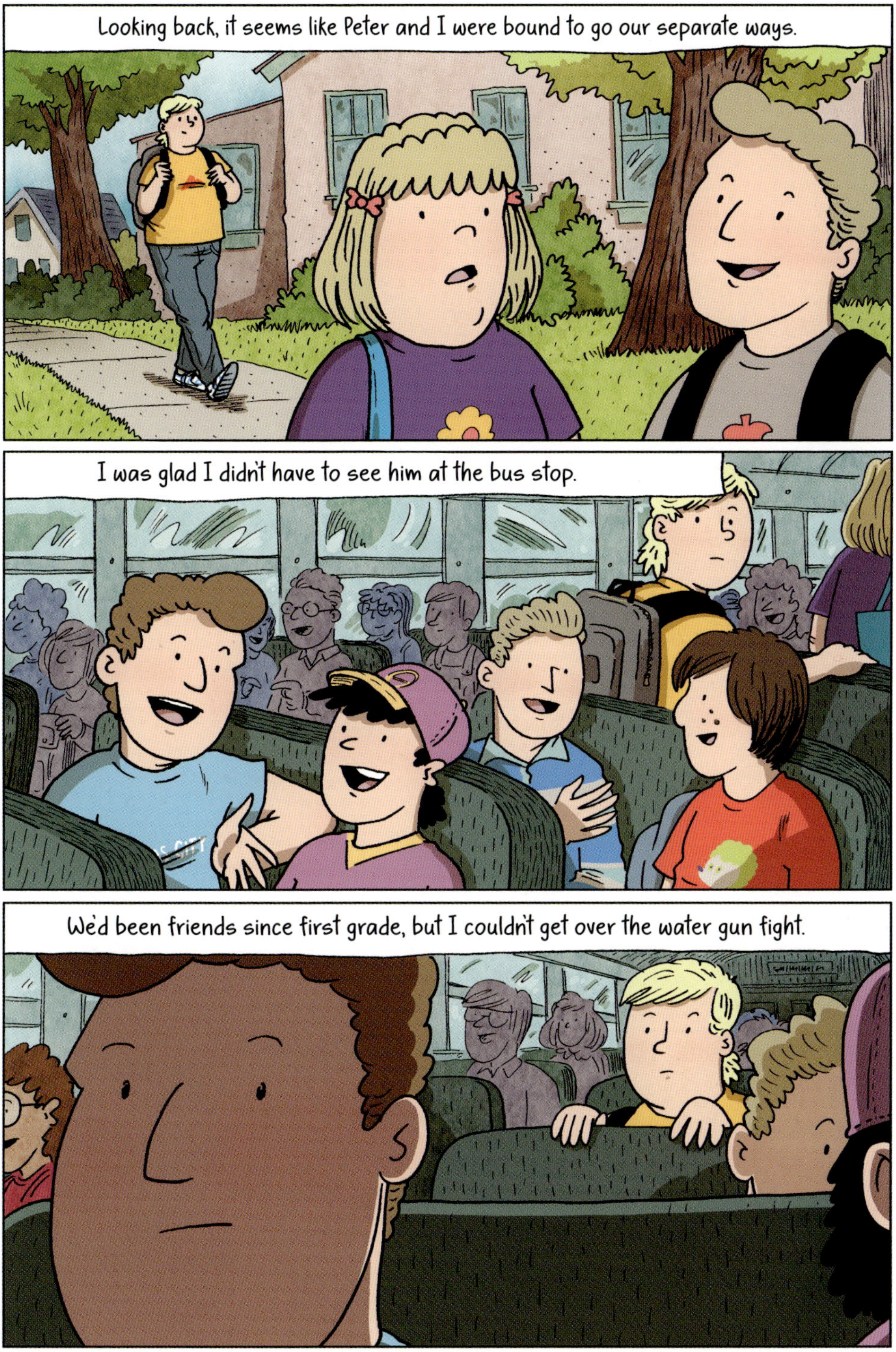
Looking back, it seems like Peter and I were bound to go our separate ways.
I was glad I didn't have to see him at the bus stop.
We'd been friends since first grade, but I couldn't get over the water gun fight.

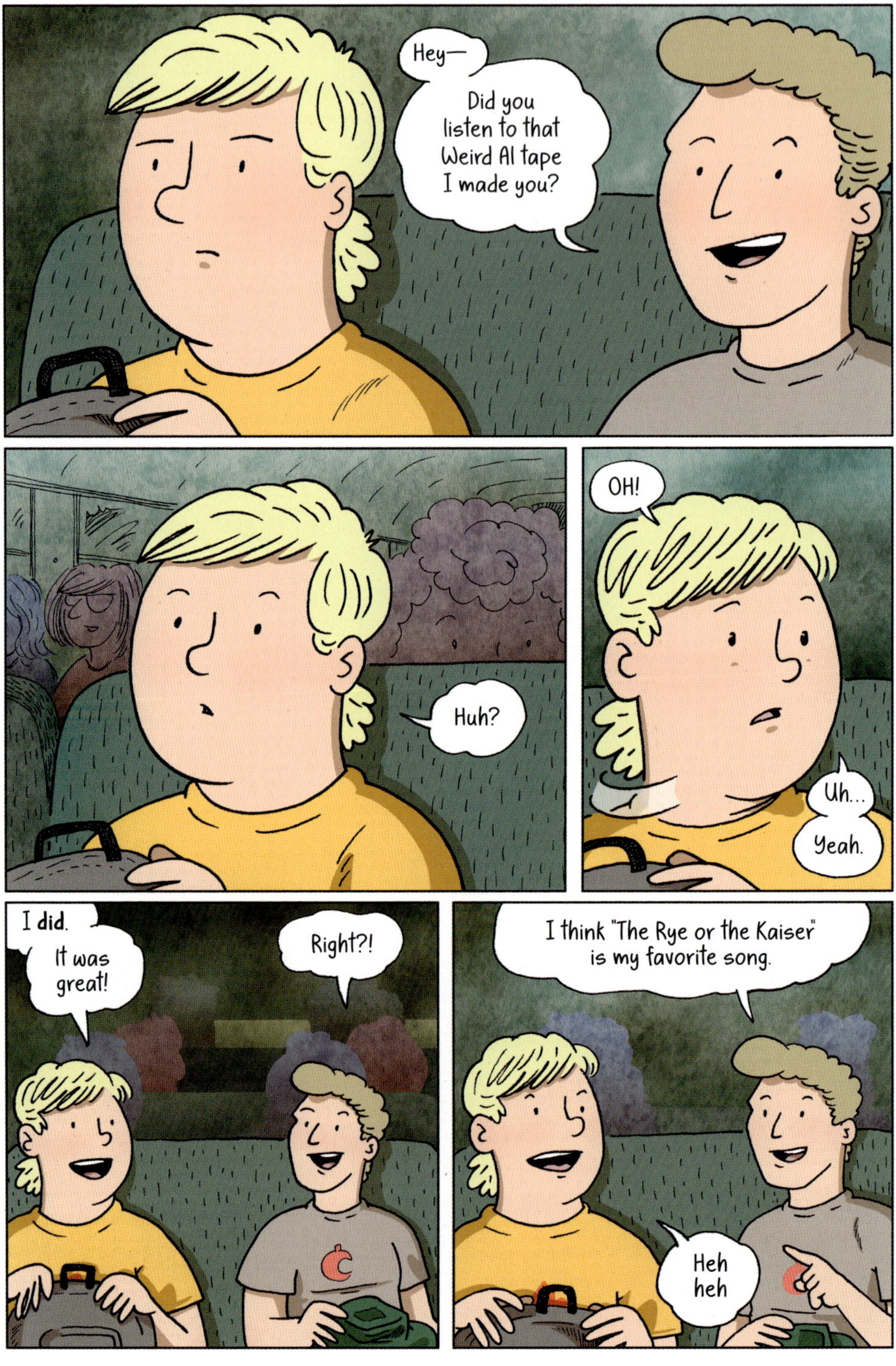
Hey—
Did you listen to that Weird Al tape I made you?
Huh?
OH!
Uh...
Yeah.
I **did**.
It was great!
Right?!
I think "The Rye or the Kaiser" is my favorite song.
Heh heh

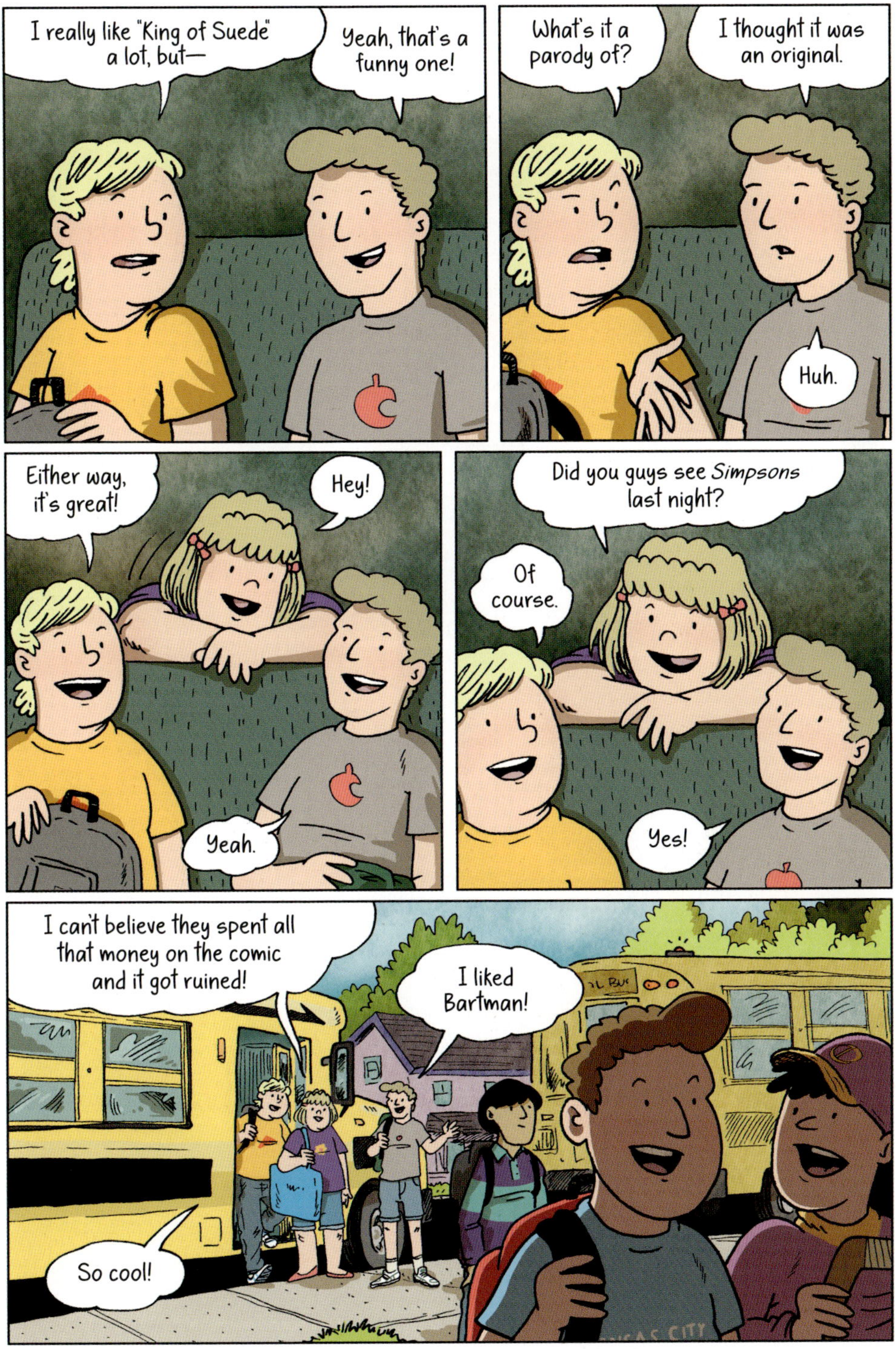
I really like "King of Suede" a lot, but—
Yeah, that's a funny one!
What's it a parody of?
I thought it was an original.
Huh.
Either way, it's great!
Hey!
Yeah.
Did you guys see *Simpsons* last night?
Of course.
Yes!
I can't believe they spent all that money on the comic and it got ruined!
I liked Bartman!
So cool!

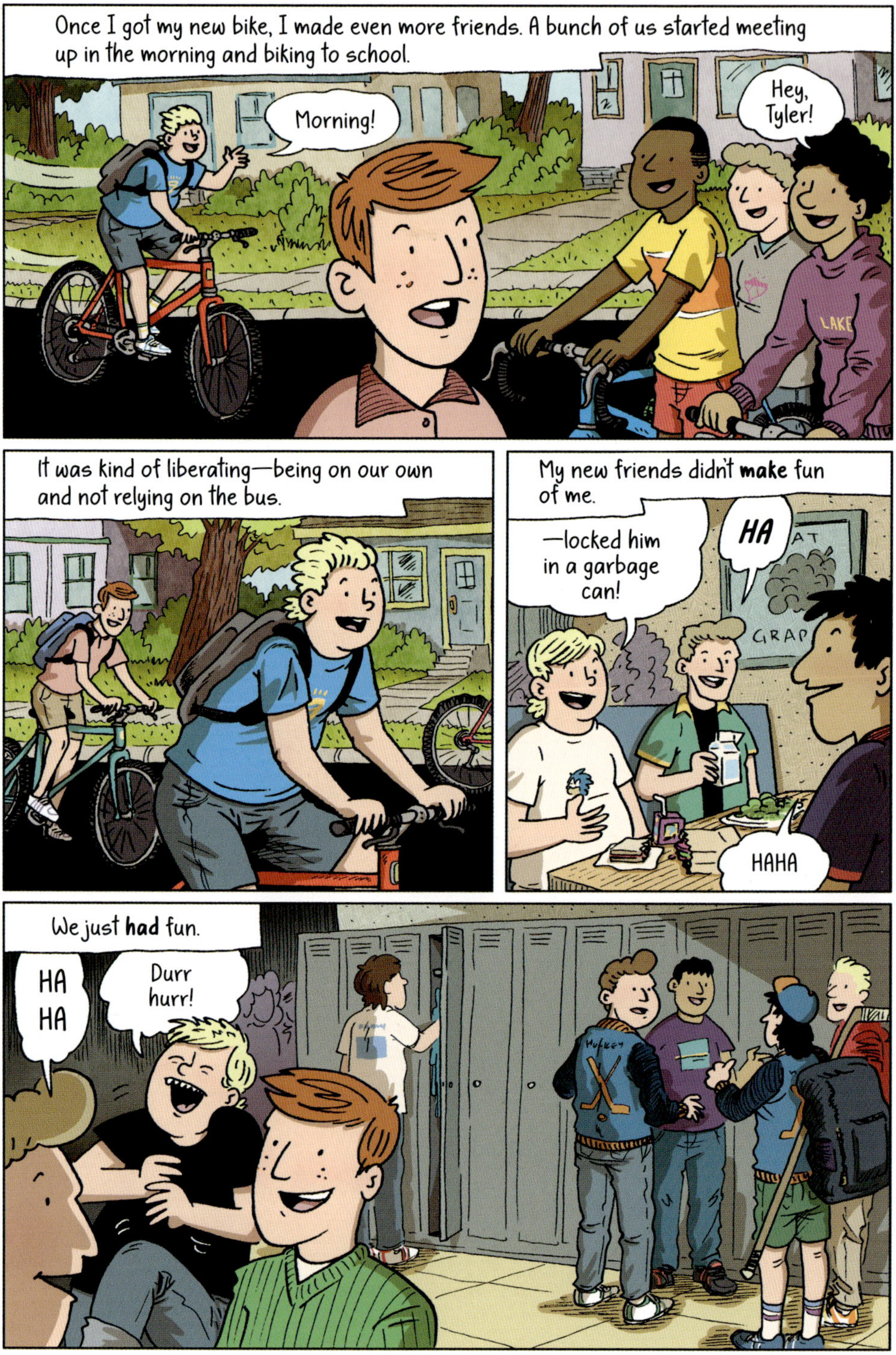
Once I got my new bike, I made even more friends. A bunch of us started meeting up in the morning and biking to school.
Morning!
Hey, Tyler!
It was kind of liberating—being on our own and not relying on the bus.
My new friends didn't **make** fun of me.
—locked him in a garbage can!
HA
HAHA
We just **had** fun.
HA HA
Durr hurr!

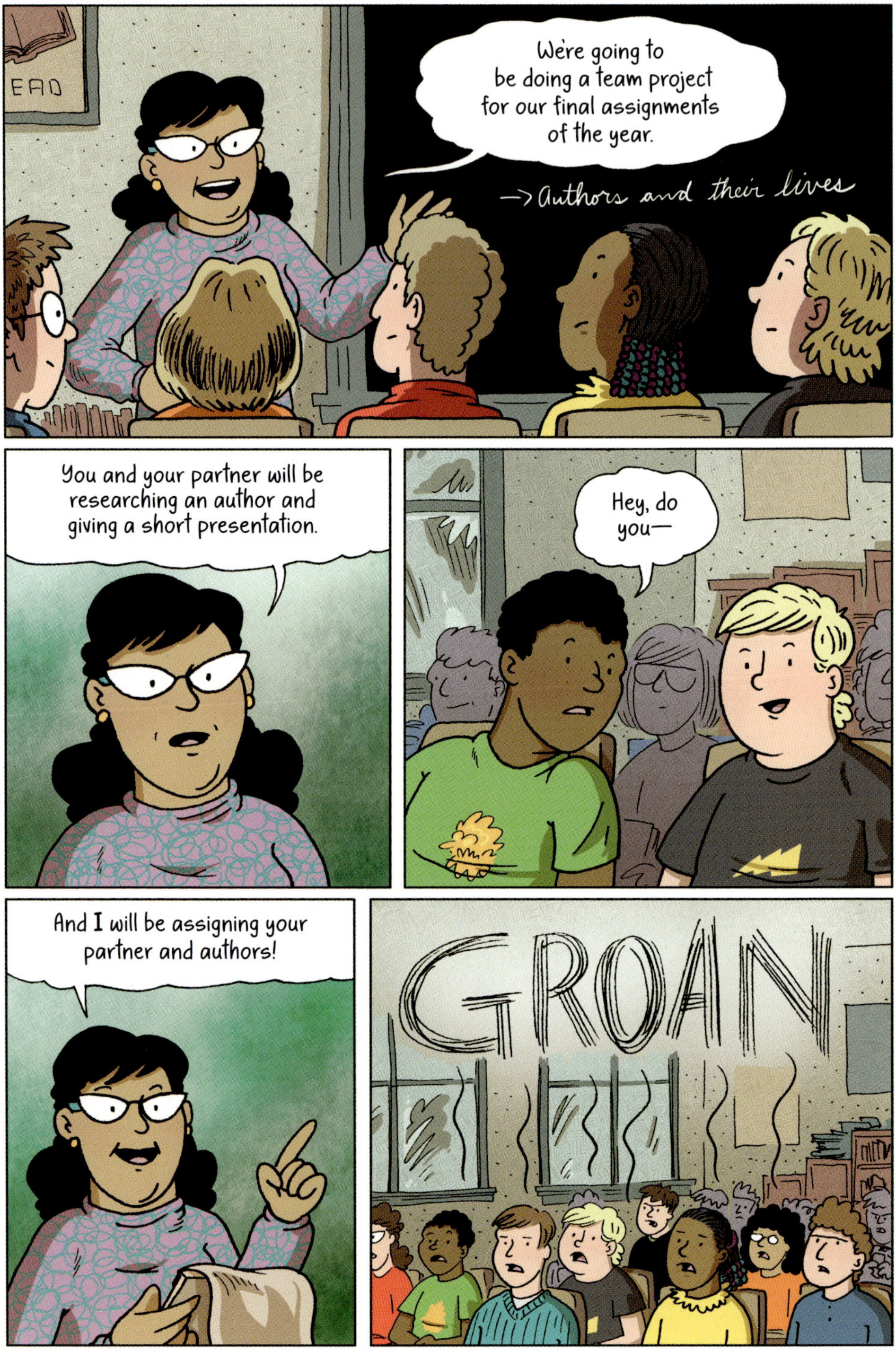
EAD
We're going to be doing a team project for our final assignments of the year.
-> Authors and their lives
You and your partner will be researching an author and giving a short presentation.
Hey, do you—
And I will be assigning your partner and authors!
GROAN

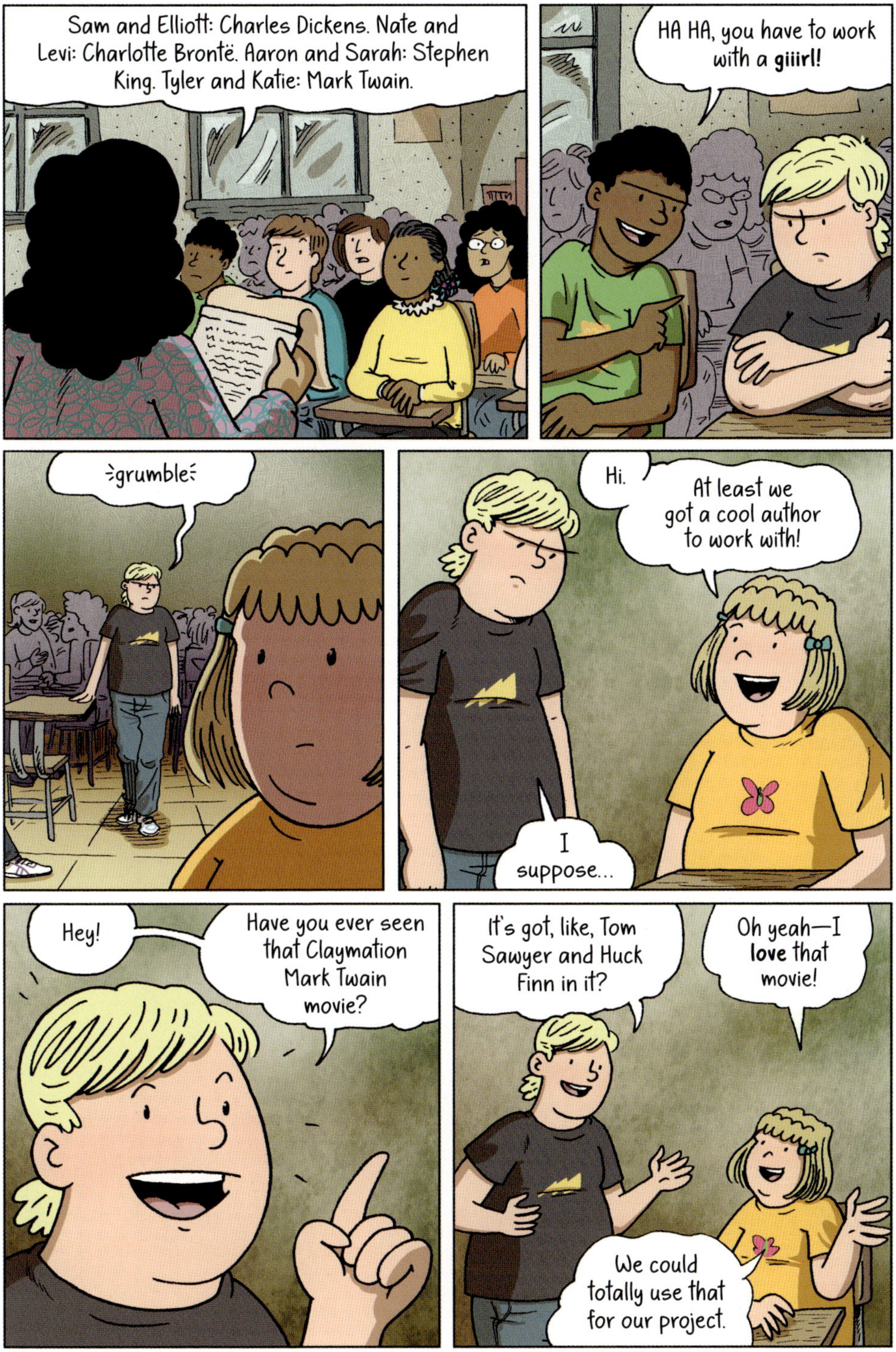
Sam and Elliott: Charles Dickens. Nate and Levi: Charlotte Brontë. Aaron and Sarah: Stephen King. Tyler and Katie: Mark Twain.
HA HA, you have to work with a **giiirl!**
grumble
Hi.
At least we got a cool author to work with!
I suppose...
Hey!
Have you ever seen that Claymation Mark Twain movie?
It's got, like, Tom Sawyer and Huck Finn in it?
Oh yeah—I **love** that movie!
We could totally use that for our project.

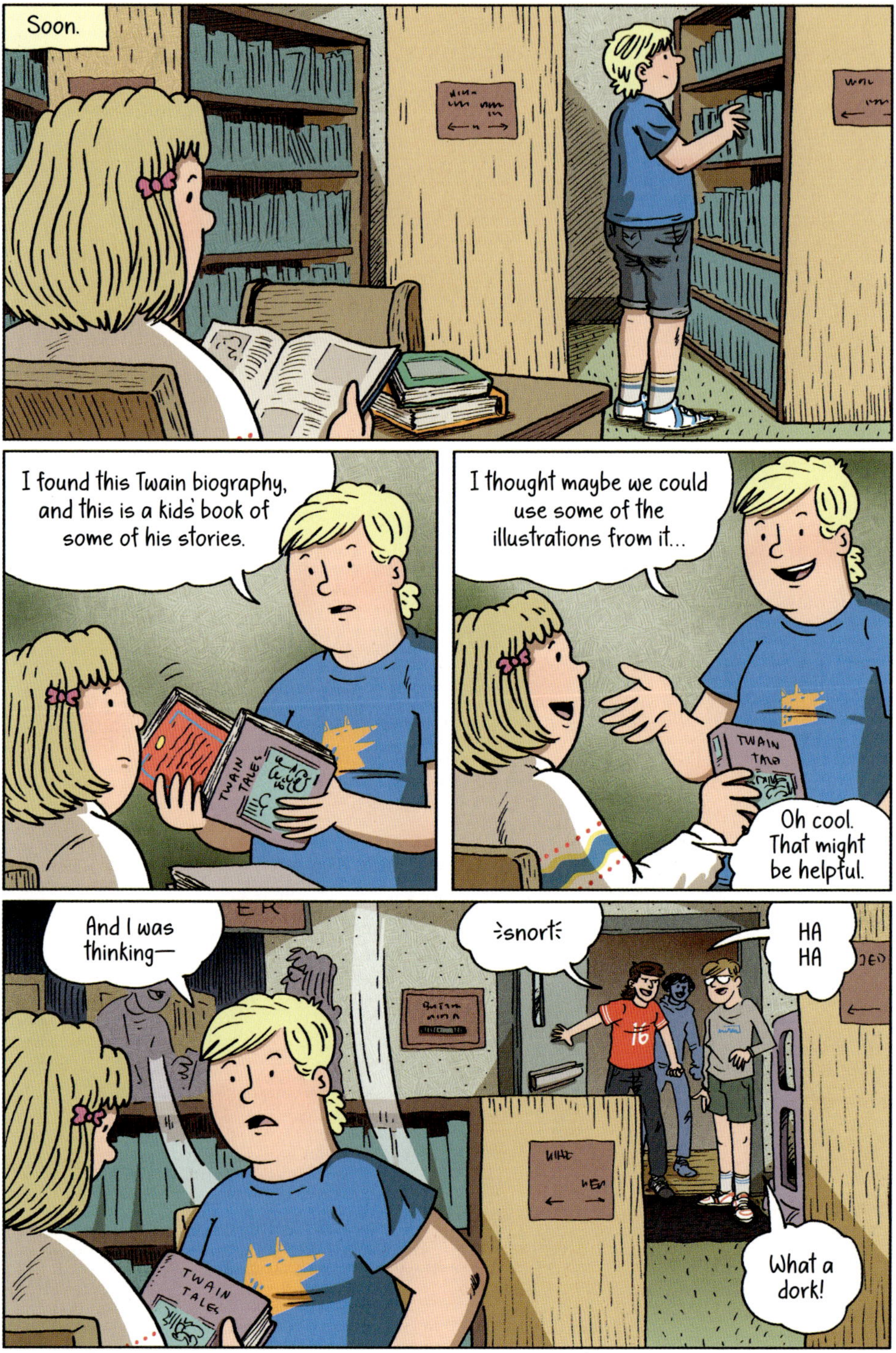
Soon.
I found this Twain biography, and this is a kids' book of some of his stories.
TWAIN TALES
I thought maybe we could use some of the illustrations from it...
Oh cool. That might be helpful.
And I was thinking—
snort
HA HA
What a dork!

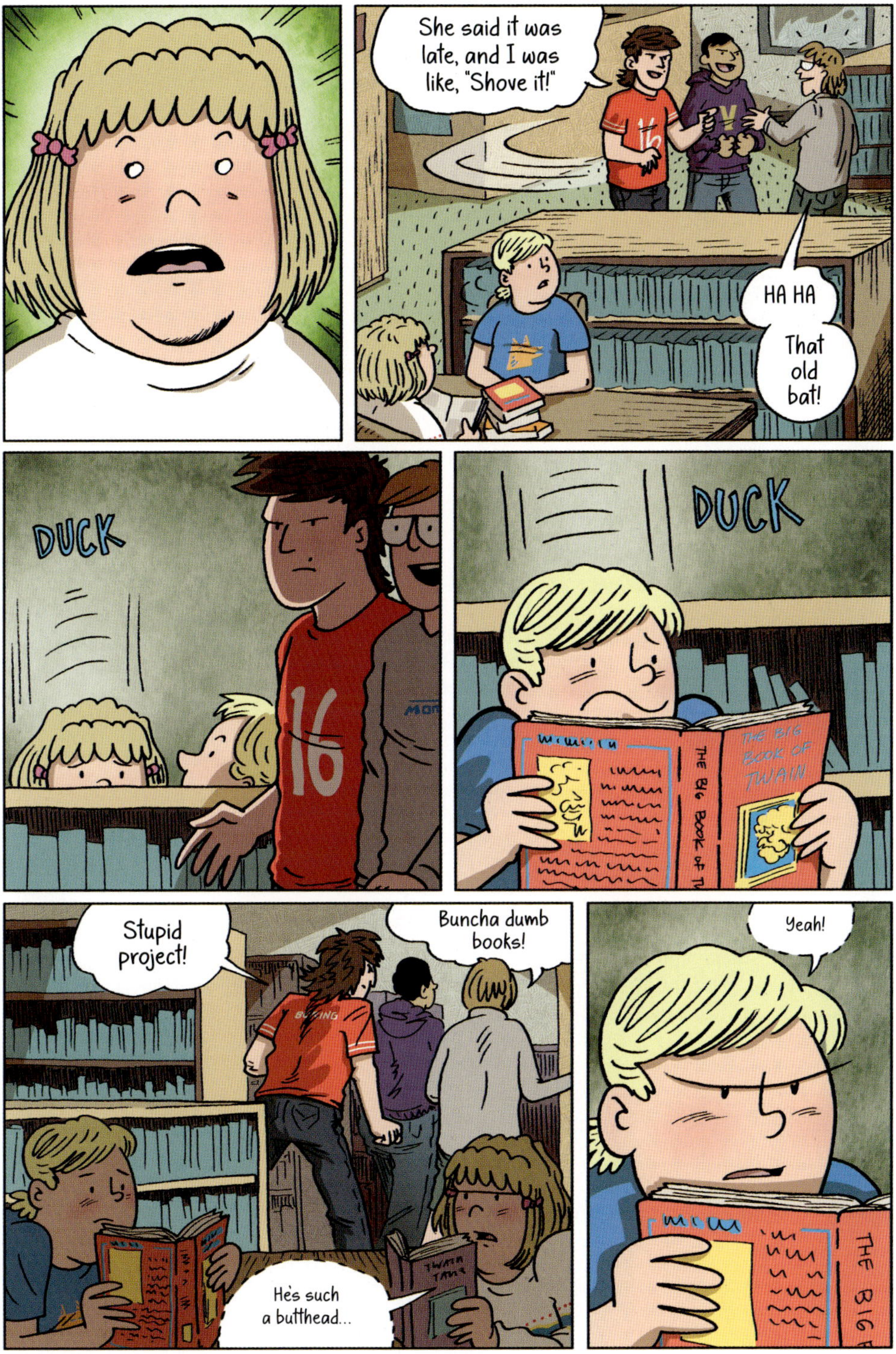
She said it was late, and I was like, "Shove it!"
HA HA
That old bat!
DUCK
DUCK
THE BIG BOOK OF TWAIN
Stupid project!
Buncha dumb books!
He's such a butthead...
Yeah!

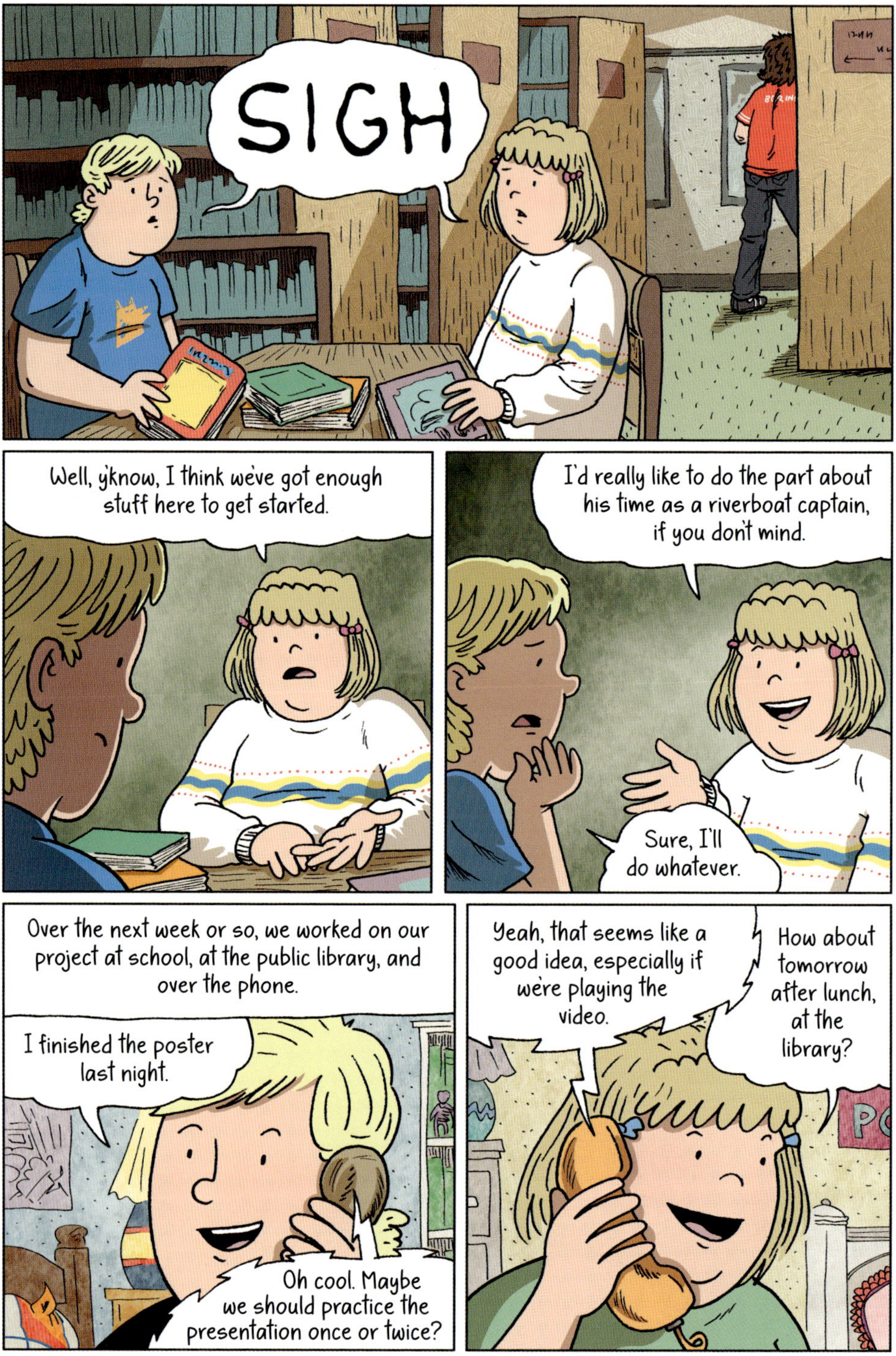
SIGH
Well, y'know, I think we've got enough stuff here to get started.
I'd really like to do the part about his time as a riverboat captain, if you don't mind.
Sure, I'll do whatever.
Over the next week or so, we worked on our project at school, at the public library, and over the phone.
I finished the poster last night.
Oh cool. Maybe we should practice the presentation once or twice?
Yeah, that seems like a good idea, especially if we're playing the video.
How about tomorrow after lunch, at the library?

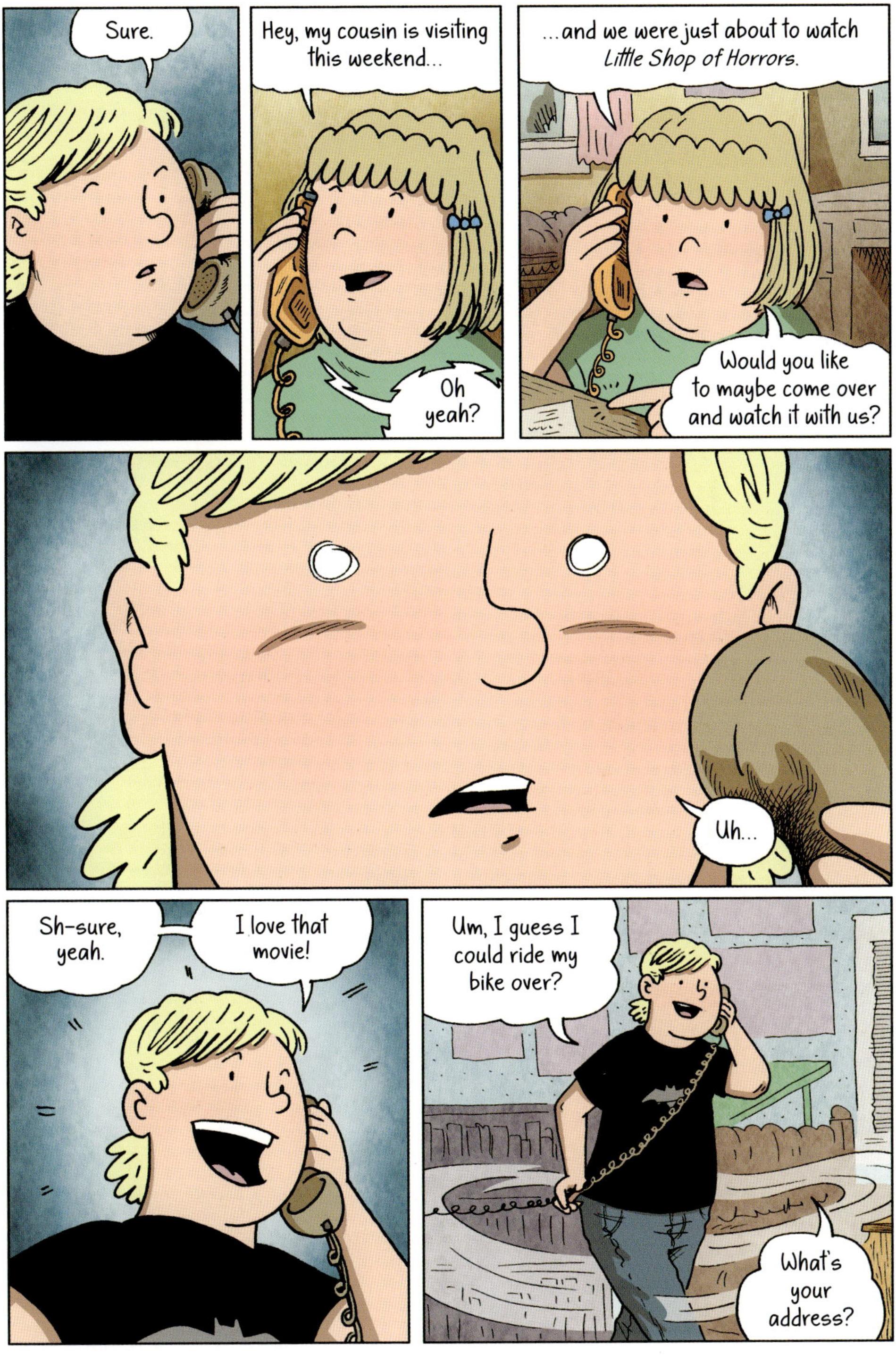
Sure.
Hey, my cousin is visiting this weekend...
Oh yeah?
...and we were just about to watch *Little Shop of Horrors*.
Would you like to maybe come over and watch it with us?
Uh...
Sh-sure, yeah.
I love that movie!
Um, I guess I could ride my bike over?
What's your address?

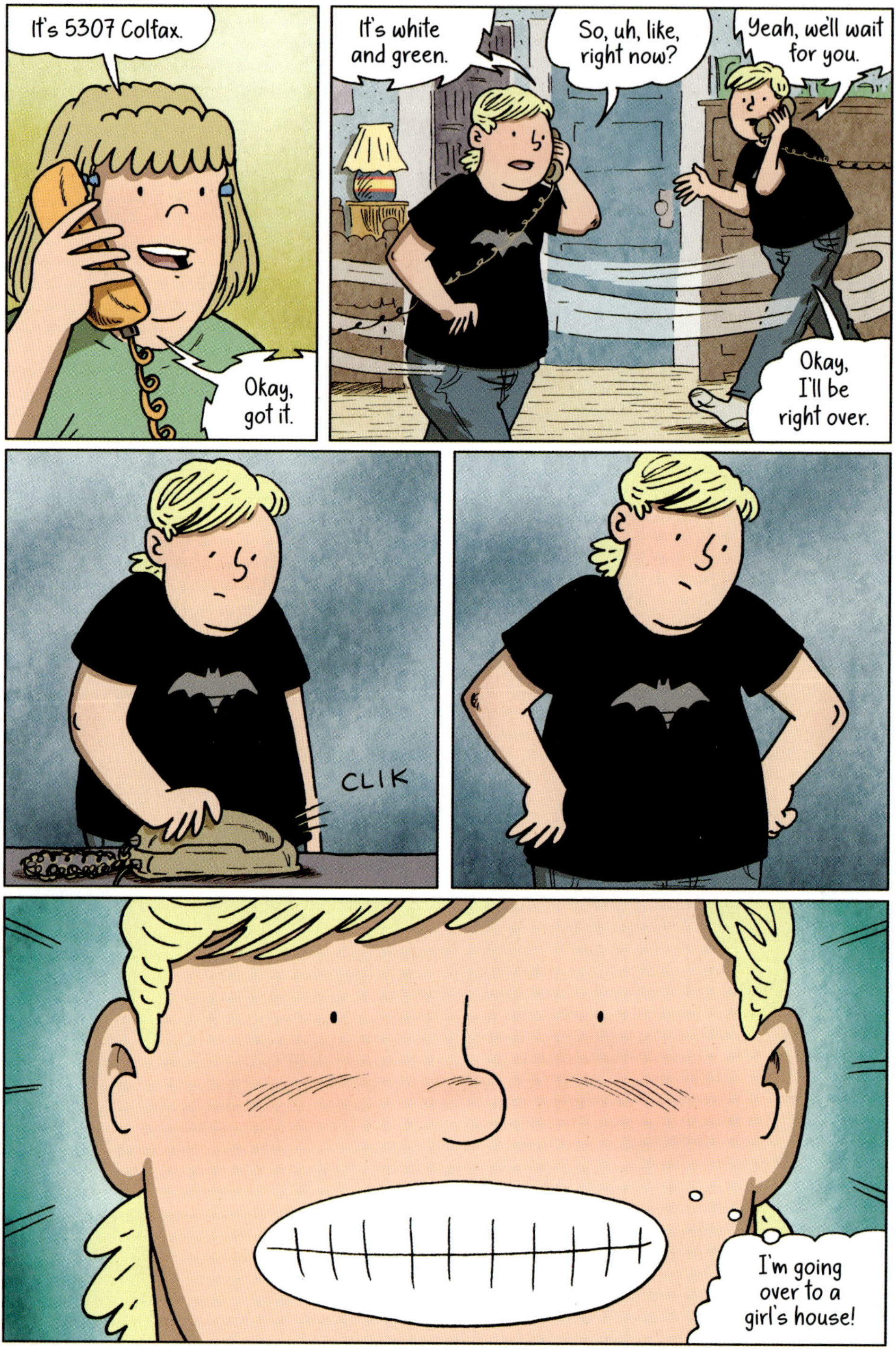
It's 5307 Colfax.
Okay, got it.
It's white and green.
So, uh, like, right now?
Yeah, we'll wait for you.
Okay, I'll be right over.
CLIK
I'm going over to a girl's house!

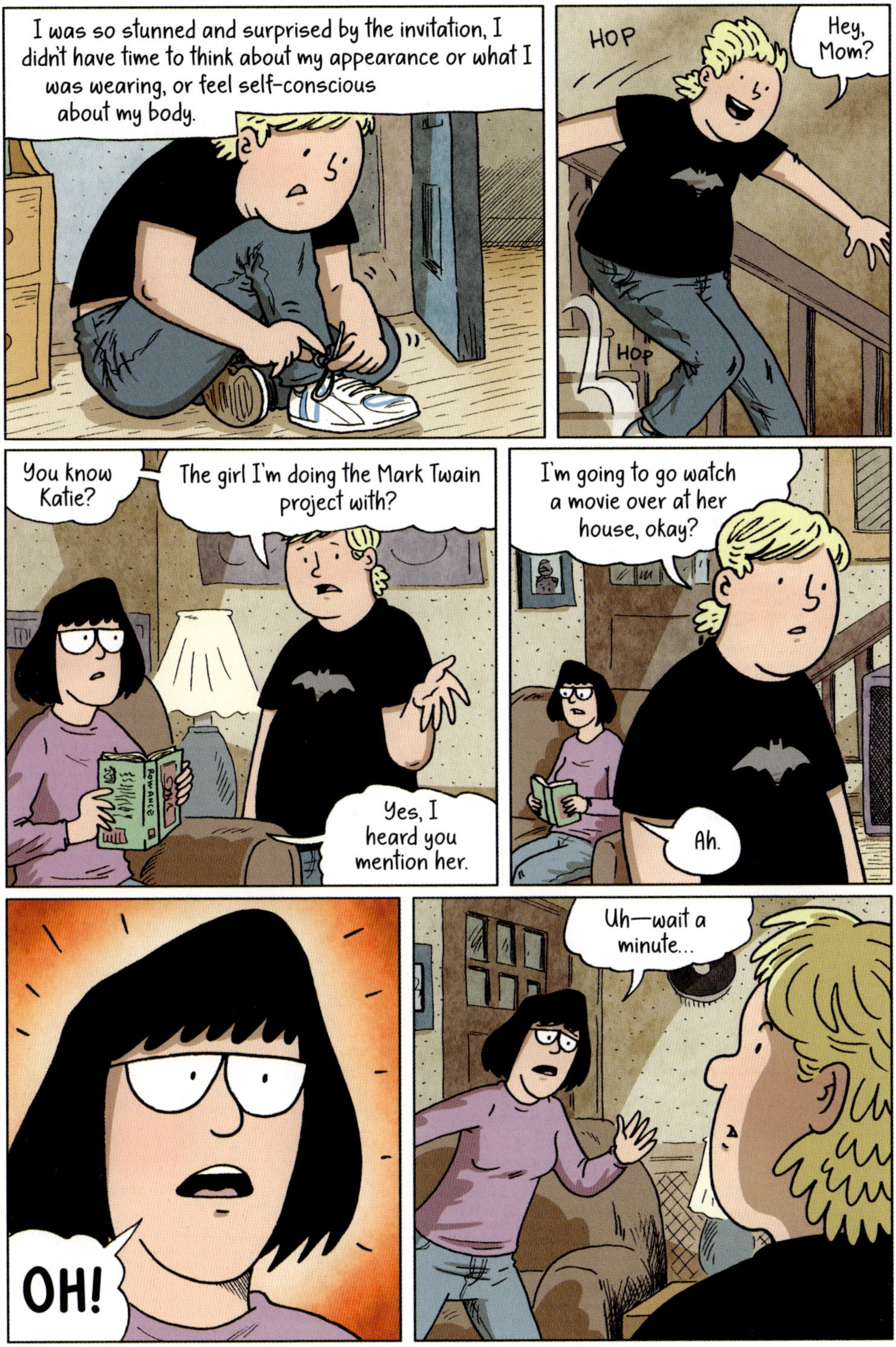
I was so stunned and surprised by the invitation, I didn't have time to think about my appearance or what I was wearing, or feel self-conscious about my body.
HOP
HOP
Hey, Mom?
You know Katie?
The girl I'm doing the Mark Twain project with?
Yes, I heard you mention her.
I'm going to go watch a movie over at her house, okay?
Ah.
OH!
Uh—wait a minute...

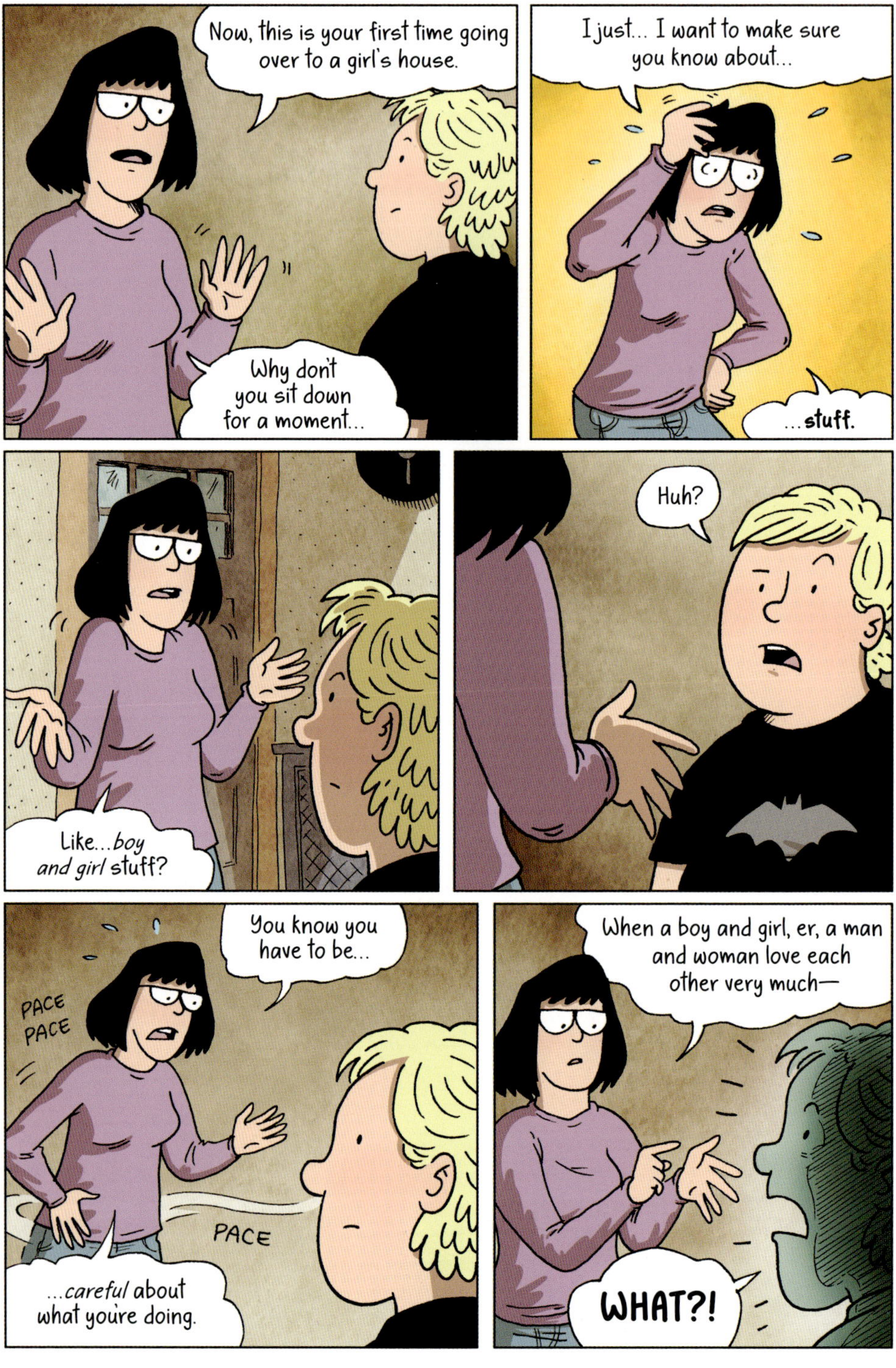
Now, this is your first time going over to a girl's house.
Why don't you sit down for a moment...
I just... I want to make sure you know about...
...**stuff.**
Like... *boy and girl* stuff?
Huh?
You know you have to be...
PACE PACE
PACE
...*careful* about what you're doing.
When a boy and girl, er, a man and woman love each other very much—
WHAT?!

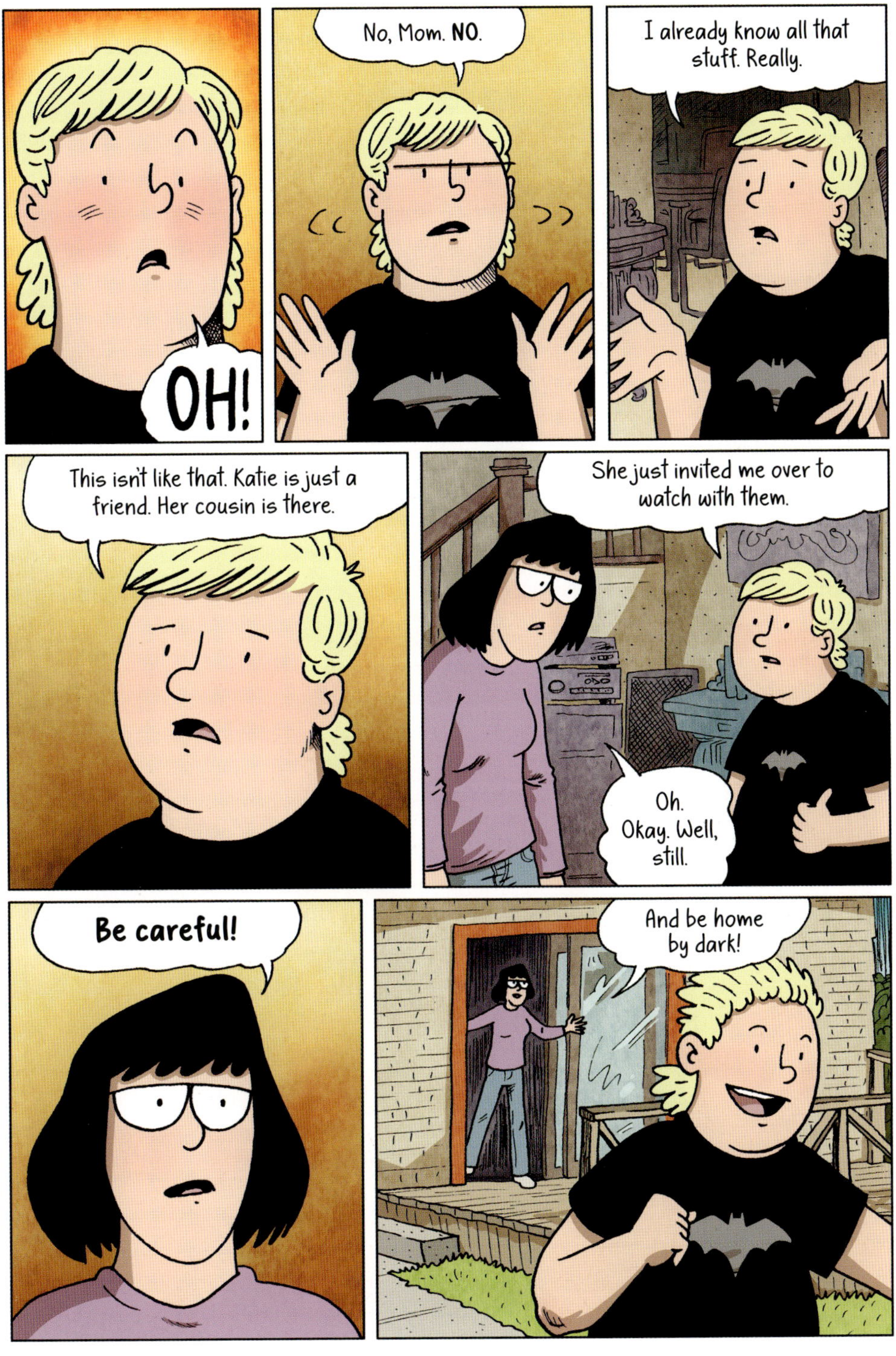
OH!
No, Mom. **NO.**
I already know all that stuff. Really.
This isn't like that. Katie is just a friend. Her cousin is there.
She just invited me over to watch with them.
Oh. Okay. Well, still.
Be careful!
And be home by dark!

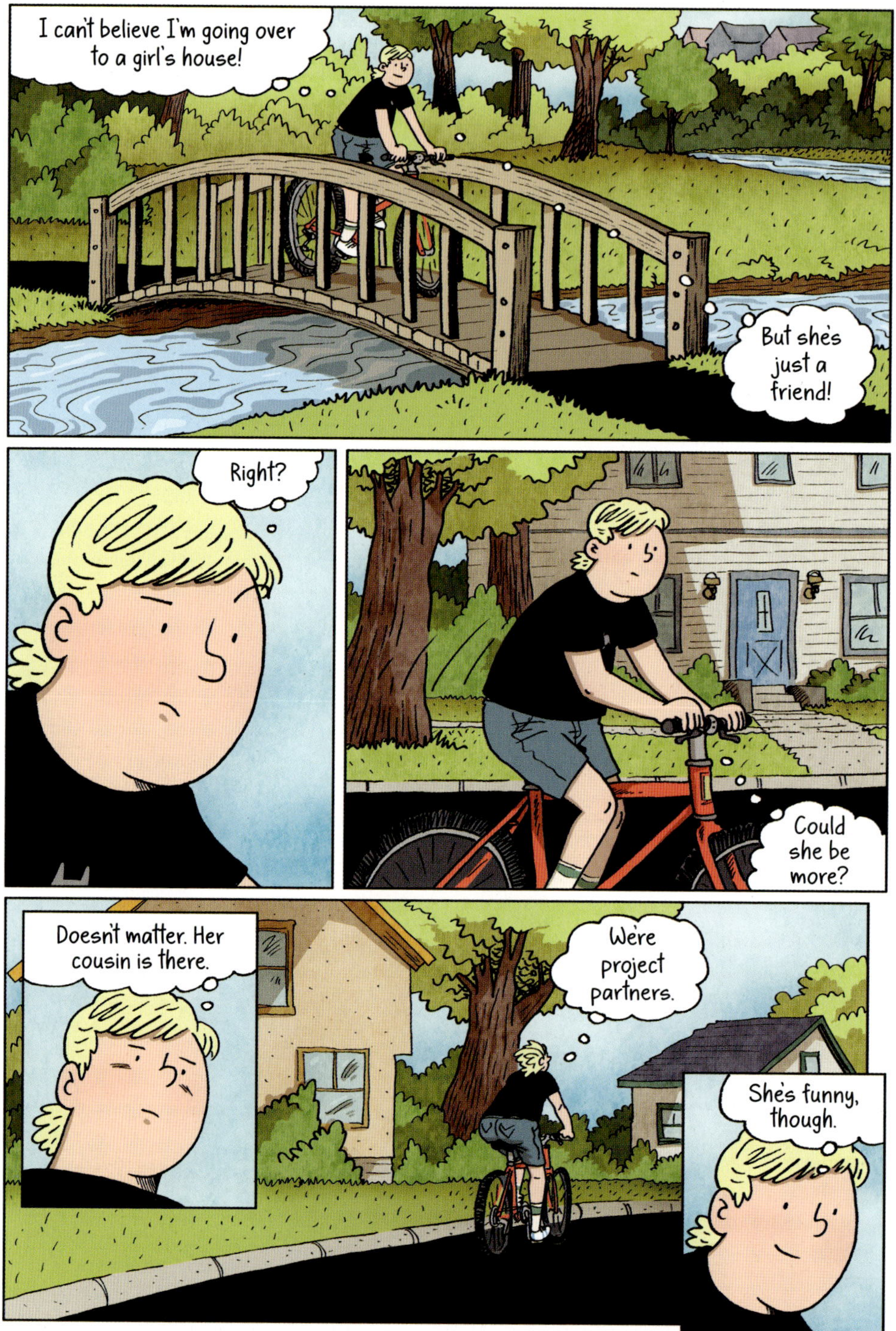
I can't believe I'm going over to a girl's house!
But she's just a friend!
Right?
Could she be more?
Doesn't matter. Her cousin is there.
We're project partners.
She's funny, though.

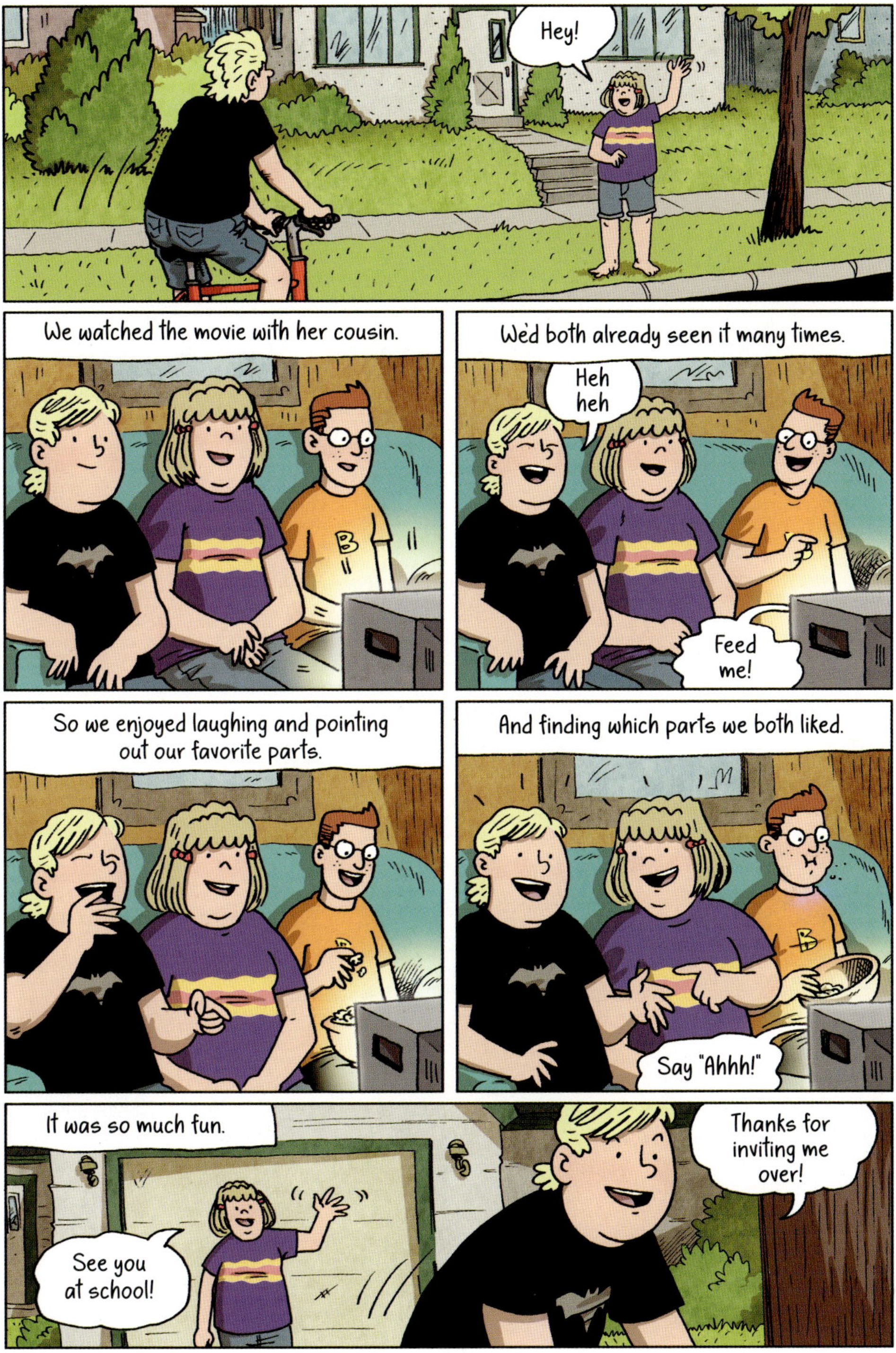
Hey!
We watched the movie with her cousin.
We'd both already seen it many times.
Heh heh
Feed me!
So we enjoyed laughing and pointing out our favorite parts.
And finding which parts we both liked.
Say "Ahhh!"
It was so much fun.
Thanks for inviting me over!
See you at school!

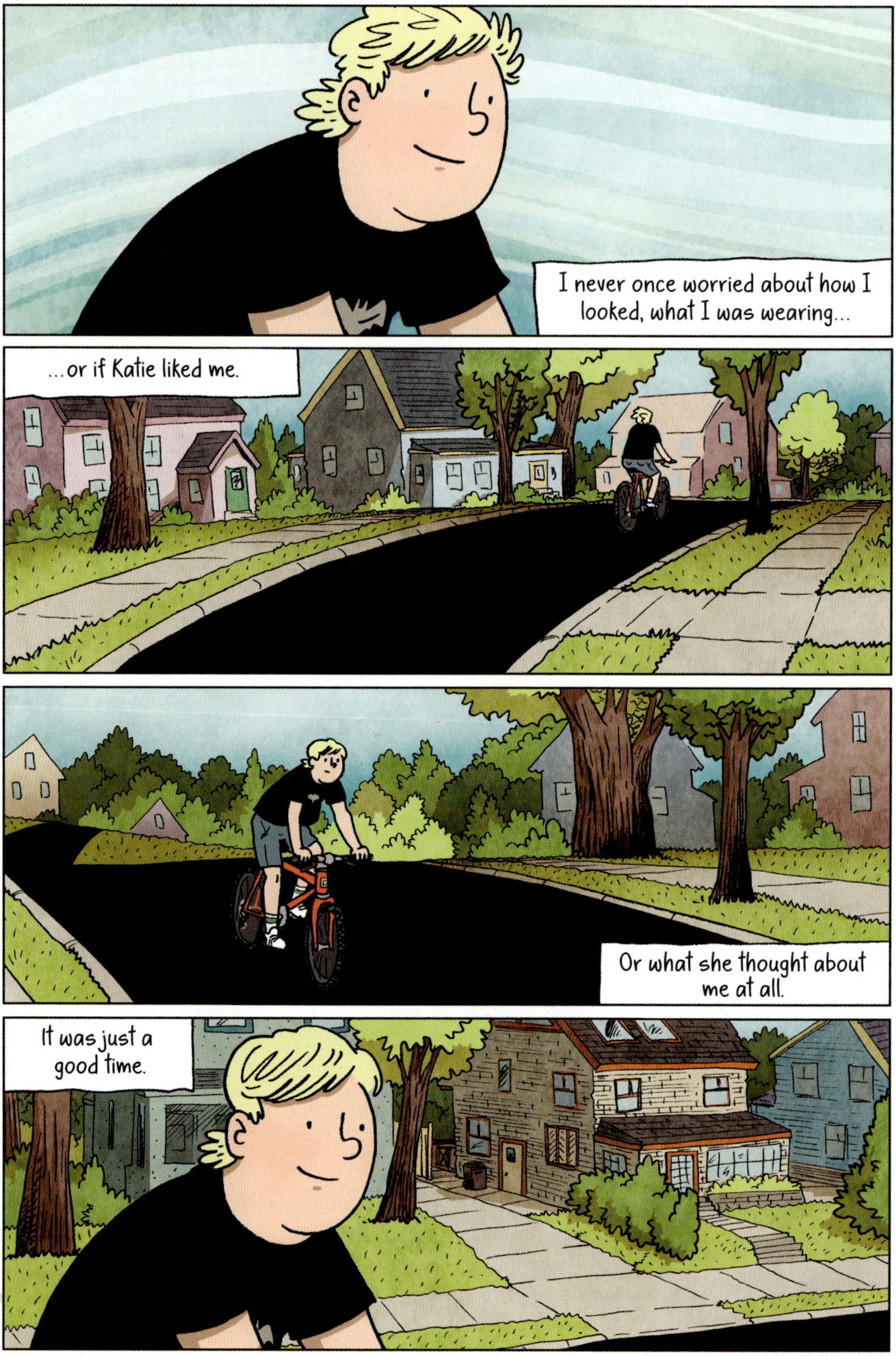
I never once worried about how I looked, what I was wearing...
...or if Katie liked me.
Or what she thought about me at all.
It was just a good time.

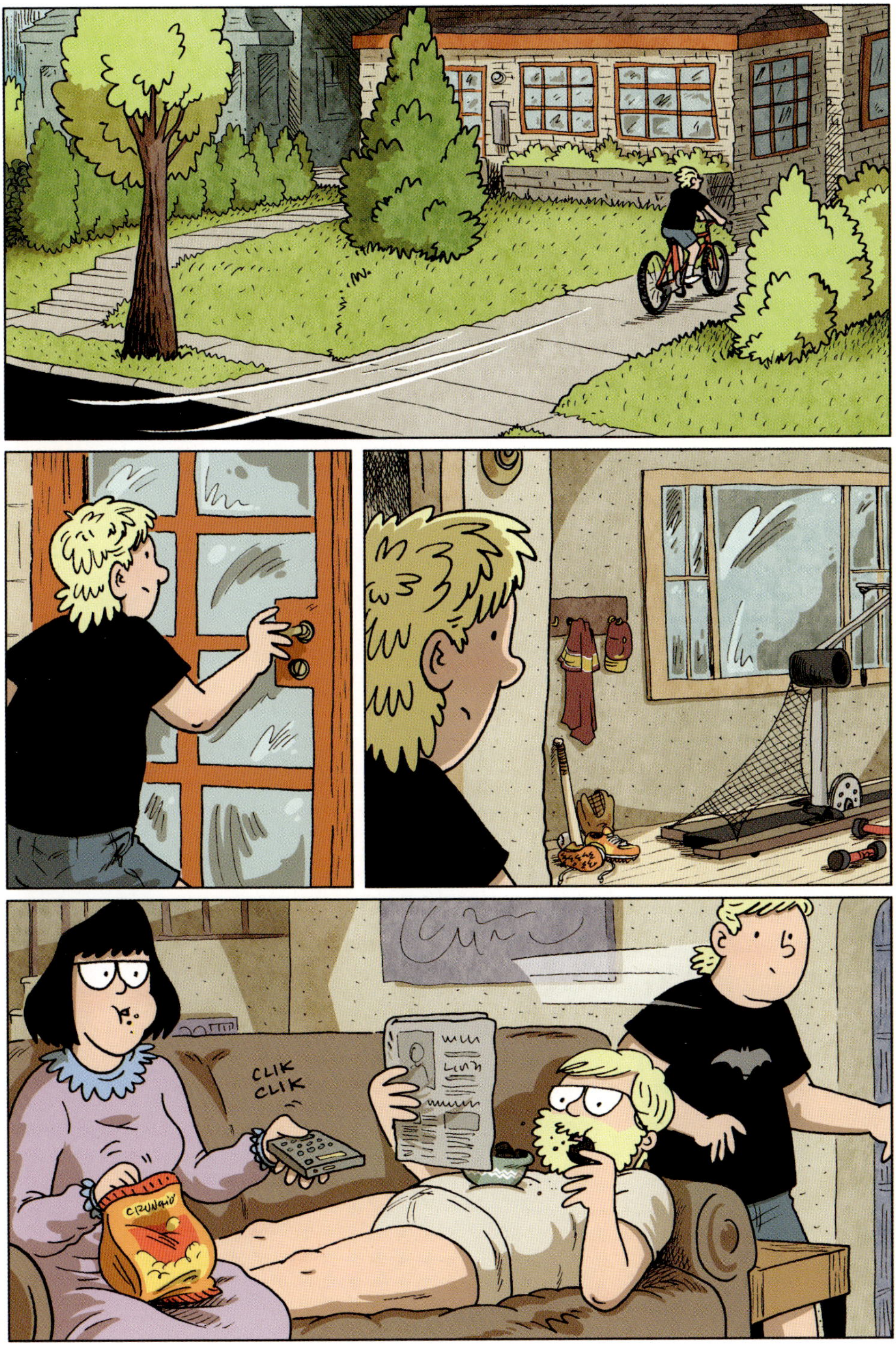
CLIK
CLIK
CRUNCHO

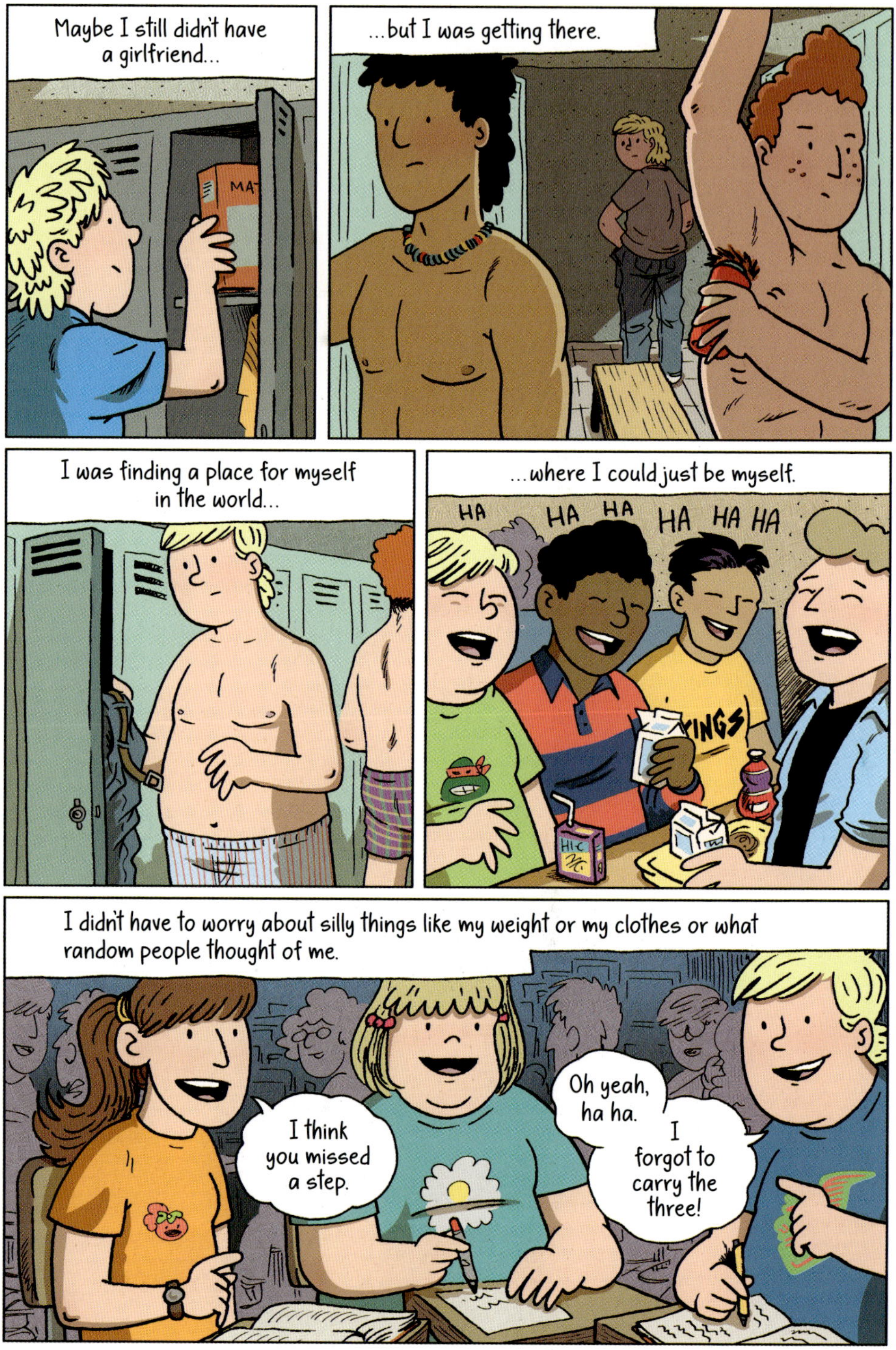

Maybe I still didn't have a girlfriend...
MAT
...but I was getting there.
I was finding a place for myself in the world...
...where I could just be myself.
HA HA HA HA HA HA
INGS
HI-C
I didn't have to worry about silly things like my weight or my clothes or what random people thought of me.
I think you missed a step.
Oh yeah, ha ha.
I forgot to carry the three!

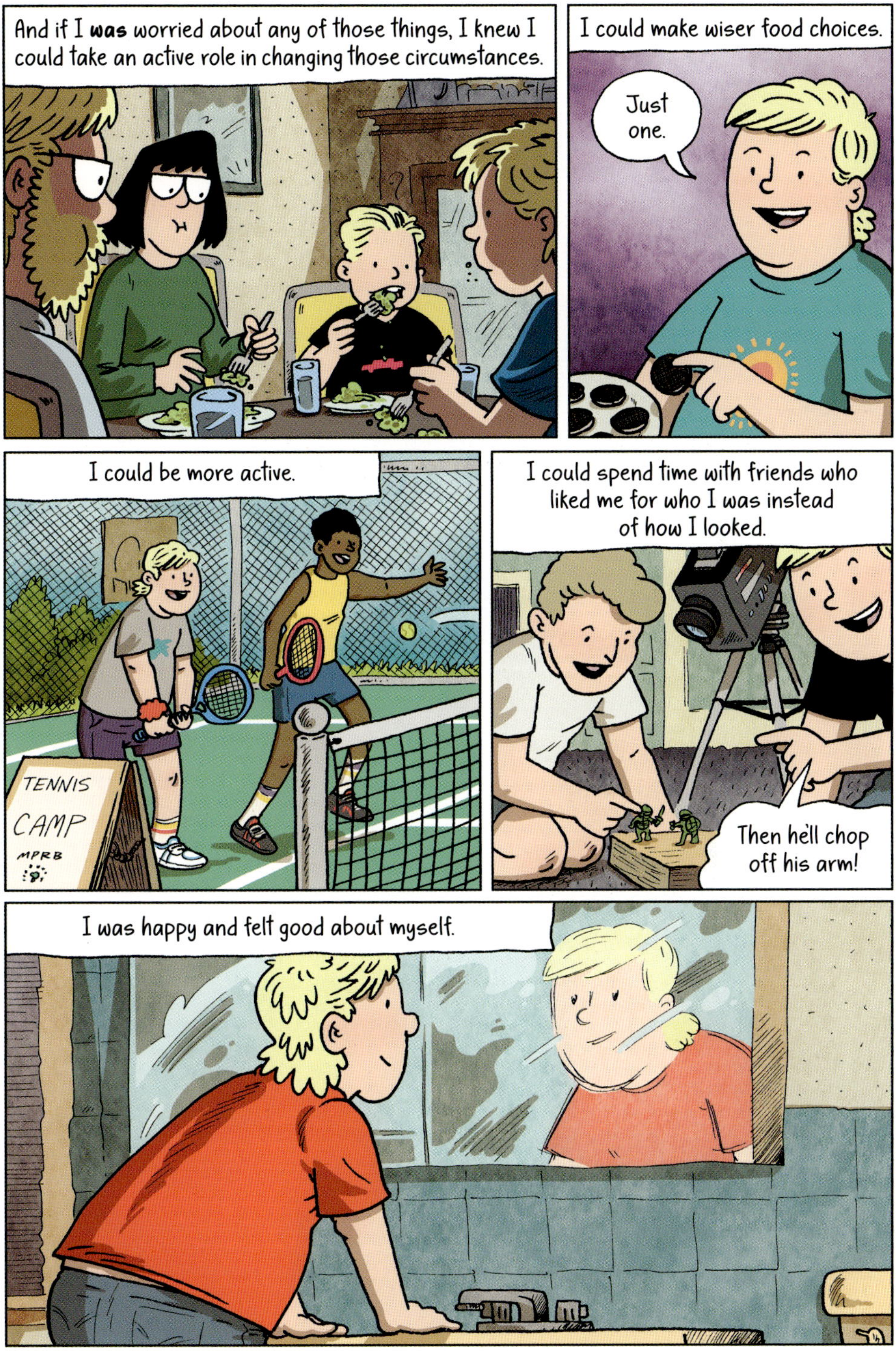
And if I **was** worried about any of those things, I knew I could take an active role in changing those circumstances.
I could make wiser food choices.
Just one.
I could be more active.
TENNIS CAMP
MPRB
I could spend time with friends who liked me for who I was instead of how I looked.
Then he'll chop off his arm!
I was happy and felt good about myself.

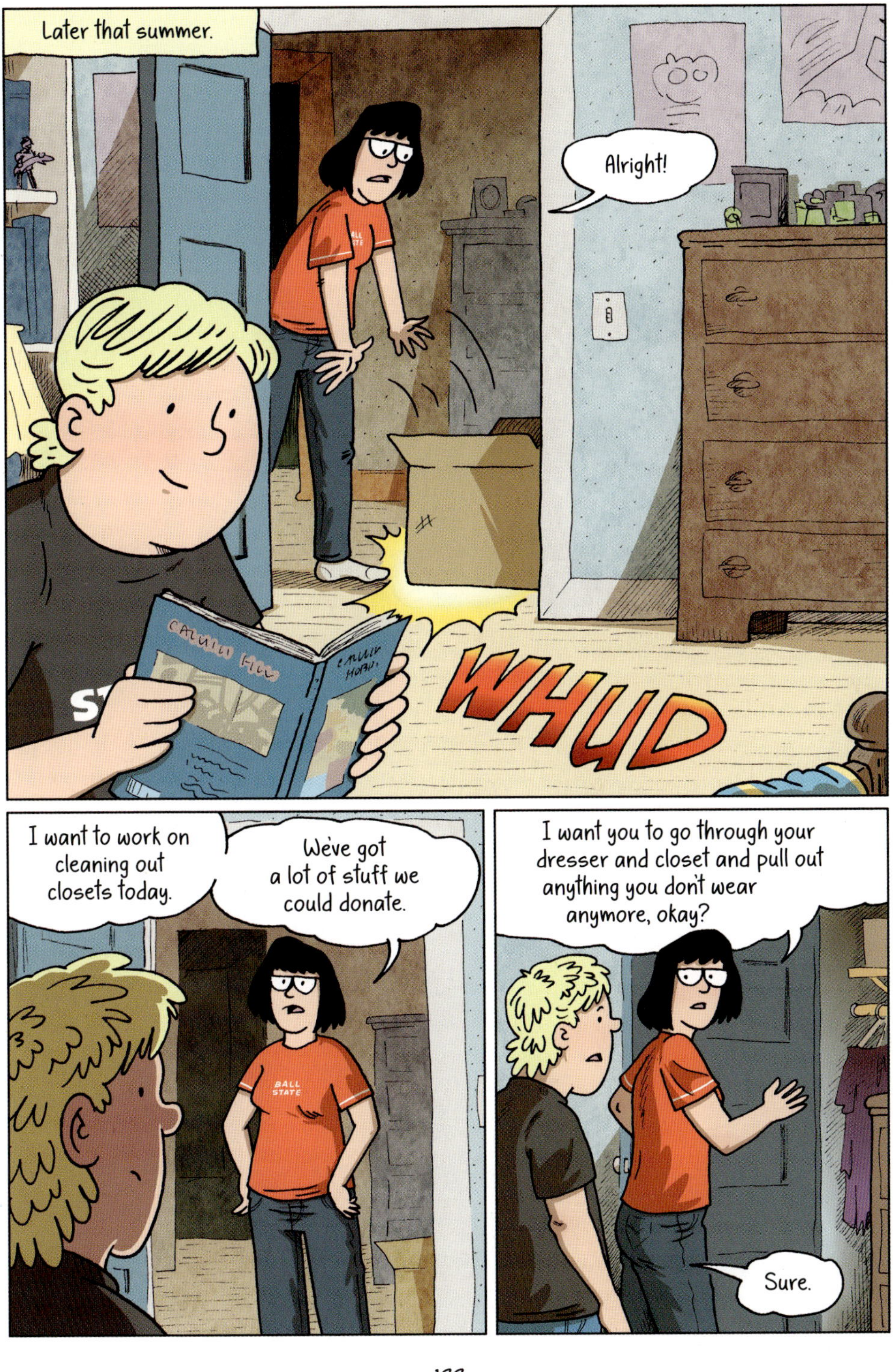
Later that summer.
Alright!
WHUD
I want to work on cleaning out closets today.
We've got a lot of stuff we could donate.
I want you to go through your dresser and closet and pull out anything you don't wear anymore, okay?
Sure.

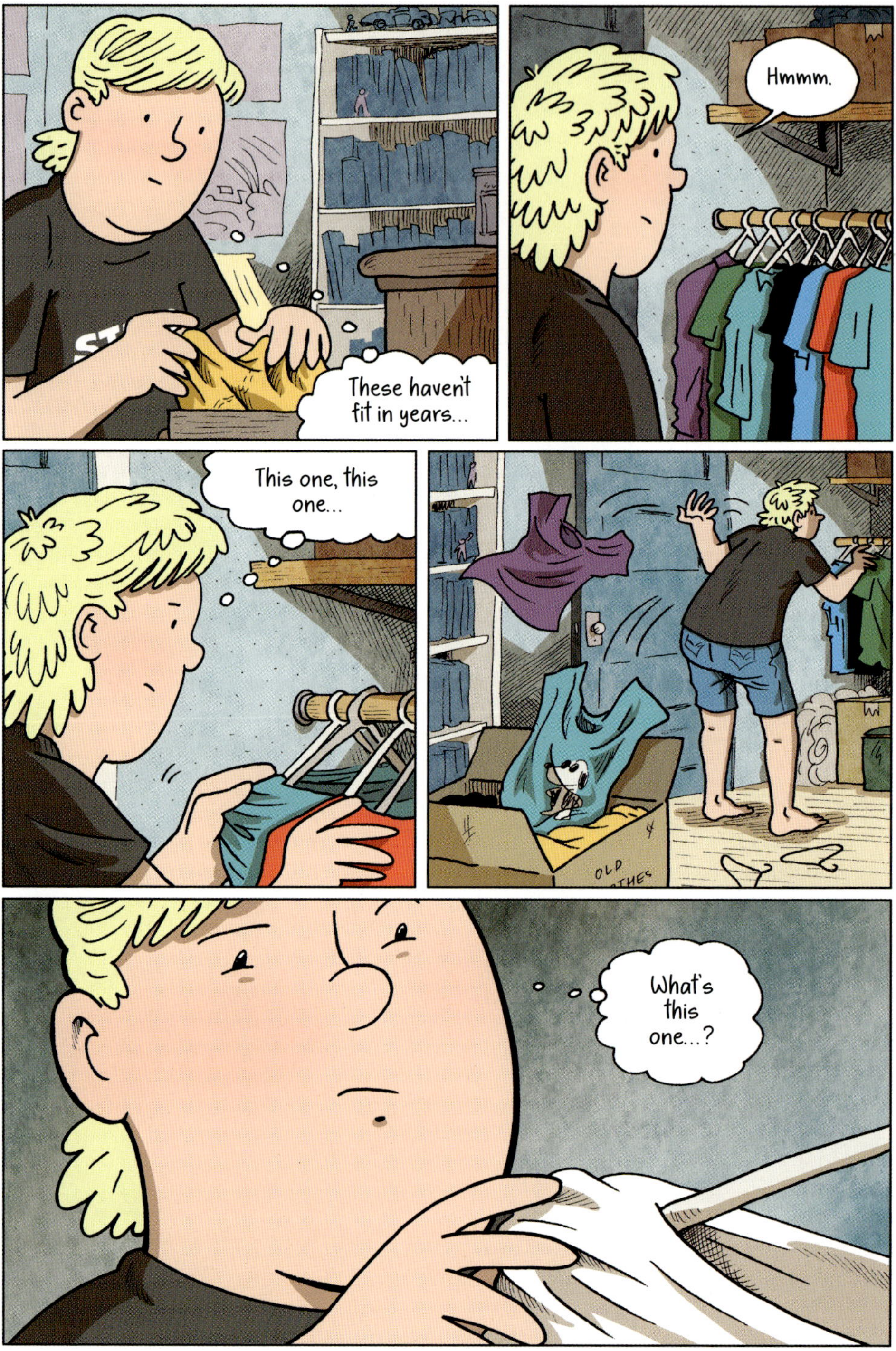
These haven't fit in years...
Hmmm.
This one, this one...
OLD CLOTHES
What's this one...?

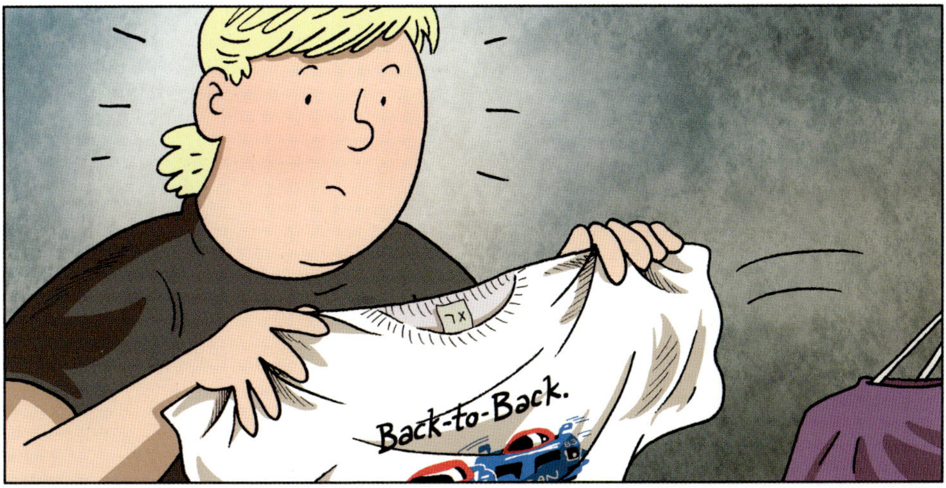
Back-to-Back.

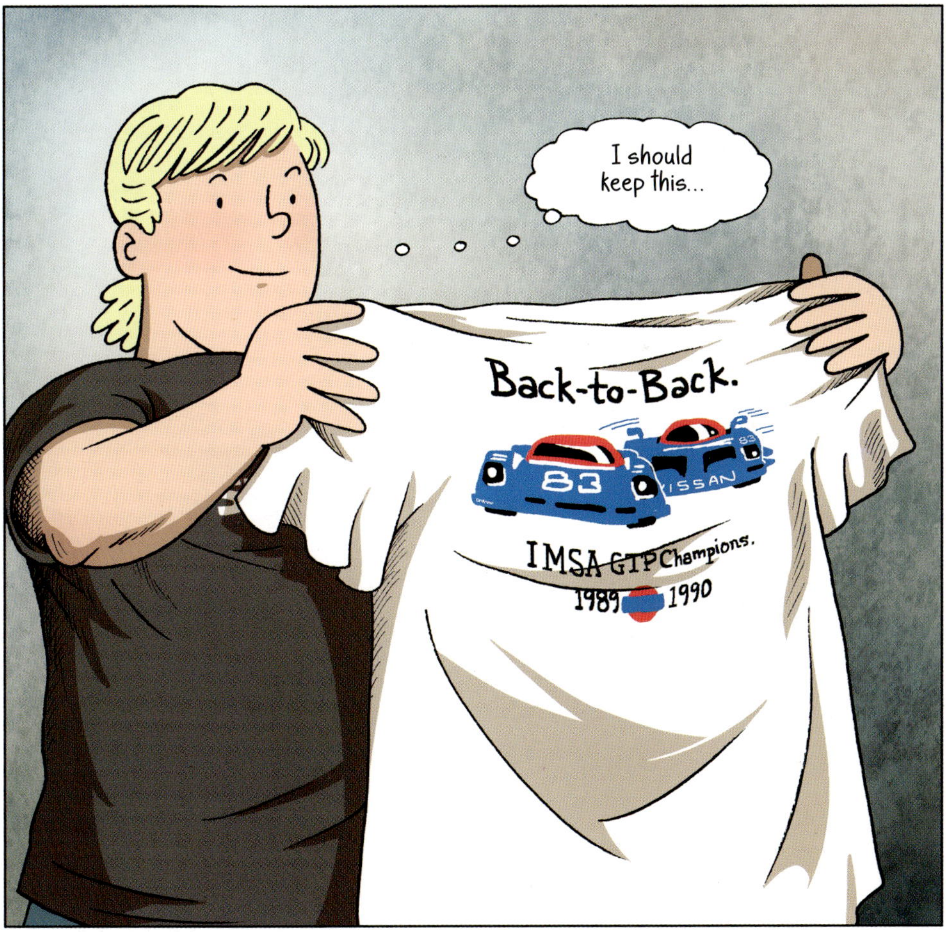
I should keep this...
Back-to-Back.
83
IMSA GTP Champions.
1989 1990

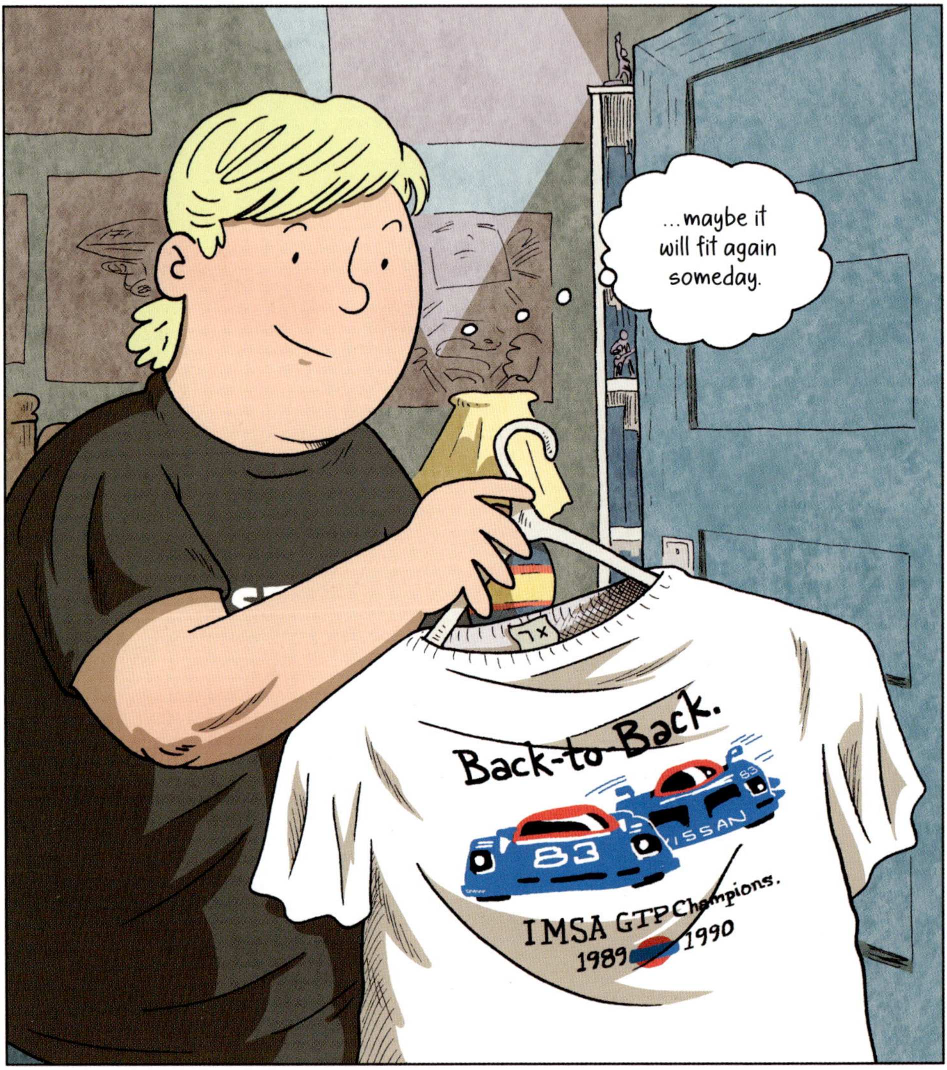
...maybe it will fit again someday.
XL
Back-to-Back.
83
NISSAN
83
IMSA GTP Champions.
1989 1990

Author's Note

To write this book, I referenced experiences from a few years of my life. I combined and rearranged events and people to tell a more focused, concentrated story. That means not everything in *Extra Large* happened to me in the same order presented here, or with the same people or places, or in the exact ways described. However, the story stays true to the emotional complexities and outcomes that I experienced in my real life.

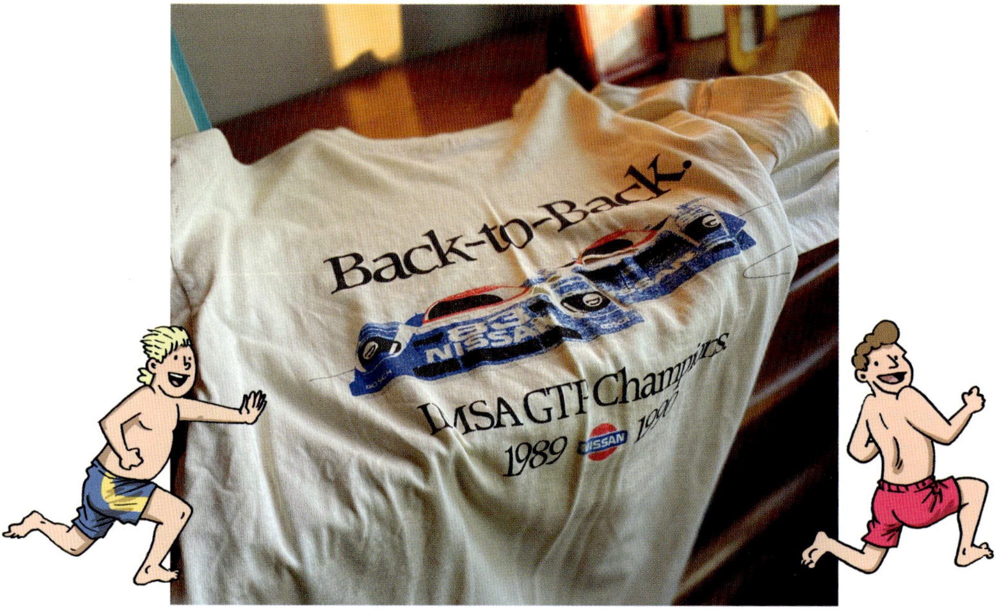
Back-to-Back.
NISSAN
1989

The Nissan shirt is real, and I still have it! I did eventually fit into it again, and then it got too big for me. By then it was too worn and threadbare to wear anymore, but I hung onto it and kept it in the back of my closet as a reminder.